Labour Law Utopias

Labour Law Utopias

Post-Growth and Post-Productive Work Approaches

Edited by

NICOLAS BUENO, BERYL TER HAAR, AND NUNA ZEKIĆ

OXFORD
UNIVERSITY PRESS

OXFORD
UNIVERSITY PRESS

Great Clarendon Street, Oxford, OX2 6DP,
United Kingdom

Oxford University Press is a department of the University of Oxford.
It furthers the University's objective of excellence in research, scholarship,
and education by publishing worldwide. Oxford is a registered trade mark of
Oxford University Press in the UK and in certain other countries

Published with the support of the Swiss National Science Foundation

Published in the United States of America by Oxford University Press
198 Madison Avenue, New York, NY 10016, United States of America

British Library Cataloguing in Publication Data

Data available

Library of Congress Control Number: 2024936109

ISBN 978–0–19–888975–5

DOI: 10.1093/oso/9780198889755.001.0001

Printed and bound by
CPI Group (UK) Ltd, Croydon, CR0 4YY

MIX
Paper | Supporting
responsible forestry
FSC® C013604

Foreword

In labour law scholarship, there appears to be something of a fashion lately for utopian thinking. At Harvard Law School, the *Clean Slate Project* proposes a 'fundamental redesign' of US labour law; 'a new labor law that is capable of empowering all workers to demand a truly equitable American democracy and a genuinely equitable American economy'.[1] In the final chapter of his recent book, *Data and Democracy: Advanced Technologies, Labor Law and the New Working Class*, Brishen Rogers presents a vision of a 'much more sustainable economy', sketching 'far-reaching sets of reforms' that would 'extend democratic norms and practices deep into the spheres of production and distribution'.[2] In the UK, the Institute of Employment Rights' more programmatic *Manifesto for Labour Law*, endorsed by the UK Labour Party when it was briefly under the leftwing leadership of Jeremy Corbyn, proposes a set of labour laws and a corresponding system of work relations that can also be seen to have a utopian flavour to them, especially at a distance of a few years.[3] There, too, labour law is cast as potentially transformative, with the potential to revolutionize 'the world of work for millions of people, reduce inequality, and build a strong, resilient, future-proofed economy'.[4] Like Rogers and the *Clean Slate* team, the Manifesto authors aim not only to inform policy debates but also to inspire collective action and lobbying efforts, providing readers with a vision of a world that is worth fighting for.

To the list, we can now add this impressive collection edited by Nicolas Bueno, Beryl ter Haar, and Nuna Zekić, in which utopian thinking is explicitly conceived of as *method*. The assembled authors are invited to imagine utopias that embody solutions to current socioeconomic and environmental challenges and crises; utopias that offer readers 'ideas about how a future world of work that is more human-centered and green may look like and what implications such a world holds for labour law'.[5] The results are wide-ranging, with

[1] Benjamin I Sachs and Sharon Block, *Clean Slate for Worker Power: Building a Just Economy and Democracy* (Harvard Law School 2020) 1 <https://clje.law.harvard.edu/app/uploads/2020/01/Clean-Slate-for-Worker-Power.pdf> accessed 30 April 2024.

[2] (MIT Press 2023) 11.

[3] Keith Ewing, John Hendy, and Carolyn Jones (eds), *Manifesto for Labour Law* (Institute for Employment Rights 2016).

[4] <https://www.ier.org.uk/Manifesto/> last accessed on 30 April 2024.

[5] Chapter 1 by Bueno, ter Haar, and Zekić in this book.

the authors turning their attention to such questions as the potential benefits that new technologies could bring to workers, creating more equal work relations and more freedom;[6] how value might be accorded to 'non-market' work, including unpaid care work and other social practices that aim to protect social and natural resources;[7] and the role of labour law in 'post-work' communities, where workers might enjoy not only the right to a basic income but a 'fundamental right to laziness'.[8]

When we consider the freedom that utopian thinking can offer scholars—to imagine a labour law and a corresponding economy and society that are radically different to what we have now—its current popularity is perhaps unsurprising. In imagining utopias, scholars can untether themselves from the detail and even the broader structures and principles of the current law and simply sidestep the potentially paralysing question of how to get there from here.[9] The worse things are, and the more convinced scholars become that radical change is necessary, the more attractive utopian thinking is therefore likely to become. Today, many of us seem to have reached precisely that conclusion. The first decades of this new century have witnessed a global financial and economic crisis, a global pandemic, steeply rising sea-levels and air temperatures, rising economic inequalities within and between nation-states, and the sometimes violent suppression of workers' rights and other civil rights and political freedoms. In the face of such monumental challenges, piecemeal and incremental reforms become patently inadequate and the argument gains force that not only new rules but new objectives—new values—are needed. Radical change appears not only desirable but perhaps even *possible*.

Though the fashion for utopian thinking in labour law scholarship is a new one, it has precursors, as new fashions often do, in earlier times and in the writings of foundational scholars in the field. In the immediate aftermath of the First World War, Hugo Sinzheimer depicted a system of labour law, which secured for labour the fundamental right to manage working relations and the economy as a whole, together with capital, with parity rights and powers.[10] At a time when revolutionary workers' councils were still engaged in violent street battles with the reactionary *Freikorps*, this vision was even included in the new Constitution of the Weimar Republic.[11] The terms of the article in

[6] Chapter 10 by Albin in this book.

[7] Chapter 8 by Tomassetti, Chapter 7 by Bueno, and Chapter 9 by Encinas de Muñagorri, all in this book.

[8] Chapter 11 by De Becker and Claus in this book.

[9] Erik Olin Wright, 'Compass Points' (2006) 41 New Left Review 93–124.

[10] Ruth Dukes, *The Labour Constitution: the Enduring Idea of Labour Law* (OUP 2014).

[11] Constitution of the German Reich, art 165.

question were never fully implemented, however, and Otto Kahn-Freund later recalled that he had always read them 'a little bit the way one reads *Alice in Wonderland*';[12] never as a realistic programme for law reform. For all his own legal scepticism, however, for which he became well-known, Kahn-Freund's early writings on British labour law also cast the system in the best possible light, underplaying its many shortcomings.[13] In the famous trilogy of works from the 1950s, we are presented with an image of industrial relations and the law that is strongly normative, if not truly utopian.[14] Like Sinzheimer before him, Kahn-Freund wrote these in a post-war context in which it felt possible or even necessary to propose and to build 'the just city', as WH Auden put it, consigning to '[y]esterday all the past'.[15]

Labour Law Utopias recalls the work of Sinzheimer and Kahn-Freund not only in its normative ambitions but also in the importance it accords to current debates in the fields of socioeconomics and political economy. Two bodies of work, in particular, are highlighted by the editors, dealing respectively with post-growth economies and post-productive labour. Each of these raises questions that strike at the very heart of the purpose and meaning of work and labour law, today and in the future, and the authors are to be congratulated for addressing them in such imaginative and productive ways.

Ruth Dukes
Edinburgh, UK
September 2023

[12] Otto Kahn-Freund, 'Postscript' in R Lewis and J Clark (eds), *Labour Law and Politics in the Weimar Republic* (Blackwell 1981) 201
[13] Dukes, *The Labour Constitution* (n 10).
[14] Otto Kahn-Freund, 'Legal Framework' in Allan Flanders and Hugh Clegg (eds), *The System of Industrial Relations in Great Britain* (OUP 1954); Otto Kahn-Freund, 'Intergroup Conflicts and their Settlement' (1954) 5 British Journal of Sociology 193–227; Otto Kahn-Freund, 'Labour Law' in Morris Ginsberg (ed), *Law and Opinion in England in the 20th Century* (Stevens 1959).
[15] WH Auden, 'Spain 1937' in *Another Time* (Faber and Faber 1940).

Acknowledgements

The idea for this book started during the Regulating for Decent Work conference, which took place in July 2019 (hosted by the International Labour Organization (ILO) in Geneva). In the breaks between sessions, we discussed developments in socioeconomic literature and what this may mean for work in general and labour law in particular. We also discussed how labour law could contribute by further developing those socioeconomic ideas. In this, we saw an opportunity to draft labour law utopias. By labour law utopias, we mean the space to address problems in our current world of work and labour law systems and explore how they could be addressed by moving beyond the existing positive law frames. To gather more ideas, we called for papers to prepare a submission for the Fifth Labour Law Research Network (LLRN) conference, which took place in June 2021 (hosted online by the University of Warsaw). We received many submissions and selected those papers that engaged with post-growth and post-productive work approaches. The four panels of this mini symposium triggered lively debates, containing many interesting suggestions, and became the foundation of this book.

After the conference, we selected the papers most strongly framed in a post-growth and post-productive work approach. Thanks to the critical but, above all, constructive and positive feedback from the reviewers of Oxford University Press on the proposal for this book, we were able to give a more balanced attention to issues of gender, race, and the perspective of the lower income countries. We are also grateful to Fay Gibbons and Matthew Williams for their patience and above all their professional, supportive, and friendly guidance throughout the publishing process.

The completion of the book would not have gone as smoothly and as quickly without the excellent collaboration of each contributor to this edited volume, and the invaluable and meticulous help with the format-editing and proofreading of the chapters of the book by Ymane Glaoua and Leo Barnard, both PhD candidates and research assistants at UniDistance Suisse. Their assistance has been made possible by the financial support of UniDistance Suisse. We are also grateful for the financial support of the Swiss National Science Foundation (SNSF), which enabled us to publish this book in Open Access and thus make it accessible to a wider audience.

Contents

Figures

Tables

Contributors

Einat Albin, Senior Lecturer in Labour Law, Faculty of Law, Hebrew University of Jerusalem, Israel.

Pushkar Anand, Assistant Professor, Faculty of Law, University of Delhi, India and PhD Candidate, Macquarie Law School, Macquarie University, Australia.

Nicolas Bueno, Professor of International and European Law, Faculty of Law, UniDistance Suisse, Switzerland.

Rodrigo Carelli, Professor of Labour Law, National Law School, Universidade Federal do Rio de Janeiro, Brazil.

Flore Claus, PhD Researcher, Faculty of Law and Criminology, Department of Criminology, Criminal Law and Social Law, University of Ghent, Belgium.

Alexander De Becker, Professor of Law, Faculty of Law and Criminology, Department of Criminology, Criminal Law and Social Law, University of Ghent, Belgium.

Élise Dermine, Professor of Labour Law, Faculty of Law and Criminology, Centre for Public and Social Law, Université libre de Bruxelles, Belgium.

Surya Deva, Professor of Law, Macquarie Law School and Director, Centre for Environmental Law, Macquarie University, Australia.

Daniel Dumont, Professor of Social Security Law, Faculty of Law and Criminology, Centre for Public and Social Law, Université libre de Bruxelles, Belgium.

Rafael Encinas de Muñagorri, Professor of Law, Faculty of Law and Political Science, Nantes Université, France.

Sergio Gamonal C., Professor of Labour Law, Faculty of Law, Universidad Adolfo Ibáñez, Chile.

Brian Langille, Professor of Law, Faculty of Law, University of Toronto, Canada.

Beryl ter Haar, Professor of International and European Labour Law, Faculty of Law, Centre for International and European Labour Law, University of Warsaw, Poland.

Paolo Tomassetti, Assistant Professor of Labour Law, University of Milan, Italy and Associate Researcher, European Trade Union Institute.

Nuna Zekić, Professor of Labour Law, Faculty of Law, University of Amsterdam, Netherlands.

1

Labour Law Beyond Growth and Productivism: An Introduction

Nicolas Bueno, Beryl ter Haar, and Nuna Zekić

The world is changing constantly, and with it so are perceptions, values, and norms in society, as well as our ideas about what kind of world we would like to live in. This regularly leads to rethinking, reconsidering, and reimagining our ways of living and the institutions that regulate our lives. Particularly since the 2008 financial and economic crisis, calls have been made for alternatives to the economic growth- and profit-driven market economy. This call was reiterated during the Covid-19 pandemic when economic priorities left more room for health concerns and a reflection on what is essential work in society.[1] These calls also reflect systemic societal challenges caused by the fear of technical replacement, climate change, demographic change, and rising inequality. All these reflections will affect labour law and a labour law perspective is needed to contribute to them.

In response to these calls and societal challenges, new ideas, or *utopias*, have gained visibility in the socioeconomic literature. The aim of this book is to engage with two alternative approaches to the current growth- and profit-driven market economy: post-economic growth and post-productive work approaches. *Labour Law Utopias: Post-Growth and Post-Productive Work Approaches* explores what these alternatives might mean for work in general, its meaning and organization, and labour law in particular. The remainder of this introduction elaborates on utopias in general (what is a utopia, what can its function be for law, and how we use this concept); why there is a need for labour law utopias; and what post-growth and post-productive work approaches entail in this book. The introduction concludes with an overview of the main trends and discussions that can be identified in the chapters for rethinking labour law beyond growth and productivism.

[1] See International Labour Organization, *The Value of Essential Work: World Employment and Social Outlook 2023* (ILO 2023).

Nicolas Bueno, Beryl ter Haar, and Nuna Zekić, *Labour Law Beyond Growth and Productivism: An Introduction* In: *Labour Law Utopias*. Edited by: Nicolas Bueno, Beryl ter Haar, and Nuna Zekić, Oxford University Press. © Oxford University Press 2024.
DOI: 10.1093/oso/9780198889755.003.0001

I. Utopias as Idealistic Alternatives

The concept of 'utopia' is often used in a historical fictional way.[2] These utopias in literary works usually have the purpose of helping the reader to imagine a completely different society, an ideal society, or an ideal way of living. However, a utopia for one person or group can be a dystopia for others. Huxley's *Brave New World* is a clear example of this. And Thomas More's *Utopia* was an ideal world for everyone who behaves in accordance with the rules as set by More. For good reasons, many utopias remain just an idea on paper. However, many utopias have also left a 'legacy'. For example, until about the mid-sixteenth century laziness was considered a virtue and the *Land of Cocagne* something every good citizen would dream of. Thomas More changed this radically. In More's *Utopia*, work was considered a virtue: every citizen ought to spend their time in a way that is useful for society. While his utopia was never realized, the idea of work being a virtue still resonates today.[3] Beyond being a virtue because it is considered as something that gives an individual person an identity, esteem, and dignity, work is also increasingly appreciated and rewarded based on its mere economic value.

Sometimes a utopia is used to visualize how the world could have been different had a certain path or paradigm been followed. Examples of these are Jurriaan Andriessen's *Eldorica*,[4] which visualizes an alternative world that considered all the recommendations of the 1972 report of the Club of Rome; and Yanis Varoufakis' *Another Now*,[5] which sketches a different world based on the idea of what could have been if, in 2008, civil society movements *Occupy* and *Extinction Rebellion* had won. By visualizing how things could have been done differently, the aim of these utopias is to facilitate different choices and get on a path towards change. Perhaps this could be considered the most important function of utopias: by imagining how things could be done differently and what kind of world that could lead to, this will make it easier to opt for change.

No matter how you look at utopias, the use of a utopia makes it clear that the goal of the author is to think beyond the existing world and imagine ideal alternatives. As such, the use of a utopia allows us to think beyond the familiar and come up with solutions that would not otherwise have been considered. Langille's chapter elaborates on the idea of labour law utopias. More generally,

[2] William Morris, *News from Nowhere or an Epoch of Rest* (Kelmscott Press 1890; first published in Commonweal Journal).
[3] Hans Achterhuis, *De Erfenis van de Utopie* (Ambo 1998) 83.
[4] Jurriaan Andriessen, *Eldorica. Met een Reisverslag naar een betere wereld* (Het Spectrum 1990).
[5] Yanis Varoufakis, *Another Now: Dispatches from an Alternative Present* (Random House 2021).

the contributions in this book use the idea of utopia as a method to offer forward-looking ideas about what a future world of work that is more human-centred and green may look like and the implications such a world holds for labour law. The future-oriented approaches that are promoted in this book aim to offer alternatives to the economic growth- and profit-driven free market economy. More concretely, this book follows two general approaches: post-growth and post-productive work. These approaches have been chosen because they respond to various important issues for the future of work, and they present serious challenges to labour law. These include environmental concerns and climate change, technological replacement, demographic change, increasing income and wealth inequality, and precariousness in a profit- and productivity-driven economic model.

II. The Need for Labour Law Utopias

With the post-growth and post-productive work approaches, we aim to do what we legal scholars are good at, namely, to ask what the law *should* or *ought* to be. This is something that some legal scholars claim to be at the heart of legal scholarship,[6] often combined with a positive law approach.[7] However, when reviewing labour law research, this 'how the law should or ought to be' approach also has its limitations. Overall, labour law research remains fragmented, dogmatically linked to positive law, and it rarely interacts with developments in other scientific fields such as economics and sociology.[8]

By fragmented, we mean that research in labour law is often focused on one particular problem or niche topic of labour law. This is usually a good thing as such an approach offers profound insights into the problem or topic addressed. This approach also serves practitioners in (labour) law, especially lawyers and judges. For example, since the rise of platform work, many labour law researchers have explored this new form of employment relationship and made suggestions on how to make this triangular contractual relationship fit within the existing and often dogmatic binary 'either employee or entrepreneur' system.[9] With an increased use of algorithms in the context of work,

[6] Jan Smits, 'Redefining Normative Legal Science: Towards an Argumentative Discipline' in Fons Coomans, Fred Grunfeld, and Menno Kamminga (eds), *Methods of Human Rights Research* (Intersentia 2009) 49.

[7] Nuna Zekić, 'The Normative Framework of Labour Law' (2019) 9 Law and Method 1.

[8] With notable exceptions: see eg Ruth Dukes, 'The Economic Sociology of Labour Law' (2019) 46(3) Journal of Law and Society 396–422.

[9] Jeremias Prassl, *The Concept of the Employer* (OUP 2015); in the context of platform work: Jeremias Prassl and Martin Risak, 'Uber, Taskrabbit, and Co.: Platforms as Employers - Rethinking the Legal

labour law researchers have also outlined the particular risks of infringements of workers' rights, such as discrimination and privacy issues, and how those risks could or should be met by existing labour law.[10] The research on precariousness, an issue that is continuously challenging labour law, especially since the proliferation of more flexible forms of employment (part-time work, fixed term contracts, temporary work contracts, zero-hour contracts, on-call contracts, but also crowd work via platforms), aims to inform practitioners, but also lawmakers, on how to improve the situation of these workers by pointing out weaknesses in the existing labour law systems and how these could be overcome with adaptations of those labour law systems.[11]

With this important type of research, labour law researchers fulfil the function of gatekeepers of the legal systems in ensuring that the positive law remains efficient and fair. However, by remaining dogmatically linked to positive labour law, one could ask whether this type of research alone is enough to question the purpose of labour law and its role in defining how we want and need to regulate work in the future. When following arguments that labour law is in crisis—some even claim it is dead[12]—it is doubtful whether labour law systems have maintained their integrity in terms of its quality and functioning. For Guy Davidov, labour law is not in crisis, however, due to incremental, piecemeal

Analysis of Crowdwork' (2016) 37(3) Comparative Labor Law and Policy Journal 619; Miriam Cherry, 'Beyond Misclassification: The Digital Transformation of Work' (2016) 37(3) Comparative Labor Law and Policy Journal 577; Valerio De Stefano and Matthias Wouters, 'Triangulaire arbeidsrelaties in de platformeconomie: een voorstel tot een vermoeden van uitzendbureau' (2019) Arbeidsrechtelijke Annotaties 3, 3; Christina Hiessl, 'The Classification of Platform Workers in Case Law: A Cross-European Comparative Analysis' (2021) 42(2) Comparative Labor Law and Policy Journal 465.

[10] Miriam Kullmann, 'Platform Work, Algorithmic Decision-Making, and EU Gender Equality Law' (2018) 34(1) International Journal of Comparative Labour Law and Industrial Relations 1–21; Valerio De Stefano, 'Algorithmic Bosses and What to Do About Them: Automation, Artificial Intelligence and Labour Protection' in D Marino and M Monaca (eds), *Economic and Policy Implications of Artificial Intelligence. Studies in Systems, Decision and Control* (Springer 2020) 65–86; Joe Atkinson, "Technology Managing People': An Urgent Agenda for Labour Law' (2021) 50(2) Industrial Law Journal 324–29; Marta Otto, 'A Step Towards Digital Self- & Co-determination in the Context of Algorithmic Management Systems' (2022) 15(1) Italian Labour Law e-Journal 51–64.

[11] Jeff Kenner, Izabela Florczak, and Marta Otto (eds), *Precarious Work: The Challenge for Labour Law in Europe* (Edward Elgar Publishers 2019); Edoardo Ales, Olaf Deinert, and Jeff Kenner, *Core and Contingent Work in the European Union. A Comparative Analysis* (Hart Publishing 2017); David Weil, *The Fissured Workplace. Why Work Became so Bad for so Many and What Can Be Done to Improve It* (Harvard UP 2004).

[12] Among various contributions: Guy Davidov and Brian Langille (eds), *The Idea of Labour Law* (OUP 2011); on the death of labour law in particular and among others: Keith Ewing, 'The Death of Labour Law?' (1988) 8 Oxford Journal of Legal Studies 293; Dennis Davies, 'Death of a Labour Lawyer?' in Joanne Conaghan, Richard Fischl, and Karl Klare (eds), *Labour Law in an Era of Globalization* (OUP 2004); Paul O'Higgins, 'The End of Labour Law as We Have Known It?' in Catherine Bernard, Simon Deakin, and Gillian Morris (eds), *The Future of Labour Law: Liber Amicorum Bob Hepple* (Hart Publishing 2004) 289.

changes that have been made to the system over the course of time, labour law's purposes and the means to achieve those purposes are no longer aligned.[13]

Others, like Ruth Dukes and Zoe Adams, argue that labour law is in crisis because the (fragmented) dogmatic studies fail to take into account the reality of the socioeconomic context in which the labour law system operates.[14] From these arguments it follows that issues in labour law should be addressed in their wider socioeconomic context, without losing sight of labour law's purpose. This may be even more the case when a forward-looking approach is taken, after all, without a broader, socioeconomic context to embed these 'labour law utopias', they risk remaining utopias forever.

Thus, while taking a forward-looking approach which puts 'dots on the horizon', these dots are embedded in the wider socioeconomic horizons of post-growth and post-productive work approaches defined below. These 'dots' may give direction to the transition that needs to be made towards new work utopias and their (cor)responding labour laws. The transition to such new work utopias and (cor)responding labour laws is very much worth exploring. However, before transitions can be made, we must have new utopias, these dots on the horizons, and currently, there is a lack of legal contributions on these dots. Therefore, the aim of the chapters in this book is to engage with doctrinal debates on post-growth and post-productive work approaches and their potential impacts on labour law.

III. Post-Growth and Post-Productive Work Approaches

History has seen many utopias. Some were translated into law and practice, at least to some extent, and therewith became socioeconomic paradigms in which work relations were shaped and labour law operated. For example, Soviet socialists and French socialists before them, envisioned a society in which each person was entitled to work and enjoy income security as the basis for economic equality.[15] In the second half of the twentieth century, the neoliberal socioeconomic paradigm emerged as a counter-ideology to socialism. Promoted particularly by Hayek and Friedman,[16] this neoliberal utopia became the new

[13] Guy Davidov, *A Purposive Approach to Labour Law* (OUP 2016).

[14] Ruth Dukes, 'Regulating Gigs', review article in (2019) 83(1) Modern Law Review 217; Zoe Adams, 'A Structural Approach to Labour Law' (2022) 46 Cambridge Journal of Economics 447.

[15] The right to work was, eg, the first fundamental right in the Soviet Constitution of 1936, art 118.

[16] Friedrich Hayek, *The Road to Serfdom* (first published 1944, University of Chicago Press 2007); Milton Friedman and Rose Friedman, *Capitalism and Freedom* (first published 1962, 40th anniversary edn University of Chicago Press 2002); Milton Friedman and Rose Friedman, *Free to Choose: A Personal Statement* (first published 1980, Harvest Book 1990).

socioeconomic paradigm since the late twentieth century. It envisions an ideal society in which individuals are free to choose work and are rewarded according to their skills, but also implies human competition for work and a growing economy able to create market jobs.

Although these two utopias seem to be in complete opposition, they share the need to rely on work as a basis for society. And, with a continuous increase in population, this has resulted in policies stimulating the creation of new jobs. States in socialist systems, as well as private companies in neoliberal market systems, have proven to be very creative and inventive in occupying an ever-increasing number of workers.[17] As ironically pictured by Bertrand Russell, in Soviet Russia the state designed admirable projects, such as making the White Sea and the northern coasts of Siberia warm, just to occupy people.[18] Alternatively, in free market societies, the state endeavours to turn individuals into socialized consumers. André Gorz described how commercial advertisement helped to artificially stimulate consumption (in order to create jobs) by making people consume, not because the products are useful or necessary, but merely as compensation for the hard work they do.[19]

Currently, the logic of ensuring more and better paid jobs requires economic growth and relies on economic productivity. This logic requires that people become economically productive by training for and taking productive jobs in the labour market, but also that they consume more, a requirement that is unlikely to respect environmental boundaries and the climate. But abandoning, collectively or individually, this economic growth and productive logic is associated with the fear of reducing employment and material security. Although consensus on a work utopia that would work for all in a globalized economy is currently non-existent, alternative economic and work models are gaining visibility. In this edited book, labour law scholars address this growth and productive dilemma by engaging with post-growth and post-productive work approaches, as outlined in the following section. Rather than offering solutions on how to solve the dilemma, the aim of the chapters in this book is to explore new avenues for work and labour law.

[17] David Graeber, *Bullshit Jobs: The Rise of Pointless Work, and What We Can Do About It* (Penguin Group 2019); Jan Lucassen, *The Story of Work: A New History of Mankind* (Yale UP 2021); James Suzman, *Work. A History of How We Spend Our Time* (Bloomsbury 2021).

[18] Bertrand Russell, *In Praise of Idleness: And Other Essays* (3rd edn, Allen & Unwin 1936) 9.

[19] André Gorz, *Critique of Economic Reason* (first published in French 1988, Verso 1989) 45.

A. Post-Growth Approaches

Post-economic growth approaches address and rethink the purpose of economic and human activities. They look beyond increasing consumption, production, and wealth as the main goals of the economy. Since most of the authors advocating a post-growth approach are educated as economists, they first describe how and why targeting economic growth, particularly in terms of GDP growth, is neither sufficient nor beneficial for most people, or even possible within planetary boundaries.[20] Some authors then propose new values, such as happiness[21] or wellbeing,[22] as the main purposes of the economy, while others aim to describe more precisely how to depart from the current growth model. To give a more concrete impression of these approaches, we briefly describe three books that have gained popular attention.

In *Less is More*, Jason Hickel focuses on the environmental and climate, as well as social, consequences of growth. He argues that the current economic order is leading humanity towards mass extinction. In order to genuinely turn things around, it is necessary to slow down the pace of extraction, production, and waste, and slow down the 'mad pace of our lives'.[23] Hence, we need a 'degrowth' policy. He suggests mobilizing behind a global Green New Deal that goes beyond the capitalist parameters and that would reduce world greenhouse gas emissions by half by 2030 and to zero by 2050. Degrowth would entail systematic downscaling of energy and resource use, to create an economy that is in 'balance with the living world in a safe and equitable way'.[24] By 'equitable', Hickel means a society where income and resources are distributed more fairly and invested in the public goods that people need to thrive and where people are 'liberated' from needless work.[25]

Kate Raworth's *Doughnut Economics* departs from the goal of achieving GDP growth that is traditionally represented by an increasing curb. Instead, Raworth replaces the traditional growth curb by a doughnut to illustrate how economic activities, from local to global, should meet the social foundation of human wellbeing (and not fall inside the hole of the doughnut) within planetary boundaries (the external limit of the doughnut).[26] Touching at the

[20] Giorgos Kallis, *Degrowth* (Agenda Publishing 2018).
[21] Bruno Frey, *Economics of Happiness* (Springer International 2018).
[22] Lorenzo Fioramonti, *Wellbeing Economy: Success in a World Without Growth* (Pan Macmillan 2017); Lorenzo Fioramonti and others, 'Wellbeing Economy: An Effective Paradigm to Mainstream Post-Growth Policies?' (2022) 192 Ecological Economics 107261.
[23] Jason Hickel, *Less is More: How Degrowth Will Save the World* (Penguin Random House 2021) 184.
[24] ibid 29.
[25] ibid 184.
[26] Kate Raworth, *Doughnut Economics: Seven Ways to Think Like a 21st-Century Economist* (Random House Business 2018) 25.

core of neoliberal market mechanisms, she rejects the idea of the rational economic man and replaces this by a vision of social and interdependent human beings.[27] She also reduces the role of markets. In her pluralistic system, the state, the household, and the commons (see for more information, particularly Chapter 8 by Tomassetti in this book), defined as shareable resources that people choose to use and govern through self-organizing, should be used to provide for human needs besides markets. In contrast to the current model that is based on the idea that we will be able to recover and redistribute after growth, she describes economies that are regenerative and distributive by design.[28]

Post-Growth by Tim Jackson is less about economic systems than about a definition of social progress and a new storytelling away from consumption and competition, as well as productive work. After presenting economic growth as a myth, including green growth, he suggests that we should strive towards other forms of prosperity, in particular health in all its physical, psychological, social, spiritual, and sexual components.[29] And for this, balance, cooperation, and love are needed more than growth, competition, and consumption. His vision of work is much broader than economically productive work and encompasses a re-evaluation of activities, such as care or craft, that offer opportunities to learn, participate, and help build the social world and our place in it.[30]

The chapters by Ter Haar (Chapter 3, Economic Paradigm Shifts for Labour Law), Zekić (Chapter 4, Labour Law for Degrowth and Meaningful Work), Carelli (Chapter 5, First Lines for an Ecological Labour Law), and Deva and Anand (Chapter 6, A Global South Perspective on Labour Rights and Supply Chains for a Post-Growth World), are mainly based on this post-growth approach.

B. Post-Productive Work Approaches

Altogether, post-growth approaches focus on the economy as a whole and its purpose, but do not yet precisely focus on work, its value and purpose, and organization. It is undeniable that transforming theories of post-growth into practice will require a clear understanding of its consequences on work. Post-productive work approaches focus more specifically on work. They include alternatives to the current work dogma or reliance on economically productive

[27] ibid ch 3.
[28] ibid chs 2, 5, 6.
[29] Tim Jackson, *Post Growth* (Wiley 2021) 61.
[30] ibid ch 7.

work for individuals and society. Two specific tracks can be distinguished. The post-work approach in the strict sense usually considers work as a form of unnecessary exploitation. Therefore, it looks for avenues to diminish its quantity as much as possible. Historically, a plethora of essays have envisioned societies that are freer from work, notably Paul Lafargue's *Right to be Lazy*,[31] or Bertrand Russel's *Praise of Idleness*.[32] More recently ideas are proposed on how technology ownership and redistribution, for example through a basic income, can liberate people from work. Two examples of the latter include Daniel Susskind's *World Without Work*[33] and Nick Srnicek and Alex Williams' *Postcapitalism and a World Without Work*.[34]

The chapters by De Becker and Claus (Chapter 11, Social Security and the Right to Laziness Beyond just Basic Income) and Gamonal (Chapter 12, Utopia, Power, and Free Labour) are based on this track of post-productive work.

The second track in the post-productive work approach goes beyond questions regarding the quantity of work. The debates focus on the purpose of work and its value for individuals and society. Whereas the current free (labour) market approach pushes individuals to compete for paid work and, thus, to train for the most economically productive and, therefore, remunerative jobs, critiques emerge on the need for more meaningful activities for individuals themselves and society altogether. The object of this approach can be defined as 'post-productive work'. The debate usually starts with a critique of some highly paid jobs that make neither the individual worker particularly happy or proud, nor the world a better place, as described in David Graeber's *Bullshit Jobs*.[35] Additionally, there is a strand of literature which is developing the concept of meaningful work, but mainly from the perspective of individuals. This literature goes beyond decent work which is at the heart of the general labour law doctrine.[36]

Beyond meaningful work for individuals, some authors also discuss the value of work (and activities beyond work) for society beyond producing wealth, or differently put, the social value of work. For instance, Chamberlain's *Undoing Work, Rethinking Community* addresses the low social esteem that is attached to unpaid activities and envisions a society, where taking responsibility for the

[31] Paul Lafargue, *The Right to Be Lazy* (first published in French 1880, Charles Kerr and Co edn 1907) 29.
[32] Russell, *In Praise of Idleness* (n 18).
[33] Daniel Susskind, *World Without Work: Technology, Automation, and How We Should Respond* (Macmillan 2020).
[34] Nick Srnicek and Alex Williams, *Inventing the Future: Postcapitalism and a World Without Work* (Verso 2016).
[35] Graeber, *Bullshit Jobs* (n 17).
[36] Andrea Veltman, *Meaningful Work* (OUP 2016).

wellbeing of others, not paid work, becomes the way to belong to society.[37] However, wellbeing remains undefined.[38] Dermine and Dumont have looked more specifically at the role of social law to promote freely chosen '(eco)socially useful activities', containing a whole range of human activities that contribute to the construction of a sustainable society, but that are not valued by the market.[39] Bueno's human economy framework reflects on the waste of human potential when someone would like to do meaningful work for society, but has no individual opportunities to do so and has to take whatever job is available on the market. In his framework, activities are personally meaningful if they are freely chosen and socially meaningful when they contribute to central human needs.[40] Finally, *Post-Growth Work* is a recent example of a book which discusses the value of work in a post-growth logic.[41]

Chapters that engage mainly with this post-productive work approach are written by Bueno (Chapter 7, Including the Non-Economic Value of Work in Labour Law), Tomassetti (Chapter 8, Labour Law and the Utopia of the Commons), Encinas de Muñagorri (Chapter 9, Labour Law for Care and Wellbeing), and Albin (Chapter 10, Channelling Technologies to Benefit Employees via Labour Law).

IV. Trends and Main Discussions of the Book

By having all the chapters grounded around post-growth and post-productive work approaches, we were able to identify several trends towards which labour law could develop. According to these trends, labour law should or could (1) become more human-centred; (2) adopt a broader socioecological approach; (3) better reconcile the individual with the collective/societal; and (4) reformulate the role of work in and for society. Despite these identifiable trends, the authors discuss different, sometimes even contrasting, ideas about work, its role, value, and meaning, and consequently about how labour law

[37] James Chamberlain, *Undoing Work, Rethinking Community: A Critique of the Social Function of Work* (Cornell UP 2018) 138.

[38] ibid.

[39] Elise Dermine and Daniel Dumont, 'A Renewed Critical Perspective on Social Law: Disentangling Its Ambivalent Relationship with Productivism' (2022) 38(3) International Journal of Comparative Labour Law and Industrial 255, 267.

[40] Nicolas Bueno, 'From the Right to Work to Freedom from Work: Introduction to the Human Economy' (2017) 33(4) International Journal of Comparative Labour Law and Industrial Relations 463–87; Nicolas Bueno, 'From Productive Work to Capability-Enhancing Work: Implications for Labour Law and Policy' (2022) 23(3) Journal of Human Development and Capabilities 354–72.

[41] Irmi Seidl and Angelika Zahrnt (eds), *Post-Growth Work: Employment and Meaningful Activities within Planetary Boundaries* (Routledge 2022).

could further develop. This section outlines the identified trends and reports the discussions for furthering research in labour law.

A. Human-Centred Labour Law

Currently, one of the main functions of labour law is to provide rights for the protection of workers. However, the focus of labour law on formally protecting the (paid) worker and the regulation of power in markets seems too narrow to be truly human-centred, as can be deduced from the chapters by Langille, Deva and Anand, and Gamonal. Many of the authors in this book take a different, more human-centred approach. They conclude in their own way that work should be defined more by how it contributes to the wellbeing of humans and society more broadly. We see this clearly in the chapter by Ter Haar who identifies a human-centred approach as opposed to a growth- and production-driven approach to work as one of the commonalities at the core of a new socioeconomic wellbeing paradigm. According to Ter Haar, this new paradigm should lead to a change in labour law's foundational principles, functions, and structure.

In Carelli's ecological labour law, a human-centred approach is expressed by the universal, all-encompassing notion of work which includes all human activities; productive and non-productive. Others re-evaluate work that is not necessarily productive but contributes to human flourishing by discussing the concepts of 'essential work' or 'meaningful work' (Zekić, Bueno, Dermine and Dumont). In this context, Bueno takes a critical view of labour law since it does not really tackle or address the fact that some types of work have a negative impact on people, such as increasing inequalities or reducing their basic human capabilities.

Encinas de Muñagorri and Albin also elaborate on some negative consequences of a labour law system that focuses on workers' productivity. Encinas de Muñagorri sketches a labour law utopia promoted by the fictional *Globalcare* programme that the United Nations (UN) will adopt in 2054. The essence of this labour law utopia is that it prioritizes care and wellbeing over considerations of productivity. Albin sketches a world in which technology is not the property of employers to be used at their will to boost productivity, but developed and used to accommodate the needs of the human worker. Hence, she also puts the human needs of the worker in the foreground.

B. Socioecological Labour Law

Many chapters in this book discuss the relevance of labour law for the environment and the climate. Labour law has traditionally been detached from questions of the environment and more concerned with providing employment and good working conditions for people. As elaborated by Ter Haar, in general the degrowth approach promotes an economic system in which all human activities, including work, respect the boundaries of the planet. Furthermore, post-growth and post-productive approaches seem to be underpinned by the idea that the interest of the planet should be respected much more in any economic system or society (Ter Haar, Tomassetti).

There seems to be a consensus that respecting the boundaries of the planet will affect production processes and result in lower production volumes. While this is accepted by some as inevitable (Ter Haar, Carelli, Zekić), Deva and Anand warn that this will have a major impact on the global supply chains and possibly hinder the development aspirations of the Global South. To overcome this problem, they introduce a 'differentiated degrowth' model, accompanied by a reorientation of corporate purpose, restoration of historical wrongs (including from colonial times), and a universal social protection for people globally.

More strongly related to the role of labour law, Zekić and Carelli in their respective chapters question whether labour law should support the logic of degrowth. More particularly, Zekić considers whether the role of labour law should be altered to foster merely production processes that are environmentally sustainable in the long run. Carelli, though, sketches an ecological labour law which balances the traditional social goals (human dignity, equality) with ecological goals (avoiding planetary cataclysm; respecting planetary boundaries). While none of the ideas presented in this book are mutually exclusive, the challenge is to figure out how to bring them together, especially when going through the transition towards a socioeconomic system that fully operates within the boundaries of the planet and takes into account the needs of society, especially the Global South.

C. The Individual and the Collective/Societal in Labour Law

There is a third underlying theme and discussion in many of the chapters. Labour law should better reconcile and further explore individual and societal interests. On one hand, labour law has a long tradition of providing collective rights to trade unions and mechanisms of collective bargaining, such to counterbalance the power of the employer. On the other hand, labour law is grounded in liberal market economies that protect the individual worker's freedom to choose work in markets and promote individual autonomy in the workplace. Beyond this current balance in labour law, some chapters further explore alternative forms of workplace democracy (Ter Haar), including through the form of the commons (Tomassetti) and the role that technology could have if it was not only an employer's property (Albin).

An important question in this book is not if, but *how* labour law can better reconcile individual and collective or societal interests. In short, how to ensure individual freedom and nevertheless promote collective outcomes for society and the environment? Ter Haar explores the collective and the individual through a change of corporate purpose, namely, to serve the needs of society and to foster the individual talents of their workers at the same time, rather than pursuing economic growth and profits. Bueno addresses further the individual and societal waste of skills when individuals, sometimes highly skilled, would like to do something meaningful for society or the environment, but must take whatever jobs are on the market. He outlines a new role for labour law that consists in reducing this mismatch by increasing individual choices for collectively meaningful work, including care work, as further developed by Encinas de Muñagorri, and reducing individual choice for collectively detrimental jobs offered in the market. De Becker and Claus, on the other hand, seek individual freedom from work by the introduction of a new fundamental right: the right to be lazy, linked to a form of basic income.

What combines the utopian visions presented in this book is the fact that work should no longer only be valued by pure market needs. Its value should also reflect the impact of work on society and the environment, its societal value. More research is needed, though, to work out what this means in terms of labour law. While Bueno and De Becker and Claus tend to be fairly concrete on labour law consequences, their focus on the individual raises questions of how to reconcile this with identifying the value of work in Tomassetti's utopias of the commons.

D. The Role of Work in and for Society

All chapters implicitly or explicitly touch upon the role of work in society. They raise questions on the meaning of work, such as: should we reconsider the purpose of work in general related to its societal meaning (Ter Haar, Tomassetti,

Encinas de Muñagorri, Albin); should we reconsider the meaning of work for its environmental impact (Ter Haar, Zekić, Carelli, Tomassetti); should we reconsider work in a more qualitative way by understanding better the social positive and negative impacts of jobs through concepts of essential or meaningful work (Bueno) or eco-socially useful work (Dermine and Dumont)?

The answers to these questions on the meaning of work raise further questions regarding its quantity and distribution in society. Will less work be needed in the utopian future (Ter Haar, Zekić, Carelli, De Becker and Claus) and how to reconsider work in terms of making us less dependent on it (De Becker and Claus)? Or what kind of work will be needed less and what kind should we have more of (Bueno, Dermine and Dumont), and how will it be distributed (Ter Haar, Deva and Anand)?

Underlying all these considerations, Deva and Anand remind us to keep in mind the impact of a changing role of work in society on the Global South. Langille, with his metaphor of the trilogy 'Voyage', 'Shipwreck', and 'Salvage', warns us to consider carefully what is good in the current system of labour law and which should therefore be salvaged as the basis for the utopias presented in this book.

E. Further Discussion

The above outlined trends also reflect the discussions that we believe can make labour law move forward in a more embedded way with a broader socio-economic-ecological context. To emphasize how this could be done, Dermine and Dumont (Chapter 13, Conclusion: Utopias for an Ecological Social Law and How to Get There) present the overall narrative that is created by the chapters in this book. Then, by further building on their own post-productive work narratives on how to promote ecosocially useful work, they explore how paths of transition can be identified from the current positive laws towards post-growth and post-productive work societies. In so doing, they illustrate how the labour law utopias presented in this book set paths for transition and how they can be used for further research.

Bibliography

Achterhuis H, *De Erfenis van de Utopie* (Ambo 1998)
Adams Z, 'A Structural Approach to Labour Law' (2022) 46(2) Cambridge Journal of Economics 447

Ales E, Deinert O, and Kenner J, *Core and Contingent Work in the European Union. A Comparative Analysis* (Hart Publishing 2017)
Andriessen J, *Eldorica, Met een Reisverslag naar een betere wereld* (Het Spectrum 1990)
Atkinson J, '"Technology Managing People": An Urgent Agenda for Labour Law' (2021) 50(2) Industrial Law Journal 324
Bueno N, 'From the Right to Work to Freedom from Work: Introduction to the Human Economy' (2017) 33(4) International Journal of Comparative Labour Law and Industrial Relations 463
Bueno N, 'From Productive Work to Capability-Enhancing Work: Implications for Labour Law and Policy' (2022) 23(3) Journal of Human Development and Capabilities 354
Chamberlain J, *Undoing Work, Rethinking Community: A Critique of the Social Function of Work* (Cornell UP 2018)
Cherry M, 'Beyond Misclassification: The Digital Transformation of Work' (2016) 37(3) Comparative Labor Law and Policy Journal 577
Davidov G, *A Purposive Approach to Labour Law* (OUP 2016)
Davidov G and Langille B (eds), *The Idea of Labour Law* (OUP 2011)
Davies D, 'Death of a Labour Lawyer?' in J Conaghan, R Fischl, and K Klare (eds), *Labour Law in an Era of Globalization* (OUP 2004)
Dermine E and Dumont D, 'A Renewed Critical Perspective on Social Law: Disentangling Its Ambivalent Relationship With Productivism' (2022) 38(3) International Journal of Comparative Labour Law and Industrial 237
De Stefano V, 'Algorithmic Bosses and What to Do About Them: Automation, Artificial Intelligence and Labour Protection' in D Marino and M Monaca (eds), *Economic and Policy Implications of Artificial Intelligence. Studies in Systems, Decision and Control* (Springer 2020)
De Stefano V and Wouters M, 'Triangulaire arbeidsrelaties in de platformeconomie: een voorstel tot een vermoeden van uitzendbureau' (2019) 13(3) Arbeidsrechtelijke Annotaties 3
Dukes R, 'Regulating Gigs' (2019) 83(1) Modern Law Review 217
Dukes R, 'The Economic Sociology of Labour Law' (2019) 46(3) Journal of Law and Society 396
Ewing K, 'The Death of Labour Law?' (1988) 8 Oxford Journal of Legal Studies 293
Fioramonti L, *Wellbeing Economy: Success in a World Without Growth* (Pan Macmillan 2017)
Fioramonti L and others, 'Wellbeing Economy: An Effective Paradigm to Mainstream Post-Growth Policies?' (2022) 192 Ecological Economics 107261
Frey B, *Economics of Happiness* (Springer International 2018)
Friedman M and Friedman R, *Capitalism and Freedom* (first published 1962, University of Chicago Press 2002)
Friedman M and Friedman R, *Free to Choose: A Personal Statement* (first published 1980, Harvest Book 1990)
Gorz A, *Critique of Economic Reason* (G Handyside and C Turner tr, first published in French 1988, Verso 1989)
Graeber D, *Bullshit Jobs: The Rise of Pointless Work, and What We Can Do About It* (Penguin Group 2019)
Hayek F, *The Road to Serfdom* (first published 1944, University of Chicago Press 2007)
Hickel J, *Less is More: How Degrowth Will Save the World* (Penguin Random House 2021)
Hiessl C, 'The Classification of Platform Workers in Case Law: A Cross-European Comparative Analysis' (2021) 42(2) Comparative Labor Law and Policy Journal 465

International Labour Organization, *The Value of Essential Work: World Employment and Social Outlook 2023* (ILO 2023)

Jackson T, *Post Growth* (Wiley 2021)

Kallis G, *Degrowth* (Agenda Publishing 2018)

Kenner J, Florczak I, and Otto M (eds), *Precarious Work: The Challenge for Labour Law in Europe* (Edward Elgar Publishers 2019)

Kullmann M, 'Platform Work, Algorithmic Decision-Making, and EU Gender Equality Law' (2018) 34(1) International Journal of Comparative Labour Law and Industrial Relations 1

Lafargue P, *The Right to Be Lazy* (first published in French 1880, Charles H Kerr tr, Charles H. Kerr & Company 1907)

Lucassen J, *The Story of Work: A New History of Mankind* (Yale UP 2021)

Morris W, *News from Nowhere or an Epoch of Rest* (Kelmscott Press 1890, first published in Commonweal Journal)

O'Higgins P, 'The End of Labour Law as We Have Known It?' in C Bernard, S Deakin, and G Morris (eds), *The Future of Labour Law: Liber Amicorum Bob Hepple* (Hart Publishing 2004)

Otto M, 'A Step towards Digital Self- & Co-Determination in the Context of Algorithmic Management Systems' (2022) 15(1) Italian Labour Law e-Journal 51

Prassl J, *The Concept of the Employer* (OUP 2015)

Prassl J and Risak M, 'Uber, Taskrabbit, and Co.: Platforms as Employers—Rethinking the Legal Analysis of Crowdwork' (2016) 37(3) Comparative Labor Law and Policy Journal 619

Raworth K, *Doughnut Economics: Seven Ways to Think like a 21st-Century Economist* (Random House Business 2018)

Russell B, *In Praise of Idleness: And Other Essays* (Allen & Unwin 1936)

Seidl I and Zahrnt A (eds), *Post-Growth Work. Employment and Meaningful Activities within Planetary Boundaries* (Routledge 2022)

Smits J, 'Redefining Normative Legal Science: Towards an Argumentative Discipline' in F Coomans, F Grunfeld, and M Kamminga (eds), *Methods of Human Rights Research* (Intersentia 2009)

Srnicek N and Williams A, *Inventing the Future: Postcapitalism and a World Without Work* (Verso 2016)

Susskind D, *World Without Work: Technology, Automation, and How We Should Respond* (Macmillan 2020)

Suzman J, *Work. A History of How We Spend Our Time* (Bloomsbury 2021)

Vandenbroucke F, Barnard C, and De Baere G (eds), *A European Social Union after the Crisis* (CUP 2017)

Varoufakis Y, *Another Now: Dispatches from an Alternative Present* (Random House 2021)

Veltman A, *Meaningful Work* (OUP 2016)

Weil D, *The Fissured Workplace. Why Work Became So Bad for So Many and What Can Be Done to Improve It* (Harvard UP 2004)

Zekić N, 'The Normative Framework of Labour Law' (2019) 9(2) Law and Method 1

2

The Coast of (Labour Law's) Utopia

Brian Langille

I. Introduction: Borrowing from Stoppard

Tom Stoppard's *The Coast of Utopia* is a trilogy of plays about Russian intellectuals in the nineteenth century. While I, like many, am an admirer of the centrality of ideas, and very clever language, in any Stoppard play, in this instance I am interested in his three titles—'Voyage', 'Shipwreck', and 'Salvage'.[1]

Let me explain the reason for this interest.

When I was asked to take part in this innovative and interestingly conceived project about *Labour Law Utopias* I began my thinking along the following lines: I was reasonably certain that most contributions would be about various labour law utopias—about the substance of those utopias and what made them worthy of being taken as a utopia. I imagined that the papers would propose, or reject, or 'interrogate' past, present, and possible future, utopias on a substantive level. They would examine the strengths and weaknesses of ambition and performance. The papers would be exercises in normative narrative and assessment. I speculated that most papers would be bold and adventurous—proposing new, comprehensive understandings of what labour law should aspire to achieve and offering answers to questions such as 'what kind of world do we wish to live in?' and 'what has labour law got to do with it?' That is, they would be the sort of papers which address the important and large questions 'head on'. In so doing they would draw, excitingly, upon *new* 'post-growth', or 'post-work' and ecologically sensitive accounts of sustainable and just economies and societies. I also anticipated that other sorts of papers in this substantive genre would be somewhat different in scope and direction of reflection, examining and critiquing *existing* and sometimes well-known utopian defences of, or attacks upon, our labour law. I was also aware of the possibility that others might take a more restricted approach—and see a particular kind of limit to the sort of utopias which labour law was permitted to dream about

[1] Tom Stoppard, *The Coast of Utopia: Voyage, Shipwreck, Salvage* (Grove Atlantic Press 2007).

Brian Langille, *The Coast of (Labour Law's) Utopia* In: *Labour Law Utopias*. Edited by: Nicolas Bueno, Beryl ter Haar, and Nuna Zekić, Oxford University Press. © Oxford University Press 2024. DOI: 10.1093/oso/9780198889755.003.0002

because they saw labour law as incarcerated in an externally imposed framework which limited our ability to think outside that particular box. This approach is perhaps on view in the introduction to this volume in the following passage:

> More generally, the contributions in this book use the idea of as a method to offer forward-looking ideas about what a future world of work that is more human-centred and green may look like and the implications such a world holds for labour law. The future-oriented approaches that are promoted in this book aim to offer alternatives to the much-criticized economic growth- and profit-driven free market economy. More concretely, this book follows two general approaches: post-growth and post- productive work. These approaches have been chosen because they respond to various important issues for the future of work, and they present serious challenges to labour law.[2]

This 'serious challenge' approach to what I will call 'the substantive genre' of thinking about labour law utopias appears to worry about an upper limit on what could be imagined by way of new utopias and what the papers could aspire to. To be sure, it leaves a lot of space to be occupied. And it may be, at the end of the day, the correct way to think about the role of any labour law utopia. That might be, for example, the path that Simon Deakin describes when he discusses labour law as a development project which evolved and evolves along with the arrival of market economies (and in his thinking about the relationship of law and markets in general).[3] But I cannot resist the thought that this possible upper limit on our role as labour lawyers is part of labour law's problem. This is reflected in numerous writings about labour law in both the domestic and international spheres. On this view the real action is elsewhere, in the domains of finance, trade, industry, and technology—which drive and create wealth. Labour law's task, it follows, is seen as offering a set of luxury goods—fairness, decency, democracy, and so on—which we can purchase, if we so desire, with the wealth created in these other spheres. That is, labour law's role is best conceived as cleaning up some of the damage done to real people after the most recent external utopia has blown through the workplace neighbourhood.[4] This way of thinking puts a real limit on labour law's possible utopias.

[2] See Chapter 1 by Bueno, ter Haar, and Zekić in this book.

[3] Simon Deakin, 'The Comparative Evolution of the Employment Relationship' in Guy Davidov and Brian Langille (eds), *The Boundaries and Frontiers of Labour Law* (Hart Publishing 2006) 89.

[4] Brian Langille, 'Imagining Post Geneva Consensus Labour Law for Post Washington Consensus Development' (2010) 31 Comparative Labor Law and Policy Journal 523; Brian Langille, 'Core Labour

But I do not wish to carry on that debate here. More precisely, I do not wish to revisit or re-enter this 'substantive' debate, nor the debate about a possible 'upper limit' on any such undertaking. Instead, I seek to offer a reflection upon the subject of 'labour law and utopias' which is independent of the substance, and the level of ambition, of any specified utopian vision and which is precisely *not* about the substance, or possible substance, of any particular utopia (despite how exciting many of the possible ones which will be discussed here may be). Essentially, I seek to enter the debate on another level and to offer another angle of attack.

And this is where Stoppard's trilogy of titles—Voyage, Shipwreck, and Salvage—helped to structure my thinking. I take them in order—and, in my view, that order is in itself worthy of reflection.

A. Voyaging

For some time, I have been interested in the idea of what I call the 'constituting narrative' of labour law.[5] I cannot review here in any detail my account of the structure of any such narrative, nor the actual content of our labour law's dominant narrative.[6] But, very briefly, labour law's constituting narrative must deliver on the three dimensions of all such narratives (for all subject matters with a way of legal life similar to that of labour law): empirical, legal, and normative. Labour law is one of those legal topics or categories not organized around, and rendered coherent by, a legal concept—such as tort, or trust, and so on. Rather, they take a 'slice' of real life like work, family, the environment, trade, and so on. But this raises the obvious issue: we need to explain why and how we legally carve reality at *this* particular joint. Such an explanation must accomplish three tasks: to make an empirical claim about what slice of reality we are after, to justify that choice from a normative point of view (show why it is important to be concerned about it), and to provide the legal conceptual framework to capture and express all of this in legal terms (ie in a way which reasonably satisfies the demands of the rule of law). Therefore, it must articulate a compelling moral

Rights—The True Story' (2005) 16 European Journal of International Law 1; Brian Langille, 'What Is International Labour Law for?' (2009) 3 Law and Ethics of Human Rights 47.

[5] I am writing this in late 2021 and early 2022.

[6] See Brian Langille, 'Labour Law's Back Pages' in Guy Davidov and Brian Langille (eds), *The Boundaries and Frontiers of Labour Law* (Hart Publishing 2006) 13.

narrative, expressed in a hard and knowable legal grammar, about *this* aspect of our lives.

Labour law's standard narrative (its 'received wisdom') has been wonderfully successful, and for a long time, by specifying employment as its empirical hunting ground (as its empirical domain), staking its legal conceptual claim on the legal ground of contract, and taking inequality of bargaining power in the negotiation of contracts (resulting in unjust processes and terms of employment (subordination, lack of dignity, and so on)) as its normative concern.

I have written about this familiar constituting narrative and our need to revise it before.[7] But here is a very important point which needs to be emphasized when thinking about normative justifications for, or of, labour law. Seeking labour law's utopia does not, in my view, consist in rustling about in an adjacent normative library, pantry, or marketplace of possible utopias for something that will be used to justify something else, which we somehow know via independent means, *is* labour law. That is a very powerful and perhaps dominant model of the project labour lawyers should undertake when they turn to basic thinking about their subject. But I think that understanding of the project at hand is deeply and importantly misconceived. Rather, seeking labour law utopias is not a matter of shopping the currently fashionable, but external, market in normative/economic/social theorizing, but rather a matter of working in the kitchen of labour law itself[8]—at the labour law workbench. Rather than imposing from without, it is about seeing the internal role of a utopia within any workable account of our discipline. Normativity is 'built in' and constructs, along with the conceptual apparatus and understood empirical reach, a unified field. These components are deeply connected and, indeed, interwoven. To illustrate my point, I will refer to a volume of essays which I edited: *The Capability Approach to Labour Law*.[9] In that volume, I wrote the following:

> A number of the chapters in this volume make the claim that the capabilities approach (CA) of Sen and/or Nussbaum cannot provide a normative justification for all of our labour law, but at most can be helpful here and there in providing the moral underpinning of bits of our labour law. But one can only say that if one has a different idea of 'justifying' labour law in mind. A different

[7] Brian Langille, 'Labour Law's Theory of Justice' in Guy Davidov and Brian Langille (eds), *The Idea of Labour Law* (OUP 2011) 101.

[8] Supriya Routh, 'The Need to Become Fashionable' in Brian Langille (ed), *The Capability Approach to Labour Law* (OUP 2019) 103.

[9] Brian Langille (ed), *The Capability Approach to Labour Law* (OUP 2019).

> picture. A different explanation of the role of the normative. On my view, the normative enters as part of our account of what labour law is. As part of our constituting narrative. It does not simply enter 'after the event'. We cannot proceed by saying 'well, here is our labour law—what in heaven's name could possibly justify that from a moral point of view?' On such a view we just know what labour law is and then scour the normative theory marketplace for a justification of it. On this view, normative theory is external to our account of labour law. That is not the view taken here. I believe that subject matters such as labour law require a constituting narrative with an internal normative dimension in order for us to know what is and is not labour law in the first place. On my view labour law does have—and must have—a normative account of the whole of labour law. Labour law's normative stance does not come in bits and pieces. Light does dawn over the whole . . . So, the role that the CA, or any normative dimension of any account of labour law plays, is part of an account of what labour law is, and not simply a normative claim about something we independently identify as labour law. That is, it is not simply a claim about justifying or criticizing labour law or various parts of it from an external point of view. It is a claim about our internal understanding of labour law.[10]

What is the link between this line of thinking and our topic of labour law utopias? It is a direct and profound one. In reaching out to new utopian understandings of the point of work (and whether those understandings come in the shape of 'doughnuts'[11] or are centred on 'happiness'[12]) we are putting not just our normative justification of labour law on the agenda but the whole of our constituting narrative, including its empirical reach and legal/conceptual structure of thought. It is 'a package deal'.[13] In what follows, I will unpack what I see as the significance of this remark.

Here is a starting point for thinking about the role of utopias in our lives. It comes from one of the most wonderful, if for many, unlikely, of radical academics: Northrop Frye, the seemingly 'old school' literary critic known mostly for his work on Shakespeare and the Bible.[14]

[10] Brian Langille, 'What is Labour Law? Implications of the Capability Approach' in ibid 122, 125–26.

[11] Kate Raworth, *Doughnut Economics: 7 Ways to Think Like a 21st-Century Economist* (OUP 2017).

[12] Bruno Frey, *The Economics of Happiness* (Springer 2018).

[13] This is, as I see it, the importance of some provocative and exciting new writing—see eg Nicolas Bueno, 'From Productive to Capability-Enhancing Work: Implications for Labour Law and Policy' (2022) 23(3) Journal of Human Development and Capabilities 354.

[14] Note: For me, what Frye is truly radical about is what it means to be an academic, what universities are for, how the academic oath 'reads', and academic freedom. See his collection of short essays, Northrop Frye, *On Education* (Fitzhenry and Whiteside 1988), for inspiration on these and other vital aspects of independent thought.

On utopias, and their role in our lives, Frye wrote the following:

> *Every person with any function in society at all* will have some kind of ideal vision of that society in the light of which he operates. One can hardly imagine a social worker going out to do case work without thinking of her as having, somewhere in her mind, a vision of the better, cleaner, healthier, more emotionally balanced city, as *a kind of mental model* inspiring the work she does. One can hardly imagine in fact, any professional person not having such a social model—a world of health for the doctor or justice for the judge—nor would such a social vision be confined to the professions.
>
> *It seems to me in fact that a Utopia should be conceived, not as an impossible dream of an impossible ideal, but as the kind of working model of society that exists somewhere in the mind of every sane person who has any social function at all.*[15]

Now, that is the expression of quite a radical and wonderful understanding of how the world works. It certainly is a long way from some common ideas about a utopia as necessarily unobtainable, a dream, literally a place which does not and cannot exist.

On the contrary, utopias are quotidian. They are functional. Every sane person's life is made possible in virtue of one. They are what make sense of the world and our (meaningful, human) place in it. They are to be found not in the libraries of the great universities, nor in academic meetings, but as Frye puts it, 'somewhere in the mind of every sane person who has any social function at all'. Think of that for a moment. What does it mean *not* to be a sane person with a social function? It means that you lack a utopia.

Labour lawyers are, for the most part at least, sane folk who have a social function. They have a utopia. It exists 'somewhere in the mind' (ie it is located where all important things are to be found). Note the 'somewhere'. I take this to mean, importantly, that it does not have to be, and perhaps cannot be, 'front of mind'. At least most of the time. This is because it is a 'social vision'—something that makes sense of what we see and do, sheds its light and makes a way of life apparent, establishes the path, tells us what it is we are doing, and why it is important to do it.

Labour law's constituting narrative is its utopia.

And now, Stoppard's titles point me to a further thought—not simply seeing or understanding the role of constituting narratives/utopias—but seeing that

[15] ibid 174 (emphasis added).

they have a life cycle. As Stoppard has it—a voyage, a shipwreck, followed by a salvage operation.[16]

As Frye put it, our utopia is simply 'somewhere in the mind'—most of the time we are simply engaged in 'living' the working model. Not creating, or contemplating, or critiquing it. We are simply *voyaging*, to use Stoppard's word, going to our work as labour lawyers, as sane people with a social role to use Frye's language, with the prevailing wind of our utopia at our back. As a result, we know which problems are our problems (and which ones are not), what content is appropriate for a law school course in labour law, which cases to read as a practising labour lawyer, which tasks our Ministries of Labour should tackle, what the International Labour Organization (ILO) is for, and so on.

This is also the problem with utopias.[17] They *are* prevailing. They are frameworks within which we carry out our social role. They offer us sanity in this world. They are *not* about the details of labour law or being a labour lawyer. They are *not* about any detail, or issue, or problem, or solution. Rather, our utopias are what make these details and these issues labour law's details and issues in the first place. They are thus hard to notice precisely because they tell us what to notice. Most of the time they simply, conveniently, and perhaps necessarily (if we are to get anything done) go without saying.

B. Shipwreck

This problem with our utopias is one Keynes famously noted: 'The difficulty lies, not in the new ideas, but in escaping from the old ones, which ramify, for those brought up as most of us have been, into every corner of our minds.'[18]

Any utopia/constitutive narrative, which exists 'somewhere in the mind' of labour lawyers, will be very difficult to get rid of.[19]

[16] Salvaging is a necessary, risky, dangerous, but sometimes profitable profession. Sometimes vessels can be saved, sometimes only (perhaps part of) the freight, and sometimes nothing.

[17] Langille, 'Theory of Justice' (n 7).

[18] John Maynard Keynes, *The General Theory of Employment, Interest and Money* (Palgrave Macmillan 1935) vii.

[19] I have recently come to use another, rather homely, metaphor to capture the structure of our narratives—that they make possible the fabric of what we know as labour law by providing the warp of conceptual apparatus required to legally frame labour law's empirical world and also providing the woof which is the normativity which answers the question: why is it morally important to be engaged with this aspect of our lives? In my language, our constituting narratives, our utopias, have a legal grammar and a moral narrative. Grammar and narrative are the warp and woof of the fabric of labour law. Grammar is legality. And, for me, the moral narrative could be capability. See Langille, *The Capability Approach* (n 9). Here I try to stick to a nautical metaphor.

Labour law's current constituting narrative/utopia has proven to be durable. In my view, too durable. It has been buffeted by many storms. Some major and recent external blasts have threatened to blow labour law onto the reef of oblivion. The force of these storms is felt so sharply because they threaten the three dimensions of our narrative/utopia: the empirical, the conceptual, and the normative. Empirically, the world of work has changed (eg think of 'fissuring', 'gigs', 'platform work', 'commodity chains', 'precarity', and so on). Conceptually, ideas such as employee or employer become the problem, not the answer (for instance, think of Uber cases around the world). Normatively, redressing inequality of bargaining power, vital as it is, seems to have its finger on one possible *means*, and not on an important *end* (such as 'capability', for example). But the ship of labour law has so far survived all tempests—often by having to jettison valuable ideas and crucial parts of the project such as the informal economy, unpaid work, sensible supply chain regulation, and so on. In my view, this is at least partly the result of refusing to set a new course to a newly imagined destination, in other words: to articulate a new utopia.

To put this point more directly: if we look carefully, we can now see that labour law's problems are not all 'external'. The most important one may be internal: labour law's own self-understanding.[20] And on this score we may have reached a critical point. The mighty storm of the economic crisis was not enough to wreck the good ship known as labour law.[21] But labour law recently ran into a new and unforeseen tempest in the form of the Covid pandemic. Labour law had to react quickly to a new set of empirical realities, take down and reset its conceptual rigging, and (at least implicitly) plot a new and radical normative course. I am thinking mainly of the following damages to our current ideas about labour law: the easy and wholesale desertion of the fundamental conceptual apparatus of employee and independent contractor, the shifts from contract to citizenship as the basis of entitlement, the reconceiving of how the value of work is determined, and so on. These are structural changes in the normative, conceptual, and empirical bulwarks of our discipline. This is not superficial damage. But the full implications have yet to be appreciated. The issue is not 'can we carry on?' It is rather: can we and should we salvage anything? This turns on our ability to rid ourselves of labour law's internal problems—its fixation on its current utopia. Only then can we see what got us

[20] Brian Langille, 'The Political Economy of Decency' in Georges P Politakis, Tomi Kohiyama, and Thomas Lieby (eds), *Law for Social Justice* (ILO 2019).

[21] Brian Langille, 'Human Freedom and Human Capital; Re-imagining Labour Law for Development' in Tonia Novitz and David Mangan (eds), *The Role of Labour Standards in Development: From Theory to Sustainable Practice?* (OUP 2011) 28.

into trouble in the first place, and should be left on the reef of history, but also which pieces of labour law's self-understanding we should be trying to salvage and take on board our new utopia.

C. Salvage

Long before the arrival of the pandemic it had been widely observed that the piece of legal fabric woven by our received view of labour law covers less and less of labour law's body, leaving more of those deserving our labour law exposed to the elements. Many forces are at work here—including the end of the post-war compromise, financialization, open currency markets, shareholder value ideology, revolutions in transportation and communication technologies, trade policy, fissuring, tax competition, rise of neoliberal politics, and so on. Many have been making these observations for some time.[22] And this is what the pandemic—and our legal reactions to it—made even more apparent. The good ship known as labour law had become a smaller and less important vessel over time, and fewer sailed on her.

A virus can be a vector for nonbiological events. It can lead to disruptive changes in other important dimensions of our lives. The pandemic has ripped both the internal and external fabric of our lives, including our labour law lives. Basic labour law categories are now more clearly rendered asunder, and old distinctions have disappeared—legally, not just in the real world. These legal developments are like canaries down labour law's mine—dead canaries telling us that we are in trouble. That our understanding of the enterprise of labour law is at risk. That we need a new understanding.

Here is a positive point: it is precisely when the fabric of our lives is ripped apart, when our ship is run on a reef, that we are offered a chance to see clearly and deeply into its basic structure. When we do look deeply into the torn fabric of our labour law, what do we see? We see the warp and woof, or, to combine metaphors, our frame and planking, of our labour law, exposed. We can see the basic structure which constitutes what we know as labour law. We see the moral narrative of anti-subordination/domination/power imbalance—or, to put it positively, some democracy, 'decency', or fairness—choose your words. We also see the legal grammar of contract. Together they create and simultaneously cover the real-world terrain of employment. Note this important point: many people interested in justice and fairness are concerned about power imbalances

[22] See Langille, 'Decency' (n 20) for a partial review.

and subordination. But attending also to the law, the legal expression of such moral concerns, is a burden we share as lawyers. Not everyone is a lawyer so not everyone shoulders this burden (philosophers and political theorists have it easy by comparison). But we are lawyers. We must not only have a moral narrative, but we also face the additional task of expressing it in a legal way, one that satisfies the demands of the rule of law. Specifically, of actually being law, rather than a philosophically or economically sophisticated essay. And law is the most important dimension of the eternal world of our lives together.

Grammar and narrative are bound together, as warp and woof, frame and planking, to make our labour law. In our standard utopia, subordination is legally captured and expressed in contract law as the power imbalance in employment contracts. That is what modern labour law does and is—and why it does and is. It is legal regulation of power imbalances in such contracts. You cannot create a new labour law without both dimensions. If you wish to change one, you must and you will change the other. And as a result, the whole of the 'package deal'.

But we have now seen, all around us, a rather large-scale abandonment of the legal grammar of the contract (of employment) in favour of a broader reach for labour law. But what is that reach now? How do we legally frame and express it? It is also true that when contracts are not at the centre, it follows that the moral imperative of redressing power imbalance in those contracts must have been swamped by something larger as well. But what is it?

To sum up. Our old utopia is a wreck. But also usefully exposed. We need a new one.

What would a new utopia for labour law look like? Can and should anything of the old story be salvaged, repurposed, and taken on board a new narrative?

This is where we are now: facing those questions. And some thoughtful salvage seems possible. For example, anti-subordination, our standard moral narrative, is an important moral goal. But it is also a modest grasp compared to what our moral reach can and should be. And, as with the moral narrative of anti-subordination, contract will likely remain an important idea—one which we need to account for. But as with anti-subordination, it need not be our fundamental legal grammar. Indeed, it cannot be if anti-subordination/power imbalance is seen as an inadequate motivator. And vice versa. Moreover, only by expanding beyond contract can we ever hope to capture non-contractual labour, or, put an end to 'de-contractualization' as a strategy for avoiding labour law.[23]

[23] ibid 525.

Therefore, one aspect of our salvaging operation may then be to relocate a possible role of the grammar of contract in some broader legal frame, and at the same time, the morality of protecting the weak in a more encompassing normative framework. This means we can, and will, cover more of the relevant empirical world of work. Indeed, that is our motivation: to carve the world at what is now a better joint. No longer the joint of employment. Salvaging of elements of the old labour law is possible—but only within the light of a new utopia. We salvage in the name of new legal grammar and a new moral narrative which can provide a labour law to better navigate the world as we now find it, and hope to make it. This makes the transition from one utopia to another difficult—it is not merely about imagining a new moral narrative—but also a new legal grammar in which to legally express it. And we do this while still at sea. This feat is only possible because of the truth of what Frye reminds us: our utopia, like the purpose of any voyage, rests 'somewhere in the mind'.

That is why this 'utopia' project is important. That is why these essays have been written: to undertake that difficult task and to begin where we are.

Bibliography

Bueno N, 'From Productive to Capability-Enhancing Work: Implications for Labour Law and Policy' (2022) 23(3) Journal of Human development and Capabilities 354

Deakin S, 'The Comparative Evolution of the Employment Relationship' in G Davidov and B Langille (eds), *The Boundaries and Frontiers of Labour Law* (Hart Publishing 2006)

Frey B, *The Economics of Happiness* (Springer 2018)

Frye N, *On Education* (Fitzhenry and Whiteside 1988)

Langille B, 'Core Labour Rights—The True Story' (2005) 16 European Journal of International Law 1

Langille B, 'Labour Law's Back Pages' in G Davidov and B Langille (eds), *The Boundaries and Frontiers of Labour Law* (Hart Publishing 2006)

Langille B, 'What is International Labour Law For?' (2009) 3 Law and Ethics of Human Rights 47

Langille B, 'Imagining Post Geneva Consensus Labour Law for Post Washington Consensus Development' (2010) 31 Comparative Labor Law and Policy Journal 523

Langille B, 'Human Freedom and Human Capital; Re-imagining Labour Law for Development' in T Novitz and D Mangan (eds), *The Role of Labour Standards in Development: From Theory to Sustainable Practice?* (OUP 2011)

Langille B, 'Labour Law's Theory of Justice' in G Davidov and B Langille (eds), *The Idea of Labour Law* (OUP 2011)

Langille B, *The Capability Approach to Labour Law* (OUP 2019)

Langille B, 'The Political Economy of Decency' in *Law for Social Justice* (ILO 2019)

Langille B, 'What is Labour Law? Implications of the Capability Approach' in B Langille (ed), *The Capability Approach to Labour Law* (OUP 2019)

Maynard Keynes J, *The General Theory of Employment, Interest and Money* (Palgrave Macmillan 1935)
Raworth K, *Doughnut Economics: 7 Ways to Think Like a 21st-Century Economist* (OUP 2017)
Routh S, 'The Need to Become Fashionable' in B Langille (ed), *The Capability Approach to Labour Law* (OUP 2019)
Stoppard T, *The Coast of Utopia: Voyage, Shipwreck, Salvage* (Grove Atlantic Press 2007)

3

Economic Paradigm Shifts for Labour Law

Beryl ter Haar

I. Introduction

The changing world, due to digitalization, climate change, demographic change, increasing inequality, and precariousness, has a profound impact on the world of work. Within the field of labour law, this has resulted in an overwhelming number of studies dealing with topics such as platform work, the gig economy, algorithmic management, fissured workplaces, precarious forms of work, and green jobs or ecological labour law, as well as the future of work in general. All these studies have improved our insight and understanding of the changing world of work and seek and suggest much-needed solutions within the existing labour law systems and positive laws.

The question remains whether these studies give enough insight and understanding about the changing world of work and what kind of adaptations to the labour law systems will be needed to deal with those changes. The question is particularly pertinent since these studies seem to presume that the dominant socioeconomic paradigm of a profit-driven neoliberal free market economy will remain unaltered. However, this seems to be unlikely. Ever since the 2008 financial crisis, and again during the Covid-19 pandemic, there have been strong societal[1] and academic critics[2] of this socioeconomic

[1] cf James A Anderson, 'Some Say Occupy Wall Street Did Nothing. It Changed Us More Than We Think', *Time* (New York, 15 November 2021); and Andrew Anthony, '"We showed it was possible to create a movement from almost nothing": Occupy Wall Street 10 years on', *The Guardian* (London, 12 September 2021). In relation to climate change, reference can be made to three cases brought before the European Court of Human Rights (ECtHR) as a sign of discontent in society and individuals claiming new rights to address their discontent: *Verein KlimaSeniorinnen Schweiz and Others v Switzerland* (No 53600/20) ECtHR; *Carême v France* (No 7189/21) ECtHR; and *Duarte Agostinho and Others v Portugal* (No 39371/20) ECtHR.

[2] Among many others, eg Wolfgang Streeck, *How Will Capitalism End?: Essays on a Failing System* (Verso Books 2017); The degrowth.info international editorial team, *Planning for Post-Corona: A Manifesto for the Netherlands* (Degrowth.info 11 May 2020); Manoj K Bhusal, 'The World After COVID-19: An Opportunity for a New Beginning' (2020) 10(5) International Journal of Scientific and Research Publications 735; Klaus Schwab with Peter Vanham, *Stakeholder Capitalism. A Global Economy that Works for Progress, People and Planet* (Wiley 2021); and Clive L Spash, '"The Economy" as if People Mattered: Revisiting Critiques of Economic Growth in a Time of Crisis' (2021) 18 Globalizations 1087.

Beryl ter Haar, *Economic Paradigm Shifts for Labour Law* In: *Labour Law Utopias*. Edited by: Nicolas Bueno, Beryl ter Haar, and Nuna Zekić, Oxford University Press. © Oxford University Press 2024. DOI: 10.1093/oso/9780198889755.003.0003

paradigm.[3] In turn, and especially in socioeconomic literature, this has fostered the development of alternative ideas, going by names such as Wellbeing Economy, Economics of Happiness, Stakeholder Capitalism, Collaborative Economy, Mission Economy, and Doughnut Economics. While each of these ideas has its own distinctive focus, they have in common that they propose a socioeconomic paradigm which is (more) concerned with the wellbeing of people and the planet rather than with making profits and aiming for growth as the main purpose of businesses and human activity. Therefore, I will draw on each of these ideas to demonstrate that there is a paradigm shift moving away from the neoliberal free market paradigm towards, what I call, a wellbeing paradigm.

This wellbeing paradigm will not only shift the focus of business and human activity but will also come with new work narratives. These work narratives, which Langille (Chapter 2) refers to as (work) utopias, shape our normative ideas of work. In other words, these work narratives determine our labour law systems, that is, its foundational principles, functions, structure, and content. The aim of this contribution is to gain insight into the wellbeing paradigm, the work narratives this will create, and what this will mean for labour law systems. To do that, the chapter is structured as follows. In Section II, the most relevant characteristics of the wellbeing paradigm are sketched by drawing on the socioeconomic ideas indicated above. Section III gives three examples of work narratives based on the wellbeing paradigm. These are compared with the work narratives from the social market and neoliberal free market paradigms in order to assess the magnitude of change. Section IV concludes with indications for possible foundational principles, functions, and structure of a redesigned labour law system for the wellbeing paradigm.

Due to the word limit for the chapters in this book, the wellbeing paradigm and work narratives are briefly sketched rather than comprehensively described. In terms of the aims of this chapter, namely to get an impression of the magnitude of change in work narratives in case of a paradigm shift and what that means for labour law, this is not a problem.

II. The Wellbeing Paradigm

Many of the new socioeconomic ideas that offer an alternative to the neoliberal free market economy take a forward-looking approach by responding to big

[3] cf Francis Fukuyama, *Liberalism and its Discontents* (Profile Books 2022) preface.

and disruptive changes the world is currently facing.[4] It is impossible to include all alternative ideas because they are numerous, and new ones are published and presented continuously. Nonetheless, when focusing on a number of them,[5] they seem to have some commonalities which could be considered as defining the essence of, what I call, the wellbeing paradigm. Therefore, the aim of this section is to identify these commonalities.

A. Commonality 1: More Human-Centred and Green

In response to the digital and green transitions, as well as rising inequality and precariousness, the alternative socioeconomic ideas are all shifting the focus away from measuring growth by GDP and profit-making for shareholders towards the wellbeing of people and the planet. Thus, instead of achieving wellbeing indirectly via an increase of (material) welfare, which was the aim of the (liberal) social market paradigm, or through the trickle-down effect of profit-making, which is the goal of the neoliberal free market paradigm, the wellbeing paradigm's aim is to achieve the wellbeing as a direct goal of human and business activities.

Although it is difficult, if not impossible, to define what wellbeing is, there are determinants, parameters, or settings, for society and economic systems that foster or facilitate the creation or achievement of wellbeing.[6] For example,

[4] Responding to all or most of the challenges are eg Lorenzo Fioramonti, *Wellbeing Economy. Success in a World without Growth* (Pan Macmillan South Africa 2017); Kate Raworth, *Doughnut Economics. Seven Ways to Think Like a 21st-Century Economist* (Penguin Random House 2018); Paul Collier, *The Future of Capitalism. Facing the New Anxieties* (Harper 2018); and Schwab, *Stakeholder Capitalism* (n 2). Responding with a broad(er) view in relation to digitalization are eg Daniel Susskind, *World Without Work: Technology, Automation, and How We Should Respond* (Macmillan 2020); Paul Mason, *Postcapitalism: A Guide to Our Future* (Farrar, Straus and Giroux 2017); Nick Srnicek and Alex Williams, *Inventing the Future: Postcapitalism and a World Without Work* (Verso 2016); and Erik Brynjolfsson and Andrew McAfee, *Race Against the Machine: How the Digital Revolution Is Accelerating Innovation, Driving Productivity, and Irreversibly Transforming Employment and the Economy* (Digital Frontier Press 2012). Responding with a broad(er) view in relation to climate change are eg Irmi Seidl and Angelika Zahrnt (eds), *Post Growth Work. Employment and Meaningful Activities within Planetary Boundaries* (Routledge 2022); and Matthias Schmelzer, Andrea Vetter, and Aaron Vansintjan (eds), *The Future is Degrowth. A Guide to a World beyond Capitalism* (Verso Books 2022). And on the concern with inequality/precariousness, eg Rebecca Henderson, *Reimagining Capitalism in a World on Fire. How Business Can Save the World* (Penguin Business 2021); Philippe Van Parijs en Yannick Vanderborght, *Basic Income. A Radical Proposal for a Free Society and a Sane Economy* (Harvard UP 2017); and Abhijit V Banerjee and Esther Duflo, *Poor Economics: A Radical Rethinking of the Way to Fight Global Poverty* (Penguin Books 2011).

[5] In particularly (in alphabetical order): Collier, *The Future of Capitalism* (n 4); Fioramonti, *Wellbeing Economy* (n 4); Bruno S Frey, *Economics of Happiness* (Springer 2018); Henderson, *Reimagining Capitalism* (n 4); Mariana Mazzucato, *Mission Economy. A Moonshot Guide to Changing Capitalism* (Harper Business 2021); Raworth, *Doughnut Economics* (n 4); and Schwab, *Stakeholder Capitalism* (n 2).

[6] cf Bruno S Frey and Alois Stutzer, *Happiness and Economics. How the Economy and Institutions Affect Well-Being* (Princeton UP 2002).

Raworth proposes an economic system that is regenerative and distributive to stay within the planet's ecological ceiling and social foundations respectively.[7] Fioramonti expresses a similar idea in the form of an economy that is 'powered by human relations, which play out in a transformed interaction with natural ecosystems. New businesses create value by connecting people, reducing ecological footprints and achieving the right size rather than pursuing maximisation in scale.'[8] More specifically, 'people will become prosumers, capable of making the most of the things they need through local systems of co-production, networks of small businesses and a new form of post-industrial artisanship'.[9] A qualified artisan would fix, upgrade, and upcycle products for the duration of a lifetime, which in turn makes professional activities personalized, care-driven, and context-specific.[10] Moreover, in such an economic system, activities that have no place or are undervalued in the social market and neoliberal free market paradigms would in fact be recognized for what they, according to Fioramonti, truly are, namely the 'core economy'. This will put families and communities at the centre of value creation and will aspire to the creation of a 'for wellbeing organisation'.[11] Henderson's idea for a collaborative economy built on shared purpose and common missions within businesses that go beyond profit maximization resonates well with Fioramonti's idea of 'for wellbeing organisations'.[12]

B. Commonality 2: Participation and Cooperation

The alternative ideas central to this study unanimously suggest strong and elaborate forms of participation (in a wide and democratic understanding of the word), either between institutional stakeholders or by stronger participation of citizens in society in general or at least by workers (and their representatives) in the workplace. While in itself the idea of stronger participation rights for workers is not new,[13] the socioeconomic context in which they are placed is what makes it interesting to reconsider and explore previously proposed and new forms of participation.

[7] Raworth, *Doughnut Economics* (n 4) chs 5 and 6.
[8] Fioramonti, *Wellbeing Economy* (n 4) 157.
[9] ibid 165.
[10] ibid 168.
[11] ibid 174.
[12] Henderson, *Reimagining Capitalism* (n 4) 83 and ch 4.
[13] cf Simon Deakin, 'Workers, Finance and Democracy' in Catherine Barnard, Simon Deakin, and Gillian S Morris (eds), *The Future of Labour Law: Liber Amicorum for Sir Bob Hepple* (Hart Publishing 2004) 79–100, esp 94ff.

In general, these ideas seek forms of direct participation by all individuals active in society or the workplace. Frey and Stutzer, for example, build in this context on the direct democracy that exists in Switzerland. Direct involvement of individuals is essential since happiness (or individual wellbeing) is subjective and therefore can only be achieved by active participation since this will enable the individual to strive for happiness.[14] Implanted in their ideas, Fioramonti and Varoufakis seek participation, or actually cooperation, in smaller group structures, such as in cooperatives and by regionalizing production and services. Henderson reimagines capitalism in the form of a collaborative economy in which companies serve common goals or purposes, often for the common good and which therefore should also create public-private alliances.

Besides public-private alliances and a stronger participation right for workers, Raworth and Schwab identify more actors that should be involved with decision-making in general and work in particular. For Raworth these are households, the market, and the state.[15] For Schwab, the stakeholders are governments, civil society, companies, and the international community (such as the United Nations (UN), International Labour Organization (ILO), and the European Union (EU)). In both ideas, these stakeholders strive each from their own perspectives and interests for the wellbeing of people, the planet, and future generations. For example, the international community is expected to represent global interests, especially the environment and the commons (those that otherwise have no voice but are in the interest of everyone). In such a model, all stakeholders have to balance their primary objectives and express the need for balance and solidarity: failing to achieve the objectives of one is considered a failure of all.[16] Underpinning this approach is a recognition that in the current economic paradigm contributions by certain stakeholders are too strong (especially shareholders) or too weak (especially civil society). This is to be restored by giving all stakeholders a 'seat at the table of decision-making' (read: inclusive democracy[17]) based on the principle of subsidiarity.[18]

Building on the ideas of cooperation as being more than mere participation, Raworth promotes a role for the commons. Deviating from the traditional economic idea that the commons will lead to a tragedy, she refers to the groundbreaking works on the commons by Elinor Ostrom who demonstrated that the

[14] Frey and Stutzer, *Happiness and Economics* (n 6) 133ff, and 174–75.
[15] Raworth, *Doughnut Economics* (n 4) 70–72.
[16] Schwab, *Stakeholder Capitalism* (n 2) 171ff.
[17] cf Raworth, *Doughnut Economics* (n 4) 86.
[18] Schwab, *Stakeholder Capitalism* (n 2) 185ff.

commons are actually creative when they operate under certain conditions.[19] Paolo Tomassetti (Chapter 8 in this book) explores the role of the commons in more detail. Varoufakis takes cooperation the furthest with his concept of corpo-syndicalism where no hierarchy exists, all workers own one share-one vote, and the company's legitimate existence is assessed by a 'Socialworthiness Index'.[20]

C. Commonality 3: Public-Private Cooperation

Partly following the second commonality is the third, namely the idea of public-private cooperation. This is not the same as public-private partnerships, because it is based on a strong conviction that wellbeing for people and the planet can only be achieved when governments and private organizations work together in constructive and mutually beneficial relationships. Henderson, for example, demonstrates with many examples that businesses thrive better economically, but especially in terms of sustainability, quality of work, products and services, and commitment of workers when they are purpose-driven. The purpose can be either related to the wellbeing of their workers, of society, or of both. However, while companies have an important role to play in achieving wellbeing for people and the planet, they can only do this when strong governments 'balance the power of the market with the power of inclusive institutions'.[21] In cooperation with governments, companies have to 'optimize for a broader objective than profits: the health and wealth of societies overall, as well as that of the planet and future generations'.[22] More generally, the four main stakeholders (governments, civil society, companies, and international community) are interconnected: 'Companies operate in the regulatory framework that governments provide for them. Civil society exerts pressure on governments and companies and contributes to their overall resilience. Finally, international organizations ensure consideration is given to consequences in one part of the world of the decisions made in another.'[23] Raworth promotes

[19] Raworth, *Doughnut Economics* (n 4) 82ff in which she follows the ideas of Elinor Ostrom, 'Coping with the Tragedies of the Commons' (1999) 2 Annual Review of Political Science 493–535.

[20] Yanis Varoufakis, *Another Now* (Melville House 2021) 41ff.

[21] Henderson, *Reimagining Capitalism* (n 4) 43ff; and similar in the function of coordinator: Collier, *The Future of Capitalism* (n 4) 147–48 and 207ff.

[22] Schwab, *Stakeholder Capitalism* (n 2) 173.

[23] ibid 178–79. Although Schwab presents this as a sort of balanced interconnection between the four main stakeholders, it reads more as how companies are controlled in ensuring that their activities contribute to a world in which the purpose is to create, protect, and ensure the wellbeing of people and the planet.

something similar by considering the State as 'the empowering, enabling economic partner' for all, that is, households, the commons, and the market.[24]

In her *Mission Economy*, Mazzucato builds on similar ideas, however, she places a strong focus on the role of governments in public-private cooperations. She first explains how governments have lost a strong position as experts with long-term views and how they can (and should) reclaim this with the example of the US's mission to get the first man on the moon. Based on this, Mazzucato builds a compelling argument for public-private cooperation to achieve common purposes. In these cooperations, governments are a 'goal-oriented stimulator of new ideas from the ground up' to fulfil public purposes.[25] To achieve this, she considers governments as defenders of public interests through the creation of regulations that are market-shaping in such a way that it rewards value creation and not value extraction.[26]

D. Commonality 4: Complexity

Traditional economic theory uses concepts that simplify elements of life and society. For example, the *homo economicus* acts in a rational and predictable manner, or the mechanical equilibrium which will be achieved by markets by balancing supply and demand. However, humans are not rational and predictable, and markets do not automatically reach a balance between supply and demand. In reality, humans and markets are complex. Therefore, they should also be acknowledged for and treated in their full complexity. This is most explicitly addressed by Raworth. Firstly, her *Doughnut Economics* is based on an embedded economy, which '*nests the economy within society and within the living world, while recognising the diverse ways in which it can meet people's needs and wants*'.[27] Such a view, although less concretely worked out, is also embraced by Fioramonti who finds the development of wellbeing in care (taking) as a core part of the relations underpinning the economic system which works for people and the planet.[28] In Mazzucato, the concept of embedded economy is presented by thinking in terms of circular economy.[29]

[24] Raworth, *Doughnut Economics* (n 4) 71 and 86. See also Collier, *The Future of Capitalism* (n 4) 147ff who considers a role of the government as mainly a facilitator for business development in an ethical, purpose driven, smart manner.

[25] Mazzucato, *Mission Economy* (n 5) 101–02.

[26] ibid 197ff.

[27] Raworth, *Doughnut Economics* (n 4) 71 (emphasis in original).

[28] Fioramonti, *Wellbeing Economy* (n 4) 167ff and 207ff. Dominique Méda, 'The Future of Work: The Meaning and Value of Work in Europe', *ILO Research Paper No 18*, 24 even presents a 'care paradigm'.

[29] Mazzucato, *Mission Economy* (n 5) 198, with reference to Raworth, *Doughnut Economics* (n 4).

Secondly, instead of the rational *homo economicus*, Raworth sees and treats humans in their diversity as socially adaptable humans who engage in different roles related to the economy, for example as citizens, employees, entrepreneurs, consumers, and parents.[30] Within these roles, people engage in a wide range of values 'many times a day as we switch from bargaining to giving to competing to sharing in our constantly changing economic landscape'.[31] Following from this, it is clear that humans are motivated by more than just cost and price, as is presumed with the *homo economicus*, indeed humans are motivated by various social dynamics, underpinned by values, heuristics, norms, and networks. From a legal point of view, this is interesting since those social dynamics can be influenced by nudges and network effects 'because they tap into underlying norms and values—such as duty, respect and care—and those values can be activated directly'.[32] Such an approach also means that governmental policies and legislative techniques need to recognize the complexity of human and collective behaviour, and as such the need for a 'hybrid approach' to modifying human behaviour using a mix of explicit (traditional) and implicit soft enforcement methods and interventions.[33]

Thirdly, the concept of mechanical equilibrium is replaced by the concept of a dynamic complexity 'based on systems thinking, summed up by a simple pair of feedback loops'.[34] Complexity, then, emerges from reinforcing (positive) and balancing (negative) feedback loops that interact with one another. To guide dealing with an ever-evolving complex system, Raworth proposes that economists should act in accordance with an ethical code, in the same way doctors do, an idea inspired by DeMartino.[35] Embracing complexity based on ethical rules, values, and purpose can also be found by others. Henderson's idea for a collaborative economy, for example, is based on the expectation that companies will be committed to 'building an organization in which every employee is treated with dignity and respect and viewed as a whole human being whose autonomy and worth is to be honored',[36] combined with economic and

[30] Raworth, *Doughnut Economics* (n 4) 128.

[31] ibid, with reference to Sy Montgomery, *The Soul of an Octopus* (Simon & Schuster 2015).

[32] Raworth, *Doughnut Economics* (n 4) 125ff.

[33] cf the pioneering work by Yuval Feldman, *The Law of Good People. Challenging States' Ability to Regulate Human Behaviour* (CUP 2018).

[34] Raworth, *Doughnut Economics* (n 4) 28 and 138ff. Similarly, Schwab, *Stakeholder Capitalism* (n 2) 193ff; and in a radical different form, Varoufakis, *Another Now* (n 20) 61ff with the Socialworthiness Index.

[35] Raworth, *Doughnut Economics* (n 4) 160–62, with reference to George F DeMartino, 'Professional Economic Ethics: Why Heterodox Economists should Care' (2012, paper given at World Economic Association Conference). Similarly, Schwab, *Stakeholder Capitalism* (n 2) 191, with reference to the 'Davos Manifesto 2020'.

[36] Henderson, *Reimagining Capitalism* (n 4) 95.

political institutions that are inclusive.[37] The same applies for Frey and Stutzer since happiness (wellbeing) cannot be achieved when humans, in their various roles, are not enabled to pursue their own happiness.[38] Collier envisions something similar with his value-based society that 'pragmatically steers capitalism' based on shared senses of belonging and identity.[39]

E. Commonality 5: Value-Based

The alternative ideas are based on values and purpose. This too is not new in itself, but the values and purpose that underpin the alternative ideas are fundamentally different from those that underpin the social market and neoliberal free market paradigms. Indeed, these ideas take a rather pragmatic approach to values, purposes, and goals, instead of one that is based on ideology. The latter, ideology, is even actively rejected as being disruptive rather than constructive.[40] Furthermore, the alternative ideas embrace an interpretation of values, purposes, and goals that is much wider than those exclusively linked to pure economic values and productivity.[41] Henderson, for example, states that a 'genuinely purpose-driven organization is in itself an act that creates shared value since it requires creating the kind of jobs that are needed to begin to address inequality and build a just society'.[42] Schwab and Mazzucato argue something similar based on a stakeholder approach which recognizes that value is created collectively, that is, not only by companies but also 'by educators, scientists, cultural actors, government institutions, ... society and the natural environment itself'.[43] For Mazzucato this also means that governments need to take the lead and set long-term missions to achieve values that are driven by public purposes from a market-shaping view.[44] Raworth argues in this context that

[37] ibid 210ff.
[38] Frey and Stutzer, *Happiness and Economics* (n 6) 171ff.
[39] Collier, *The Future of Capitalism* (n 4) 206ff.
[40] These are rejected explicitly by Schwab and Collier (supported by Banerjee and Duflo in their *Poor Economics* (n 4) and implicitly by Frey, Mazzucato, and Raworth.
[41] See on this also the Introduction of this book, especially the ideas of Jackson.
[42] Henderson, *Reimagining Capitalism* (n 4) 87; and similarly, Collier, *The Future of Capitalism* (n 4) 69ff with the idea of an *ethical firm*. See on this also Alain Supiot, 'Labour Is Not a Commodity: The Content and Meaning of Work in the Twenty-First Century' (2021) 160(1) International Labour Review 8.
[43] Schwab, *Stakeholder Capitalism* (n 2) 184, with reference to Mariana Mazzucato, *The Value of Everything* (Penguin Random House 2018). See also Mazzucato, *Mission Economy* (n 5) 194.
[44] Mazzucato, *Mission Economy* (n 5) 181 and 207ff; and similarly, Collier, *The Future of Capitalism* (n 4) 147ff; and Henderson, *Reimagining Capitalism* (n 4) 208ff (inclusive economy and political institutions).

the success of the economy will not be reflected in 'the metric of money but in the metric that reflects human prosperity in a flourishing web of life'.[45]

F. Commonality 6: Degrowth and Post (Productive) Work

The shift of values, purposes, and goals of human and business activities away from pure profit-making and productivity to what is important for the wellbeing of people and the planet, is accompanied by a sense of degrowth. Especially when the wellbeing of the planet is to be taken into account, there seems to be no other conclusion than that economic systems should become 'agnostic about growth'. For Raworth, agnostic means the design of an economy 'that promotes human prosperity whether GDP is going up, down or holding steady'.[46] However, this refers only to 'monetary' growth, growth in the old sense of profit-making in which not all costs of production are included. But, when the alternative ideas are examined closely, it is clear that growth is no longer a purely monetary idea, instead growth is related to the achievement of certain values, purposes, and goals. Growth is, therefore, more related to how societies (communities) use the resources of the planet and maintain a balance between what is good for the planet and the needs of people. This approach is particularly strong in the ideas of Fioramonti, Varoufakis, and Andriessen, and can also be linked to Hickel and Jackson (see the Introduction of this book).

With the focus of human and business activities on what is good for the planet and needed by people, the new alternative ideas can also be situated in ideas of post-productive work, such as addressed by Graeber and presented by Chamberlain (see the Introduction of this book). The ideas of Fioramonti, Varoufakis, and Andriessen especially fit with this approach.

III. Examples of New Work Narratives of the Wellbeing Paradigm

Rather than speaking in terms of productive work activities, the wellbeing paradigm focuses on how human and business activities can contribute to

[45] Raworth, *Doughnut Economics* (n 4) 279; and similarly, Varoufakis, *Another Now* (n 20) with his Socialworthiness Index; and Frey and Stutzer, *Happiness and Economics* (n 6), with their recognition that happiness is subjective and can only be achieved when people are enabled to reach for what makes them happy.

[46] Raworth, *Doughnut Economics* (n 4) 245.

the achievement of happiness or wellbeing of people within the boundaries of the planet.[47] Wellbeing in this context is to be understood as something to be achieved at the level of society as a whole (people and planet) and the individual person.[48] Hence, new work narratives are created. The three example work narratives have been selected because they are the most characteristic narratives of the social market and neoliberal free market paradigms. Each narrative is concluded with an indication of what the narrative means for the foundational principles and functions of the labour law system.

A. Work Narrative Example 1: From Labour Is Not a Commodity to Human Capital to Human Centred

Capitalist markets treat labour, land, and money as commodities; as if they were products that could be traded on the market.[49] However, they are in fact the basic conditions for production and trade and therefore, in order to be sustainable, they need to be regulated to match reality. When it comes to labour, the reality is that 'it cannot be separated from the person of the worker and its performance involves a physical commitment, intelligence and competences that form part of the historical specificities of each human life'.[50] Therefore, the phrase 'labour is not a commodity' is one of the foundational principles of the ILO, reiterated in its 1944 Philadelphia Declaration.[51] It was also the leading phrase for the development of the post-war welfare states, a period Fudge indicated as 'labour law's golden years',[52] a period that was characterized by the ideas of social democracy.[53] Therefore, the main foundational principles of the

[47] This is particularly strong in the ideas by Collier, *The Future of Capitalism* (n 4); Fioramonti, *Wellbeing Economy* (n 4); Varoufakis, *Another Now* (n 20); Jurriaan Andriessen, *Eldorica* (Het Spectrum 1990); and Raworth, *Doughnut Economics* (n 4) 280–84 (new aspirations). To a lesser extent also in the ideas by Henderson, *Reimagining Capitalism* (n 4); Mazzucato, *Mission Economy* (n 5); Frey and Stutzer, *Happiness and Economics* (n 6) 36–40; and Schwab, *Stakeholder Capitalism* (n 2) esp 234–36 where he refers to New Zealand which moved away from GDP towards a wellbeing approach based on four capitals: natural capital, human capital, social capital, and financial and physical capital.

[48] Esp Collier, *The Future of Capitalism* (n 4); and Andriessen, *Eldorica* (n 47).

[49] cf Supiot, 'Labour Is Not a Commodity' (n 42) 6, with reference to Karl Polanyi, *The Great Transformation: The Political and Economic Origins of Our Time* [1944] (Beacon Press 2001) ch 6, 'The Self-Regulating Market and the Fictitious Commodities: Labor, Land, and Money', 71–80.

[50] Supiot, 'Labour Is Not a Commodity' (n 42) 6.

[51] ibid; and, in more detail, Sandrine Kott, 'L'OIT en tension: entre travail humain et productivisme' in Pierre Musso and Alain Supiot (eds), *Qu'est-ce qu'un régime de travail réellement humain?* (Hermann 2018) 399–413.

[52] Judy Fudge, 'Labour as a "Fictive Commodity": Radically Reconceptualizing Labour Law' in Guy Davidov and Brian Langille (eds), *The Idea of Labour Law* (OUP 2011) 122.

[53] ibid. See also Bob Hepple and Bruno Veneziani (eds), *The Transformation of Labour Law in Europe: A Comparative Study of 15 Countries 1945–2004* (Hart Publishing 2009).

labour law system were social justice, human dignity, and equality, with protection and balancing the power between the workers and the employer by law and collective labour relations as its main functions.[54]

In the neoliberal free market paradigm, the phrase 'labour is not a commodity' has been pushed to the background by the notion of 'human capital'. This notion refers to the idea that human labour is seen as 'natural capital' on which a market price can be placed.[55] This is not only within companies but also by governments and the EU, especially with their focus on employment policies, which include investment policies.[56] Besides more traditional investment 'costs', such as those related to occupational health and safety measures, this includes costs for training and (personal) development (eg the EU's lifelong learning policy) to keep their workers employable within the company and on the labour markets in general. The 'human capital' approach also fosters an environment in which the human contribution to work is measured by productivity, and investments are therefore aimed at increasing the productivity of its human workers. Investments in digitalization and robotization are striking examples of this.[57] In a sense, the inclusion of capability (albeit not in the sense as understood in the works of Sen and Nussbaum[58]) as a foundational principle for labour law can be seen as an expression of this change, as well as the inclusion of labour markets policies as a function of the labour law system.[59]

In the wellbeing paradigm, the attention will be fully on the human. Instead of seeing the human worker as part of the production process—in other words: what can the human with their labour, intellect, etc mean for the company and productivity—the question will be what work has to offer to the individual human being as well as society. Individuals will be looking for work activities that will give them satisfaction in terms of esteem, belonging, and self-realization. Preferably, such work activities will also contribute to the wellbeing of society, since this increases the feelings of esteem and belonging. As Bueno explores in more detail in Chapter 7 of this book, this requires us

[54] cf Fudge, 'Labour as a "Fictive Commodity"' (n 52) 123; and Frank Henderickx, 'Foundations and Functions of Contemporary Labour Law' (2012) 3(2) European Labour Law Journal 108.

[55] Supiot, 'Labour Is Not a Commodity' (n 42) 7; and more generally Gary S Becker, *Human Capital: A Theoretical and Empirical Analysis with Special Reference to Education* (3rd edn, University of Chicago Press 1993).

[56] eg Beryl ter Haar, 'Design and Influence of the EU's Youth OMC. A Case Study of the NEET's Needs and The Netherlands' (2020 and 2021) Hungarian Labour Law e-Journal, 2020/1 (part 1) and 2021/1 (part 2).

[57] cf Albin, Chapter 10 in this book.

[58] See, for more detail on the capability approach in the context of labour law, Brain Langille (ed), *The Capability Approach in Labour Law* (OUP 2019).

[59] Frank Henderickx, 'Foundations and Functions' (n 54).

to evaluate and regulate work activities by completely different standards. The quality of work activities will no longer be evaluated by elements such as minimum wage, health and safety, decent working time, and autonomy only. It will also be evaluated on how such activities contribute to society as a whole (destructive or constructive[60]) as well as the extent to which undertaking those activities will enable the individual to realize their talents and perform the work activities of their own choice. Therefore, the foundational principles of the labour law system in the wellbeing paradigm would include at least social purpose and capability (as understood in the works of Sen and Nussbaum). The function of the labour law system in the wellbeing paradigm would be to foster esteem, belonging, and self-realization, such to be achieved by a labour law system that is more enabling and facilitating rather than purely protective in nature.

B. Work Narrative Example 2: From a Standard Employment Contract to Flexicurity to Free from Income from Work

Under the social market paradigm, a full-time open-ended employment contract was the standard. Such a contract was based on the idea that an employee would serve most of his working life with one employer. Because it was not common to change jobs, losing a job had a major impact on the life of the employee, often the breadwinner, and his family. Consequently, dismissal protection was an important element of the labour law system. Since dismissal often resulted in long-term unemployment, a rigorous social protection system was needed, supported by passive labour market policies, that is, only providing the benefits and leaving it up to the individual to find their way back on to the labour market. Dismissal protection and social protection are therefore characteristic contents of the protective function of the labour law system. They give expression to the foundational principles of social justice and human dignity.

The full-time open-ended employment contract is no longer the standard in the neoliberal free market paradigm. Instead, a wide variety of employment contracts and employment relationships have developed. Contracts vary in working hours (part-time, zero-hour, on-call), duration (fixed term, seasonal, projects), contractual construction (work-mediators like temporary works agencies, payrolling, intra-concern posting), and qualification (employee,

[60] See on this also David Graeber, *Bullshit Jobs: The Rise of Pointless Work, and What We Can Do About It* (Penguin 2019) 210ff.

dependent self-employed, employee-like worker). This proliferation of atypical or non-standard work arrangements is, among other things, the result of the flexibilization of the labour market. This means flexibility for the employer to increase and decrease its workforce with the demand for products and services. For the employee, flexibility is a means to better combine work and private life. Within the EU in particular, flexibility is combined with security: flexicurity.[61] Security is about keeping workers employable (via training), assisting the unemployed in their transition to a new job, and providing adequate unemployment benefits. These rather fundamental changes have resulted in weaker labour law protections of non-standard employment relationships,[62] and in social security systems which are accompanied by active labour market policies, including penalties in case of non-cooperation by the unemployed in their transition to a new job. These changes have also resulted in a changed meaning of the foundational principles of social justice,[63] human dignity,[64] and equality. The latter refers not only to equality between men and women, but also in income and employment security, employment opportunities, etc. The inclusion of capability as a foundational principle can also be seen as an element of flexicurity since fast transitions between jobs can only be realized when the individual worker remains employable.[65] The functions of the labour law system have changed from mainly providing dismissal protection and passive labour market policies to also facilitating flexibility and active labour market policies.

The basic idea in the wellbeing paradigm is to make everyone less dependent on income from work. To achieve this, ideas are proposed to distribute wealth. For Raworth, for example, 'distribution' concerns especially the wealth that 'lies in controlling land, enterprise, technology, knowledge and the power to create money'.[66] Ideas to realize such distribution of wealth include changes to tax systems[67] and forms of a universal basic

[61] European Commission, Communication *Towards Common Principles of Flexicurity: More and better jobs through flexibility and security* (COM(2007) 359).

[62] In many legal systems a-typical workers are not or not fully covered by labour law. cf Judy Fudge, Shae McChristal, and Kamala Sankaran (eds), *Challenging the Legal Boundaries of Work Regulation* (Hart Publishing 2012); and Guy Davidov, *A Purposive Approach to Labour Law* (OUP 2016) 98ff.

[63] eg with a change of the division of risk between the employer and employee, depending on the deviation from the standard employment contract. cf David Weil, *The Fissured Workplace* (Harvard UP 2017).

[64] See, indirectly on this, Nuna Zekić, *Werkzekerheid in het Arbeidsrecht* (Kluwer Academic Press 2014).

[65] cf Virginia Mantouvalou, 'Work, Human Rights, and Human Capabilities' in Brian Langille (ed), *The Capability Approach to Labour Law* (OUP 2019) 210, who considers employability as a right that is part of the right to work.

[66] Raworth, *Doughnut Economics* (n 4) 177.

[67] eg Thomas Piketty, 'Capital and Wealth Taxation in the 21st[t] Century' (2015) 68(2) National Tax Journal 449; and Raworth, *Doughnut Economics* (n 4) 278–79 who proposes taxing the use of non-renewable resources instead of labour; Collier, *The Future of Capitalism* (n 4) 132, 142–44, and 187 who

income.[68] Varoufakis introduces a radically new idea, namely Personal Capital, which consists of three components: Accumulation (income deposits generated with work activities); Legacy (which is a kind of trust fund every baby receives from the Sate); and Dividend (a universal right to the proceeds of society's capital which is made possible by monthly payments by the State).[69] While the idea to free people from income from work is not new per se, it was hard or even impossible to realize during the other two paradigms,[70] it could work within the wellbeing paradigm because of the fundamental re-valuation of human and business activities that comes with it (see Example 1 in Section III.A). When humans are no longer dependent on income from work, there will be hardly any need for dismissal protection. There will also be no need for adequate unemployment benefits or labour market policies to guide the transition from work to work. There might be more need for policies to facilitate the realization of talents so they can be used for the benefit of society and the wellbeing of the individual. That means that the foundational principle of social justice will be more about the distribution of wealth (and not redistribution), human dignity will be more about the fulfilment of values and norms that bring people esteem, belonging, and satisfaction, and capability will become the most important foundational principle, with equality as an independent principle possibly becoming obsolete. This will come with new functions of the labour law system, such as distributing wealth (in the form of something like a basic income), facilitating the realization of talents, and facilitating the fulfilment of values and norms that bring people esteem, belonging, and satisfaction. It would make social security, dismissal protection laws, and labour market policies for full employment obsolete.

argues for taxation guided by ethics and efficiency, leading to eg tax on economic rents and financial transactions. See also DeBecker and Claus, Chapter 11 in this book, in which they propose a tax on consumption instead of income.

[68] Besides Raworth, among many others, Rutger Bregman, *Utopia for Realists: And How We Can Get There* (Bloomsbury 2017); Philip Alston, 'Universal Basic Income as a Social Rights-Based Antidote to Growing Economic Insecurity in Katharina Young (ed), *The Future of Economic and Social Rights*, foreword by Amartya Sen (CUP Press 2019) 377; and Daniel Dumont, 'Universal Basic Income as a Source of Inspiration for the Future of Social Protection Systems? A Counter-Agenda' (2022) 24(4) European Journal of Social Security 299.

[69] Varoufakis, *Another Now* (n 20) 52–55.

[70] cf Dumont, 'Universal Basic Income' (n 68).

C. Work Narrative Example 3: From Social and Collective to Human Rights and Individual to Values and Purposes

The social market paradigm is characterized by a sense of collectivity, both towards society as well as to workplace organization.[71] With the need for rebuilding, many private business activities were linked to public goals, such as building houses and infrastructures. Thus, a sense of social purpose was present in many jobs, which often justified the lack of personal satisfaction in performing that job.[72] Workplaces, with jobs for life, were also communities with people that were taking care of each other. Hence, a sense of collective organization in trade unions, works councils, and other forms was strongly present and promoted and protected in labour laws. Therefore, the freedom of association and the right to collective bargaining can be considered labour law's function to balance the power between the employer and the workers which is part of the foundational principle of social justice.

The changes that came with the shift to the neoliberal free market paradigm are multiple, but they can be summarized as a change to individualism and human rights. Individualism at the workplace is fostered and facilitated by the development of flexible employment relationships leading to fewer people working in jobs for life, but also by the outsourcing of ancillary work activities (like security, cleaning, and catering), and the globalization of the work processes. Thus, instead of one integrated workplace where everyone is a member of the same 'family', the workplace is fissured in various ways reducing the sense of community and the feeling of belonging.[73] Furthermore, some flexible work arrangements, for example self-employment, remote working, and platform labour, have complicated collective organization and bargaining.[74]

[71] cf Bob Hepple and Bruno Veneziani, 'Introduction' in Hepple and Veneziani (eds), *The Transformation of Labour Law in Europe* (n 53).

[72] Something that is still strongly felt in communist countries, especially China where everyone has a moral duty to contribute to the economic wellbeing of China. Consequently, a standard six-day working week of twelve hours per day (from 9–9) is accepted by the majority of the population. cf Weidong Zhang, *Achieving Decent Work in China. A Case Study of Decent Working Time* (Dissertation, Leiden University 2023).

[73] cf Guy Mundlack, *Organising Matters. Two Logics of Trade Union Representation* (Edward Elgar Publishing/ILO 2020), who discusses similar developments to address the decline in trade union membership.

[74] cf Iacopo Senatori and Carla Spinelli (eds), *Litigation (Collective) Strategies to Protect Gig Workers' Rights. Comparative Perspectives* (G. Giappichelli Editore 2022); Teun Jaspers, 'Collective Bargaining and Competition Law' in Beryl ter Haar and Attila Kun (eds), *EU Collective Labour Law* (Edward Elgar Publishers 2021) 376–95; and Joanna Unterschütz, 'Digital Work—Real Bargaining: How Can the Sustainability of Social Dialogue Be Ensured in the Digital Era?' in Jeff Kenner, Izabela Florczak, and Marta Otto (eds), *Precarious Work. The Challenge for Labour Law in Europe* (Edward Elgar Publishing 2019) 222–41.

A loss of collectivism is also due to the neoliberal ideology in which the State—the collective—shifts certain responsibilities to its citizens. For example, entitlements to unemployment and social benefits are linked to obligations on the individual for a fast transition back to work (see section III.B on active labour market policies). The individualization of society and the workplace has also been contributed to the rise of human rights, which takes the individual as the primary subject, hence it favours the interests of the individual, even when dealing with collective labour rights.[75] While much more can and ideally should be said about this, the bottom line of the shifts that came with the neoliberal free market paradigm is one that favours the individual over the collective, enforced by a mantra of human rights over labour rights. In labour law's foundational principles, this change is reflected in a human rights interpretation of human dignity, enforced by its facilitating function to regulate flexible work arrangements, and the inclusion of active labour market policies with additional requirements to keep entitlements to unemployment and social benefits. The ordering function of collective labour rights seems to have a less prominent position in the labour law system of this paradigm.

The wellbeing paradigm moves back to the idea of societal purpose and collectivity (belonging) as found in the social market paradigm, but takes it a step further. Indeed, the wellbeing paradigm is fully built on values, purposes, and goals for society as a whole and for the individual. Therefore, the balance between interests is not between those of the worker and the employer, but it is between those of society and the individual. Given that all human and business activities are to take place within the boundaries of the planet, those interests also need to be considered. The interests of the individual include the opportunity to develop, realize, and give expression to one's talents and the freedom to decide how to use those talents for the benefit of society. One way to achieve the balance between the three main interests is by strong participation rights for all stakeholders, including workers, which would be one of the foundational principles for the wellbeing labour law system. Other foundational principles

[75] Kevin Kolbin, 'Labor Rights and Human Rights' (2010) 50(2) Virginia Journal of International Law Association 449; Keith Ewing, 'Law Against Strikes Revisited' in Catherine Barnard, Simon Deakin, and Gillian S Morris (eds), *The Future of Labour Law* (n 13) esp 50–59; Bob Hepple, 'The Freedom to Strike and its Rationale' in Bob Hepple, Rochelle Le Roux, and Silvana Sciarra (eds), *Laws Against Strikes. The South African Experience in an International and Comparative Perspective* (Franco Angeli 2015) 27–44; and Viginia Mantouvalou, 'Are Labour Rights Human Rights?' (2012) 3(2) European Labour Law Journal 18.

that have been suggested in the context of values, purposes, and goals include socioecological justice,[76] self- realization,[77] care,[78] and accommodation.[79]

IV. Conclusions: Foundational Principles, Function, and Structure of a Wellbeing Labour Law System

The brief sketches of the work narratives and indications of what that means for labour law's foundational principles and functions in Section III make clear the significant magnitude of change that comes with the wellbeing paradigm. To make this more visible, the work narratives, foundational principles, and functions have been summarized in Table 3.1. Table 3.1 also gives an indication of the structure of the labour law system that can be deduced from the foundational principles and functions.

What stands out in this table is that there are more foundational principles in the wellbeing paradigm. This was to be expected because in this paradigm, the interests of society, individuals, and the planet are central, rather than subjective to the interests of the market. Furthermore, there is little overlap in terminology and even where there is overlap, the meaning has changed (see eg capability).

Secondly, the function of the wellbeing labour law system is radically different, except for the ordering function. The function of labour law in the wellbeing paradigm seems to be about fostering, distributing (not *re*distributing), enabling, and facilitating. This reflects Feldman's ideas for a hybrid legislative approach to modify human behaviour. Modify means in this context to influence the behaviour of people in a desired direction. Such an approach is also needed when the complexity of society and human nature is fully recognized, both in the socioeconomic system, like it is in the wellbeing paradigm, and by legislative techniques.

Thirdly, the structure of the labour law system in the wellbeing paradigm is also radically different from that of the other two paradigms. Given the information collected in this chapter, I have chosen to structure the system by the type of regulatory techniques. With more examples and more details, it may be imagined that other structures are also possible. What is clear, though, is that

[76] cf Carelli, Chapter 5 in this book.

[77] Although approached differently, see for more detailed ideas on this, Zekić (Chapter 4 in this book) and Bueno (Chapter 7 in this book). See also Mantouvalou, 'Work, Human Rights' (n 65) 203–04, 210.

[78] Méda, 'The Future of Work' (n 28).

[79] cf Albin, Chapter 10 in this book.

Table 3.1 Overview work narratives, foundational principles, functions, and structures of labour law systems

	Socioeconomic Paradigm	Social Market Paradigm	Neoliberal Free Market Paradigm	Wellbeing Paradigm
Labour law system	Keywords work narratives	Labour is not a commodity	Human capital	Human
		Standard employment contract	Flexicurity	Free from income of work
		Social/Collective	Human rights/ Individualistic	Values/Purposes
	Foundational principles	Social justice (balancing social and market)	Social justice	Socioecological justice (balancing social, individual, and planetary needs)
		Human dignity (social interpretation)	Human dignity (human rights interpretation)	Pragmatic (universal) values and norms
		Equality	Equality	Social purpose
			Capability (aimed at increasing productivity)	Capability (self-realization)
				Participation and cooperation
				Care and Accommodating approaches
	Functions	Protective	Protective	Fostering (feelings of belonging and self-esteem)
		Ordering	Ordering	Ordering (participation, cooperation, balancing interests)
		Passive labour market policies	Active labour market policies Facilitating flexibility	Distributive (wealth/income) Enabling (self-realization)
				Facilitating care and accommodating approaches
	Structure	Individual Collective Social Protection	Individual Collective Labour market policies Social Protection	Fostering Ordering Distributing Enabling Facilitating

with a likely loss of importance of the employment contract (after all, we will no longer be dependent on work for income), it is less likely that the wellbeing labour law system will follow a structure that is strongly related to the employment contract.

To conclude, based on only three examples of work narratives that are created with the wellbeing paradigm, it is already clear that the shift in paradigm requires a radical redesigning of the labour law system. Radical enough that it creates space to realize labour law utopias, such as those presented in the other chapters of this book.

Bibliography

Alston P, 'Universal Basic Income as a Social Rights-Based Antidote to Growing Economic Insecurity' in K Young (ed), *The Future of Economic and Social Rights* (CUP 2019)

Anderson JA, 'Some Say Occupy Wall Street Did Nothing. It Changed Us More Than We Think', *Time* (New York, 15 November 2021)

Anthony A, '"We showed it was possible to create a movement from almost nothing": Occupy Wall Street 10 years on', *The Guardian* (London, 12 September 2021)

Banerjee AV and Duflo E, *Poor Economics: A Radical Rethinking of the Way to Fight Global Poverty* (Penguin Books 2011)

Becker GS, *Human Capital: A Theoretical and Empirical Analysis with Special Reference to Education* (3rd edn, University of Chicago Press 1993)

Bhusal MK, 'The World After COVID-19: An Opportunity for a New Beginning' (2020) 10(5) International Journal of Scientific and Research Publications 735

Bregman R, *Utopia for Realists: And How We Can Get There* (Bloomsbury 2017)

Brynjolfsson E and McAfee A, *Race Against the Machine: How the Digital Revolution is Accelerating Innovation, Driving Productivity, and Irreversibly Transforming Employment and the Economy* (Digital Frontier Press 2012)

Collier P, *The Future of Capitalism: Facing the New Anxieties* (Harper 2018)

Davidov G, *A Purposive Approach to Labour Law* (OUP 2016)

Deakin S, 'Workers, Finance and Democracy' in C Barnard, S Deakin, and GS Morris (eds), *The Future of Labour Law: Liber Amicorum for Sir Bob Hepple* (Hart Publishing 2004)

DeMartino GF, 'Professional Economic Ethics: Why Heterodox Economists should Care' (2012, Paper given at World Economic Association Conference)

Dumont D, 'Universal Basic Income as a Source of Inspiration for the Future of Social Protection Systems? A Counter-Agenda' (2022) 24(4) European Journal of Social Security 299

European Commission, Communication *Towards Common Principles of Flexicurity: More and better jobs through flexibility and security* (COM(2007) 359)

Ewing K, 'Law Against Strikes Revisited' in C Barnard, S Deakin, and GS Morris (eds), *The Future of Labour Law: Liber Amicorum for Sir Bob Hepple* (Hart Publishing 2004)

Feldman Y, *The Law of Good People: Challenging States' Ability to Regulate Human Behaviour* (CUP 2018)

Fioramonti L, *Wellbeing Economy: Success in a World without Growth* (Pan Macmillan 2017)

Frey BS, *Economics of Happiness* (Springer 2018)

Frey BS and Stutzer A, *Happiness and Economics: How the Economy and Institutions Affect Well-Being* (Princeton UP 2002)

Fudge J, 'Labour as a "Fictive Commodity": Radically Reconceptualizing Labour Law' in G Davidov and B Langille (eds), *The Idea of Labour Law* (OUP 2011)

Fudge J, McChristal S, and Sankaran K (eds), *Challenging the Legal Boundaries of Work Regulation* (Hart Publishing 2012)

Fukuyama F, *Liberalism and its Discontents* (Profile Books 2022)

Graeber D, *Bullshit Jobs: The Rise of Pointless Work, and What We Can Do About It* (Penguin 2019)

Haar B ter, 'Design and Influence of the EU's Youth OMC. A Case Study of the NEET's Needs and The Netherlands' (2020 and 2021) Hungarian Labour Law e-Journal, 2020/1 (part 1) and 2021/1 (part 2)

Henderickx F, 'Foundations and Functions of Contemporary Labour Law' (2012) 3(2) European Labour Law Journal 108

Henderson R, *Reimagining Capitalism in a World on Fire: How Business Can Save the World* (Penguin Business 2021)

Hepple B, 'The Freedom to Strike and its Rationale' in B Hepple, R Le Roux, and S Sciarra (eds), *Laws Against Strikes. The South African Experience in an International and Comparative Perspective* (Franco Angeli 2015)

Hepple B and Veneziani B, 'Introduction' in B Hepple and B Veneziani (eds), *The Transformation of Labour Law in Europe: A Comparative Study of 15 Countries 1945–2004* (Hart Publishing 2009)

Hepple B and Veneziani B (eds), *The Transformation of Labour Law in Europe: A Comparative Study of 15 Countries 1945–2004* (Hart Publishing 2009)

Jaspers T, 'Collective Bargaining and Competition Law' in B ter Haar and A Kun (eds), *EU Collective Labour Law* (Edward Elgar Publishers 2021)

Kolbin K, 'Labor Rights and Human Rights' (2010) 50(2) Virginia Journal of International Law Association 449

Kott S, 'L'OIT en tension: entre travail humain et productivisme' in P Musso and A Supiot (eds), *Qu'est-ce qu'un régime de travail réellement humain?* (Hermann 2018)

Langille B (ed), *The Capability Approach in Labour Law* (OUP 2019)

Mantouvalou V, 'Are Labour Rights Human Rights?' (2012) 3(2) European Labour Law Journal 18

Mantouvalou V, 'Work, Human Rights, and Human Capabilities' in B Langille (ed), *The Capability Approach to Labour Law* (OUP 2019)

Mason P, *Postcapitalism: A Guide to Our Future* (Farrar, Straus and Giroux 2017)

Mazzucato M, *The Value of Everything* (Penguin Random House 2018)

Mazzucato M, *Mission Economy: A Moonshot Guide to Changing Capitalism* (Harper Business 2021)

Méda D, 'The Future of Work: The Meaning and Value of Work in Europe', ILO Research Paper No 18

Montgomery S, *The Soul of an Octopus* (Simon & Schuster 2015)

Mundlack G, *Organising Matters: Two Logics of Trade Union Representation* (Edward Elgar Publishing/ILO 2020)

Ostrom E, 'Coping with the Tragedies of the Commons' (1999) 2 Annual Review of Political Science 493

Piketty T, 'Capital and Wealth Taxation in the 21st Century' (2015) 68(2) National Tax Journal 449.

Polanyi K, *The Great Transformation: The Political and Economic Origins of Our Time* (Beacon Press 2001 [1944])
Raworth K, *Doughnut Economics. Seven Ways to Think Like a 21st-Century Economist* (Random House 2018)
Schmelzer M, Vetter A, and Vansintjan A (eds), *The Future is Degrowth. A Guide to a World beyond Capitalism* (Verso Books 2022)
Schwab K with Vanham P, *Stakeholder Capitalism: A Global Economy that Works for Progress, People and Planet* (Wiley John and Sons 2021)
Seidl I and Zahrnt A (eds), *Post Growth Work: Employment and Meaningful Activities within Planetary Boundaries* (Routledge 2022)
Senatori I and Spinelli C (eds), *Litigation (Collective) Strategies to Protect Gig Workers' Rights: Comparative Perspectives* (G. Giappichelli Editore 2022)
Spash CL, '"The Economy" as if People Mattered: Revisiting Critiques of Economic Growth in a Time of Crisis' (2021) 18 Globalizations 1087
Srnicek N and Williams A, *Inventing the Future: Postcapitalism and a World Without Work* (Verso 2016)
Streeck W, *How Will Capitalism End?: Essays on a Failing System* (Verso Books 2017)
Supiot A, 'Labour Is Not a Commodity: The Content and Meaning of Work in the Twenty-First Century' (2021) 160(1) International Labour Review 1
Susskind D, *World Without Work: Technology, Automation, and How We Should Respond* (Macmillan 2020)
The degrowth.info international editorial team, *Planning for Post-Corona: A Manifesto for the Netherlands* (Degrowth.info 11 May 2020)
Unterschütz J, 'Digital Work—Real Bargaining: How Can the Sustainability of Social Dialogue Be Ensured in the Digital Era?' in J Kenner, I Florczak, and M Otto (eds), *Precarious Work. The Challenge for Labour Law in Europe* (Edward Elgar Publishing 2019)
Van Parijs P and Vanderborght Y, *Basic Income. A Radical Proposal for a Free Society and a Sane Economy* (Harvard UP 2017)
Varoufakis Y, *Another Now* (Melville House 2021)
Weil D, *The Fissured Workplace* (Harvard UP 2017)
Zekić N, *Werkzekerheid in het Arbeidsrecht* (Kluwer Academic Press 2014)
Zhang W, *Achieving Decent Work in China: A Case Study of Decent Working Time* (Dissertation, Leiden University 2023)

4

Labour Law for Degrowth and Meaningful Work

Nuna Zekić

I. Introduction

As labour law scholars, we often either start or finish our scholarly work with the explanation that the 'world of work' is changing and note that labour law needs to adapt to those changes. The challenges that the field faces are not trivial: Globalization and intensified market competition, technological changes and the use of artificial intelligence (AI), falling unionization rates, growing economic inequality, climate change and the need to transition to a truly sustainable economy—they all affect the workplace and work relations. Thinking in terms of utopias (for labour law) can seem to be wishful thinking, because many of these challenges have been debated for a long time, while seeing too little improvement. However, the Covid-19 pandemic has taught us that big changes can happen fast and that ideas for a better future are never wasted.

When we think about how labour law should look in an ecologically sustainable and just future, we need to include the question of what meaning paid work has in people's lives and in our societies. After all, paid work is a powerful driver of the economy. Most governments have always pursued, and still pursue, full employment as one of their main social policy objectives. However, as will be explained below, an economy dependent on continuous economic growth (eg measured as Gross Domestic Product (GDP)) comes with costs and is ecologically not sustainable. Greenhouse gas emissions, waste, and pollution are causing environmental problems for the entire globe. In the end, we must prioritize the environment, as both society and economy are dependent on it.[1]

[1] Halliki Kreinin and Ernest Aigner, 'From "Decent Work and Economic Growth" to "Sustainable Work and Economic Degrowth": A New Framework for SDG 8' (2022) 49 Empirica 283.

Nuna Zekić, *Labour Law for Degrowth and Meaningful Work* In: *Labour Law Utopias*. Edited by: Nicolas Bueno, Beryl ter Haar, and Nuna Zekić, Oxford University Press. © Oxford University Press 2024. DOI: 10.1093/oso/9780198889755.003.0004

A transition to an economy that is in balance with planetary boundaries will most likely have to involve some kind of degrowth policy.

This chapter further explains that argument and explores the implications for labour law. First, the post-growth approach and the degrowth strategy will be explained (Section II). Next, it unfolds how current labour law is bound up with growth dynamics (Section III). The chapter then explores what role labour law can play in a post-growth society (Section IV). Section V concludes.

II. Post-Growth Approach and Degrowth Strategy

Climate change is a global problem and is, therefore, on top of the agenda of many international organizations. It has led to important international treaties and declarations, such as the Paris Climate Accords of 2015, the UN 2030 Agenda for Sustainable Development, the 2023 UN High Seas Treaty, the 2015 ILO Guidelines for a Just Transition, and the 2019 EU 'Green Deal'. There seems to be consensus—at least based on these documents—on the need to change the (fossil-fuelled) economy to address climate change, even though this consensus is yet to be reached on many national levels where most of the concrete steps need to be taken.

These steps towards a different kind of economy are good steps in terms of ecological sustainability. The so-called 'new' economy seeks to develop a sustainable economic system. By contrast, the 'old' market economy, which is in fact the economy we are still living in, does not take into account the adverse environmental impacts. There is, however, no way to escape the evidence that greenhouse gas emissions have been rising globally, resulting in climate change. The fossil-driven industries are especially problematic in this regard, also because natural resources are not inexhaustible. It has become clear that our fossil-fuelled economies of production and consumption have led to a 'climate emergency' including habitat and biodiversity loss.[2]

Businesses in the old and still dominant capitalist economy have one purpose above all others: to make a profit. Building on the concepts of 'use-value' and 'exchange-value' from Marx's *Capital*, Hickel (and many others) have shown that under capitalism, it is not enough to generate a steady profit.[3] Because there is no end point—the profit is not meant to satisfy particular

[2] eg Subhabrata Bobby Banerjee and others, 'Theoretical Perspectives on Organizations and Organizing in a Post-Growth Era' (2021) Organization 338.

[3] Jason Hickel, *Less is More: How Degrowth Will Save the World* (Penguin Random House 2021) 81–83.

concrete (human) needs—the goal becomes to reinvest that profit (that has become *capital*) to expand the production process and generate more profit than the year before. If capital sits still, it loses value due to inflation, depreciation, etc. That is why our economy relies on *growth*. And growth, as Kallis and others argue, requires continuous enumeration and valorization of unmonetized 'goods' and services—environmental, caring, and relational—and their integration into the market.[4]

But it's not only how the capitalist system works that ensures the focus is on growth. There are all kinds of (legal) infrastructures created to facilitate the expansion of capital: limited liability, corporate personhood, shareholder value rules, etc.[5] In addition, governments have placed GDP growth at the centre of their economic policies for decades, even though GDP is a system that reveals the monetary value of all the goods and services produced in the economy, but does not care whether these economic activities are useful or destructive.[6] It says nothing about possible adverse effects of those economic activities on the environment or society. In addition, GDP only counts the activities that are exchanged on the *market*. As Hickel explains: 'If you cut down a forest for timber, GDP goes up.... If you grow your own food, clean your own house or care for your ageing parents, GDP says nothing. It only counts if you pay companies to do these things for you.'[7]

National governments have not been alone in using GDP growth to manage economies, thus internalizing the interests of capital. International organizations, such as the Organisation for Economic Cooperation and Development (OECD) and the International Monetary Fund (IMF), have also focused on reducing all possible barriers to making a profit and to advance GDP growth. Many industries that were once in public hands have become privatized in the last few decades, including the financial industry, where states have removed important national decisions (eg money supply) from the realm of democratic choice and attributed them to markets and independent bodies (eg Central Banks).[8] This (neoliberal) policy has also—or perhaps, especially—been pushed across the Global South.[9] Policies advancing economic growth—pursued even in societies that have attained relatively high levels of income and

[4] Giorgos Kallis, Christian Kerschner, and Joan Martinez-Alier, 'The Economics of Degrowth' (2012) Ecological Economics 173.
[5] eg Katharina Pistor, *The Code of Capital. How the Law Creates Wealth and Inequality* (Princeton UP 2019).
[6] Hickel, *Less is More* (n 3) 87.
[7] ibid.
[8] Kallis and others, 'The Economics of Degrowth' (n 4) 173.
[9] See Chapter 6 by Deva and Anand in this book

wealth—are still justified by saying that GDP growth is the only way to reduce poverty, to create jobs, and to improve people's lives. A second justification often used for the pursuit of economic growth, as Rose explains, is that it spurs ongoing innovation, which enhances people's opportunities and protects a society against future risks.[10] Finally, continued economic growth is supposed to foster attitudes of openness, tolerance, and generosity, which are essential to the functioning of a liberal democratic society. However, Rose and many others argue that it is possible to achieve these goals through other means and policies.

A. Green Growth

There are indeed steps being taken to include aspects *other* than GDP growth when looking at economic progress. More importantly, more attention is being given to the adverse (ecological) effects of the 'old' economy. In the treaties, agreements, and declarations, like the UN 2030 Agenda for Sustainable Development, the Paris Climate Agreement, and others mentioned above, governments commit themselves to lower the environmental costs, for example by reducing carbon dioxide emission. A transition to a 'green economy' is the main focus of this currently dominant view, which is now also supported by influential organizations such as the OECD and the World Bank.[11] However, this conception of the green economy has been greatly criticized. In this green economy, the focus is still on economic growth, but it should be 'green growth'. The underlying premise is that society can keep expanding production and consumption while achieving a reduction of emissions and material demands on the planet. There are, for instance, contradictions within the UN 2030 Sustainable Development Goals (SDGs) that, on the one hand, aim to fight climate change (SDG 13) and to promote 'sustainable consumption and production patterns' (SDG 12), but on the other hand also promote 'sustainable growth'. SDG 8 aims to 'promote sustained, inclusive and sustainable economic growth, full and productive employment and decent work for all'.[12] However, long-term economic growth is at odds with ecological sustainability.[13] In this

[10] Julie Rose, 'On the Value of Economic Growth' (2020) Politics, Philosophy & Economics 128.

[11] In 2011, the OECD launched the 'Green Growth Strategy', see OECD, *Towards Green Growth*, 25 May 2011. See also World Bank, *Toward a Green, Clean, and Resilient World for All: A World Bank Group Environment Strategy 2012–2022*, 1 May 2015.

[12] UN General Assembly, Res 70/1, *Transforming Our World: The 2030 Agenda for Sustainable Development*, 25 September 2015, 14.

[13] Kreinin and Aigner, 'From "Decent Work"' (n 1) 282.

green growth idea, a lot of trust is being put in technological innovation, for example renewable energy, and the market to 'decouple' the economy from fossil fuel and to create economic growth with new (green) jobs, but it remains unclear whether this is possible and how it will happen.

Moreover, the underlying mechanisms of the market economy that not only exacerbate ecological degradation and climate change, but also perpetuate social inequality and global injustice, do not seem to be addressed.[14] An important critique has been that the green economy 'reconfigures power structures through the economization and monetization of nature, and the ecologization of the economy'.[15] In addition, specifically regarding the UN 2030 Agenda for Sustainable Development, disagreement has been expressed on the way in which 'decent work' is coupled with economic growth.[16]

It should be noted that there is no *one* coherent green growth approach. To scrutinize the green growth approach, which is *not* the aim of this contribution, would require taking into account the concrete (proposed) policies under this heading. The main point for our purpose is, however, that the green economy seems to assume that continuous growth of production and consumption is desirable and necessary, but that production should be organized differently.

B. Degrowth

The post-growth approach departs from the premise that continuous economic growth and sustainability are irreconcilable. There are different strategies within the post-growth approach, but they all have in common that they do not place (GDP) growth—even if green—at the centre. The degrowth strategy is perhaps the best known. The degrowth strategy criticizes global capitalism and continuous growth policies for not only having accelerated environmental degradation, but also for having failed to bring about greater prosperity for all. Instead, they have caused greater economic inequality and 'a radical reduction in workers' bargaining power'.[17] In turn, growing economic inequality has, for example, caused social mobility to fall.[18]

[14] See Ariel Salleh, 'Climate, Water, and Livelihood Skills: A Post Development Reading of the SDGs' (2016) 13(6) Globalizations 952–59.

[15] Beate Littig, 'Good Work? Sustainable Work and Sustainable Development: A Critical Gender Perspective from the Global North' (2018) 15(4) Globalizations 567.

[16] Gillian MacNaughton and Diane Frey, 'Decent Work for All: A Holistic Human Rights Approach' (2011) 26(2) American University International Law Review 468.

[17] Aaron Benanav, *Automation and the Future of Work* (Verso 2020) 9.

[18] ibid 63. Benanav refers to UN, *Human development report 2019: Beyond Income. Beyond Averages, beyond Today: Inequalities in Human Development in the 21st Century*, 2019.

Just like with the green economy, there is no *one* coherent degrowth strategy. Besides a shared underlying critique of growth-based approaches, the different strategies proposed also have in common that they rely on two pillars: they address environmental degradation on the one hand and economic and social inequality on the other. The degrowth strategy proposed by Hickel[19] has become known as a strategy that purposes a planned, coherent policy to reduce the ecological impact of the economy, reduce inequality, and improve wellbeing.[20] Its intention is to slow down the pace of material production and consumption by, for example, ending 'planned obsolescence'[21] or introducing a right to repair.[22] This resembles the circular economy, but it has a broader scope. Slowing down the pace of material production and consumption would moreover mean gradually scaling down ecologically destructive and 'socially less necessary' production, such as fossil fuels, mass-produced meat and dairy, fast fashion, advertising, cars and aviation, including private jets, while expanding other sectors that are socially important like healthcare and education.[23] Scaling down ecologically destructive industries and scaling down on material throughput will eventually lead to employment loss, at least in some sectors, as Hickel acknowledges. However, degrowth is different from a recession, because it is planned and has specific goals, namely to address climate change effectively while at the same time reducing inequality and improving wellbeing. Various solutions are proposed to reach this goal.

To offset the negative consequences of employment losses in some sectors, Hickel proposes all kinds of redistributive measures, notably shortening working hours, redistributing work more evenly, maintaining high enough wages, as well as investing in and expanding public goods so that people can live well. These measures are in fact close to some existing models; the measures are not that 'radical' as degrowth strategy would, at first glance, seem to some. However, a radical reduction of income and wealth inequality through a progressive tax system forms an integral part of the degrowth strategy, at least as Hickel and others propose.[24] In addition, the degrowth strategy proposed would only mean degrowth for wealthy economies; the Global South could still

[19] Hickel, *Less is More* (n 3).
[20] ibid.
[21] This is when products are designed with an artificially limited useful life.
[22] The European Commission presented its proposal for a Right to Repair in March 2023, see COM(2023) 155 fin.
[23] Jason Hickel and others, 'Degrowth Can Work—Here's How Science Can Help' (2022) 612 Nature 401.
[24] ibid.

expand its production and consumption.[25] This approach resonates with the literature on ecologically unequal exchange between high-income countries and low-income countries as a persistent feature of the global economy from 1990 to 2015.[26] High-income countries depend on resource-intensive industrial technologies and infrastructures whose efficient functioning is contingent on annual net transfers of biophysical resources from distant areas.[27] Or, in the words of David Doorey: 'Large and powerful business enterprises produce a substantial proportion of greenhouse gases, and citizens of wealthy nations contribute far more to climate harm than do citizens of poor nations.'[28]

It could very well be that even without adopting a deliberate degrowth strategy, the economies in the Global North will need to adjust to low- or zero-growth, since growth has been slowing down in high-income countries for decades.[29] From the 1970s onwards, rates of manufacturing-output growth stagnated in most countries, resulting in a true global deindustrialization.[30] Instead, the service sector has expanded. However, the service sector is generally characterized by low-productivity jobs. Overall, this has resulted in a slowdown in GDP growth rates. Such a slowdown already gives rise to serious challenges in economic policies and we see many industrialized countries struggling to grow their economies.

However, a deliberate degrowth strategy is politically extremely complicated. As Kallis and others argue, growth economies—and mainstream economics—simply do not know how to degrow. According to them, the core question for twenty-first-century economics is no longer how nations get rich, but how they 'manage without growth'.[31] In recent years, many academic contributions have been written concerning limits to growth and alternative pathways to wellbeing. These scholars maintain that a form of degrowth is humanity's best bet to avoid global warming's devastating effects, as predicted in the reports by

[25] The policies for low- and middle-income countries would also have to include cancelling unfair and unpayable debts and curbing unequal exchange in international trade. See also Chapter 6 by Deva and Anand in this book.

[26] Christian Dorninger and others, 'Global Patterns of Ecologically Unequal Exchange: Implications for Sustainability in the 21st Century' (2021) 179 Ecological Economics 1–14.

[27] ibid 2.

[28] David Doorey, 'Just Transitions Law: Putting Labour Law to Work on Climate Change' (2017) 30(2) Journal of Environmental Law and Practice 226.

[29] eg Kate Raworth, *Doughnut Economics: Seven Ways to Think Like a 21st-Century Economist* (Random House 2017) 221.

[30] Benanav, *Automation and the Future of Work* (n 17) 28.

[31] Kallis and others, 'The Economics of Degrowth' (n 4) 172.

the UN Intergovernmental Panel on Climate Change (IPCC).[32] Nevertheless, many challenges lie ahead.

III. Labour Law and the Growth Economy

A. Labour Law as a Legal Framework for Wage Labour

Paid work is a powerful driver of economic growth.[33] Therefore, considerable attention is paid to *work* in the post-growth literature. Scholars are exploring how work is bound up with growth dynamics, explaining the adverse effects of this, and exploring what role work will play in a post-growth society.[34] However, existing (labour) laws are often neglected in such scholarly works (ie usually economic literature), even though some authors acknowledge that 'paid work in the growth society not only represents a "phenomenon" (as an activity), but also an "institution", and an "ideology"—with effects on welfare and the environment'.[35] This is probably because these observers often focus on other disciplines and treat law as a sideshow.[36] However, as Pistor argues in her influential book *Code of Capital*, capitalism cannot function without legal institutions or what she calls 'legal codes': capital owes its wealth-creating capacity to its legal coding.[37] So, what role does labour law play in the growth economy?

Just like other legal domains, labour law plays a role in determining the 'rules of the game' when it comes to how our economies function. As Dermine and Dumont explain, labour law, including social security law (ie social law), is fully integrated into the legal structure of—what they call—the productivist model and what boils down to the ideology of economic growth, as explained above.[38] According to Dermine and Dumont, social law is a tool that serves the end pursued by the productivist model, namely to continually increase

[32] Kreinin and Aigner, 'From "Decent Work"' (n 1) 282; Dominique Méda, 'Work and Employment in a Post-Growth Era' in Isabelle Cassiers, Kevin Maréchal, and Dominique Méda, *Post-Growth Economics and Society* (Routledge 2018) 14.

[33] Irmi Seidl and Angelika Zahrnt, 'Employment, Meaningful Activity and the Post-Growth Society' in Irmi Seidl and Angelica Zahrnt (eds), *Post-Growth Work* (Routledge 2022) 4.

[34] eg Simon Mair, Angela Druckman, and Tim Jackson, 'A Tale of Two Utopias: Work in a Post-Growth World' (2020) 173 Ecological Economics 1; Seidl and Zahrnt, *Post-Growth Work* (n 33).

[35] Kreinin and Aigner, 'From "Decent Work"' (n 1) 295.

[36] Pistor, *The Code of Capital* (n 5) 4.

[37] ibid 12. Pistor shows in depth how land, firms, debt, and know-how have been legally coded as capital.

[38] Elise Dermine and Daniel Dumont, 'A Renewed Critical Perspective on Social Law: Disentangling Its Ambivalent Relationship with Productivism' (2022) 38(3) International Journal of Comparative Labour Law and Industrial Relations 239. According to Dermine and Dumont, productivism is an ideology inherited from the Industrial Revolution, based on the belief that continually increasing

production within society.[39] Indeed, at its core, labour law allows for human labour to be exchanged on the labour market, making work itself a commodity. Labour law is constructed around labour exchanged on the market, but it also puts a legal structure in place for wage labour.

In addition to establishing a legal framework for wage labour, labour law institutionalizes power relations and converts factual power into structural power.[40] Control by the employer over the employee is an integral part of the employment contract, the central feature of labour law. Subordination of the worker to the employer is the distinctive and central element of the legal definition of the employment contract. Even though we can explain this by pointing to the embeddedness of the employment contract in a specific production system, we cannot deny the fact that labour law plays its supporting role for that very same system. The employment contract as a legal institution first distributes power to the employer before it is curtailed by the laws governing the employment contract.

However, labour law is most often defined as *protective* law. And indeed, labour law (albeit implicitly) recognizes the unequal and vulnerable position of workers and gives them a protected status in order to protect their human dignity. By providing different minimum norms and procedures that need to be respected in employment relationships, such as minimum wages and collective bargaining, labour law also modifies the way profits are distributed. However, it is important to stress that the protective goals of labour law have been developed in the framework of a growth- and profit-driven productive system, in the framework of a market economy.[41] As Fudge has put it: 'Labour law, even during its golden period, was concerned with *production* and *protection*.'[42] At the same time that labour law limits the employer's legal right to command, it also constitutes the legal authority of the employer and the subordination of the worker.[43] The subordination is not a natural phenomenon, it needs to be created—and coded—in law. Subordination and wage labour are

production in society is both possible and desirable, and that economic growth should be the central objective of all human organization.

[39] ibid 246.

[40] Marc Rigaux, *Labour Law or Social Competition Law? On Labour in Its Relation with Capital through Law* (Intersentia 2009) 23.

[41] Nuna Zekić, 'The Normative Framework of Labour Law' (2019) 9(2) Law and Method 9–10.

[42] Judy Fudge, 'Labour as a "Fictive Commodity"' in Guy Davidov and Brian Langille (eds), *The Idea of Labour Law* (OUP 2011) 123.

[43] Simon Deakin, 'The Many Futures of the Contract of Employment' in Joanne Conaghan, Richard Michael Fischl, and Karl Klare (eds), *Labour Law in an Era of Globalization: Transformative Practices and Possibilities* (OUP 2002) 187.

very important for economies focused on growth. As Dermine and Dumont explain, it is this form of organization of work that is best able to create value at large scale, because it enables the division of labour.[44] The employer can purchase the labour needed for production and then break down the complex tasks into smaller, simple tasks carried out by specialized and therefore more efficient workers. These workers can also be steered easily towards (professional) changes according to the company's needs.

Moreover, property relations between employers (ie capital owners) and workers are for the most part left untouched within this system. Employers are *automatically* owners of the fruit of labour. This is often an implicit aspect of labour law, but it is usually made explicit in the legal regulation of the ownership of intellectual property rights. For example, copyright laws will usually stipulate that the person who creates a work becomes the owner of the copyright vested in that work. But when a work is created by an employee in the course of his employment, copyright law stipulates that the employer is the owner of the copyright, unless the parties explicitly agree otherwise. The employees are supposed to be compensated by their wages only. The contribution of labour in a company does not lead to a right to acquire shares in that company. It needs no explanation that next to legal subordination, this is also an important element of the market economy and capital accumulation.

B. Labour Law as Protective, but also Indifferent Law?

We now turn back to the protective side of labour law. As indicated earlier, although labour law legitimizes labour as a commodity exchanged on the market, it also recognizes that labour cannot be separated from the worker and that the worker is dependent on employment. Protection of the worker as the weaker party to the employment contract is therefore one of the main goals of labour and employment law. This is a well-known side of labour law. However, when put against the ecological crisis, a deficit in this approach becomes visible. Some aspects of workers' needs as human beings are protected, but others are not. Similar to the GDP system, which reveals the monetary value of all the goods and services produced in the economy but does not care whether these economic activities are useful or destructive, labour law is designed in a way that it protects workers in formal employment in terms of, for example, income and job security, but it doesn't care whether the work performed (*as*

[44] Dermine and Dumont, 'A Renewed Critical Perspective on Social Law' (n 38) 252.

an activity) is useful or destructive for the planet, society, or the individual workers involved.

Admittedly, when it comes to adverse environmental impacts, it's the companies, the organizations, and the institutions we should look at in the first place, not the individual jobs. However, having a legal framework in place for the exchange of labour on the market that is practically indifferent to the end that labour is used for has resulted in the situation where the most profitable companies can offer the most profitable jobs and can thus attract some of the best workers. Many of the most profitable jobs are to be found in environmentally destructive industries. Labour law has paid little to no attention to the environmental consequences of productive employment. As long as jobs meet the criteria of decent work, labour law is not concerned with the possible environmental effects of remunerated work, even though the ecological effects of some activities performed in paid employment have historically been damaging. This indifference—or neutrality—towards work as an activity that workers perform contributes to capitalist growth economies.

As important as jobs generally are, at the same time, many jobs do little to enhance individual, family, or community wellbeing.[45] In addition, they can be dangerous, demoralizing, demeaning, or just plain boring.[46] Even when a job is stable and relatively well paid, it may still do little for one's own wellbeing. Jobs described by Graeber in his book, *Bullshit Jobs*, are good examples of such jobs.[47] Graeber's main claim is that in contemporary developed service economies there are many pointless and even pernicious jobs. While usually well paid, people in these jobs do very little of—what Graeber calls—social value, but the jobs themselves take an enormous 'spiritual' toll on the workers. There is, however, no space for such considerations in labour law. Also Graeber's *bullshit jobs* are good jobs, according to labour law standards, because they are stable and relatively well paid.

Why is this problematic? Because, at the same time, labour law and more broadly the social security systems do promote wage labour actively. 'Jobs, jobs, jobs' has been the mantra for many governments in the past few decades. We see a coupling of the growth economy and the right to work, one of the most important notions in labour law. It has a place in many constitutions, and a prominent one in the European Social Charter since it is in the first article. Many ILO Declarations can be seen as an elaboration of this right.[48] The right is

[45] See also Bas Rombouts and Nuna Zekić, 'Decent and Sustainable Work for the Future?' (2020) 24(2) UCLA Journal of International Law and Foreign Affairs 353.

[46] MacNaughton and Frey, 'Decent Work for All' (n 16) 633.

[47] David Graeber, *Bullshit Jobs: A Theory* (Allen Lane 2018).

[48] See eg ILO Declaration No 122 and No 168.

understood as an obligation on the part of the government to put measures in place that promote and stimulate employment.[49] It entails an obligation for the state to have a labour market policy in place, which is targeted towards full employment. Income security of individuals depends on performing productive labour. In fact, the realization of a large number of social rights and social security are linked to (having performed) wage labour, like unemployment benefits, pensions, disability allowances. In turn, all kinds of activation policies in social security are geared towards reintegrating individuals as soon as possible back into employment.[50] This strongly steers individuals to seek employment.

Even though labour law can be described as indifferent to some effects of wage labour, it does, however, identify what type of labour is considered to create economic value and thus should be protected.[51] Labour law only protects 'market work', also called 'wage labour' or 'productive work': work that is remunerated on the market and controlled by an employer. 'Market work' also includes paid employment at public and non-profit organizations that are necessary for a market economy to function. Non-market forms of work, notably reproductive and domestic work, mostly done by women, but also communal work and participation in common affairs, fall outside the scope of labour law. This has been a long-standing critique from the feminist legal scholarship, but it has also been picked up in the post-growth literature.[52] Feminist scholars have discussed the exclusion of 'family labour' (eg domestic housework and taking care of families), notably from labour law regulation. Family labour is not granted the protection wage labour receives, even though family work is productive work and very necessary for the functioning of the economy. Furthermore, many of its forms converge with conventional employment, such as work performed by housekeepers, nurses, nannies, etc.[53] Volunteer work and work done by trainees or interns also falls (largely) outside the boundaries of protection by labour and social security law. Concluding, while labour and social security law strongly promote subordinate wage work, they are indifferent to advancement of meaningful work.

[49] See eg Colm O'Cinneide, 'The Right to Work in International Human Rights Law' in Virginia Mantouvalou (ed), *The Right to Work: Legal and Philosophical Perspectives* (Hart Publishing 2015) 121.

[50] Also see Dermine and Dumont, 'A Renewed Critical Perspective on Social Law' (n 38) 253.

[51] ibid 245.

[52] Hickel, *Less is More* (n 3). See also Chapter 9 by Encinas de Muñagorri in this book.

[53] Noah Zatz, 'The Impossibility of Work Law' in Guy Davidov and Brian Langille (eds), *The Idea of Labour Law* (OUP 2011) 234, 235.

IV. What Role for Labour Law in a Post-Growth Society?

For a long time, labour law scholars were largely absent from climate discussions. That has been changing in the last couple of years.[54] As Dermine and Dumont argue, the scientific and social consensus around what they call 'productivism' is beginning to crumble; there is currently a crucial momentum for a revival of the critical movement in law.[55] It is important to think about how labour law can be deployed to support a degrowth strategy. However, for many, one of the important questions is whether degrowth means fewer jobs. Not necessarily. As explained, degrowth means scaling down the production and consumption in ecologically destructive industries and investing in others. It also means redistributing work and income more equally. Furthermore, degrowth is a strategy to stabilize economies; hardly anyone in the degrowth literature is preaching eternal degrowth.[56] It is important to think about decoupling our labour laws and welfare systems in general from growth. To make them, as it were, agnostic to growth.[57] So, what role is there for labour law in this post-growth future?

When studying the different degrowth strategies proposed, it quickly becomes clear that the proposed ecological and redistributive measures are inherently connected. The proposed strategies are not only about degrowth, but also about inequality. It can be said that degrowth is in fact about reorienting the economy towards societal welfare. While maintaining that improvements of human welfare and wellbeing can be achieved without GDP growth, Hickel states in his book: 'It's not income itself that matters, but how it's distributed.'[58] This corresponds with the longstanding labour law goals of distributive justice, income security, social inclusion,[59] and solidarity.[60] As explained above, labour law (re)distributes resources, power, and risks to compensate for unequal bargaining power. Whereas tax law (and to some extent social security law) is more about the redistribution of market *outcomes*, labour law directly determines the rules of the labour market. It intervenes in the contractual freedom of the parties because it presupposes that labour exchange cannot be left to market

[54] eg Doorey, 'Just Transitions Law' (n 28) 223; see also eg special issue 'Work Regulation and Environmental Sustainability' in (2018) 40(1) Comparative Labor Law and Policy Journal, edited by Ania Zbyszewska.

[55] Dermine and Dumont, 'A Renewed Critical Perspective on Social Law' (n 38) 244–45.

[56] Kallis and others, 'The Economics of Degrowth' (n 4) 173.

[57] Raworth, *Doughnut Economics* (n 29).

[58] Hickel, *Less is More* (n 3).

[59] Guy Davidov, *A Purposive Approach to Labour Law* (OUP 2016) 57–59.

[60] Wolfgang Däubler, 'Labour Law and Competition' in Marc Rigaux, Jan Buelens, and Amanda Latinne (eds), *From Labour Law to Social Competition Law?* (Intersentia 2014) 58–59.

forces alone. One could say that this is not redistribution, but rather 'pre-distribution'.[61] However, this function of labour law is no longer guaranteed.

Before the neoliberal era and mainly in the 1970s, what might have been the 'golden period' for labour law in European countries, (re)distribution was a prominent policy theme. In many countries, but also globally, there was the idea that the state had to play a significant role in redistributing income. Moreover, the fact that some individual citizens have incomes that are too low, and the scarcity of resources, were considered to be a collective problem. With the rise of the neoliberal economy, the resource scarcity problem has been strongly individualized; one's fate has to a large degree—once again—become one's own problem; this corresponded with the gradual replacement of stable employment relationships with flexible ones, also referred to as non-standard forms of work.[62]

Strengthening the distributive role of labour law should be one of the core aims of labour law if it is to support a degrowth strategy. But does that mean that the 'standard' employment relationship should once again become the norm in a post-growth future? Probably not the old standard employment relationships of lifelong employment, working forty hours per week. In fact, an overall reduction of working hours is one of the recurring proposals for a post-growth future. As stated by Kreinin and Aigner: 'A reduction in the *quantity* of paid or "productive" employment is necessary to stay within the planetary boundaries, as well as *a qualitative* change in work itself—towards societally and environmentally necessary work.'[63] Méda argues, as well, that in a post-growth future, quality should have priority over quantity: 'Absolute priority must now be given to producing goods and services with lighter ecological and carbon footprints and making the quality of goods and services the crucial criterion.'[64]

If we scale down environmentally destructive industries, consume less, make products that last longer, share products among each other, and reduce food waste, employment in some sectors will inevitably decline. For Hickel, shortening the working week is 'the way out' of mass unemployment that might follow a degrowth agenda; it is 'key to building a humane, ecological economy'.[65] He proposes introducing a job guarantee (coupled with a 'living

[61] Nick Bunker, 'What is predistribution?' June 2015 <http://equitablegrowth.org/equitablog/predistribution/> accessed 11 June 2023.
[62] David Weil, *The Fissured Workplace: Why Work Became So Bad for So Many and What Can Be Done to Improve It* (Harvard UP 2014).
[63] Kreinin and Aigner, 'From "Decent Work"' (n 1) 296–98.
[64] Méda, 'Work and Employment' (n 32) 22.
[65] Hickel, *Less is More* (n 3) 197, 199.

wage' that is adequate for people to live well) and rolling out retraining programmes so that redundant workers from shrinking industries can transition easily to other sectors, such as renewable energy and public services. The necessary labour can be distributed more evenly among the working population and in this way full employment can be maintained.

Benanav argues that despite the stories of robots replacing humans in almost every activity, it is unlikely that technological progress will lead to a future in which machines have fully substituted human labour.[66] Even in, what he calls, a post-scarcity world—a world where all people have adequate means of income and access to enough healthcare, education, and welfare to reach their full potential—we will need to find other ways to allocate the necessary labours that serve as the foundation for all other activities. After all, in this post-scarcity world, people would not be in a position where they eventually have to accept the best possible job offered on the labour market to make a living. Following Karl Marx, Thomas More, Ėtienne Cabet, and Peter Kropotkin, Benanav divides social life into two separate but interrelated spheres: a realm of necessity and one of freedom. The extent of the necessary labour (eg the provision of housing, food, clothing, sanitation, water, electricity, healthcare, education, child and elderly care, or transportation) would need to be decided democratically. Estimates are that these 'common labours' would take up around three to five hours a day.[67]

The focus should be on the quantity of work (reduction of work, more free time) and the quality of work (for the individual and the planet).[68] It's important to realize that the degrowth proposals are more in the stage of ideas than detailed plans. Most scholars, however, believe that there will remain work that needs to be performed, but people will not have to devote so much time to it as they currently do. There are different ways to distribute this 'necessary labour' that remains to be performed. But it is certain that when labour *needs* to be performed, there is a need for labour laws. Benanav admits there could still be sanctions to ensure that necessary work is actually undertaken.[69] Indeed, it is plausible that within a society, there will always be work that has to be performed because of its necessity. It is likely that work relations will remain power relations, even though the dynamics would be different than they are

[66] Benanav, *Automation and the Future of Work* (n 17) 83.

[67] ibid 86. Hickel thinks the reduced working week would be 'thirty or perhaps even twenty hours' per week, Hickel, *Less is More* (n 3) 197.

[68] On quality of work, see eg Chapter 7 by Bueno in this book.

[69] Benanav, *Automation and the Future of Work* (n 17) 89.

today.[70] Existing principles established as part of labour law will still be relevant, for example the right to work or free choice of occupation.[71]

For Dermine and Dumont, the right to free choice of work can 'relativize and even challenge' productivism.[72] Free choice of work is a component of the right to work, which is enshrined in several human rights documents and constitutions. Dermine and Dumont rightly emphasize that the right to work does not only entail the obligation for the state to keep increasing the number of jobs available but also obligations for the authorities to respect and protect individuals' free choice of employment.[73] Through its component of freely chosen work, the right to work sets out limits on the duty to work. With free choice of employment, labour law wants to promote individual autonomy and self-fulfilment. This is important in an economy focused on growth, but also in a post-growth economy.

Promoting autonomy and self-fulfilment might be characterized as the 'old' goals of labour law, but they will not lose their relevance in a post-growth world. However, linking labour rights to ecological sustainability does bring about a new way of looking at remunerated work, and this new way might lead us to broadening the concept of work in law and policy.[74] A starting point could be to think about broadening our understanding of 'good jobs'. Already in the Philadelphia Declaration, both the material and immaterial dimensions of work were acknowledged: 'All human beings, irrespective of race, creed or sex, have the right to pursue both their material wellbeing and their spiritual development in conditions of freedom and dignity, of economic security and equal opportunity.'[75] The immaterial (or social) dimension of work, however, has not yet been fully addressed in the regulation of work. We need to find ways to align the 'necessary labour' in the post-growth world with work through which people can find self-fulfilment.[76] The existing concept of 'decent work' needs to be extended beyond the material needs, including human development and workers' wellbeing. For many people, work is not just a way to make a living but also a way to contribute to society; work can be important as an act of self-expression, self-fulfilment, and a venue for socialization.[77] There are

[70] On power relations, see Chapter 12 by Gamonal in this book.
[71] See Chapter 5 by Carelli in this book.
[72] Dermine and Dumont, 'A Renewed Critical Perspective on Social Law' (n 38) 255.
[73] ibid 256.
[74] Paolo Tomassetti, 'Labour Law and Environmental Sustainability' (2018) 40(1) Comparative Labor Law and Policy Journal 61, 64.
[75] Annex to ILO-Constitution sub II a.
[76] Nicolas Bueno, 'From Productive Work to Capability-Enhancing Work: Implications for Labour Law and Policy' (2022) 23(3) Journal of Human Development and Capabilities 354–72.
[77] Virginia Mantouvalou, 'Introduction' in Virginia Mantouvalou (ed), *The Right to Work: Legal and Philosophical Perspectives* (Hart Publishing 2015) 1.

no reasons to think this will change in a post-growth future where 'necessary labour' remains, even though the importance of work in this context will probably diminish if the working time is (drastically) reduced. Instead of only focusing on (material) working conditions, an effort should be made to include 'meaningful work' in the labour law discourse.

Vocational training could, for example, be directed more towards the needs of the workers themselves. In the recent years, vocational training and 'lifelong learning' have been used mostly in the framework of employability and worker's adaptability.[78] The credo is: In a flexible (or volatile) market, workers need to be adaptable. However, a right to training and development—provided that it is 'robust' enough and gives an individual a right to get training according to one's own choice—can also be placed within the framework of personal development and autonomy. The workers gain more options to choose work that fits best with their personal interests.

Moreover, the discussion on the division between market work and non-market work and how we treat the two in labour and social security law has not lost its importance. On the contrary, it is increasingly important to investigate the justifications for such divisions, especially if we want to redirect the economy towards meeting the needs of all humans and respecting planetary boundaries. The importance of non-market forms of work, such as caring and communal work, cannot be stressed enough. The same is true of work in public services. During the Covid 19-period, it became clear how important—nay, essential—some jobs are for society.[79] If reducing working hours were to become a reality, people will have more time to devote themselves to caring, communal, and voluntary work when they find it personally meaningful;[80] or they will simply have more leisure time. We need to find ways to recognize and reward types of meaningful work other than formal employment, for example by granting tax and social security benefits to workers performing such work.

V. Conclusion

Degrowth is an *agenda*,[81] and as such it needs to be developed and made concrete in a democratic conversation. Ultimately, it's a matter of politics. Until

[78] Nuna Zekić, *Werkzekerheid in het arbeidsrecht* (Kluwer 2011).
[79] ILO, *World Employment and Social Outlook 2023: The Value of Essential Work*, March 2023.
[80] See, for more on this, Chapter 7 by Bueno in this book.
[81] Federico Savini, 'Post-growth, degrowth, the doughnut and circular economy: a short guide', 7 November 2022 <http://www.planetamateur.com>> accessed 26 March 2023.

now, no real degrowth policies seem to have been embraced on a significant scale, probably because most politicians think it is unrealistic to hope their electorate will give up on growth. That might be a correct assessment of the current situation. However, in the meantime, our thinking in natural and social sciences about a (global) economic system that is not dependent on growth continues to develop, and labour law scholarship is catching up as well. Even though post-growth thinking is very convincing in the statement that unlimited expansion of production and consumption is impossible on a finite planet, it is only an approach, and it does not have a strategy or an agenda yet.[82] Degrowth can be that strategy, and doughnut economics[83] an analytical tool, but as said: that will depend on political actions taken. *How* a post-growth future can be achieved remains a profound challenge for theorists and for society.

That does not remove the need to think about and investigate possible avenues in which labour law can play a role to facilitate a post-growth society. Many of the 'old' goals and principles of labour law, like (re)distribution, the right to work, and free choice of occupation will remain relevant. We will, however, need to fundamentally rethink the role of work in our society in order to bring the economy back in balance with planetary boundaries and to redistribute labour, income, and wealth more fairly. In this chapter an attempt was made to do just that by bringing degrowth and post-growth thinking in labour law discourse.

Bibliography

Banerjee S and others, 'Theoretical Perspectives on Organizations and Organizing in a Post-Growth Era' (2021) 28(3) Organization 337

Benanav A, *Automation and the Future of Work* (Verso 2020)

Bueno N, 'From Productive Work to Capability-Enhancing Work: Implications for Labour Law and Policy' (2022) 23(3) Journal of Human Development and Capabilities 354

Bunker N, 'What is predistribution?' June 2015 <http://equitablegrowth.org/equitablog/predistribution/>

Däubler W, 'Labour Law and Competition' in M Rigaux, J Buelens, and A Latinne (eds), *From Labour Law to Social Competition Law?* (Intersentia 2014)

Davidov G, *A Purposive Approach to Labour Law* (OUP 2016)

Deakin S, 'The Many Futures of the Contract of Employment' in J Conaghan, RM Fischl, and K Klare (eds), *Labour Law in an Era of Globalization: Transformative Practices and Possibilities* (OUP 2002)

[82] ibid.

[83] Raworth, *Doughnut Economics* (n 29).

Dermine E and Dumont D, 'A Renewed Critical Perspective on Social Law: Disentangling Its Ambivalent Relationship With Productivism' (2022) 38(3) International Journal of Comparative Labour Law and Industrial Relations 237

Doorey D, 'Just Transitions Law: Putting Labour Law to Work on Climate Change' (2017) 30(2) Journal of Environmental Law and Practice 201

Dorninger C and others, 'Global Patterns of Ecologically Unequal Exchange: Implications for Sustainability in the 21st Century' (2021) 179 Ecological Economics 106824

Fudge J, 'Labour as a "Fictive Commodity"' in G Davidov and B Langille (eds), *The Idea of Labour Law* (OUP 2011)

Graeber D, *Bullshit Jobs: A Theory* (Allen Lane 2018)

Hickel J, *Less is More: How Degrowth Will Save the World* (Penguin Random House 2021)

Hickel J and others, 'Degrowth Can Work—Here's How Science Can Help' (2022) 612 Nature 400

Kallis G, Kerschner C, and Martinez-Alier J, 'The Economics of Degrowth' (2012) 84 Ecological Economics 172

Kreinin H and Aigner E, 'From "Decent Work and Economic Growth" to "Sustainable Work and Economic Degrowth": A New Framework for SDG 8' (2022) 49 Empirica 281

Littig B, 'Good Work? Sustainable Work and Sustainable Development: A Critical Gender Perspective from the Global North' (2018) 15(4) Globalizations 565

MacNaughton G and Frey D, 'Decent Work for All: A Holistic Human Rights Approach' (2011) 26(2) American University International Law Review 441

Mair S, Druckman A, and Jackson T, 'A Tale of Two Utopias: Work in a Post-Growth World' (2020) 173 Ecological Economics 106653

Mantouvalou M (ed), *The Right to Work: Legal and Philosophical Perspectives* (Hart Publishing 2015)

Méda D, 'Work and Employment in a Post-Growth Era' in I Cassiers, K Maréchal, and D Méda, *Post-Growth Economics and Society* (Routledge 2018)

Pistor K, *The Code of Capital. How the Law Creates Wealth and Inequality* (Princeton UP 2019)

Raworth K, *Doughnut Economics: Seven Ways to Think Like a 21st-Century Economist* (Random House 2017)

Reuter N, 'Employment in the Tension between Ecology and Distributive Justice. The Role of Trade Unions' in I Seidl and A Zahrnt (eds), *Post-Growth Work* (Routledge 2022)

Rigaux M, *Labour Law or Social Competition Law? On Labour in Its Relation with Capital through Law* (Intersentia 2009)

Rombouts B and Zekić N, 'Decent and Sustainable Work for the Future?' (2020) 24(2) UCLA Journal of International Law and Foreign Affairs 317

Rose J, 'On the Value of Economic Growth' (2020) 19(2) Politics, Philosophy & Economics 128

Salleh A, 'Climate, Water, and Livelihood Skills: A Post Development Reading of the SDGs' (2016) 13(6) Globalizations 952

Savini F, 'Post-growth, degrowth, the doughnut and circular economy: a short guide', 7 November 2022 <http://www.planetamateur.com>

Seidl I and Zahrnt A, 'Employment, Meaningful Activity and the Post-Growth Society' in I Seidl and A Zahrnt (eds), *Post-Growth Work* (Routledge 2022)

Tomassetti P, 'Labour Law and Environmental Sustainability' (2018) 40(1) Comparative Labor Law and Policy Journal 61

Weil D, *The Fissured Workplace: Why Work Became So Bad for So Many and What Can Be Done to Improve It* (Harvard UP 2014)

Zatz N, 'The Impossibility of Work Law' in G Davidov and B Langille (eds), *The Idea of Labour Law* (OUP 2011)
Zbyszewska A (ed), 'Work Regulation and Environmental Sustainability' in (2018) 40(1) Comparative Labor Law and Policy Journal
Zekić N, *Werkzekerheid in het arbeidsrecht* (Kluwer 2011)
Zekić N, 'The Normative Framework of Labour Law' (2019) 9(2) Law and Method 1

5

First Lines for an Ecological Labour Law: A Social Utopia for the Anthropocene

Rodrigo Carelli

I. Introduction

We live in a time that is called the Anthropocene;[1] a time of environmental and civilizational crisis of anthropogenic causes and catastrophic consequences[2] representing the sunset of the capitalist economy based on fossil fuel technology that some call global civilization.[3] This denomination indicates that our species passes from biological agent to geological force[4] and also represents a process of massive, rapid, and planetary destruction of the fragile conditions of life on this planet.[5] The Anthropocene presents us with the prospect of an end of the world in the sense of 'a radical change in the material conditions of existence of the species',[6] which can range from a dramatic shift in our way of living to the simple extinction of the human species due to the end of the special and rare conditions that enable it to exist in this unique niche of negentropy that is planet Earth.[7] Ecology represents the 'changing alterations of the relationship with the world', being 'a new madness and a new way of fighting against previous madnesses'.[8]

It's clear that the current model is completely unsustainable, based on the endless exploitation of labour (ie human beings) and land (ie finite natural resources of planet Earth) for the purposes of production and consumption with the assumption and pretension of exponential and continuous growth.

[1] Dipesh Chakrabarty, 'Anthropocene Time' [2008] History and Theory 57.
[2] Débora Danowski and Eduardo Viveiros de Castro, *Há mundo por vir? Ensaio sobre os medos e os fins* (Desterro, Cultura e Barbárie and Intituto Socioambiental 2014) 11.
[3] ibid 20.
[4] ibid 25.
[5] Bernard Stiegler, 'Sortir de l'anthropocène' [2015] Multitudes 60.
[6] Danowski and Viveiros de Castro, *Há mundo por vir?* (n 2) 44.
[7] Bruno Latour, *Diante de Gaia. Oito conferências sobre a natureza do Antropoceno* (Ateliê de Humanidades and Ubu Editora 2020).
[8] ibid 32.

Rodrigo Carelli, *First Lines for an Ecological Labour Law: A Social Utopia for the Anthropocene* In: *Labour Law Utopias.* Edited by: Nicolas Bueno, Beryl ter Haar, and Nuna Zekić, Oxford University Press.
DOI: 10.1093/oso/9780198889755.003.0005

Its most updated version is the passage from neoliberalism to ultraliberalism (which is nothing more than the former with its intentions and methods in the open, such as authoritarianism and plutocracy).[9] But perhaps more important than noting the failures, is to identify that the global tragedy is embedded in the industrial or consumer society, based on a continuous, compound, and everlasting growth:[10] 'a root driver of both the climate and biodiversity crises'.[11] Growth goes hand in hand with mounting inequalities and the economic sacrifices of the poorest for the benefit of the top of the social pyramid.[12]

This is a very important lesson: ecological disasters assume catastrophic proportions due to, and directly result from, the model of industrial society adopted.[13] But that is not all: the realization is not only that the magnitude of the crisis is due to the model adopted until now, but also that our economic model is absolutely incapable of getting us out of this crisis, not to mention that it will only make things worse. Thus, we should build a new reason of the world, a new utopia to follow.

In this chapter it will be argued that the new reason for the world may well be based on a post-growth society, including the construction of a labour law with combined and not mutually excluding goals: the traditional social one, reducing inequalities and guaranteeing human dignity; and the ecological one, helping to avoid planetary cataclysm, built on a purposive approach of labour law, matching purposes and means.[14]

This chapter will demonstrate this by first addressing the current ecological crisis, including its central social character, in Section II. Then, Section III will present an ecological labour law, which will be an essential part of a possible solution to the ecological crisis. Finally, Section IV will draft and elaborate on the core issues of labour law with an ecological approach.

This chapter is a first sketch of an ecological labour law, which could serve as a template for further research, addressing, among other things, the underlying complexities.

[9] Alain Supiot, *La gouvernance par les nombres* (Seuil 2015).

[10] Giorgos Kallis and others, *The Case for Degrowth* (Polity Press 2020) 34.

[11] Diana Stuart, Ryan Gunderson, and Brian Petersen, *The Degrowth Alternative: A Path to Address Our Environmental Crisis?* (Routledge 2021).

[12] David Reidmiller and others (eds), *Impacts, Risks, and Adaptation in the United States: Fourth National Climate Assessment, Volume II* (US Global Change Research Program 2018); EPA, *Climate Change and Social Vulnerability in the United States: A Focus on Six Impacts* (US Environmental Protection Agency 2021).

[13] Éloi Laurent, 'The European Green Deal: From Growth Strategy to Social-Ecological Transition?' in Bart Vanhercke, Slavina Spasova, and Boris Fronteddu (eds), *Social Policy in the European Union: State of Play 2020* (European Trade Union Institute (ETUI) and European Social Observatory (OSE) 2021).

[14] Guy Davidov, *A Purposive Approach to Labour Law* (OUP 2016).

II. The Ecological Crisis We Live (and Deny)

The notion that humans are a powerful and growing geological force[15] allows us to realize that the climate crisis we are experiencing stems from the model behind the Industrial Revolution. This model is based on a consumer society structured around the use of fossil fuels, with an economy dependent on growth, represented by the motto 'grow or die'.[16] To support this model, continuous and supposedly eternal exploitation of natural resources and human beings is needed. Consequently, these are turned into commodities by the fiction of labour power, whose lack of adequate regulation inevitably leads to the destruction of society.[17] This construction is only possible by viewing nature as external to humanity and opposed to culture.[18]

The persistence of a society based on growth will inevitably lead to the destruction of our planet or, rather, the extinction of our species and thousands of others that depend on our actions. Therefore, an effective change in the way of life on Earth must be made in the Anthropocene,[19] moving away from the illogical and insane axiom of eternal and continuous growth on a finite planet,[20] with its finite resources and capacities. This axiom is even more insane when you realize that this planet is governed by the second law of thermodynamics, that is, that a system needs low entropy[21] to maintain its equilibrium and that low entropy is rare and never reverted to the original state except from a new source of low entropy, or free energy.[22] This assumption of eternal growth can only inexorably cause more and more crises, which will progressively become more serious and traumatic.

Economists are beginning to realize the need to review the bases of traditional economics stipulated on top of the dogma of growth, as well as to include the ecological issue. For example, Raworth's idea of a Doughnut

[15] Chakrabarty, 'Anthropocene Time' (n 1) 5.

[16] Murray Bookchin, *Social Ecology and Communalism* (AK Press 2006).

[17] Karl Polanyi, *The Great Transformation: The Political and Economic Origins of Our Time* (Beacon Press 2001).

[18] Stiegler, 'Sortir de l'anthropocène' (n 5).

[19] Etienne Turpin, 'O antropoceno é um alerta sobre as ações humanas no planeta' Interview with Ricardo Machado (2018) IHU <http://www.ihu.unisinos.br/159-noticias/entrevistas/582885-o-antropoceno-e-um-alerta-sobre-as-acoes-humanas-no-planeta-entrevista-especial-com-etienne-turpin> accessed 19 September 2018.

[20] Tim Jackson, *Prosperity Without Growth. Foundations for the Economy of Tomorrow* (2nd edn, Routledge 2017).

[21] Entropy is commonly defined as a measure of the amount of disorder or randomness of a system. A highly ordered system, like a diamond, will have a very low entropy, and a very disordered system, like a mixture of gases at a high temperature, will have a high entropy. Bernard Stiegler, *The Negathropocene* (Open Humanities Press 2018).

[22] Nicholas Georgescu-Roegen, *La Décroissance* (2nd edn, Éditions Sang de la terre 1995) 40, 45.

Economy, which meets—and is built to observe—the ecological limits of our planet, without forgetting social issues.[23] To this end, a Doughnut Economy abandons the idea of prosperity based on growth measured by Gross Domestic Product (GDP) only. Furthermore, the idea of a Doughnut Economy redefines prosperity as the possibility of 'human beings to flourish, to achieve greater social cohesion, to find higher levels of wellbeing and yet still to reduce their material impact on the environment'.[24] Thus, the necessary 'degrowth'[25] will not be seen as an evil, as it is in the current economy, but as a path, a method, and an objective to achieve in order to face our ecological problems and preserve the planet for future generations. Such a path would only be possible with a paradigm shift in economic and political thinking: changing from the unlimited growth mantra towards a more growth-agnostic one, based on redistribution and 'predistribution' of wealth and income,[26] through a series of instruments to socially share the awards of the public investment made in risky business.[27] A society based on postulates such as free trade (and all that is premised on it and follows from it) is definitely out of the question if we are to survive as a species.[28]

Virtually all ecological problems stem from major social issues, and economic, ethnic, cultural, and gender conflicts are at the heart of the issue.[29] Attacking the ecological crisis without confronting the social question, with an apolitical 'environmentalist'[30] approach, is 'focusing on the symptoms of perverse social pathology rather than (confronting) the pathology itself'.[31] It also means perpetuating the illusory and ideologically constructed separation between humans and nature, and simply remaining in the misconception that has brought us to the situation we find ourselves in. The battleground is the social one, between corporate power and the long-term interests of humanity as a whole. Thus, ecology must act in the field of politics, resituated in the knowledge of our critical situation on Earth.[32]

The fight against climate disaster also requires attention to the anti-colonial struggle: the colonial fracture, which separates colonized from colonizers plus

[23] Kate Raworth, *Economia Donut. Uma alternativa ao crescimento a qualquer custo* (Zahar 2019).
[24] Jackson, *Prosperity Without Growth* (n 20) 102.
[25] Stefania Barca, 'The Labour of Degrowth' [2019] Capitalism Nature Socialism 30.
[26] Raworth, *Economia Donut* (n 23) 178, 179.
[27] Mariana Mazzucato, *Mission Economy: A Moonshot Guide to Changing Capitalism* (Penguin 2022) 173.
[28] Naomi Klein, *On Fire: The Burning Case for a Green New Deal* (Alfred A. Kopf Canada 2019).
[29] Bookchin, *Social Ecology and Communalism* (n 16) 19.
[30] Malcom Ferdinand, *Une écologie décoloniale* (Seuil 2019) 13.
[31] Bookchin, *Social Ecology and Communalism* (n 16) 20.
[32] Chakrabarty, 'Anthropocene Time' (n 1) 5.

central and peripheral spaces on the planet, racializes the world, taking precedence over the man-nature fracture.[33] The colonial fracture of modernity reduces people's experience to the vision of the colonizer and separates anti-colonial and environmentalist movements. Colonial problems are unsolvable without attacking this cleavage which has been in continuous accomplishment and repetition for over five centuries. The colonial fracture, and the boomerang effect of ecological issues, are also demonstrated by the dualization of the world concerning the Covid-19 vaccine, to which the poor world does not have access, thus generating new viral variants, which in turn hinders the eradication of the disease across the planet.[34] Inequality goes hand in hand with environmental imbalance since outsourcing the causes of the climate crisis to other countries is only possible because of the poverty generated by the colonial situation of these nations.[35] It was asserted above that there is no real ecology without social justice because it is crucial to take the postcolonial ecocriticism axiom of 'there is no social justice without ecological justice' into account since the burden to address the consequences of climate change—and expropriation of people and land—is heavier in exploited parts of the world.[36] Using electric cars to run on European streets produced from a global chain involving the extraction of raw materials powered by the dirtiest energy sources, such as those of Chilean or Congolese origin, is nowhere near a solution. If the Chilean and Congolese environmental situations get bad, the effects on the world are not the best either.[37]

Examples of the impossibility of isolated local solutions in response to global crises include Norway's case; they have the highest number of electric-powered vehicles in the world, but at the same time, are one of the largest exporters of fossil fuels that cause the greenhouse effect.[38] Another illustration of a failing local policy is the import by Germany of Brazilian fruits that bring back the pesticides sold by the Germans but banned in Europe. In this new world that we must build, it is thus essential to recognize both social and ecological limits, which are ultimately intertwined. The ecological limits are known to

[33] Ferdinand, *Une écologie coloniale* (n 30) 10.

[34] Marina Rossi, 'Frutas exportadas pelo Brasil levam agrotóxicos proibidos na Europa à mesa dos alemães' (2021) <https://brasil.elpais.com/brasil/2021-06-08/frutas-exportadas-pelo-brasil-levam-agrotoxicos-proibidos-na-europa-a-mesa-dos-alemaes.html> accessed 8 June 2021.

[35] Laurent, 'The European Green Deal' (n 13).

[36] Graham Huggan and Hellen Tiffin, *Postcolonial Criticism: Literature, Animals, Environment* (Routledge 2010) 35.

[37] Nadia Krieger, 'Will Your Electric Car Save the World or Wreck It?' (2018) <https://www.engineering.com/story/will-your-electric-car-save-the-world-or-wreck-it> accessed 26 January 2023.

[38] Lars Taralden, 'The world's electric-car capital is having nasty fights over oil' (2021) <https://www.bloomberg.com/news/features/2021-06-10/norway-s-climate-contradiction-fuels-debate-over-oil> accessed 10 June 2021.

scientists: destruction of the ozone layer, air pollution, loss of biodiversity, land conversion, freshwater withdrawals, nitrogen and phosphorus loads, chemical pollution, acidification of the oceans, and climate change.[39] As ecological labour law is linked to a new way of organizing society guided by planetary limits, all those limits will have to be met by ecological labour law. However, the limit that is put at risk and exceed the most is climate change. It is this limit that we will stick to in this chapter.

The scientific consensus is that human activity causes climate change, and to reverse or prevent even greater damage to life on Earth, there is a need to control the increase in temperature on Earth, which can only happen by limiting new anthropogenic greenhouse gas (GHG) emissions to zero.[40] This will only be achieved if fossil fuels are replaced by other, less impactful technologies that require less harmful energy sources. However, a merely technological solution is a mirage: as stated above, replacing individual vehicles powered by combustion with *new* individual vehicles powered by electric batteries is far from being a solution. Indeed, they are rather the re-creation of social problems, the perpetuation of the logic of growth and the displacement of the global focus of GHG emissions.[41] Electric cars could be part of a solution, but only if this includes ecological and social awareness: about the extraction of the materials needed for their production and about the manufacturing process itself (1); about the impact of replacing the entire global fleet and the fate of the resulting material waste (2); and maybe the most important, about whether the mass use of individual vehicles is a viable solution over that of mass transportation or even the adoption of public policies that would reduce the need for circulation altogether (3). There must be a change in the way we produce, the way we live, and ultimately the way we work and value work. Only then will it be possible to achieve the goal put forward by the scientific consensus.

III. The Ecological Labour Law

Michel Serres,[42] in his work *The Natural Contract*, points to three 'worldless' rights as the legal foundation of modernity. The world, in this legal vision, is

[39] Will Steffen, 'Planetary Boundaries: Guiding Human Development on a Changing Planet' [2015] Science 347.
[40] Intergovernmental Panel on Climate Change, *Climate Change 2021: The Physical Science Basis* (IPCC 2021).
[41] Jamie Morgan, 'Electric Vehicles: The Future We Made and the Problem of Unmaking It' (2020) 44 Cambridge Journal of Economics 4.
[42] Michel Serres, *Le contrat naturel* (François Boutin 1990).

considered as a mere object to be dominated and possessed. Human beings—or some of them—are the only subjects that appear in this law. These three rights are the social contract, natural law, and the Declaration of the Rights of Man. The social contract, an agreement, either actually reached or merely virtually, makes us abandon the natural state to form a society wherein the only recognized subjects are human beings. The (modern) natural law, formed from a 'set of rules that would exist outside any formulation', is derived from human nature and from reason. Nature, as such, in this formulation of law, is reduced to human nature, which in turn is reduced to history, that is, the world (and its history) are in a constant state of disappearing.[43] The Declaration of the Rights of Man also ignores the world as an ecological system in favour of human nature, that defeats external nature through reason 'monopolised by science and the set of techniques'.[44] Human beings thus enjoy all rights, but are 'necessarily condemned to destroying the things of the world'. Our pact being exclusively social, thus leads us to the obliteration of nature, which is 'the set of conditions of human nature itself'.[45]

The ecological labour law should be thought of as a negentropic instrument, that is, a tool in favour of the decrease of entropy, which is designed, understood, and used as a positive pharmacology in order to enable the deceleration of energy dispersion.[46]

The ecological labour law will be central to the necessary degrowth, for two basic reasons: (1) there is no ecology, or degrowth, or zero emissions without the resolution of social problems;[47] and (2) labour is at the heart of our way of living (and producing, and consuming, and accelerating entropy). Just like the 'doughnut' proposed by Raworth for the economy, it will have to respect both the social and the ecological limits.[48] So, it will be a labour law with a socioecological basis, with a new dual theory of justice: social protection and ecological purpose, in intense interconnection, which must be balanced so that one does not overlap or completely exclude the other. For example, if an action meets a social objective (eg the preservation of jobs through the operation of a highly polluting company), but at the same time overrides an ecological objective (ie the reduction of the emission of pollutants), this action would be prohibited. The reduction of pollutants, in turn, must meet social objectives, such as the

[43] ibid 60.
[44] ibid 61.
[45] ibid.
[46] Stiegler, 'Sortir de l'anthropocène' (n 5) 146.
[47] European Environment Agency, Eurofound, *Exploring the Social Challenges of Low-Carbon Energy Policies in Europe* (Eurofound 2021).
[48] Raworth, *Economia Donut* (n 23).

protection of those who lost jobs or those who survived around a company after the closure of a certain economic activity.

David Doorey, primarily for the same purposes as this chapter, proposes the creation of a new branch of law called just transitions law, which would encompass environmental law and labour law and be based on three normative claims (NC): NC1 is that states should respond through public policy and law; NC2 is that public policy should encourage a transition towards 'greener' less carbon-concentrated economies; and NC3 is that governments should minimize the economic and social harms associated with the desired transition, redistributing those harms and resulting benefits.[49] The proposal of the present chapter differs from Doorey's in two aspects: (1) the broader perspective of ecological labour law in relation to ecological needs, which go beyond the issue of climate change; and (2) the active role for labour law in the ecological issue, as an indispensable instrument for current and future challenges.

As a premise, in order to be functional, the ecological labour law must be universal and encompass all human activities in the world. This universality must be seen from two perspectives: (1) the labour law must assume its innate global vocation, as described and repeated in the documents of the International Labour Organization (ILO);[50] and (2) its addressees cannot be classified with the aim of excluding any person from its scope.

To those ends, the ILO must be widely redesigned, among other things, by ceasing to be tripartite by extending its constituents with the inclusion of the representatives of the ecological movement. The committee of experts should have a stronger role and decision-making power, including the power of veto. This is crucial so that the immediate interests of workers, business, or nations cannot endanger the protection of the life and wellbeing of human beings, which is the highest goal of ecological labour law. The ILO should also make its documents binding on its member countries and should, finally, have sanctioning powers. A planetary climate crisis can only be solved with global actions.[51] The non-fulfilment of ecological-labour precepts in one part

[49] David Doorey, 'Just Transitions Law: Putting Labour law to Work on Climate Change' [2017] Journal of Environmental Law and Practice 201.

[50] 'Whereas also the failure of any nation to adopt humane conditions of labour is an obstacle in the way of other nations which desire to improve the conditions in their own countries' in the Preamble to the ILO's Constitution.

[51] As reaffirmed at COP27: 'Acknowledging that climate change is a common concern of humankind, Parties should, when taking action to address climate change, respect, promote and consider their respective obligations on human rights, the right to a clean, healthy and sustainable environment, the right to health, the rights of indigenous peoples, local communities, migrants, children, persons with disabilities and people in vulnerable situations and the right to development, as well as gender equality, empowerment of women and intergenerational equity.' COP 27, *Sharm el-Sheikh Implementation Plan* (UN 2022).

of the planet affects everyone in the world. Labour-environmental arbitrage, by selecting countries with less labour and environmental protection, must be completely abolished.

Moreover, the recipients of the ecological labour law must be broadened and universalized. The categories of employee, self-employed, casual worker, entrepreneur, independent contractor, worker, cooperative, domestic worker, volunteer, intern, should all lose their validity and meaning. A radical change in what should be considered as work is central to the ecological labour law. We should adopt an overarching concept of work as a 'meaningful activity', taking into account the 'diversity of possible kinds of work', including formal employment, besides the fact that people carry out different kinds of work sequentially or in parallel, and that work should aspire 'to be meaningful for the person carrying it out and for society as a whole'.[52] Adapting the 'Four-in-One Perspective' of Frigga Haug,[53] which acknowledges that different areas of human activities are interconnected: care work, personal development activities, leisure activities, and political participation activities would also be considered work, besides formal employment.

The deepening of our relationship with virtual and online tools makes us increasingly aware that many activities previously seen as leisure can now be considered work: live-streamings, posts, likes, videos, texts, messages, photos, memes; all of this is work that generates wealth and value in society and should be considered labour. Not considering these activities as work means not understanding (or not wanting to understand) how current technocapitalism works.[54] Personal hygiene and healthcare, such as going to the doctor, or dentist, getting a haircut or pedicure, physical exercise, meditation, yoga, therapy, reading or watching the news, putting on clothes and uniforms and protective equipment, or even sunbathing, are also essential human activities that should be considered as labour, as they benefit the whole of society by bringing health to its members. Education, as a personal development necessary not only for formal employment but also for political and civic life, must also be considered work. While recognizing that these various activities make up the economy and that it is unfair to exclude them from the concept of work, the aim is also

[52] Irmi Seidl and Angelika Zahrnt, 'Employment, Meaningful Activity and the Post-Growth Society' in Irmi Seidl and Angelika Zahrnt (eds), *Post-Growth Work: Employment and Meaningful Activities with Planetary Boundaries* (Routledge 2022) 9.

[53] Stefanie Gerold, 'Revaluations of Work: Enabling and Combining a Diversity of Activities' in Irmi Seidl and Angelika Zahrnt (eds), *Post-Growth Work: Employment and Meaningful Activities with Planetary Boundaries* (Routledge 2022).

[54] Hamid Ekbia and Bonnie Nardi, *Heteromation, and Other Stories of Computing and Capitalism* (The MIT Press 2017).

to solve social and ecological problems; clearly, it is only through the distribution of work (or the expansion of what is considered work) to reach the greatest number of people that we can achieve degrowth.[55]

Thus, the definition of work should change to include any form of human activity with a recognized social value. However, this does not mean that every form of work should automatically be remunerated proportionally to the task performed or that all those benefitting from work are considered employers, but rather that all work should be valued in some way (in the form of public services, for example), and that all those benefitting directly or indirectly from the work of others, whether from a defined person or the crowd, are responsible and should contribute to this valorization, either by compensating the worker or by paying taxes that will be reverted to society as a whole which will, naturally, reach those who performed the work.[56] The second form of remuneration is, arguably, the most suitable for crowdwork where sometimes invisible microtasks are distributed throughout society,[57] for example, making posts on social networks and WhatsApp messages or work mechanisms like Re-Captcha. The concept of the employer should also change back to the simple and effective 'employing or using someone in their economic activity', giving rise to the figure of the co- or joint employers when a specific work benefits an entire production or value chain, meaning a work process containing various forms of value extraction and modes of production.[58] Both direct and indirect beneficiaries will be fully responsible for the rights of the one who works. The aim is to better distribute the wealth created by society, which is currently appropriated by a handful of people; to enable a better understanding of the impact of human activities on Earth; and to distribute responsibilities effectively and fairly. The mere redistribution of wealth is not enough since it is also necessary to meet human and planetary needs. This means that it is paramount to encourage people to carry out their activities within the socio-ecological limits and objectives.

[55] Lonnie Golden and Stuart Glosser, 'Work Sharing as a Potential Policy Tool for Creating More and Better Employment: A Review of the Evidence' in John Messenger and Naj Ghosheh (eds), *Work Sharing: New Developments during the Great Recession and Beyond* (Edward Elgar Publishing and ILO 2012).

[56] Raworth, *Economia Donut* (n 23) 191, 192.

[57] Ekbia and Nardi, *Heteromation* (n 54).

[58] Christian Fuchs, 'Theorising and Analysing Digital Labour: From Global Value Chains to Modes of Production' (2013) 2 The Political Economy of Communication 1. There is an example of this idea, still very limited, in US labour legislation, which is called joint-employment. See <https://www.nlrb.gov/news-outreach/news-story/nlrb-issues-notice-of-proposed-rulemaking-on-joint-employer-standard> accessed 26 January 2023.

IV. The Core Points of a Labour Law with a Socioecological Matrix

Ecological labour law would be based on a tripod of actions: the strict regulation of working time; the guarantee of a universal basic income; and the protection of the work environment.

Even if the regulation of working time is not the only strategy to reduce GHG emissions, it is always central. It has been proven that the number of hours currently worked far exceeds the levels that could be considered sustainable and that much lower weekly working hours compared to the current ones would be adequate to reach the objectives agreed upon in the climate treaties.[59] GHG emissions and labour time are presumed to have a proportional relationship because the United Nations (UN) Framework Convention on Climate Change links GHG emissions to units of GDP, and GDP correlates to waged working time in one way or another.[60] It is calculated that a 1 per cent decrease in working hours could lead to a 1.46 per cent decrease in the carbon footprint and a 0.42 per cent decrease in CO_2 emissions.[61] Other research shows, taking into account the redistribution of work and spending on leisure activity, that in a 'half-day society', the reduction in carbon emissions would reach 10 per cent and, combined with greater transport efficiency, a system of incentives and sanctions to ensure participation in socially important activities and energy efficiency could further improve the reduction in carbon emissions.[62]

Universal basic income is required to guarantee each person a fair income which would make exploitation, either of individuals themselves or the ecological boundaries of the planet, less pervasive. As such, a universal basic income would meet both objectives of ecological labour law.

The third pillar of ecological labour law, the protection of the working environment, is necessary because it is the very soul of it. 'Environment' in ecological labour law is to be understood broadly: the conditions of life on the planet, which are inseparable from human activities that are in continuous communication, action, and reaction. The following will outline some ideas for each part of the tripod; this stems from the author's original proposal, based on

[59] Philipp Frey, *The Ecological Limits of Work: on Carbon Emissions, Carbon Budgets and Working Time* (Autonomy 2019).

[60] Ibid

[61] Kyle Knight, Eugene Rosa, and Juliet Schor, 'Reducing Growth to Achieve Environmental Sustainability: The Role of Work Hours' in Jeannette Wicks-Lim and Robert Pollin (eds), *Capitalism on Trial* (Edward Elgar Publishing 2013).

[62] Axel Schaffer and Carsten Stahmer, 'Die Halbtagsgesellschaft—ein Konzept für nach-haltigere Produktions- und Konsummuster' (2005) 14 GAIA – Ecological Perspectives for Science and Society 3.

the objectives of an ecological labour law presented above, and it is still in an embryonic phase.

A. Regulation of Working Time

Ecological labour law will be central to the new paradigm needed to tackle the climate crisis because it is essential not only for, as we saw above, the valorization of activities (and people) until now segregated from the world of rights, but also for the reduction of production and consumption, that is, of labour as we conceive it today, which must be readjusted to the new paradigm.

We currently not only consume too much, but we also work excessively.[63] The two things are intertwined, and this is central to the impact on our society.[64] Two hours of traffic on the way to work, two hours on the way back, and twelve-hour shifts are completely devastating actions for life on Earth. Not only for the worker whose life is colonized, but also indirectly for all those who suffer from the ecological cataclysm. Moreover, today there is an encroachment of paid and unpaid working time over living time that is completely unacceptable.[65] In some peripheral countries, such as Brazil, overtime is no longer something out of the ordinary, where more than 36 per cent of workers, mainly in low-paid jobs, permanently work well over the legal weekly limit, often without due remuneration.[66] The spread of digital tools has made us reachable at any time and in any place, but also allows workers to be available for work at any time. This problem has been examined in the literature, which proposes the creation of the right to disconnect.[67] Moreover, the reduction of working time is essential in the redistribution of paid work in the actions required for degrowth.[68] A first step is precisely to remove the excuse that there is not enough work for everyone. As we have seen, this stems from the use of a deliberately narrow concept of work, which eliminates the value of a range of human activities, most of which are performed by women. Thus, the

[63] Will Stronge and Kyle Lewis, *Overtime. Why We Need A Shorter Working Week* (Verso 2021).

[64] As stated in COP 27. COP 27, *Sharm el-Sheikh Implementation Plan* (UN 2022).

[65] James Suzman, *Work: A Deep History, from the Stone Age to the Age of Robots* (Penguin 2020); Matteo Avogaro, 'Right to Disconnect: French and Italian Proposals for a Global Issue' [2019] Revista Direito das Relações Sociais e Trabalhistas 9.

[66] Ana Luíza Matos de Oliveira, *Brazil: Case Study on Working Time Organization and Its Effects in the Health Services Sector* (ILO 2015).

[67] Facundo Chiuffo, 'The "Right to Disconnect" or "How to Pull the Plug on Work" [2019] <https://ssrn.com/abstract=3422283> accessed 26 January 2023; this new right is already provided for in France and Italy.

[68] David Spencer, *Making Light Work: An End to Toil in the Twenty-First Century* (Polity 2022) 59.

elimination of the gender bias from the current concept of work, in addition to other biases, most of them racial, which prevent other activities from being recognized as work, would immediately increase existing work.[69] After that, we would start distributing it. But how should we distribute it? Well, one of the main variables for employment is working time. The longer the working day in a country is, the fewer people will hold jobs. Conversely, the shorter the maximum working day is, the more people may be employed.[70] Approached like this, unemployment is, in fact, a political choice. Weekly hours should be reduced to an ideal point to fulfil the ecological labour law goals. Ecological labour law also means an ecological right to work. Obviously, in this system, overtime will not be allowed as a possible instrument of subterfuge for social-ecological protection, even if it is in the immediate self-interest of workers to increase their remuneration.

This strict limitation of working hours must be carried out in relation to workers as individuals and not in relation to a job. Thus, if a worker provides services to more than one employer or contractor, those hours should count towards the total working hour limitation. Universal basic income, as proposed below, could reduce the temptation or need to add work hours. But the limit should be explicit, as people will still have desires for accumulation or consumption that would incite them to work more than the permitted limit. The focus goes from the job or even the workplace to the person who works, always aiming towards social ecology. As noted above, this regulation will apply to all kinds of workers, and the qualification of self-employed or employees will no longer be relevant. The Covid-19 pandemic showed us that some values of safety and the health of society prevail over individual interests. Workers should not have the right to exceed the maximum amount of daily/monthly/yearly working hours, for the protection of their and everyone else's health, and for the protection of the environment, besides the social interest in the

[69] For in-depth study, see Gaëlle Ferrant, Luca Maria Pesando, and Keiko Nowacka, *Unpaid Care Work: The Missing Link in the Analysis of Gender Gaps in Labour Outcomes* (OECD 2014); Claudia Mazzei Nogueira and Rachel Gouveia Passos, 'A divisão sociossexual e racial do trabalho no cenário da epidemia do Covid-19: considerações a partir de Heleieth Saffioti' [2020] Cadernos CRH 33; Ursula Huws, 'The Reproduction of Difference: Gender and the Global Division of Labour (2014) 6 Work Organisation, Labour & Globalisation 1; Romina Lerussi and Francisco Trillo Párraga, 'Un nuevo derecho del trabajo para el mundo actual: ensanchar la base y expandir la imaginación (2021) 6 Revista Teoria Jurídica Contemporânea 1; Romina Lerussi, 'Orientaciones feministas para um nuevo derecho del trabajo (2020) 11 Revista Direito e Práxis 4; Noopur Raval and Joyojeet Pal, 'Making a "Pro": 'Professionalism after Platforms in Beauty-work' (2019) 3 Proceedings of the ACM on Human-Computer Interaction 175; Eneida Maria dos Santos and Rodrigo de Lacerda Carelli, 'As plataformas digitais de trabalhos e o lugar do negro no mercado de trabalho: o racismo nas configurações institucionais do trabalho no Brasil do século XXI [2022] Revista Jurídica Trabalho e Desenvolvimento Humano 5.

[70] Spencer, *Making Light Work* (n 68) 85.

distribution of work. A person's freedom begins and ensures its effectiveness in the very delimitation of everyone's acts. Freedom, in fact, is established by law based on the democratic delimitation of the interdictions, as shown by Fabre-Magnam.[71]

Furthermore, there should be a meeting of the two 'times' that Michel Serres[72] tells us about. In French, as in the Latin languages, *le temps* means both time and weather. Thus, Serres wants the two meanings of the French word *temps* to once again become one, as they were in the past. First of all, this means that clock time will be reconnected to the natural *temps* (weather, in English): light, dark, cold, hot, seasons, rain, snow, drought, flood. Second, it means that climatic conditions must be taken into consideration when establishing the working time. The worker will once again reunite the two *temps* in the form of the peasant and the sailor that Serres speaks of, making it possible for the worker to be connected with the world. Of course, because it stems from the principle itself, this rule is adaptable to each place. In regions where the climate is very cold or very hot for the whole year the two *temps* will not be treated in the same way as in regions where the seasons change regularly.

To achieve the goals of ecological labour law, remuneration by task or by output must be prohibited because it has been a known form of ultra-exploitation of the worker for more than 150 years.[73] Therefore, the regulation of working hours assumes a much greater character than it does currently, where it has very restricted objectives and is submitted to the particular and immediate interests and needs of the worker and employer. Also, the working hours cannot be left to collective self-regulation, except to obtain a reduction of working time, taking into account any specificity of the represented parties. The organizations representing society, including unions, must expand and take multidisciplinary and holistic views of the problems to perceive all of their facets. Trade unions, thus, would gain new, broader attributions, in a scope of action inside and outside the strict work environment, increasing their political role but ceasing to be representatives only of specific workers' economic interests.

[71] Muriel Fabre-Magnan, *L'institution de la liberte* (PUF 2018).
[72] Serres, *Le contrat naturel* (n 42).
[73] Karl Marx, *O Capital. Livro I* (Boitempo 2013) 411, 415.

B. Guaranteeing a Universal Basic Income

The scenes reported by the press of the pathetic desperation of entrepreneurs, and even of workers, who wished to reopen their businesses and return to work in the midst of the Covid-19 pandemic, even at the risk of their own lives, health, and that of the entire population, are proof of the failure of the current economic model.[74] People, of course, should not have to choose between their material survival and the risk of death by illness, wondering which would be the lesser evil. To prevent such undesirable situations, the right to live should be given an expanded meaning. Among other means, it could be guaranteed by a permanent universal basic income that guarantees people's unconditional monetary means for worthy existence in all situations and stages of life. The aim is precisely to prevent people from being forced to accept any job, under any conditions, by giving them a real opportunity to exercise of their free will, and not the laughable version of this we have today. Obviously, this minimum income should be independent of free basic public services, such as health, education, housing, and transportation, which should be universalized. Only with a universal income will it be possible to achieve degrowth and prevent people from competing for jobs, and accepting starvation or death wages.

How can this be achieved? One possibility is by economically compensating the poorest countries for the destruction of living conditions on the planet that enriched the countries at the centre of capitalism. This is a debt that must be paid and is essential to implement the conditions of ecological labour law in a universal way. The principle of 'no one left behind', on which the European mechanisms for the green and digital transitions are based, must take on a planetary dimension if we want a chance to resolve the global ecological crisis we are currently experiencing.[75] This can be done, for example, through the transfer of Special Drawing Rights (SDRs), the international currency issued by the International Monetary Fund (IMF), from the responsible core nations to the countries colonized in the past.[76] These SDRs are a kind of 'coupon' that are distributed to central banks and treasuries of countries around the world

[74] Joseph Stiglitz, *Recovering from the Pandemic: An Appraisal of Lessons Learned* (FEPS 2020); Mariana Mazzucato, 'Covid, uma doença do Antropoceno' <https://www.ihu.unisinos.br/sobre-o-ihu/78-noticias/603575-covid-uma-doenca-do-antropoceno-artigo-de-mariana-mazzucato> accessed 26 January 2023.

[75] Dimitris Stevis and Romain Felli, 'Planetary Just Transition? How Inclusive and How Just?' [2020] Earth System Governance 6.

[76] Cynthia Lucas Hewitt, 'One Capital Indivisible Under God: The IMF and Reparation for in a Time of Globalized Wealth' (2004) 47 American Behavioral Scientist 7.

that can be exchanged for money. There should be a redesign with the fair allocation of these SDRs for planetary ecological protection in a just way.[77]

C. Defence of the Work Environment

Ecological labour law will understand labour in a holistic way, as part of the broad relations between people and the other elements of this planet. The worker will become a universal subject and not just someone circumstantially linked to a specific relationship. Moreover, the worker will be respected as one more element of Earth, and seen as a central element for being the main geological force of the planet today. Thus, the working environment must be fully integrated with the environment in general. The health and hygiene of the worker must be guaranteed inside, and outside, the restricted and direct work environment, and there can be no differentiation. An uncontrolled work environment necessarily causes disturbances in the environment and vice versa. The environmental principles of precaution and prevention must be taken seriously and take precedence over axioms such as innovation, productivity, or progress. Life, both inside and outside the company or factory (a concept which is itself completely outdated, since the use of modern remote working tools and digital platforms makes us wonder where a company begins and where it ends), is the ultimate legal good to be preserved, and is inalienable and non-negotiable. Negri's concept of the social factory, broadening the idea of a place of production to include all social relations in all spaces, makes perfect sense in today's world, and for ecological labour law purposes.[78] Health hazard and risk premiums, as facets of the commodification of health, will be replaced by positive and negative incentives to reduce risks. In situations where risks could not be reasonably contained, robots, aided by artificial intelligence (AI), could be used. Production, as it loses its function of growth being substituted by that of preservation, will have the protection of the work environment as its main objective, which will see the protection of workers trickle down to the other inhabitants of this planet.

The environment will be considered to be the entire working environment, and thus, considered in a truly complete and socioecologically correct manner. An industrial activity will not only have the workers as subjects to be

[77] Michael Franzak and Olúfémi Táíwò, 'Here's how to repay developing nations for colonialism—and fight the climate crisis' (2022) <https://www.theguardian.com/commentisfree/2022/jan/14/heres-how-to-repay-developing-nations-for-colonialism-and-fight-the-climate-crisis> accessed 3 March 2022.

[78] Antonio Negri, *Cinco lições sobre Império* (DP&A 2003).

considered, but also the whole world. The factory, together with the workers, is reinserted into the world, at the same time as the other inhabitants of the Earth are inserted into the factory.

V. Conclusion

Obviously, ecological labour law is only one possibility and there is no determinism that will impose these solutions. Other choices can be made by society, including the deepening of ultraliberalism and the consequent extinction of the human species in a relatively short time. Everything is politics, and all politics is choice. It is also evident that these first lines are only initial ideas, which may prove to be impossible, or even wrong, and can only be verified after much discussion. The idea is precisely that: let us discuss this alternative. Some may see these ideas as utopian. And to appease those people, we could simply recite Fernando Birri's quote, made famous by Eduardo Galeano: '[U]topia is on the horizon. I know that I will never reach it. If I walk ten steps, it will move ten steps away. The more I seek it, the less I will find it, because it moves away as I get closer. So what is utopia for? It is precisely for that: to walk.'

Bibliography

Avogaro M, 'Right to Disconnect: French and Italian Proposals for a Global Issue' [2019] Revista Direito das Relações Sociais e Trabalhistas 9

Barca S, 'The Labour of Degrowth' [2019] Capitalism Nature Socialism 30

Bookchin M, *Social Ecology and Communalism* (AK Press 2006)

Chakrabarty D, 'Anthropocene Time' [2008] History and Theory 57

Danowski D and Viveiros de Castro E, *Há mundo por vir? Ensaio sobre os medos e os fins* (Desterro, Cultura e Barbárie and Intituto Socioambiental 2014)

Davidov G, *A Purposive Approach to Labour Law* (OUP 2016)

Doorey D, 'Just Transitions Law: Putting Labour Llaw to Work on Climate Change' [2017] Journal of Environmental Law and Practice 201

Ekbia H and Nardi B, *Heteromation, and Other Stories of Computing and Capitalism* (The MIT Press 2017)

EPA, *Climate Change and Social Vulnerability in the United States: A Focus on Six Impacts* (US Environmental Protection Agency 2021)

European Environment Agency, Eurofound, *Exploring the Social Challenges of Low-Carbon Energy Policies in Europe* (Eurofound 2021)

Fabre-Magnan M, *L'institution de la liberte* (PUF 2018)

Ferdinand M, *Une écologie décoloniale* (Seuil 2019)

Ferrant G, Maria Pesando L, and Nowacka K, *Unpaid Care Work: The Missing Link in the Analysis of Gender Gaps in Labour Outcomes* (OECD 2014)

Franzak M and Táíwò O, 'Here's how to repay developing nations for colonialism—and fight the climate crisis' (2022) <https://www.theguardian.com/commentisfree/2022/jan/14/heres-how-to-repay-developing-nations-for-colonialism-and-fight-the-climate-crisis>

Frey P, *The Ecological Limits of Work: on Carbon Emissions, Carbon Budgets and Working Time* (Autonomy 2019)

Fuchs C, 'Theorising and Analysing Digital Labour: From Global Value Chains to Modes of Production' (2013) 2 The Political Economy of Communication 1

Georgescu-Roegen N, *La Décroissance* (2nd edn, Éditions Sang de la terre 1995)

Gerold S, 'Revaluations of Work: Enabling and Combining a Diversity of Activities' in Seidl I and Zahrnt A (eds), *Post-Growth Work: Employment and Meaningful Activities with Planetary Boundaries* (Routledge 2022)

Golden L and Glosser S, 'Work Sharing as a Potential Policy Tool for Creating More and Better Employment: A Review of the Evidence' in J Messenger and N Ghosheh (eds), *Work Sharing: New Developments during the Great Recession and Beyond* (Edward Elgar Publishing and ILO 2012)

Huggan G and Tiffin H, *Postcolonial Criticism: Literature, Animals, Environment* (Routledge 2010)

Huws U, 'The Reproduction of Difference: Gender and the Global Division of Labour (2014) 6 Work Organisation, Labour & Globalisation 1

Intergovernmental Panel on Climate Change, *Climate Change 2021: The Physical Science Basis* (IPCC 2021)

Jackson T, *Prosperity Without Growth. Foundations for the Economy of Tomorrow* (2nd edn, Routledge 2017)

Kallis G and others, *The Case for Degrowth* (Polity Press 2020)

Klein N, *On Fire: The Burning Case for a Green New Deal* (Alfred A. Kopf Canada 2019)

Knight K, Rosa E, and Schor J, 'Reducing Growth to Achieve Environmental Sustainability: The Role of Work Hours' in J Wicks-Lim and R Pollin (eds), *Capitalism on Trial* (Edward Elgar Publishing 2013)

Krieger N, 'Will Your Electric Car Save the World or Wreck It?' (2018) <https://www.engineering.com/story/will-your-electric-car-save-the-world-or-wreck-it>

Latour B, *Diante de Gaia. Oito conferências sobre a natureza do Antropoceno* (Ateliê de Humanidades and Ubu Editora 2020)

Laurent E, 'The European Green Deal: From Growth Strategy to Social-Ecological Transition?' in B Vanhercke, S Spasova, and B Fronteddu (eds), *Social Policy in the European Union: State of Play 2020* (European Trade Union Institute (ETUI) and European Social Observatory (OSE) 2021)

Lerussi R, 'Orientaciones feministas para um nuevo derecho del trabajo (2020) 11 Revista Direito e Práxis 4

Lerussi R and Trillo Párraga F, 'Un nuevo derecho del trabajo para el mundo actual: ensanchar la base y expandir la imaginación (2021) 6 Revista Teoria Jurídica Contemporânea 1

Lucas Hewitt C, 'One Capital Indivisible Under God: The IMF and Reparation for in a Time of Globalized Wealth' (2004) 47 American Behavioral Scientist 7

Maria dos Santos E and de Lacerda Carelli R, 'As plataformas digitais de trabalhos e o lugar do negro no mercado de trabalho: o racismo nas configurações institucionais do trabalho no Brasil do século XXI [2022] Revista Jurídica Trabalho e Desenvolvimento Humano 5

Marx K, *O Capital. Livro I* (Boitempo 2013)

Matos de Oliveira A, *Brazil: Case Study on Working Time Organization and Its Effects in the Health Services Sector* (ILO 2015)

Mazzei Nogueira C and Gouveia Passos R, 'A divisão sociossexual e racial do trabalho no cenário da epidemia do Covid-19: considerações a partir de Heleieth Saffioti' [2020] Cadernos CRH 33

Mazzucato M, *Mission Economy: A Moonshot Guide to Changing Capitalism* (Penguin 2022)

Mazzucato M, 'Covid, uma doença do Antropoceno' (8 October 2020) <https://www.ihu.unisinos.br/sobre-o-ihu/78-noticias/603575-covid-uma-doenca-do-antropoceno-artigo-de-mariana-mazzucato>

Morgan J, 'Electric Vehicles: The Future We Made and the Problem of Unmaking It' (2020) 44 Cambridge Journal of Economics 4

Negri A, *Cinco lições sobre Império* (DP&A 2003)

Polanyi K, *The Great Transformation: The Political and Economic Origins of Our Time* (Beacon Press 2001)

Raval N and Pal J, 'Making a "Pro": 'Professionalism after Platforms in Beauty-work' (2019) 3 Proceedings of the ACM on Human-Computer Interaction 175

Raworth K, *Economia Donut. Uma alternativa ao crescimento a qualquer custo* (Zahar 2019)

Reidmiller and others (eds), *Impacts, Risks, and Adaptation in the United States: Fourth National Climate Assessment, Volume II* (US Global Change Research Program 2018)

Rossi M, 'Frutas exportadas pelo Brasil levam agrotóxicos proibidos na Europa à mesa dos alemães' (2021) <https://brasil.elpais.com/brasil/2021-06-08/frutas-exportadas-pelo-brasil-levam-agrotoxicos-proibidos-na-europa-a-mesa-dos-alemaes.html>

Schaffer A and Stahmer C, 'Die Halbtagsgesellschaft—ein Konzept für nach-haltigere Produktions- und Konsummuster' (2005) 14 GAIA – Ecological Perspectives for Science and Society 3

Seidl I and Zahrnt A, 'Employment, Meaningful Activity and the Post-Growth Society' in I Seidl and A Zahrnt (eds), *Post-Growth Work: Employment and Meaningful Activities with Planetary Boundaries* (Routledge 2022)

Serres M, *Le contrat naturel* (François Boutin 1990)

Spencer D, *Making Light Work: An End to Toil in the Twenty-First Century* (Polity 2022)

Steffen W, 'Planetary Boundaries: Guiding Human Development on a Changing Planet' [2015] Science 347

Stevis D and Felli R, 'Planetary Just Transition? How Inclusive and How Just?' [2020] Earth System Governance 6

Stiegler B, 'Sortir de l'anthropocène' [2015] Multitudes 60

Stiegler B, *The Negathropocene* (Open Humanities Press 2018)

Stiglitz J, *Recovering from the Pandemic: An Appraisal of Lessons Learned* (FEPS 2020)

Stronge W and Lewis K, *Overtime. Why We Need A Shorter Working Week* (Verso 2021)

Stuart D, Gunderson R, and Petersen B, *The Degrowth Alternative: A Path to Address our Environmental Crisis?* (Routledge 2021)

Supiot A, *La gouvernance par les nombres* (Seuil 2015)

Suzman J, *Work: A Deep History, from the Stone Age to the Age of Robots* (Penguin 2020)

Taralden L, 'The world's electric-car capital is having nasty fights over oil' (2021) <https://www.bloomberg.com/news/features/2021-06-10/norway-s-climate-contradiction-fuels-debate-over-oil>

Turpin E, 'O antropoceno é um alerta sobre as ações humanas no planeta' Interview with Ricardo Machado (2018) <http://www.ihu.unisinos.br/159-noticias/entrevistas/582885-o-antropoceno-e-um-alerta-sobre-as-acoes-humanas-no-planeta-entrevista-especial-com-etienne-turpin>

6

A Global South Perspective on Labour Rights and Supply Chains for a Post-Growth World

Surya Deva and Pushkar Anand

I. Introduction

The current economic growth model relies heavily on supply chains in the Global South.[1] The supply chains are deeply problematic for several reasons. For example, although they create jobs and economic opportunities (including for socially marginalized groups) in the Global South, they also exploit various intersectional vulnerabilities of workers[2] and export the Global North's share of environmental pollution to the Global South. Various international soft standards have generally failed to address these problems. That has led to the recent push for European states to enact mandatory human rights due diligence (HRDD) laws with an extraterritorial effect.[3] However, the efficacy of even these laws in bringing a positive change in the lives of supply chain workers in the Global South is suspect.[4] More critically, such laws—manufactured in the Global North without participation of stakeholders from the Global South—again reflect the power dynamics in setting the 'rules of the game' in a way that might perpetuate the colonial legacy.[5]

[1] We use the terms 'Global South' and 'Global North' merely as convenient labels to reflect power imbalances, inequalities, and exclusions—both historical and current—linked to the current economic model and global governance rather than taking these terms indicating sharp geographical divisions, eg there may be a Global South in the Global North and vice versa.

[2] These vulnerabilities may be social, economic, cultural, personal, or structural, eg poverty, illiteracy, patriarchal values, and discrimination on the basis of class, caste, sex, sexual orientation, gender identity, disability, age, colour, ethnicity, religion, language, marital status, migration, and indigenous status.

[3] See Claire Bright and Nicolas Bueno, 'Mandatory Human Rights Due Diligence' in Anthony Ewing (ed), *Teaching Business and Human Rights* (Edward Elgar 2023) 144.

[4] Ingrid Landau, 'Human Rights Due Diligence and the Risk of Cosmetic Compliance' (2019) 20 Melbourne Journal of International Law 221; Surya Deva, 'Mandatory Human Rights Due Diligence Laws in Europe: A Mirage for Rightsholders?' (2023) 36 Leiden Journal of International Law 389.

[5] Caroline Omari Lichuma, '(Laws) Made in the "First World": A TWAIL Critique of the Use of Domestic Legislation to Extraterritorially Regulate Global Value Chains' (2021) 81 Zeitschrift für

Surya Deva and Pushkar Anand, *A Global South Perspective on Labour Rights and Supply Chains for a Post-Growth World*
In: *Labour Law Utopias*. Edited by: Nicolas Bueno, Beryl ter Haar, and Nuna Zekić, Oxford University Press.
 DOI: 10.1093/oso/9780198889755.003.0006

While we have been struggling to create fair and humane supply chains, the idea of degrowth or post-growth has started taking root in the Global North in recent years.[6] The post-growth model seeks to shift the focus away from gross domestic product (GDP) as a measure of economic development. It also promotes restricting overconsumption of the scarce resources of the world as well as reducing resource and energy demands. The degrowth idea is perhaps the need of the hour to avert the climate crisis and build an inclusive and sustainable society. However, it is the Global North—which has already achieved economic development and continues to maintain very high levels of consumption of food and energy per capita[7]—that needs degrowth more than the Global South.

Nevertheless, due to the interconnected nature of the global economy and the continued dominance of the Global North in setting regulatory agendas, the degrowth idea might once again deprive the Global South of its legitimate development aspirations. For instance, a post-growth economic model that requires cutting down production and consumption is likely to result in Global South suppliers receiving fewer manufacturing orders. Moreover, the push for a zero-carbon economy and resort to automated manufacturing will disproportionately impact the Global South.

Against this backdrop, this chapter critiques the current state of labour rights within supply chains from a Global South perspective. The dominant narrative augmenting support for supply chain capitalism is that they create jobs and facilitate the economic development of the countries in the Global South. We expose this 'win-win' narrative and argue that supply chains reflect a business model that prioritizes profit over people and the planet. If supply chains merely create exploitative jobs, entrench economic inequality, and promote unsustainable development, they do not deserve celebration. Moreover, supply chains allow multinational corporations (MNCs), most of them headquartered

ausländisches öffentliches Recht und Völkerrecht (Heidelberg Journal of International Law) 497; Debadatta Bose, 'Decentring Narratives around Business and Human Rights Instruments: An Example of the French Devoir de Vigilance Law' (2023) 8 Business and Human Rights Journal 18.

[6] See eg Jason Hickel, *Less is More: How Degrowth Will Save the World* (Penguin 2021).

[7] 'Privileged lifestyles in Europe, North America and other nations in the Global North produce a carbon footprint 100 times greater than that of the world's poor nations combined.' Generation Climate Europe, 'Global North and Global South: How Climate Change Uncovers Global Inequalities' (10 May 2022) <https://gceurope.org/global-north-and-global-south-how-climate-change-uncovers-global-inequalities/> accessed 9 May 2024. See also Jason Hickel and others, 'Imperialist Appropriation in the World Economy: Drain from the Global South through Unequal Exchange, 1990–2015' (2022) 73 Global Environmental Change 102467; Jason Hickel and Aljosa Slamersak, 'Existing Climate Mitigation Scenarios Perpetuate Colonial Inequalities' (2022) 6(7) The Lancet Planetary Health 628.

in the Global North, to export risks to the Global South, avoid legal responsibilities, and exploit power imbalances.

As a potential solution, we develop an alternative vision of labour rights and supply chains which is responsive to the needs and aspirations of the Global South. We argue that a 'differentiated degrowth' model should be adopted—what degrowth means in the Global North should not be identical to what it entails in the Global South. Moreover, a reorientation in the corporate purpose is required, otherwise, companies will continue to exploit vulnerable workers to maximize profit for shareholders. States, MNCs, and consumers in the Global North should also internalize responsibilities for the outsourcing and exporting of risks to the Global South.[8] At the same time, they should account for historical wrongs (including during the colonial era) and contribute to developing universal social protection for people globally. Only by taking these steps, could a just and equitable post-growth model be developed.

Section II of the chapter sets the context by analysing current literature concerning supply chains in the Global South and the post-growth theories. In Section III, we provide a critique of the current supply chains model. This critique is then used in Section IV to offer an alternative vision of supply chains and labour rights in the post-growth economy. Some concluding thoughts are offered in Section V.

II. Locating Economic Globalization, the Global South, and Supply Chains in 'Post-Growth' Theories

Globalization has been a key component of the neoliberal global ordering, effected through what is characterized as the 'Washington consensus' prioritizing deregulation of markets, privatization of public sector undertakings, liberalization of trade and foreign investment, and legal security for property rights.[9] The neoliberal market policies adopted by states have had deleterious effects on workers' rights and have precipitated a race to the bottom concerning labour rights for attracting global capital.[10] The dismantling of trade and investment barriers, technological and informational advancements, and

[8] In line with our usage of the terms Global North and Global South, MNCs and affluent consumers in the Global South should also bear this responsibility.

[9] See John Williamson, 'The Washington Consensus as Policy Prescription for Development' (2004) <https://www.piie.com/sites/default/files/publications/papers/williamson0204.pdf> accessed 9 May 2024.

[10] Robert G Blanton and Dursun Peksen, 'Economic Liberalisation, Market Institutions and Labour Rights' (2016) 55 European Journal of Political Research 474, 482.

improvements in transportation have led to geographical dispersion and fragmentation of the production processes, triggering the proliferation of global supply chains across the world and coordinated by MNCs.[11] The inability or the unwillingness of the host states in the Global South, where the production and extraction take place, and the home states in the Global North, where most MNCs have their headquarters, to regulate the corporate conduct violating labour and human rights has created a governance gap in the regulation of these supply chains.[12]

In addition to being the situs of governance and accountability gaps, supply chains have also contributed to the resource drain from the Global South. The appropriation of the southern resources and labour by the developed economies in the Global North amounts to USD10.8 trillion in 2015 and USD242 trillion during 1990–2015.[13] Dorninger and others find that the high-income countries were the net appropriators of all types of embodied resources, that is, material, energy, land, and labour, during the same period, with all other world regions serving as net exporters of such resources, leading to the perpetuation of an unequal exchange relation.[14]

At least 70 per cent of the world's industrial labour force today resides in the Global South,[15] due to the proliferation of the global commodity chains constituting almost 80 per cent of international trade.[16] Despite the contribution to most of the industrial production by the Global South workers, including the high-technology productions such as automobiles and computers, the inequality in the wages for labour is extreme. Intan Suwandi argues that the global value or commodity chains led by the MNCs centred in the Global North represent the new form of economic imperialism.[17] MNCs ask the smaller suppliers in the chain to adopt stringent labour management and control practices, such as open-cost systems, international price benchmarking, and regulation of suppliers' profit margins, to maximize labour productivity designed to maximize extraction, while simultaneously shielding themselves from accountability for the oppressive policies that the supplier companies

[11] See Daniel Brinks and others, 'Private Regulatory Initiatives, Human Rights, and Supply Chain Capitalism' in Daniel Brinks and others (eds), *Power, Participation, and Private Regulatory Initiatives* (University of Pennsylvania Press 2021) 3, 9.

[12] ibid 8.

[13] Hickel and others, 'Imperialist Appropriation' (n 7) 6.

[14] Christian Dorninger and others, 'Global Patterns of Ecologically Unequal Exchange: Implications for Sustainability in the 21st Century' (2019) 179 Ecological Economics 106824.

[15] See ILOSTAT, 'Statistics on the Population and Labour Force' <https://ilostat.ilo.org/topics/population-and-labour-force/> accessed 9 May 2024.

[16] Hickel and others, 'Imperialist Appropriation' (n 7).

[17] Intan Suwandi, *Value Chains: The New Economic Imperialism* (Monthly Review Press 2019).

might adopt.[18] Suwandi further shows that the MNCs in the Global North put pressure on companies in the South to maintain 'competitive' wage rates or to improve the workers' efficiency if wages are increased.[19] Workers are hired on insecure, zero-hour contracts, and paid a legal minimum wage leaving them below the poverty line.[20]

The post-growth idea[21] challenges this current global socioeconomic order shaped by the neoliberal competitive market economy: it is a project against the system celebrating unabated economic expansion that disproportionately benefits a small minority of the rich.[22] It argues that the relentless expansion of production and consumption has led to overshooting of the planetary boundaries and is unsustainable as the natural resources driving such expansion are finite.[23] Post-growth problematizes using GDP as a proxy for social wellbeing, as it does not distinguish between the activities contributing to wellbeing and those that do not.[24] Nor does it take into account the non-market activities in society, such as community engagement, the functioning of ecosystems, or the income inequality in society.[25]

Broadly, implementing the post-growth approach requires moving beyond growth-based economies and reforming a number of socioeconomic structures.[26] Such restructuring, argues Hickel, involves a 'planned reduction of energy and resource throughput designed to bring the economy back into balance with the living world in a way that reduces inequality and improves human wellbeing'.[27] In other words, it means scaling back on consumption, and production, while adapting to an alternative simpler way of living.[28] However, this reduction in consumption and production might negatively affect millions of

[18] See Intan Suwandi, R Jamil Jonna, and John Bellamy Foster, 'Global Commodity Chains and the New Imperialism' (2019) 70(10) Monthly Review 1.

[19] Suwandi, *Value Chains* (n 17).

[20] See Kate Raworth, *Trading Away Our Rights: Women Workers in Global Supply Chains* (Oxfam International 2004).

[21] The term post-growth in this chapter refers to and includes various post-economic growth approaches such as degrowth, doughnut economics, steady-state economics, post-development, etc, which look beyond increasing consumption, production, and wealth as the main goal of the economy. See Chapter 1 by Bueno, ter Haar, and Zekić in this book.

[22] Jason Hickel, 'What Does Degrowth Mean? A Few Points of Clarification' (2021) 18(7) Globalizations 1105.

[23] See Kate Raworth, *Doughnut Economics: Seven Ways to Think like a 21st -Century Economist* (Random House Business 2018).

[24] See Samuel Alexander, *Prosperous Descent: Crisis as Opportunity in an Age of Limits* (Simplicity Institute 2015) 40.

[25] ibid. See also Chapter 7 by Bueno in this book.

[26] See Simon Mair, Angela Druckman, and Tim Jackson, 'A Tale of Two Utopias: Work in a Post-Growth World' (2020) 173 Ecological Economics 106653.

[27] See Hickel 'What Does Degrowth Mean?' (n 22).

[28] See Ted Trainer <http://thesimplerway.info/> accessed 9 May 2024.

workers of the Global South employed in the supply chains. Additionally, since the objective of the post-growth approach is to achieve a sustainable and equitable society, this raises an important question of how the post-growth theories address the inequitable accumulation of wealth by MNCs operating through supply chains in the Global South.

Further, implementing the post-growth approach also requires radical reforms in the institution of work. Paid work in a growth-based society is not just a phenomenon but an institution and an ideology that significantly affects the welfare and the environment.[29] The institution of work is, presently, bound with the growth dynamics.[30] In attempting to maximize their profit and reduce costs, the firms aim at increasing labour productivity leading to a requirement of fewer people to do the same amount of work, which may, in turn, lead to unemployment as well as displacement towards jobs that are less well-paid.[31] Since unemployment means not only the loss of social status but also material necessities and social welfare, the only imperative is that the economies should continually grow, thus straining and overshooting the planetary boundaries.[32] The consequence of reducing economic activity pursuant to the post-growth approach would be a reduction in employment opportunities or the availability of work. In order to address this concern, several policies to prevent unemployment and to even improve employment have been suggested by the advocates of a post-growth approach, such as working time reduction, introducing a job guarantee with a living wage, and rolling out retention programmes to shift people out of sunset sectors.[33] These policies will require substantial institutional restructuring[34] as well as financial support from the states. While the states in the Global North may be able to support such a transition, those in the Global South might not. This is yet another question which the post-growth approach needs to address. While a comprehensive survey of post-growth literature would be beyond the scope of this chapter, we look at some of the recent popular works on post-growth.

The applicability of the post-growth approach to the Global South has been debated, with several economists holding the view that post-growth should only apply to the Global North. For instance, Herman Daly argued that it

[29] Halliki Kreinin and Ernest Aigner, 'From "Decent Work and Economic Growth" to "Sustainable Work and Economic Degrowth": A New Framework for SDG8' (2022) 49 Empirica 281.

[30] See Mair, Druckman, and Jackson, 'A Tale of Two Utopias' (n 26).

[31] ibid.

[32] ibid. See also Timothée Parrique, *The Political Economy of Degrowth* (Stockholm University 2019).

[33] See Jason Hickel and others, 'Degrowth Can Work—Here's How Science Can Help' (2022) 612 Nature 400–02.

[34] See Max Koch, 'The State in the Transformation to a Sustainable Postgrowth Economy' (2020) 29(1) Environmental Politics 115.

would be 'morally backward to preach steady-state doctrines to underdeveloped countries' before the developed countries themselves take measures aimed at reducing the consumption of resources.[35] Similarly, Jason Hickel argues that only the 'high-income countries exceeding per capita fair-shares of planetary boundaries' need to degrow, not the rest of the 'economies that are not characterized by excess resources and energy use'.[36] The material and energy consumption in the Global North has disproportionate consequences for the Global South, both in terms of carbon emissions as well as material extraction.[37] Hickel asserts that excessive consumption in the Global North 'relies on patterns of colonization' through 'appropriation of South's fair share of atmospheric commons, and the plunder of southern ecosystems' and that degrowth in the Global North would mean decolonization in the South.[38]

Responding to the concerns of the negative impact of degrowth in the Global North on the economies of the Global South that are dependent on the export of raw materials and manufactured products, Hickel questions the logic underlying this concern, that is, 'the consumption in the global north must continue to rise even if it causes ecological breakdown in the global south as it is necessary for its development'.[39] Rather than sticking to more growth leading to exploitation, the focus should be on ensuring economic justice to the Global South, that is, ensuring fair prices for the labour and resources that they provide.[40] Degrowth in the Global North would create space for the economies in the Global South to shift away from their 'enforced role as exporters of cheap labour and raw materials' and to focus on building economies based on sovereignty, self-sufficiency, and human wellbeing.[41] Importantly, the Global South could use degrowth in the North as an opportunity to collectively organize in a manner that led to the call for a New International Economic Order (NIEO),[42] and demand increased prices for their labour and resources, fairer terms of trade and finance, and better representation in the global governance.[43] However, some disagree with this line of argument.

Ted Trainer finds Hickel's view on the applicability of degrowth to the Global South as suggesting the continuity of the third world on the same path of development characterized by economic growth, which is a 'resource squandering

35 Herman E Daly, *Steady State Economics* (Island Press 1991) 148.
36 See Hickel, 'What Does Degrowth Mean?' (n 22) 1109.
37 ibid.
38 ibid.
39 ibid.
40 ibid 1110.
41 ibid.
42 ibid.
43 ibid.

road to affluent lifestyles and complex energy-intensive debt-fuelled systems, by prospering through trading within a globalized trade-intensive economy'.[44] It is indeed doubtful whether the states in the Global South will be able to ensure the wellbeing of their citizens and provide them with equitable living conditions if they continue on the same trajectory. Trainer argues instead that *all* the economies 'must abandon affluence, centralization, urbanization, large scale and globalization, and must adopt as the basic social form the small scale highly self-sufficient, self-governing and cooperative community'.[45] He urges the economies to be needs-based rather than profit-driven because 'most production could be via privately owned small firms and farms'.[46] That would also require us to envision a change in the value and purpose of work in society. For instance, Bueno argues that labour law and policy should shift their focus from productive work to activities that foster human development and social wellbeing.[47] The path advocated by Trainer resonates with Serge Latouche, who urges the Global South to adopt a model for developing differently by not 'rushing up the blind alley of growth economics'. However, Latouche argued that this *different* development of the Global South was possible only when the Global North adopted some form of economic contraction.[48]

A specific proposal comes from Gerber and Raina, who argue that post-growth approach as a mix of degrowth, agrowth, steady-state economics, and post-development is very relevant to the Global South.[49] They propose various ways of thinking about post-growth in the Global South. They start by recognizing that the current growth patterns in the Global South are ecologically, financially, and socially unsustainable. Second, they argue that rather than thinking about post-growth in terms of geographical boundaries, a 'class-based perspective' must be adopted, considering a global ruling class, also referred to as the transnational capitalist class,[50] as sharing similar lifestyles and consumption patterns.[51] Thirdly, they challenge the narrative that more growth is

[44] See Ted Trainer, 'What Does Degrowth Mean? Some Comments on Jason Hickel's 'A Few Points on Clarification' (2021) 18(7) Globalizations 1112, 1114.
[45] ibid.
[46] ibid.
[47] Nicolas Bueno, 'From Productive Work to Capability-Enhancing Work: Implications for Labour Law and Policy' (2022) 23(3) Journal of Human Development and Capabilities 354.
[48] See Serge Latouche, 'Degrowth Economics' Le Monde Diplomatique (14 November 2004) <https://mondediplo.com/2004/11/14latouche> accessed 9 May 2024.
[49] See Julien-François Gerber and Rajeswari S Raina, 'Post-Growth in the Global South? Some Reflections from India and Bhutan' (2018) 150 Ecological Economics 353.
[50] William I Robinson, *A Theory of Global Capitalism: Production, Class, and State in a Transnational World* (The John Hopkins University Press 2004); William I Robinson and Jerry Harris, 'Towards a Global Ruling Class? Globalization and the Transnational Capitalist Class' (2000) 64(1) Science and Society 11.
[51] Gerber and Raina, 'Post-Growth in the Global South?' (n 49).

essential to overcome poverty. Taking the example of the lopsided economic growth in India, they illustrate that the adoption of pro-growth policies has been counter-productive, leading to increasing income inequality, jobless growth, creation of new poverties by undermining meaningful local activities, fostering accumulation by dispossession and contamination, and destruction of the livelihood of people formerly directly dependent on ecosystems.[52] Further, they suggest that the focus of the policies should be on the satisfaction of basic needs and that this does not necessarily require a general increase in wealth but a better redistribution[53] and change in the value and purpose of work in society.[54]

However, despite the differences in the ways of thinking about and implementing the post-growth agenda, there are certain commonalities. First, there seems to be concurrence on the requirement of economic contraction, that is, reduction of production and consumption. Second is the necessity of moving away from profit-making as the focus of policies and reorienting the goal to satisfaction of basic needs of the people. Third is the requirement of adopting policies aimed at redistributing the accumulated wealth.

In the context of redistributing income and wealth, Kate Raworth, in *Doughnut Economics*, criticizes the rise of shareholder capitalism for entrenching the culture of shareholder primacy. The primary obligation of a corporation to maximize the profit for its shareholders relegates the employees as the outsiders, and treats them as 'a production cost that is to be minimised'.[55] Raworth suggests flipping the dominant ownership model of businesses by creating employee-owned companies and member-owned cooperatives.[56] She argues for a bottom-up redesigning of the business model that will democratize the 'access of economic power' from few to many and will reorient the purpose of business from 'social indifference to social benefit'.[57] While Raworth's distributive design of the economy does offer a broad and general insight into what an alternative business environment would look like, it does not delve deep into the specific question of supply chain capitalism. In this regard, the work of Belén Payán-Sánchez and others is insightful. From a management perspective, they argue that apart from the change in the political and economic perspective, innovations in the operations management and supply

[52] ibid.
[53] ibid.
[54] See Bueno, 'From Productive Work to Capability-Enhancing Work' (n 47) and Chapter 7 by Bueno in this book.
[55] Raworth, *Doughnut Economics* (n 23) 189.
[56] ibid.
[57] ibid.

chain management by engaging stakeholders, in the decision-making process, can gear the current form of 'corporate governance towards a more sustainable management that is compatible with situations of economic degrowth'.[58]

However, despite some insights and the broad critique of the neoliberal market-based globalization, the post-growth literature does not seem to have addressed the precise questions of accumulation of wealth by MNCs through supply chains and how, if the economies are to contract, the Global South deals with this transition's impact on the workers. In fact, while charting a future research agenda for a post-growth approach, Hanaček and others find that 'little work has focused on relevance of such [post-growth] policies outside Europe and North America. How can work sharing (reduction of paid working hours) be implemented, for example, in economies that are not fully industrialized? Is there a place for a carbon tax (or dividend) or a basic income in low-income economies? If not, what policies would work in such contexts, and steer these economies to more sustainable, post-growth trajectories?'[59]

III. Critique of the Current Supply Chain Model

The current supply chain model is inherently exploitative for workers and the entire ecosystem, generally in the Global South. Below, we focus on certain dimensions of this exploitative nature.

A. Focusing on Economic Efficiency

Maximizing profit requires companies to reduce the cost of production as much as possible. Alford notes that 'major corporations have worked out ways to reduce their costs by locating different stages of their products' design, production, and assembly in various countries'.[60] This rationale explains the presence of MNCs' supply chains in the Global South: the availability of

[58] Belén Payán-Sánchez, Miguel Pérez-Valls, and José Antonio Plaza-Úbeda 'Supply Chain Management in a Degrowth Context: The Potential Contribution of Stakeholders' in Natalia Yakovleva, Regina Frei, and Sudhir Rama Murthy (eds), *Sustainable Development Goals and Sustainable Supply Chains in the Postglobal Economy* (Springer 2019) 31.

[59] See Ksenija Hanaček and others, 'Ecological Economics and Degrowth: Proposing a Future Research Agenda from the Margins' (2020) 169 Ecological Economics 106495.

[60] Matthew Alford, 'Labour and Work' in Nicola Phillips (ed), *Global Political Economy* (OUP 2023) 281, 282.

abundant cheap labour.[61] In fact, even within the Global South, MNCs move their supply chains from one country to another to cut down the cost of producing goods. For example, when wages in China increased, many companies moved their sourcing factories to Bangladesh, Cambodia, and Vietnam.[62] The uneven spread of supply chains in the Global South is also driven by the desire of MNCs to maximize the economic efficiency of production.[63]

The corporate focus on achieving economic efficiency in production also means that negative impacts on the rights of workers, the environment, and the climate are often not given the same importance as maximizing profit for the shareholders. Since the Global South is the world's manufacturing hub, these negative impacts are disproportionately borne by people in the Global South, whereas the gains of economic efficiency are enjoyed by the actors in the Global North. Moreover, multiple developing states competing to secure production facilities results in a race to the bottom regarding labour standards,[64] thus undermining the goal of inclusive and sustainable development. Many MNCs have adopted codes of conduct governing their global supply chains and put in place certification and auditing processes. One may think that adopting such measures should result in a 'race to the top' regarding social and environmental standards around the globe.[65] However, it is doubtful that this has happened in practice on a significant scale.

B. Evading Legal Responsibility by Outsourcing

MNCs consciously operate through a complex global web of subsidiaries and suppliers. In addition to achieving economic efficiency, outsourcing operations (production, assembling, manufacturing, selling, servicing, etc) allows parent companies and brands to evade legal responsibility for the wrongful conduct

[61] 'A significant and straightforward explanation for this is that corporations want to increase profits to appease their shareholders. The simple fact is that labour and production costs tend to be much cheaper in developing and emerging countries based in the Global South.' ibid.

[62] MacDonald notes that 'rapidly rising wages in China have contributed to recent manufacturing shifts towards countries such as Cambodia, Vietnam, and Bangladesh'. Kate MacDonald, 'Production and Business' in Nicola Phillips (ed), *Global Political Economy* (OUP 2023) 135, 138.

[63] 'Many companies have chosen to concentrate their offshore sourcing in relatively large, low-cost production sites close to major East Asian manufacturing centres. Smaller countries that are geographically further away from these hubs, such as less-developed countries in sub-Saharan Africa, find it increasingly difficult to compete with large and established suppliers.' ibid 142.

[64] Alessandro Guasti and Mathias Koenig-Archibugi, 'Has Global Trade Competition Really Led to a Race to the Bottom in Labor Standards?' (2022) 66(4) International Studies Quarterly saqc61.

[65] UNCTAD, *Better Trade for Sustainable Development: The role of voluntary sustainability standards* (2021) 5–6 <https://unctad.org/system/files/official-document/ditctab2021d2_en.pdf> accessed 9 May 2024.

of their subsidiaries and suppliers. It is well-documented how companies have misused the twin principles of separate corporate personality and limited liability to deny, delay, or altogether avoid responsibility for human rights abuses by their subsidiaries.[66] Research indicates that parent companies assigned their risky businesses to subsidiaries to insulate themselves from potential liability.[67]

Sourcing through independent contractors takes the outsourcing model of business to the next level. This model allows MNCs to outsource their risks and responsibilities to suppliers spread across the globe. Companies creating and using gig platforms should also be seen in this light because this business model is deepening the distancing of responsibility for creating 'precarious work'.[68]

The evolution of parent companies' direct duty of care offers some hope in holding these companies liable for abuses linked to their subsidiaries.[69] This principle may potentially be extended against MNCs' suppliers (as discussed below). Yet, this pathway only offers a case-by-case determination in specific cases, and there is still inadequate political appetite to bring fundamental changes to the rules of the game that allow MNCs to legally evade their responsibility for human rights abuses in their operations.[70] Moreover, self-regulation tools adopted by MNCs—such as reporting, certification, and social auditing—often fail to address an issue as serious as modern slavery,[71] and companies continue to adopt innovative business models of modern slavery.[72]

The failure of both self-regulation and soft international standards in encouraging most MNCs to respect human rights (including the labour rights

[66] Amnesty International, *Injustice Incorporated: Corporate Abuses and the Human Rights to Remedy* (Amnesty International 2014) 115–17; Surya Deva, 'Fictitious Separation, Real Injustice: Why and How to Tame the Twin Principles of Corporate Law?' in *Creating a Paradigm Shift: Legal Solutions to Improve Access to Remedy for Corporate Human Rights Abuse* (Amnesty International and BHRRC 2017) 21, 21–22. See also Charlotte Villiers, 'A Game of Cat and Mouse: Human Rights Protection and the Problem of Corporate Law and Power (2023) 36 Leiden Journal of International Law 415.

[67] Henry Hansmann and Reinier Kraakman, 'Toward Unlimited Shareholder Liability for Corporate Torts' (1991) 100 Yale Law Journal 1879, 1891.

[68] Alford, 'Labour and Work' (n 60) 284.

[69] *Vedanta Resources plc v Lungowe* [2019] UKSC 20; *Okpabi v Royal Dutch Shell plc* [2021] UKSC 3. See also Richard Meeran, 'Multinational Human Rights Litigation in the UK: A Retrospective' (2021) 6 Business and Human Rights Journal 255.

[70] Radu Mares, 'Liability Within Corporate Groups: Parent Companies' Accountability for Subsidiary Human Rights Abuses' in Surya Deva and David Birchall (eds), *Research Handbook on Human Rights and Business* (Edward Elgar 2020) 446.

[71] See Justine Nolan and Nina Frishling, 'Australia's Modern Slavery Act: Towards Meaningful Compliance' (2019) 37 Company and Securities Law Journal 104; Jolyon Ford and Justine Nolan, 'Regulating Transparency on Human Rights and Modern Slavery in Corporate Supply Chains: The Discrepancy between Human Rights Due Diligence and the Social Audit' (2020) 26 Australian Journal of Human Rights 27.

[72] Andrew Crane and others, 'Confronting the Business Models of Modern Slavery' (2022) 31(3) Journal of Management Inquiry 264.

of workers in their supply chains) has triggered the enactment of mandatory HRDD laws in Europe.[73] Protecting the labour rights of supply chain workers by requiring selected large MNCs to conduct HRDD in consultation with the relevant stakeholders is at the heart of these laws.[74] These laws also provide for administrative sanctions and/or civil liability for breaching legal provisions. In short, mandatory HRDD laws appear as a silver lining. However, their value in improving the conditions of workers in the Global South or providing them with a viable pathway to remediation remains suspect at this early stage because these laws do not seek to dismantle the business model of irresponsibility or address power imbalances which create a permissive environment for exploitation.[75]

C. Exporting Risks to the Global South

Global North states and their MNCs consciously export risks to the Global South. This is done by exploiting various vulnerabilities in the Global South such as poverty, high rates of unemployment, lack of awareness about rights, lower safety standards, corruption, and weak enforcement of laws.

Let us take the shipbreaking industry in South Asia as an example. Due to 'stricter social and environmental laws in the Global North', the shipbreaking industry has flourished in South Asia, with more than 70 per cent of the estimated 800 decommissioned ships being scrapped in Chittagong (Bangladesh), Alang (India), and Gadani (Pakistan).[76] Workers in these shipbreaking

[73] ECCJ, 'Comparative Table: Corporate Due Diligence Laws and Legislative Proposals in Europe' (May 2021) <https://corporatejustice.org/publications/comparative-table-due-diligence-proposals-europe/> accessed 9 May 2024. In addition, states such as the UK, Canada, and Australia have enacted modern slavery laws, while New Zealand is considering doing so.

[74] See Sandra Cossart, Jérôme Chaplier, and Tiphaine Beau de Lomenie, 'The French Law on Duty of Care: A Historic Step Towards Making Globalization Work for All' (2017) 2 Business and Human Rights Journal 317; Markus Krajewski, Kristel Tonstand, and Franziska Wohltmann, 'Mandatory Human Rights Due Diligence in Germany and Norway: Stepping, or Striding, in the Same Direction?' (2021) 6 Business and Human Rights Journal 550; Nicolas Bueno and Christine Kaufmann, 'The Swiss Human Rights Due Diligence Legislation: Between Law and Politics' (2021) 6 Business and Human Rights Journal 542.

[75] For a critique, see Deva, 'Mandatory Human Rights' (n 4).

[76] Afsana Rubaiyat, 'South Asia's hazardous ship recycling industry must transition to a more sustainable future' (6 June 2022) <https://scroll.in/article/1025094/south-asias-hazardous-ship-recycling-industry-must-transition-to-a-more-sustainable-future> accessed 9 May 2024. See also 'Ship Breaking around the world' <https://shipbreakingbd.info/ship-breaking-around-the-world/> accessed 9 May 2024.

yards—many of whom are children and/or migrants[77]—are exposed to significant occupational health and safety risks.

For instance, Bangladesh's shipbreaking industry is labelled by the International Labour Organization (ILO) as 'amongst the most dangerous of occupations, with unacceptably high levels of fatalities, injuries and work-related diseases'.[78] A study 'revealed that workers lack basic facilities and are exposed to occupational health hazards due to working in a risky environment' and that more 'than 60% of workers reported being injured or suffering from various physical problems such as blurred vision, abdominal pain, and skin problems'.[79] It is also estimated that 'one third of workers in local shipbreaking yards face a high risk of lung diseases thanks to their exposure to asbestos'.[80] Moreover, child labour is prevalent in these shipbreaking yards.[81]

Shipbreaking is also 'a highly polluting industry' because large amounts of carcinogens and toxic substances are 'dumped into the soil and coastal waters'.[82] Moreover, as 'the majority of yards have no waste management systems or facilities to prevent pollution, shipbreaking takes an enormous toll on the surrounding environment, the local communities, fishery, agriculture, flora and fauna'.[83] In other words, the local communities who depend on the coastal ecosystem 'are devastated by toxic spills and other types of pollution caused by the breaking operations'.[84]

It is generally extremely difficult to hold the Global North MNCs accountable for such conscious export of hazards to the Global South. A glimmer of hope is provided by the direct duty of care principle developed by the UK courts. The UK Court of Appeal decision in *Begum v Maran* is a case in point.[85] In 2017, Maran, a UK company, sold one of its ships to a company for demolition, which in turn sent the ship to a shipbreaking yard in Chattogram in

[77] 'South Asian Shipbreakers Continue to Dominate Scrap Trade' (6 February 2022) <https://maritime-executive.com/article/south-asian-shipbreakers-continue-to-dominate-scrap-trade> accessed 9 May 2024.

[78] ILO, 'Ship-breaking: A hazardous work' <https://www.ilo.org/safework/areasofwork/hazardous-work/WCMS_110335/lang--en/index.htm> accessed 9 May 2024.

[79] Abu Faisal Ahamad and others, 'Livelihood Assessment and Occupational Health Hazard of the Ship-Breaking Industry Workers at Chattogram, Bangladesh' (2021) 9(7) Journal of Marine Science and Engineering 718.

[80] 'One-third of shipbreakers in Bangladesh at risk from lung diseases' (3 February 2017) <https://splash247.com/one-third-shipbreakers-bangladesh-risk-lung-diseases/> accessed 9 May 2024.

[81] NGO Shipbreaking Platform, 'Child labour' <https://shipbreakingplatform.org/issues-of-interest/child-labor/> accessed 9 May 2024.

[82] ILO, 'Ship-breaking' (n 78).

[83] ibid.

[84] NGO Shipbreaking Platform, 'The Environmental Costs' <https://shipbreakingplatform.org/our-work/the-problem/environmental-costs/> accessed 9 May 2024.

[85] [2021] EWCA Civ 326.

Bangladesh. Mohammed Khalil Mollah, a shipbreaker, fell to his death while working on the ship. Mollah's wife sued Maran in the UK for the death of her husband, alleging that 'by knowingly selling its vessel to be demolished in a manner that endangered the lives of the shipbreakers, including Mollah, Maran violated its duty of care'.[86] The Court held that Maran owed a duty of care to a Bangladeshi worker who suffered fatal injuries while breaking up the ship. In so holding, the Court 'applied an established exception to the principle that a defendant is not liable for the acts of a third party, in circumstances where the defendant has created the danger'.[87] The Court reasoned that Maran 'arguably played an active role by sending the vessel to Bangladesh, knowingly exposing workers (such as the deceased) to the significant dangers which working on this large vessel in Chattogram entailed'[88] and that Maran 'could, and should, have insisted on the sale to a so-called "green" yard, where proper working practices were in place'.[89]

Although the decision in *Begum* offers a potential pathway for corporate accountability, it is not practical to successfully pursue all cases of human rights abuses or environmental pollution related to the shipbreaking industry in the Global North. In short, people in the Global South continue to bear disproportionately the cost of economic development.

D. Exploiting and Perpetuating Power Imbalances

Supply chains are full of power imbalances: between home and host states of MNCs, brands and suppliers, and suppliers and workers. For our purposes, the second type of power imbalance is the most relevant. A typical example of such imbalance results in brands adopting unethical or irresponsible purchasing practices.[90] While such practices are common in normal times, the Covid-19 pandemic exacerbated the situation. For example, the Global North apparel brands cancelled billions of dollars' worth of orders from readymade garment suppliers in Bangladesh,[91] which directly affected vulnerable workers at the

[86] See <https://corpaccountabilitylab.org/calblog/2021/5/17/hamida-begum-v-maran-uk-limited-shipbreakers-death-turning-the-tide-in-third-party-liability-claims-under-english-law> accessed 9 May 2024.

[87] Meeran, 'Multinational Human Rights Litigation in the UK' (n 69) 262.

[88] [2021] EWCA Civ 326, para 64.

[89] ibid para 67.

[90] See Mark Anner, 'Squeezing Workers' Rights in Global Supply Chains: Purchasing Practices in the Bangladesh Garment Export Sector in Comparative Perspective' (2020) 27(2) Review of International Political Economy 320.

[91] Sushmita S Preetha and Zyma Islam, 'Is foul play the new normal?' (30 June 2020) <https://www.thedailystar.net/business/news/you-suffer-we-survive-1920733> accessed 9 May 2024.

bottom of the supply chains.[92] Despite some brands in the readymade garment sector committing to achieve a living wage for workers[93] and/or adopt responsible purchasing practices,[94] a wider systemic impact of these commitments on the ground remains suspect.[95]

Another power imbalance dimension is reflected in how the workers' contribution is valued much less than 'the tasks performed at the beginning (design) and end (marketing) of the production process'.[96] This then results in workers, and their host countries, remaining poor because the gains of production are mostly reaped by actors in the Global North.

Although the third type of power imbalance (between suppliers and workers) is not our focus here, it is worth noting that the power imbalance between brands and suppliers has a ripple effect on the conditions of workers. For instance, when brands reduce the turnaround time of their orders due to fast fashion trends, this contributes to the creation of precarious work conditions for workers in the Global South.[97]

While several regulatory approaches have been tried to create decent work in supply chains, most have failed to make a systematic change in the condition of workers. One of the reasons for this failure is that these regulatory initiatives often do not address the power imbalances noted above, which are the root cause of exploitation in supply chains in the Global South.[98] Enhancing the power of suppliers vis-à-vis buyers as well as of the workers' bargaining power will be vital to address these power imbalances.[99]

[92] See SANEM and Fair Wear, *The Impact of the Covid Pandemic on the Cost of Production and Orders in Bangladesh* (April 2021) <https://api.fairwear.org/wp-content/uploads/2021/07/The-Impact-of-the-Covid-19-Pandemic-on-the-Cost-of-Production-and-Orders-in-Bangladesh.pdf> accessed 9 May 2024.

[93] 'H&M pledges living wage for textile workers in Bangladesh and Cambodia' (26 November 2013) <https://www.theguardian.com/business/2013/nov/25/h-m-living-wage-textile-workers-bangladesh-cambodia> accessed 9 May 2024.

[94] H&M Group, 'Responsible purchasing practices' <https://hmgroup.com/sustainability/leading-the-change/transparency/responsible-purchasing-practices/> accessed 9 May 2024. See also the Better Buying initiative: <https://betterbuying.org/> accessed 9 May 2024.

[95] See eg Clean Clothes campaign, 'Not a single worker is making a living wage yet H&M claims to have done an amazing job' <https://cleanclothes.org/news/2019/not-a-single-worker-is-making-a-living-wage-yet-hm-claims-to-have-done-an-amazing-job> accessed 9 May 2024.

[96] Eduardo Ortiz-Juarez and Andy Sumner, 'Inequality' in Nicola Phillips (ed), *Global Political Economy* (OUP 2023) 223, 234.

[97] MacDonald, 'Production and Business' (n 62) 147.

[98] IHRB and Chowdhury Center for Bangladesh studies at UC Berkeley, 'The Weakest Link in The Global Supply Chain: How the Pandemic is Affecting Bangladesh's Garment Workers' (May 2021) <https://www.ihrb.org/focus-areas/covid-19/bangladesh-garment-workers> accessed 9 May 2024; Deva, 'Mandatory Human Rights' (n 4).

[99] Ashok Kumar, 'A Race from the Bottom? Lessons from a Workers' Struggle at a Bangalore Warehouse' (2019) 23(4) Competition & Change 346.

IV. An Alternative Vision of Supply Chains and Labour Rights in a Degrowth Era

Embracing a degrowth model by itself will not address the inherently exploitative and unsustainable nature of current global supply chains, some elements of which are highlighted above. In fact, this might exacerbate the exploitation by moving back production to the Global North due to automation[100] and/or reduction in the manufacturing orders received by suppliers in the Global South due to ethically conscious consumers deciding to consume less.

Therefore, the current modes of production adopted by businesses and consumption patterns would require a systemic overhaul. Moreover, labour rights as well as labour standards applicable to businesses—such as the ILO Tripartite Declaration of Principles concerning Multinational Enterprises and Social Policy (MNE Declaration)—would require reimagination for an era in which people may have a right to work but no work or no capacity to upgrade their skills to secure new forms of work. In this section, we focus on three aspects of an alternative vision of labour rights and supply chains in a degrowth era: what degrowth should mean for the Global South, how businesses can contribute to creating humane supply chains, and what reimagined labour standards should look like.

A. A Differentiated Degrowth Model

As discussed in Section II, scholars take different views as to the applicability of degrowth to the Global South. Daley and Hickel, for instance, contend that developing countries in the Global South need not embrace the degrowth model. On the other hand, Trainer and Latouche argue that all countries should adopt degrowth policies, though the Global South countries need not adopt a degrowth pathway identical to that of developed countries in the Global North. We argue that the world needs a 'differentiated' degrowth model to accommodate different levels of economic development and diverse aspirations of what development means in practice. Such an approach will be aligned with

[100] Lessons from the Covid-19 pandemic and the current geopolitical situation might also be pushing for such a move. See Elia Stefano and others, 'Post-Pandemic Reconfiguration from Global to Domestic and Regional Value Chains: The Role of Industrial Policies' (2021) 28(2) Transnational Corporations 67.

the principle of 'common but differentiated responsibilities'[101] and the people's right to development in the Global South.

Three elements of differentiated degrowth are worthy of consideration. First, if reduced consumption in the Global North results in a reduction in the existing production and manufacturing footprints in the Global South, such a change should be accompanied by more decent and sustainable jobs. Even if a lesser number of people get to work in the Global South due to such degrowth in the interest of the global community, those people would have safer and stable jobs with a living wage, thus reducing poverty and inequality.

Second, while pursuing degrowth, the Global North countries, as well as their MNCs, should account for historical wrongs of slavery, exploitation, and expropriation that contributed to the current level of economic development. This may take many shapes and forms—from offering a public apology to the restoration of historical treasures, offering technical assistance, providing development aid, facilitating peer learning, and exporting green technologies.

Third, the Global South need not copy the development trajectory followed by the Global North, which focuses on 'self', 'individuality', 'accumulation', 'consumption', and 'commodification'. Rather, countries in the Global South may skip unsustainable steps of development. They could, for example, promote a collective and communitarian way of living in which sharing is encouraged.[102] Similarly, going 'back to bikes'—wherever feasible—instead of 'battery operated vehicles' would better support degrowth and also ensure a healthier lifestyle, reduced environmental pollution, and a lesser number of fatal road accidents.

B. Humane Supply Chains

Although supply chains have created many jobs in the Global South, 'most of these jobs are insecure and low-paid compared to those in the Global North'.[103] Existing regulatory approaches are struggling to create supply chains free from exploitation and abuses because they are not addressing them at the root. For instance, the preventive element of mandatory HRDD laws is not trying to

[101] Dipa Patel, '"Common but differentiated responsibilities': A beacon of realism' (29 July 2020) <https://blogs.lse.ac.uk/internationaldevelopment/2020/07/29/common-but-differentiated-responsibilities-a-beacon-of-realism/> accessed 9 May 2024.

[102] See Bronwyn Hayward and Joyashree Roy, 'Sustainable Living: Bridging the North-South Divide in Lifestyles and Consumption Debates' (2019) 44 Annual Review of Environment and Resources 157.

[103] Alford, 'Labour and Work' (n 60) 282.

address the root causes of exploitation in supply chains; the HRDD obligation in Europe may translate into contractual obligations akin to existing third-party certification or auditing practices. Nor is the remediation aimed at offering full and effective reparations in line with international human rights law. Moreover, any attempt to put in place more robust laws has faced stiff opposition due to corporate lobbying.

We, therefore, propose three fundamental structural changes to create humane supply chains: reorienting the purpose of corporations in society, reimagining the HRDD process to centre the role of rightsholders, and adopting a red-line approach in suitable cases or circumstances.

A change in the very purpose of corporations in society is required because corporations, a key beneficiary of exploitative supply chains, have to be an integral part of the required shift. The shareholder primacy model often pushes directors and corporate managers to maximize profit without paying much attention to the rights of workers in their supply chains. Villiers argues that 'directors' duties must be rewritten to pursue not a prioritized members' interests, but an overarching goal of social benefit'.[104] She further contends that any breach of such duties 'should perhaps come with the potential for personal liability for those directors who fail to adhere'.[105] In a similar vein, Sjåfjell argues that the 'failure of company law lies notably in what company law does *not* say about the purpose of the company and the duties of the decision-makers' and that this gap results in 'an extreme externalization of social costs of production onto people, notably a lack of respect for human rights'.[106]

Because of increasing scholarly critique of the shareholder primacy model and civil society demands,[107] corporate leadership has started to respond to the issue. For example, in the last few years, the Chief Executive Officer (CEO) of BlackRock, Larry Fink, in his annual letter to CEOs of companies that BlackRock invests trillions of dollars in, has raised issues related to social purpose, climate change, and sustainability of business.[108] More notably, the Business Roundtable in August 2019 released 'a Statement on the Purpose of

[104] Villiers, 'A Game of Cat and Mouse' (n 66) 435.
[105] ibid 436.
[106] Beate Sjåfjell, 'How Company Law has Failed Human Rights—and What to Do About It' (2020) 5 Business and Human Rights Journal 179, 182–83 (emphasis in original).
[107] See eg Frank Bold, 'The Purpose of the Corporation Project' <http://www.purposeofcorporation.org/en> accessed 9 May 2024.
[108] See 'Larry Fink's 2022 Letter to CEOs: The Power of Capitalism' <https://www.blackrock.com/corporate/investor-relations/larry-fink-ceo-letter> accessed 9 May 2024. For a critical analysis, see Surya Deva, 'From "Business or Human Rights" to "Business and Human Rights": What Next?' in Surya Deva and David Birchall (eds), *Research Handbook on Human Rights and Business* (Edward Elgar 2020) 1, 7–8.

a Corporation signed by 181 CEOs who commit to lead their companies for the benefit of all stakeholders—customers, employees, suppliers, communities and shareholders'.[109] In other words, 'stakeholder capitalism' is fast becoming the new corporate mantra.[110] However, this shift appears mostly symbolic because no changes have been introduced to the core principles of corporate law, which are part of the problem. The real shift would require, for instance, imposing binding duties on directors to respect the rights of workers throughout business operations, allowing non-shareholders to enforce such duties, and abolishing incentive-based remuneration of directors and CEOs.

Brinks and others argue that 'in order to contest the unequal distribution of power and resources along supply chains, the workers and local communities most directly affected by supply chain capitalism should be at the forefront' of private regulatory initiatives.[111] We apply this reform call to reimagine the HRDD process outlined in Pillar II of the UN Guiding Principles on Business and Human Rights (UNGPs), which puts corporations in charge of identifying, mitigating, and preventing adverse human rights impacts. Although corporations are expected to consult the relevant rightsholders, consultations are mostly on terms, timing, and narrative set by the relevant corporations. To centre rightsholders, HRDD should not be conducted by businesses or consultants hired by them.[112] Rather, it should be done by rightsholders, as they are in a better position to make an informed decision about the actual or potential adverse impacts of business activity on their rights. Rightsholders are not merely victims of corporate abuses; they also have an agency, and HRDD processes should recognize this.

Under our proposed model, rightsholders will not be merely consulted by corporations. Instead, rightsholders will design and own the entire HRDD process and invite corporations for a consultation to provide input about the proposed business activity or project.[113] That would, for example, mean that

[109] Business Roundtable, 'Business Roundtable Redefines the Purpose of a Corporation to Promote "An Economy That Serves All Americans"' <https://www.businessroundtable.org/business-roundtable-redefines-the-purpose-of-a-corporation-to-promote-an-economy-that-serves-all-americans> accessed 9 May 2024.

[110] See James M Loree, 'COVID-19 is Accelarating Stakeholder Capitalism' (30 July 2021) <https://www.weforum.org/agenda/2021/07/covid-19-has-accelerated-stakeholder-capitalism/> accessed 9 May 2024.

[111] Daniel Brinks and others, 'Private Regulatory Initiatives and Beyond: Lessons and Reflections' in Daniel Brinks and others (eds), *Power, Participation, and Private Regulatory Initiatives* (University of Pennsylvania Press 2021) 258, 268.

[112] Surya Deva, 'Reimagining Business and Human Rights' in Judith Schrempf-Stirling, Tricia Olsen, and Harry J Van Buren III (eds), *A Research Agenda for Business and Human Rights* (Edward Elgar 2024) (forthcoming).

[113] Surya Deva and Harpreet Kaur, 'Business and Human Rights: From "Tokenism" to "Centring" Rights and Rightsholders' in Marianna Leite and Matti Kohonen (eds), *Righting the Economy* (Agenda Publishing Limited 2024) 43.

workers will decide on living wages and safety conditions at work. In conducting HRDD, rightsholders should be assisted by independent CSOs, trade unions, lawyers, and academia to address power imbalances concerning access to information, financial resources, and legal expertise between rightsholders and corporations. The relevant corporations should bear the cost of conducting such reimagined HRDD.

The third element to create more humane supply chains will be for states to start drawing 'red lines' about certain business activities. Unless supply chains create decent jobs, assist in reducing economic inequality, and contribute to an inclusive and sustainable economy, they should face regulatory 'red lines'. The case of gig economy workers illustrates this. Even if HRDD conducted by a gig platform corporation finds concerns about workers' rights, those are likely to be addressed within an inherently exploitative business model which seeks to turn employees into autonomous entrepreneurs to maximize profit.[114] For this reason, regulating the gig economy may be a superficial and symbolic exercise, as this business model is rooted in exploiting vulnerabilities and converting workers into independent contractors in the guise of flexibility and empowerment.[115]

C. Reimagined Labour Standards

The existing labour standards directed towards businesses, such as the MNE Declaration, are premised on the assumption that work is available and that the proposed tools, such as HRDD, the freedom of association, and collective bargaining, can secure decent work. These standards also see formalization as the primary way to address decent work deficits in the informal economy.

Taking a cue from the UNGPs, the MNE Declaration embraces the idea of the HRDD process 'to identify, prevent, mitigate and account for how they address their actual and potential adverse impacts' on labour rights.[116] The relevant stakeholders should be able to participate meaningfully in the process to make HRDD effective. However, many workers are either not informed about their rights as well as the responsibilities of companies or lack empowerment. Independent trade unions should be able to bridge various power imbalances between companies and workers. But many Global South countries with huge

[114] Deva, 'Mandatory Human Rights' (n 4) 402.

[115] International Labour Organization (ILO), *Non-Standard Employment Around the World: Understanding Challenges, Shaping Prospects* (ILO 2016).

[116] MNE Declaration, para 10(d).

supply chains have no independent trade unions (eg China and Vietnam) or ones that operate in a highly constrained environment (eg Bangladesh and India). In the absence of independent trade unions, HRDD might end up becoming merely a tick-box exercise and might not make substantial improvements in the lives of workers.[117] Moreover, the MNE Declaration does not explicitly endorse the goal of MNCs paying a living wage in the Global South.[118] To ensure workers fully realize their right to development,[119] they should have agency and ownership over policies and processes determining their work conditions rather than merely being consulted by companies that do not respect the right to collective bargaining. Our reimagined HRDD should be able to achieve this.

Labour rights, as well as labour standards, should also take cognizance of both 'no work' scenarios (eg due to automation; reduction in production contracts due to degrowth) and 'work from home' scenarios (eg the new normal for certain workers in the post-Covid economy). A provision for universal social security will be vital to deal with the former, but the MNE Declaration is again very weak in terms of expectations from companies.[120] De Schutter, the UN Special Rapporteur on extreme poverty and human rights, in his 2021 report, proposed the setting up of a 'global fund for social protection' to increase the level of support to low-income countries.[121] Companies which make economic gains, for instance, from introducing automation must be required to contribute to such a fund. For the latter scenarios, the protection of labour rights, such as occupational health and safety, should be extended to workers working from home. The ILO's Violence and Harassment Convention 2019 seems to move in this direction in that it prohibits violence and harassment in 'the world of work'.[122] However, despite its extensive revision in 2017, the MNE

[117] See Deva, 'Mandatory Human Rights' (n 4) 405.

[118] It merely says that the MNEs 'should provide the best possible wages, benefits and conditions of work' considering, among others, 'the needs of workers and their families, taking into account the general level of wages in the country, the cost of living, social security benefits, and the relative living standards of other social groups'. MNE Declaration, para 41.

[119] 'The right to development is an inalienable human right by virtue of which every human person and all peoples are entitled to participate in, contribute to, and enjoy economic, social, cultural and political development, in which all human rights and fundamental freedoms can be fully realized.' Declaration on the Right to Development, art 1.

[120] 'Multinational and other enterprises *could complement* public social security systems and help to stimulate further their development, including through their own employer-sponsored programmes.' MNE Declaration, para 22 (emphasis added).

[121] Report of the Special Rapporteur on extreme poverty and human rights, Olivier De Schutter, 'Global fund for social protection: international solidarity in the service of poverty eradication', A/HRC/47/36 (22 April 2021).

[122] Violence and Harassment Convention 2019 (No 190), arts 2 and 3.

Declaration is still rooted in the traditional idea of formal work between employers and employees in a defined workplace.

The informal economy is a substantial part of the economy in the Global South. For instance, as per the ILO's estimates, about 1.3 billion people—which is about 68 per cent of the employed population—in the Asia Pacific are part of the informal economy.[123] Moreover, a significant number of workers in vulnerable situations in the Global South—such as migrant workers, low-skill workers, workers from marginalized groups, and undocumented workers—are part of the informal economy. Yet, the MNE Declaration hardly responds to this reality. It merely says: 'Governments should develop and implement an integrated policy framework to facilitate the transition to the formal economy, recognizing that decent work deficits are most pronounced in the informal economy. Multinational and other enterprises should also contribute to this aim.'[124]

Formalization of the informal economy is thus the main mantra proposed by the MNE Declaration. However, this formalization will take several decades or may not solve the problem because decent work deficits continue to be pervasive even in the formal sector. More importantly, from a degrowth perspective, small-local-informal business models might be more viable economically and more environmentally sustainable. In other words, alternative approaches and tools should be developed to ensure dignified work in the informal economy.

V. Conclusion

Degrowth is the need of the hour because the current model of economic growth does not respect planetary boundaries and is, therefore, unsustainable. While the degrowth idea is more prevalent in the Global North, this is also relevant for the Global South due to the interconnected nature of global economies. For example, reduced consumption in developed countries would impact the supply chains and employment levels in developing countries. However, in view of colonization and historical injustices, as well as continued power imbalances between the Global North and the Global South, degrowth should not mean the same thing everywhere.

[123] ILO, 'Informal economy: More than 68 per cent of the employed population in Asia-Pacific are in the informal economy' <https://www.ilo.org/resource/news/more-68-cent-employed-population-asia-pacific-are-informal-economy> accessed 9 May 2024.

[124] MNE Declaration, para 21.

Against the backdrop of growing degrowth literature (again, mostly produced in the Global North), this chapter provides a critique of the current supply chains model, which is inherently exploitative of vulnerable workers, most of whom are from the Global South. As an alternative, we propose a 'differentiated degrowth' model, ways to create more humane supply chains, and articulate how labour rights and standards should evolve in the degrowth era. Our proposals are admittedly informed by the Global South's perspectives so as to contribute to a just and equitable degrowth trajectory.

Bibliography

Ahamad AF and others, 'Livelihood Assessment and Occupational Health Hazard of the Ship-Breaking Industry Workers at Chattogram, Bangladesh' (2021) 9(7) Journal of Marine Science and Engineering 718

Alexander S, *Prosperous Descent: Crisis as Opportunity in an Age of Limits* (Simplicity Institute 2015)

Alford M, 'Labour and Work' in N Phillips (ed), *Global Political Economy* (OUP 2023)

Anner M, 'Squeezing Workers' Rights in Global Supply Chains: Purchasing Practices in the Bangladesh Garment Export Sector in Comparative Perspective' (2020) 27(2) Review of International Political Economy 320

Blanton RG and Peksen D, 'Economic Liberalisation, Market Institutions and Labour Rights' (2016) 55 European Journal of Political Research 474, 482

Bose D, 'Decentring Narratives around Business and Human Rights Instruments: An Example of the French Devoir de Vigilance Law' (2023) 8 Business and Human Rights Journal 18

Bright C and Bueno N, 'Mandatory Human Rights Due Diligence' in A Ewing (ed), *Teaching Business and Human Rights* (Edward Elgar 2023)

Brinks D and others, 'Private Regulatory Initiatives and Beyond: Lessons and Reflections' in D Brinks and others (eds), *Power, Participation, and Private Regulatory Initiatives* (University of Pennsylvania Press 2021)

Brinks D and others, 'Private Regulatory Initiatives, Human Rights, and Supply Chain Capitalism' in D Brinks D and others (eds), *Power, Participation, and Private Regulatory Initiatives* (University of Pennsylvania Press 2021)

Bueno N, 'From Productive Work to Capability-Enhancing Work: Implications for Labour Law and Policy' (2022) 23(3) Journal of Human Development and Capabilities 354

Bueno N and Kaufmann C, 'The Swiss Human Rights Due Diligence Legislation: Between Law and Politics' (2021) 6 Business and Human Rights Journal 542

Cossart S, Chaplier J, and Beau de Lomenie T, 'The French Law on Duty of Care: A Historic Step Towards Making Globalization Work for All' (2017) 2 Business and Human Rights Journal 317

Crane A and others, 'Confronting the Business Models of Modern Slavery' (2022) 31(3) Journal of Management Inquiry 264

Daly HE, *Steady State Economics* (Island Press 1991)

Deva S, 'Fictitious Separation, Real Injustice: Why and How to Tame the Twin Principles of Corporate Law?' in *Creating a Paradigm Shift: Legal Solutions to Improve Access to Remedy for Corporate Human Rights Abuse* (Amensty International and BHHRC 2017) 21

Deva S, 'From "Business or Human Rights" to "Business and Human Rights": What Next?' in S Deva and D Birchall (eds), *Research Handbook on Human Rights and Business* (Edward Elgar 2020) 1

Deva S, 'Mandatory Human Rights Due Diligence Laws in Europe: A Mirage for Rightsholders?' (2023) 36 Leiden Journal of International Law 389

Deva S, 'Reimagining Business and Human Rights' in J Schrempf-Stirling, T Olsen, and HJ Van Buren III (eds), *A Research Agenda for Business and Human Rights* (Edward Elgar 2024) (forthcoming)

Deva S and Kaur H, 'Business and Human Rights: From "Tokenism" to "Centring" Rights and Rightsholders' in M Leite and M Kohonen (eds), *Righting the Economy* (Agenda Publishing Limited 2024)

Dorninger C and others, 'Global Patterns of Ecologically Unequal Exchange: Implications for Sustainability in the 21st Century' (2019) 179 Ecological Economics 106824

Ford J and Nolan J, 'Regulating Transparency on Human Rights and Modern Slavery in Corporate Supply Chains: The Discrepancy between Human Rights Due Diligence and the Social Audit' (2020) 26 Australian Journal of Human Rights 27

Gerber J-F and Raina RS, 'Post-Growth in the Global South? Some Reflections from India and Bhutan' (2018) 150 Ecological Economics 353

Guasti A and Koenig-Archibugi M, 'Has Global Trade Competition Really Led to a Race to the Bottom in Labor Standards?' (2022) 66(4) International Studies Quarterly saqc61

Hanaček K and others, 'Ecological Economics and Degrowth: Proposing a Future Research Agenda from the Margins' (2020) 169 Ecological Economics 106495

Hansmann H and Kraakman R, 'Toward Unlimited Shareholder Liability for Corporate Torts' (1991) 100 Yale Law Journal 1879

Hayward B and Roy J, 'Sustainable Living: Bridging the North-South Divide in Lifestyles and Consumption Debates' (2019) 44 Annual Review of Environment and Resources 157

Hickel J, *Less is More: How Degrowth Will Save the World* (Penguin 2021)

Hickel J, 'What Does Degrowth Mean? A Few Points of Clarification' (2021) 18(7) Globalizations 1105

Hickel J and Slamersak A, 'Existing Climate Mitigation Scenarios Perpetuate Colonial Inequalities' (2022) 6(7) The Lancet Planetary Health 628

Hickel J and others, 'Imperialist Appropriation in the World Economy: Drain from the Global South through Unequal Exchange, 1990–2015' (2022) 73 Global Environmental Change 102467

Koch M, 'The State in the Transformation to a Sustainable Postgrowth Economy' (2020) 29(1) Environmental Politics 115

Krajewski M, Tonstand K, and Wohltmann F, 'Mandatory Human Rights Due Diligence in Germany and Norway: Stepping, or Striding, in the Same Direction?' (2021) 6 Business and Human Rights Journal 550

Kreinin H and Aigner E, 'From "Decent Work and Economic Growth" to "Sustainable Work and Economic Degrowth": A New Framework for SDG8' (2022) 49 Empirica 281

Kumar A, 'A Race from the Bottom? Lessons from a Workers' Struggle at a Bangalore Warehouse' (2019) 23(4) Competition & Change 346

Landau I, 'Human Rights Due Diligence and the Risk of Cosmetic Compliance' (2019) 20 Melbourne Journal of International Law 221

Lichuma CO, '(Laws) Made in the "First World": A TWAIL Critique of the Use of Domestic Legislation to Extraterritorially Regulate Global Value Chains' (2021) 81 Zeitschrift für ausländisches öffentliches Recht und Völkerrecht (Heidelberg Journal of International Law) 497

MacDonald K, 'Production and Business' in N Phillips (ed), *Global Political Economy* (OUP 2023) 135

Mair S, Druckman A, and Jackson T, 'A Tale of Two Utopias: Work in a Post-Growth World' (2020) 173 Ecological Economics 106653

Mares R, 'Liability Within Corporate Groups: Parent Companies' Accountability for Subsidiary Human Rights Abuses' in S Deva and D Birchall (eds), *Research Handbook on Human Rights and Business* (Edward Elgar 2020)

Meeran R, 'Multinational Human Rights Litigation in the UK: A Retrospective' (2021) 6 Business and Human Rights Journal 255

Nolan J and Frishling N, 'Australia's Modern Slavery Act: Towards Meaningful Compliance' (2019) 37 Company and Securities Law Journal 104

Ortiz-Juarez E and Sumner A, 'Inequality' in Nicola Phillips (ed), *Global Political Economy* (OUP 2023)

Payán-Sánchez B, Pérez-Valls M, and Plaza-Úbeda JA, 'Supply Chain Management in a Degrowth Context: The Potential Contribution of Stakeholders' in N Yakovleva, R Frei, and S Rama Murthy (eds), *Sustainable Development Goals and Sustainable Supply Chains in the Postglobal Economy* (Springer 2019)

Raworth K, *Trading Away Our Rights: Women Workers in Global Supply Chains* (Oxfam International 2004)

Raworth K, *Doughnut Economics: Seven Ways to Think like a 21st -Century Economist* (Random House Business 2018)

Robinson WI, *A Theory of Global Capitalism: Production, Class, and State in a Transnational World* (The John Hopkins University Press 2004)

Robinson WI and Harris J, 'Towards a Global Ruling Class? Globalization and the Transnational Capitalist Class' (2000) 64(1) Science and Society 11

Sjåfjell B, 'How Company Law Has Failed Human Rights—and What to Do About It' (2020) 5 Business and Human Rights Journal 179

Stefano E and others, 'Post-Pandemic Reconfiguration from Global to Domestic and Regional Value Chains: The Role of Industrial Policies' (2021) 28(2) Transnational Corporations 67

Suwandi I, *Value Chains: The New Economic Imperialism* (Monthly Review Press 2019)

Suwandi I, Jonna JR, and Foster JB, 'Global Commodity Chains and the New Imperialism' (2019) 70(10) Monthly Review 1

Trainer T, 'What Does Degrowth Mean? Some Comments on Jason Hickel's 'A Few Points on Clarification' (2021) 18(7) Globalizations 1112

Villiers C, 'A Game of Cat and Mouse: Human Rights Protection and the Problem of Corporate Law and Power' (2023) 36 Leiden Journal of International Law 415

7

The Value of Work in Labour Law

Nicolas Bueno

I. Introduction

Economic liberals in the eighteenth century distinguished between serfdom and slavery, on the one hand, and free labour operating in the labour market, on the other hand. The distinction created an entire category of workers who suddenly appeared as free because they had some choice of occupation. In the twentieth century, economic neoliberals reemphasized this liberating potential of labour markets. By focusing on market mechanisms, however, economic liberals and neoliberals also consolidated the idea that productive work on the market (market work) is more valuable than any other occupation. To what extent do wages and incomes reflect the value of work? Is it normal that activities that seem meaningful or even essential, such as a cleaning, taking care of others, or restoring the environment are valued less than jobs in finance, corporate law, and trading firms? Why is this the case and how should labour law address this without reducing free choice of occupation? Building on post-economic growth and post-productive work theories, this chapter discusses how and when labour law should intervene in the valuation of work.

Section II explains the influence of economic ideology on the purpose and value of work. This section describes the evolution of the value of work from classical liberalism and Soviet socialism until neoliberalism. With respect to neoliberalism, it discusses the works of Friedrich Hayek in *The Road to Serfdom*,[1] and Milton Friedman in *Capitalism and Freedom*[2] and *Free to Choose*.[3] Neoliberal views, which resonate today, value work according to its economic value as determined by the market. Section III shows the implication of these ideologies for the function of labour law. It shows that labour law tends

[1] Friedrich Hayek, *The Road to Serfdom* (first published 1944, University of Chicago Press 2007).
[2] Milton Friedman and Rose Friedman, *Capitalism and Freedom* (first published 1962, 40th anniversary edn, University of Chicago Press 2002).
[3] Milton Friedman and Rose Friedman, *Free to Choose: A Personal Statement* (first published 1980, Harvest Book 1990).

Nicolas Bueno, *The Value of Work in Labour Law* In: *Labour Law Utopias*. Edited by: Nicolas Bueno, Beryl ter Haar, and Nuna Zekić, Oxford University Press. © Oxford University Press 2024. DOI: 10.1093/oso/9780198889755.003.0007

to promote the type of work considered as the most useful by the predominant ideology. Currently, that is productive market work under neoliberalism. Identifying what makes an activity useful (for whom) and designing a corresponding system of value has not yet been part of the function of labour law.

Section IV offers a vision of what the value of work and the function of labour law in this respect could be in a post-growth logic, that is, an invitation to think with other goals in mind than increasing material wealth (which is unequally distributed anyway), such as living on an environmentally healthy planet and in a less unequal environment. When the goals change, the purpose and value of work to achieve them necessarily change as well. In a more systematic manner, this section suggests that what makes work valuable should be dictated less by whether there is a market (consumers with purchasing power) for the job and more by its (positive and negative) impact on people's lives. The current market-based valuation of work has great advantages, but also two major shortcomings for labour law to address. It wastes human skills for the realization of non-market objectives and may encourage work that is detrimental to people and the environment through high pay. There is, therefore, a need for labour law to intervene more systematically in the value of work.

II. The Value of Work in Economic Ideologies

A. The Market Value of Work in Liberalism

During the eighteenth and nineteenth centuries, classical liberals had the idea of creating markets for labour which impacted how work is valued today. The establishment of labour markets was a progress and a new source of freedom away from the system of serfdom where people worked for a lord in return for protection.[4] The liberal logic of labour markets also abolished privileges of regulated trades in order to expand access to work. In *The Wealth of Nations* (1776), Adam Smith dreamed, for example, of a society 'where every man was perfectly free both to choose what occupation he thought proper, and to change it as often as he thought proper'.[5] As he put it: 'to hinder [a poor man] from employing his strength and dexterity in what manner he thinks proper without injury to his neighbour is a plain violation of this most sacred property'.[6] This

[4] Alessandro Stanziani, *Bondage: Labor and Rights in Eurasia from the Sixteenth to the Early Twentieth Centuries* (Berghahn 2018) 31.

[5] Adam Smith, *The Wealth of Nations* (first published 1776, Penguin Classics 1999) 201.

[6] ibid 225; see also Pierre Rosanvallon, *Le capitalisme utopique: Histoire de l'idée de marché* (3rd edn, Seuil 1999) 72.

emancipatory narrative of labour markets was echoed by many others at the time. In *Richesse Commerciale* (1803), Sismondi also considered labour markets as a way for everyone to secure liberty, wealth, and happiness by relying on their capacity to achieve, on their own, a level of income favouring economic and social insertion.[7] In short, labour markets were historically thought to free the poor by reducing the barriers they faced when competing for (paid) work in a world regulated by trades and corporations.[8] Historically, it was a social and liberating device.[9]

The other side of the coin is that labour markets radically transformed the value of work and its purpose in society. Adam Smith and John Stuart Mill, for example, started to divide workers between *productive* and *unproductive*, according to whether a worker creates value by producing vendible commodities in the market or not. For Smith, productive labour included any activity that adds to the value of a vendible commodity, 'whereas unproductive labour, such as the labour of military officers, churchmen, lawyers, physicians, men of letters of all kinds and musicians, does not fix or realise itself in any particular ... vendible commodity'.[10] Mill tried to depart from this distinction. According to him, unproductive labour could also be useful and, indeed, even more useful than productive labour. As he deplored, a pure productive logic would lead to such conclusion that 'the labour of saving a friend's life is not productive, unless the friend is a productive labourer'.[11] However, he was unable to attach a specific and measurable value to unproductive labour and decided not to depart from Smith. He only extended the notion of productive labour to all kinds of labour that directly *and* indirectly contributes to the production of material wealth, such as the labour of teaching a trade or of ensuring public security.[12] This gave some value to public work, but only in relation to its contribution to productive market work.

The purpose of work also changed. From serving the needs of a community (or the personal needs of a lord for protection), market work became a private instrument for receiving an income and a societal instrument for increasing

[7] Jean Charles de Sismondi, '*De la richesse commerciale ou Principes d'économie politique appliqués à la législation du commerce*' in Pascal Bridel and others (eds), *Oeuvres économiques completes*, vol 2 (Economica 2012).

[8] See also Rosanvallon, *Le capitalisme utopique* (n 6) 71.

[9] Pascal Bridel, 'D'un marché libérateur (1803) à un marché despotique (1837): Une note de synthèse sur le concept de marché chez Sismondi' (2020) 9(1) Revue d'histoire de la pensée économique 237, 239.

[10] Smith, *The Wealth of Nations* (n 5) 430.

[11] John Stuart Mill, The *Principles of Political Economy with Some of Their Applications to Social Philosophy* (first published 1848, 7th edn, Longmans 1909) 31–45; for the chapter 'Of Unproductive Labour', ibid 50.

[12] ibid.

'the wealth of the nation'. Smith's objective was ultimately to increase the wealth of the nation and to him, there was therefore no other option than to increase the number of productive workers or their productivity. As a result, productive market work became valuable while unproductive work, such as public work or care work,[13] started to be considered as a cost for society at least when it did not indirectly contribute to increasing material wealth.

B. The Problematic Value of Work in Soviet Socialism

In the first half of the twentieth century, soviet socialists took power in Russia. They abruptly abolished the system of labour markets and experimented with a new system of valuing work.

By the end of the nineteenth century, mechanization increased both in agriculture and industry in most parts of Europe.[14] In England, the pressure on workers increased even more after the repeal of economic safety nets during this period. As presented by Polanyi in *The Great Transformation*, the Poor Law Amendment Act of 1834 in England prohibited existing wage supplementation and it repealed outdoor relief for the able-bodied unemployed in rural areas. According to Polanyi, this made workers feel the consequences of a labour market in which there was no impediment to the free operation of supply and demand.[15]

The commodification of labour had gone too far. Even classical liberals changed their minds concerning the liberating power of labour markets. Commenting on the nature of the English industrial system in *Etudes sur les sciences sociales* (1817), Sismondi found that this system of market for labour 'turns man and his labour into mere market tradable goods'.[16] 'Since the abolition of slavery, all manual labour is carried out by men who are not motivated by free choice. Pressed as they are by necessity and needs, they are not free in the market to deliver their labour.'[17] It is in this context that the socialist ideology gained influence. French socialists first required a right to guaranteed

[13] See Chapter 9 by Encinas de Muñagorri in this book.

[14] Stanziani, *Bondage* (n 4) 145.

[15] Karl Polanyi, *The Great Transformation: The Political and Economic Origins of Our Time* (Joseph Stiglitz and Fred L Block trs, 2nd edn, Beacon Press 2001) 81, 89.

[16] J-J Gislain, 'La conversion de Sismondi' (2013) 64(1) Cahiers d'Économie Politique 111; Bridel, 'D'un marché libérateur' (n 9) 239.

[17] Jean Charles de Sismondi, 'Études sur les sciences sociales' in Pascal Bridel and others (eds), *Œuvres économiques complètes* (Economica 2018) 63–64; Bridel, 'D'un marché libérateur' (n 9) 239.

work.[18] Karl Marx published *Capital* explaining how companies extract value from workers in a dual market system opposing workers and producers.

Against this ideological backdrop, Soviet Russia abruptly suppressed labour markets in 1918 after the Bolshevik revolution and introduced a new system of value. At first during the Bolshevik period, the central government introduced a rigid system of wage tariffs. For each sector, workers were divided into groups and categories according to the skill or training required.[19] By September 1918, salaries were fixed for the whole of Russia in a more centralized way. Pursuant to the Russian Code of Labour Laws of 1919, tariffs had to be drafted by the trade unions, in agreement with the management (from the state). The standards that had to be taken into consideration when establishing the tariffs were the kind of labour, the danger of the conditions, the complexity of the work, the degree of independence and experience, as well as the standard of education and experience required for the performance of the work.[20] Clearly, the criteria were not democratically established. They aimed to favour manual labour, in the name of whom the revolution was made, and sectors, for example construction and agriculture, considered of utmost importance for the state.

By 1922, it became clear that the various experiments regarding the value of work were not delivering their promises. After the New Economic Plan, all wage policies were repudiated. The jobs that were needed were determined by the central government according to its needs, particularly after the five-year plans of the Soviet Union. The Labour Code of 1922 introduced a general system of collective contracts, defined as agreements between a trade union and an employer (usually the state), laying down the remuneration in public undertakings and public institutions.[21] The use of collective agreements became general in the Soviet Union with 87 per cent of workers covered by 1926, although collective agreements were less widespread in the public institutions and organs of the state.[22] The value of work much depended, therefore, on the bargaining power of workers in front of the state and therefore the importance of the sector or the public undertaking for the state.

[18] Louis Blanc, *Le Socialisme: Droit au travail* (3rd edn, Nouveau Monde 1849).
[19] International Labour Office, *Labour Conditions in Soviet Russia: Systematic Questionnaire and Bibliography Prepared for the Mission of Enquiry in Russia* (Harrison 1920) 16.
[20] Russian Code of Labour Law, art VI, r 59.
[21] Code of Labour Law of 1922, art IV, r 15.
[22] International Labour Office, *The Trade Union Movement in Soviet Russia* (ILO 1927) 165.

C. The Problematic Value of Work in Neoliberalism

After the Second World War, economists invited by Friedrich Hayek founded the Société du Mont Pelerin, named after a small Swiss village. Their annual meetings aimed to use the momentum to shape a new liberal order after a decade of authoritarian regimes. Neoliberalism was born.[23]

During the war, Hayek wrote *Road to Serfdom* (1944) because he was alarmed at seeing societies progressively abandoning the individual and liberal idea of freedom and moving in the direction of socialism.[24] He was concerned that by giving the power to the state to plan what must be produced, what socialism promised as a road to freedom from economic necessity was in fact 'a high road to servitude'.[25] Like Adam Smith, his goal was to free the individual in the economic sense.[26] Concerning work, anybody should be free to make anything that can be produced or sold at all. Trades should be open to all on equal terms, and the law should not tolerate any attempts by individuals or groups to restrict entry to work.[27] In return for freedom, people must take individual responsibility to train and compete for paid market work. He also observed that the free exercise of human ingenuity led to the undesigned free growth of economic activities and contributed to reaching a degree of material comfort, security, and personal independence, all of which seemed scarcely possible in the middle of the nineteenth century.[28] In short, there was no question of intervening on the value of work. According to this ideology, a free market for work is the best system of selecting and rewarding the most useful work. Its remuneration simply depends on the needs expressed by others in the market.

In *Capitalism and Freedom* (1962) and *Free to Choose* (1980), Milton Friedman describes the advantages of free markets to expand individual freedom, including that of workers. He aimed to establish what he called 'competitive capitalism', defined as the organization of economic activity through private enterprise operating in a free market.[29] In order to establish competitive capitalism, he suggested removing all barriers to competition for productive activities. That included not only legal requirements for jobs, but also labour rights, such as minimum wage or trade unions rights, that may favour

[23] For a discussion on the concept of neoliberalism itself and its critique, Damien Cahill and Martijn Konings, *Neoliberalism* (Polity 2017) or Julie Wilson, *Neoliberalism* (Routledge 2018).
[24] Hayek (n 1) 67.
[25] ibid 78.
[26] ibid 77.
[27] ibid 86.
[28] ibid 70.
[29] Friedman and Friedman, *Capitalism and Freedom* (n 2) 4.

workers and exclude others.[30] Interestingly, neither the value nor purpose of work is addressed by Friedman. This is due do to the fact that neoliberals take for granted that the market perfectly reflects what people want in society since they can express their needs through their consumption in the market.

In the neoliberal ideology, the value of a job therefore depends on the needs that are expressed in the market and the purpose of work is to fulfil these needs. The concept of marginal productivity of labour has also eliminated any possible debate on the value of work beyond the labour market. The marginal productivity of labour states that the value of labour is measured by its economic return in the labour market. In other words, the wage that an employer is ready to pay reflects the value of work. As Mazzucato puts it, 'defining everything that commands a price as valuable led to the marginalists' conclusion that what you receive is what you are worth'.[31] This is the source of unfairness in the valuation of labour.

III. The Value of Work in Labour Law?

Liberals, socialists, and neoliberals all had their vision about the value of work. But where is the debate on the value of work in labour law? For classical liberals, the goal was to organize work in labour markets and promote productive market work. In this ideology, the main function of labour law should therefore be to remove legal barriers that hindered competition for work.[32] This was legally implemented with the abolition of the privileges of corporations and statutes of apprenticeships that protected members of regulated trades.[33] For soviet socialists, the main function of labour was quite different. It consisted in providing economic security for workers through guaranteed work by the state and setting legal minimum working conditions.[34] The right to work was a pillar of this ideology.[35]

For neoliberals, the function of labour law should, by contrast, be to facilitate access to productive market work, not only for the poor. The law should

[30] Friedman and Friedman, *Free to Choose* (n 3) ch 8.

[31] Mariana Mazzucato, *The Value of Everything: Making and Taking in the Global Economy* (Penguin Books 2018) 69. See also Jake Rosenfeld, *You're Paid What You're Worth: And Other Myths of the Modern Economy* (Harvard UP 2021).

[32] Elise Dermine, *Droit au travail et politiques d'activation des personnes sans emploi: Étude critique du rôle du droit international des droits humains* (Bruylant 2017) 69, 81.

[33] Stanziani, *Bondage* (n 4) 25.

[34] See Blanc (n 18) 9 and *Le droit au travail à l'Assemblée nationale: recueil complet de tous les discours prononcés dans cette mémorable discussion* (Joseph Garnier ed, 1848).

[35] Russian Labour Code of 1919, art I; Soviet Constitution of 1936, art 118.

systematically unleash the productive skills of people by removing legal requirements for a job. Hayek and Friedman were also opposed to minimum wage legislation that would hurt low-skilled workers by excluding them from competition in the market because employers will not hire them above their market value.[36] They also identified a monopolistic effect of labour union activities. For Friedman, raising the wage rate of a particular industry would reduce the amount of employment available in that industry.[37] He concluded that one main role of governments should be to foster competitive markets by removing legislation that creates or supports labour or industry monopolies.[38]

Today, labour law in most countries is somewhere in-between, probably closer to the neoliberal view. In market economies, labour law is traditionally described in the legal literature as a countervailing force against the inequality of bargaining power that is inherent in the employment relationship.[39] It aims at guaranteeing a functioning labour market, which is too limited. Focusing on processes and minimum standards is essential, but a discussion on the value of work in a market is equally important to maintain some level of fairness. Several scholars in this book discuss the value of work in labour law. Enciñas de Muñagorri discusses the value of care work.[40] Dermine and Dumont develop the broader notion of eco-socially useful work in labour law.[41] It is along those lines that this chapter offers a more systematic manner to understand the positive and negative value of work in labour law.

IV. Defining the Value of Work for Labour Law

This chapter has so far explained the influence of economic ideology on the value of work. In the current ideology, work is mainly valuable because there is a (private) market for it, and the more a job is paid, the more it seems to be needed. The focus on productive market work is problematic because many activities outside the private market, including public work, non-profit work, and unpaid or unpaid care work, contribute to human flourishing or environment goals and are therefore also valuable. Other highly paid activities by contrast

[36] Hayek (n 1) 154; Friedman and Friedman, *Capitalism and Freedom* (n 2) 35, 180.

[37] Friedman and Friedman, *Free to Choose* (n 3) 232, 234.

[38] Friedman and Friedman, *Capitalism and Freedom* (n 2) 2,132; Friedman and Friedman, *Free to Choose* (3) 234.

[39] Guy Davidov, *A Purposive Approach to Labour Law* (OUP 2016) 52.

[40] See Chapter 9 by Enciñas de Muñagorri in this book, for an overview.

[41] Elise Dermine and Daniel Dumont, 'A Renewed Critical Perspective on Social Law: Disentangling Its Ambivalent Relationship with Productivism' (2022) 38(3) International Journal of Comparative Labour Law and Industrial 237. See also Chapter 13 by Dermine and Dumont in this book.

may be detrimental to them. In order to discuss the value of work in a different, but systematic way, it is important to distinguish first between the private and the social value of work and then between the individual and the societal value of work.

A. The Private and Societal Value of Work

The market logic is very much linked to the economic growth paradigm. The narrative of economic growth is that by producing more, people will have more work, which will generate more income from which they will be able to consume more, which means having more individual choices for products on the market. In this narrative, work has a mainly private value for the worker. It has become a mere instrument to generate an income for the worker in order to buy products and have market choices in life. This reflects the idea of individual freedom through work.[42]

There are many questions along the way, though. For example, producing more does not necessarily mean more jobs if technology is used to replace workers. More work does not mean more income if the economic outputs of work are not redistributed to the worker but appropriated by employers and investors.[43] Finally, it is questionable whether more choice in market products is worth it if one has to live in a polluted environment as a consequence. Finally, neoliberals also overlook the fact that workers are free to choose only market work and that most workers have no choice at all, but must take whatever is available in the market.[44] As Hayek recognized, most people have, in practice, never enjoyed much choice with respect to work.[45] Workers are currently 'free' to choose work in a limited way and their freedom of choice is limited by the income of their work, its private value.

There is no real discussion about the societal value (positive and negative) of work in a market logic. Currently, the market selects what needs to be produced and people work according to what is consumed. The main societal purpose of work is therefore to serve the interests of consumers with purchasing

[42] Nicolas Bueno, 'Freedom at, through, and from Work: Rethinking Labour Rights' (2021) 160(2) International Labour Review 31 doi: 10.1111/ilr.12192.

[43] See Tim Jackson, *Post Growth: Life after Capitalism* (Polity 2021) 18. See also Giorgos Kallis, *Degrowth* (Agenda 2018) 87–90 for the limits of economic growth. Kate Raworth, *Doughnut Economics* (Penguin 2017) 177 and 188–89 on stagnant wages.

[44] Timothy Weidel, 'Moving Towards a Capability for Meaningful Labour' (2018) 19(1) Journal of Human Development and Capabilities 70–88; see also Francesco Laruffa, 'Re-thinking Work and Welfare for the Social-Ecological Transformation' (2022)16 Sociologica 143.

[45] Friedman and Friedman, *Capitalism and Freedom* (n 2) 12.

power who can reflect their needs on the market. This is a very narrow way of understanding the societal value of work. Jobs produce certain outcomes that obviously have an impact on the life of others. Some of these impacts can be negative or positive regardless of the remuneration of a job. In fact, the exact same job can have very different societal impacts. One can think of a farmer producing either exotic fruits for foreign markets or local food for the community; a lawyer working *pro bono* to defend a poor community affected by water pollution or for the company responsible for the pollution. The societal impact of architects and construction workers is also different depending on whether they construct chalets for holidays or homes for people who need one.

In all these examples, the remuneration of the work depends on the existence of a market for the good or the service. The problem is that there is usually no market value attributed, and no market, to serve the needs of people without purchasing power or the environment. As a result, the market-based model of valuing work forces people to train for and take productive market work. The fact that the societal value of work is not recognized and rewarded deters people from training and using their skills. The system becomes clearly inefficient when people have the skills and would find it personally meaningful to use them for positive societal outcomes, but lack of opportunities hinders them from doing so. This is the example of the farmer who would prefer to produce locally for the community or the engineers at Airbus and Boeing who could, and would like to, develop a CO_2 neutral airplane but are kept busy by their employers to compete for market shares. This results in a waste of human potential, and it is questionable if humanity can afford to waste such valuable resources.[46] There is, therefore, a need to better define and measure the societal value of work, which requires thinking about the potential societal goals.

B. The Positive and Negative Societal Value of Work

In previous research, I discussed the societal value of work based on its impact on basic needs by referring to the concept of central human capabilities.[47] Human capabilities, as defined by Amartya Sen in *Development as Freedom*,[48]

[46] Nicolas Bueno, 'From the Right to Work to Freedom from Work: Introduction to the Human Economy' 33(4) International Journal of Comparative Labour Law and Industrial Relations (2017) 480; Bueno, 'Rethinking Labour Rights' (n 42) 323.

[47] Nicolas Bueno, 'From Productive Work to Capability-Enhancing Work: Implications for Labour Law and Policy' (2022) 23(3) Journal of Human Development and Capabilities 354.

[48] Amartya Sen, *Development as Freedom* (OUP 1999) 14, 75.

are the positive freedom of a person to achieve what she or he may value doing or being. In *Creating Capabilities*,[49] Martha Nussbaum suggested starting with a list of ten central human capabilities that people could all agree on. She included, for instance, being able to have good health, adequate nourishment, shelter, and education; to move freely and live in relation to the world of nature, and to play and enjoy recreational activities.[50] I discussed the direct impact (positive and negative) of work on these central human capabilities and argued that on moral grounds, it would be fairer to value work by taking into account the impact of a specific job on these central human capabilities rather than its market value.

Taking the central capability of being in good health as a new objective of the economy, for example, would lead us to reconsider the value of care work beyond the market. Elsewhere, I considered the impact of jobs on our capability to play and enjoy recreational activities. I made the argument that if people became more efficient in realizing basic needs (for which most people must currently work), they would also become freer from the need to work (freedom *from* work) and could enjoy more time to live outside work.[51]

The International Labour Organization (ILO) applied a similar minimum approach to discuss the positive value of work beyond its market value in *The Value of Essential Work*.[52] In this post-pandemic report, the ILO listed all workers defined as essential in the domestic pandemic legislation. Most countries included activities safeguarding essential needs, such as access to food, water, electricity, sanitation and healthcare, and ensuring public order. More concretely, the report identifies eight specific groups of occupations that were essential in the pandemic context: food system workers, health workers, retail workers, security workers, manual workers, cleaning and sanitation workers, transport workers, and technician and clerical workers.[53] It shows that essential workers earn, on average, 26 per cent less than other workers.[54] This gap shows that the market is not a good indicator of the positive societal value of work.

So far, this section has discussed the positive societal value of certain activities on certain societal goals. In reality, not all jobs have such positive societal value. High-value market work can have a negative impact on basic needs or central human capabilities. I define these activities as 'capability-reducing

[49] Martha Nussbaum, *Creating Capabilities: The Human Development Approach* (Harvard UP 2011)
[50] ibid 33–34.
[51] Bueno, 'Introduction to the Human Economy' (n 46).
[52] ILO, *The Value of Essential Work: World Employment and Social Outlook 2023* (ILO 2023).
[53] The report only reported essential frontline occupations, which means that they could not be teleworkable, such as educational work.
[54] ILO, *The Value of Essential Work* (n52) 84.

work'.[55] Take the example of speculation on food or housing prices. The activity consists in buying cheap and selling at a high price on the market. There are big markets for these activities that are highly remunerated, yet they may increase living costs and reduce access to food and housing for most people. Access to food and housing are essential needs, and in fact international human rights. Here again, market mechanisms are not a good indicator for the negative social value of work.

There is a question of what standards to use for measuring the societal value of work. Impact on basic needs, central human capabilities, or freedom from work are some examples. Other goals could be more specific or relate more specifically to the environment. Another question is how these goals should be determined. At least two conditions must be met. First, the value of work should relate to existing needs in a community, a country, or the international community. It cannot relate only to the needs expressed on the market by those who have purchasing power. It also cannot relate only to the national interest of a state. Second, it should be the result of public deliberation. All systems of work valuation thus far did not respect these two conditions. These needs and the value of work should not be identified externally by the government, *à la* Soviet socialism, nor by the market itself, *à la* neoliberalism.

Pragmatically, I suggest starting with a minimum approach and identifying first, and after public deliberation, the needs that can be defined as essential for people and the environment. Prioritizing needs is nothing new. For example, governments already set societal targets for education, health, or environment and climate protection.[56] The Sustainable Development Goals are an example of such basic societal goals. This first step requires thinking more in terms of missions than in economic growth, as recommended by Mariana Mazzucato,[57] such as reducing climate emissions, reducing poverty or inequality, or guaranteeing essential needs. The second step should consist in identifying jobs and activities that can be qualified as essential or detrimental to achieve them. The ILO report on the value of *essential work* is also a good example of an international body prioritizing needs around essential needs for people. The same task could be done for identifying the value of green jobs. Finally, it is necessary to determine when labour law should intervene to promote or discourage certain jobs, which is the subject of the following section.

[55] Bueno, 'From Productive Work to Capability-Enhancing Work' (n 47) 361.

[56] See Chapter 3 by Beryl ter Haar in this book, for policies prioritizing values other than economic growth.

[57] Mariana Mazzucato, *Mission Economy: A Moonshot Guide to Changing Capitalism* (Allen Lane 2021).

C. When Should Labour Law Intervene?

Governments usually strike some balance between individual freedom and societal needs. Currently, the main strategy consists in regulating labour markets through minimum working standards, creating (any kind of) jobs by stimulating investment and consumption,[58] and providing unemployment benefits when necessary.[59] In this logic, typical labour rights mainly aim to regulate the labour market and labour law allows questions of value to be answered by the market alone. Labour law itself is sometimes presented as the law of the labour market[60] despite some discussions about its role on expanding human capabilities.[61] But generally, there is not much debate about the purpose of labour law beyond regulating the labour market.[62]

The suggestion of this chapter is that labour law should play some role in shaping the societal value of work beyond the market. A post-growth approach to labour law should lead to expanding opportunities and individual free choice for work with positive societal impacts at the same time, but also reducing individual free choice for detrimental work offered in the market. No system can function without a conciliation of individual and societal interests. Very few people would feel free with a personally meaningful essential job from which they cannot survive. Conversely, very few would also feel free if they were forced to conduct essential work if they did not want to do it. In order to reconcile these interests, labour law must move beyond its mere labour market regulatory function.

So far, labour law only intervenes in the market, through minimum wage for example, when the value of work set by the market is considered too low to be decent. In the future, labour law should continue to do so, but it should also valorize low paid or unpaid work that positively contributes to societal and environmental goals. In his recent report to the UN General Assembly, UN Special Rapporteur on extreme poverty and human rights Olivier de Schutter suggested to include this element of societal value in the universal right to fair remuneration.[63]

[58] Kerry Rittich, 'The Right to Work and Labour Market Flexibility: Labour Market Governance Norms in the International Order' in Virginia Mantouvalou (ed), *The Right to Work: Legal and Philosophical Perspectives* (Hart Publishing 2015).

[59] Dermine, *Droit au travail et politiques d'activation des personnes sans emploi* (36) 97.

[60] S Deakin and F Wilkinson, *The Law of the Labour Market* (OUP 2005).

[61] See generally Brian Langille (ed), *The Capability Approach to Labour Law* (OUP 2019) and Bueno, 'From Productive Work to Capability-Enhancing Work' (n 47) 336, for an overview of the capability approach to labour law.

[62] See generally Davidov, *A Purposive Approach to Labour Law* (n 39).

[63] Special Rapporteur on extreme poverty and human rights, Olivier De Schutter, 'The Working Poor: A Human Rights Approach to Wages', UN Doc A/78, paras 49–54.

Expanding individual opportunities for such work is crucial to avoid the waste of human skills referred to above when people have to take any job in the market although they would personally prefer to use their skills more meaningfully. Should the farmer have a real choice and opportunity to produce food for a local community; the lawyer to advise poor communities affected by the water pollution; the engineer to design carbon neutral planes; the psychologist to help the poor; the architect and construction worker to build homes for people who really need one? It is commonly accepted that the right to freely choose work does not mean that everyone should have the exact job they desire.[64] This would be unrealistic and impracticable.[65] Nevertheless, I believe that in the cases listed above, the answer should be yes and that there is a role for labour law to make sure that these activities can be done even if the market does not allow them.

On the other hand, not everyone should support the costs of creating individual opportunities for meaningful work. This would be particularly unfair considering the many high-paying jobs with a negative societal and environmental impact. Labour law should also intervene to discourage highly paid market work that has a negative impact on people and the planet, at least when the market value of a job cannot be justified in light of its negative societal value. Should labour law discourage highly paid market activities, such as food or housing price speculation when they impact essential needs of most people? I believe that labour law should ensure that this is the case by taxing these activities in order to create opportunities for more meaningful jobs for society and the environment.

V. Conclusion

Economic liberals praised labour markets for their liberating potential. Historically, one goal was to reduce barriers to compete for paid work, particularly for the poor. Friedman and Hayek championed this liberating narrative of labour markets for workers during the second half of the twentieth century. The introduction of markets for work, however, has radically transformed the purpose and value of work. The purpose of work has been reduced to receiving an income and its value has become determined by the market regardless of

[64] Jeremy Sarkin-Hughes and Mark Koenig, 'Developing the Right to Work: Intersection and Dialoguing Human Rights and Economic Policy' (2011) 33 Human Rights Quarterly 1, 10.
[65] Weidel, 'Moving Towards a Capability for Meaningful Labour' (n 44).

its impact on people's lives. This system ignores the fact that work has a societal value. It ignores the fact that work can positively or negatively impact lives and the environment. It also overlooks the fact that valuable human skills and resources are wasted when people cannot carry out activities which would be valuable for people or the environment, but have to take whatever job is offered in the market.

Labour law should, therefore, introduce a debate on the societal value of work by discussing concepts of essential work and detrimental work. This chapter suggests new ways for labour law to intervene more systematically in market mechanisms when the gap between the societal and the market value of work becomes too wide.

Bibliography

Blanc L, *Le socialisme: droit au travail* (3rd edn, Nouveau Monde 1849)

Bridel P, 'D'un marché libérateur (1803) à un marché despotique (1837): Une note de synthèse sur le concept de marché chez Sismondi' (2020) 9(1) Revue d'histoire de la pensée économique 237

Bueno N, 'From the Right to Work to Freedom from Work: Introduction to the Human Economy' (2017) 33(4) International Journal of Comparative Labour Law and Industrial Relations 463

Bueno N, 'Freedom at, through and from Work: Rethinking Labour Rights' (2021) 160(2) International Labour Review 311

Bueno N, 'From Productive Work to Capability-Enhancing Work: Implications for Labour Law and Policy' (2022) 23(3) Journal of Human Development and Capabilities 354

Cahill D and Konings M, *Neoliberalism* (Polity 2017)

Collins H, 'Is there a Human Right to Work?' in V Mantouvalou (ed), *The Right to Work: Legal and Philosophical Perspectives* (Hart Publishing 2015)

Deakin S and Wilkinson F, *The Law of the Labour Market* (OUP 2005)

Dermine E, *Droit au travail et politiques d'activation des personnes sans emploi: Étude critique du rôle du droit international des droits humains* (Bruylant 2017)

Dermine E and Dumont D, 'A Renewed Critical Perspective on Social Law: Disentangling Its Ambivalent Relationship with Productivism' (2022) 38(3) International Journal of Comparative Labour Law and Industrial 237

De Schutter O, Report of the Special Rapporteur on extreme poverty and human rights, The working poor: a human rights approach to wages, October 2023 UN Doc A/78, paras 49–54

Elster J, 'Is There (or Should There Be) a Right to Work?' in Amy Gutman (ed), *Democracy and the Welfare State* (Princeton UP 1988)

Friedman M and Friedman R, *Capitalism and Freedom* (first published 1962, 40th anniversary edn, University of Chicago Press 2002)

Friedman M and Friedman R, *Free to Choose: A Personal Statement* (first published 1980, Harvest Book 1990)

Gislain J-J, 'La conversion de Sismondi' (2013) 64(1) Cahiers d'Économie Politique 111

Hayek F, *The Road to Serfdom* (first published 1944, University of Chicago Press 2007)
ILO, *The Value of Essential Work: World Employment and Social Outlook 2023* (ILO 2023)
Jackson T, *Post Growth: Life after Capitalism* (Polity 2021)
Kallis G, *Degrowth* (Agenda 2018)
Langille B (ed), *The Capability Approach to Labour Law* (OUP 2019)
Laruffa F, 'Re-thinking Work and Welfare for the Social-Ecological Transformation' (2022)16 Sociologica 123
Marx K, *Capital: Critique of Political Economy, Vol I* (Penguin Classics 1990)
Mazzucato M, *The Value of Everything: Making and Taking in the Global Economy* (Penguin Books 2018)
Mill, JS, *The Principles of Political Economy with Some of Their Applications to Social Philosophy* (first published 1848, 7th edn, Longmans 1909)
Nussbaum M, *Creating Capabilities: The Human Development Approach* (Harvard UP 2011)
Polanyi K, *The Great Transformation: The Political and Economic Origins of our Time* (2nd edn, Beacon Press 2001)
Raworth K, *Doughnut Economics* (Penguin 2017)
Rittich K, 'The Right to Work and Labour Market Flexibility: Labour Market Governance Norms in the International Order' in V Mantouvalou (ed), *The Right to Work: Legal and Philosophical Perspectives* (Hart Publishing 2015)
Rosanvallon P, *Le capitalisme utopique: Histoire de l'idée de marché* (3rd edn, Seuil 1999)
Rosenfeld, J, *You're Paid What You're Worth: And Other Myths of the Modern Economy* (Harvard UP 2021)
Sarkin-Hughes J and Koenig M, 'Developing the Right to Work: Intersection and Dialoguing Human Rights and Economic Policy' (2011) 33 Human Rights Quarterly 1
Saul B, Kinley D, and Mowbray J, *The International Covenant on Economic, Social and Cultural Rights: Commentary, Cases and Materials* (OUP 2014)
Sen A, *Development as Freedom* (OUP 1999)
Sismondi (de) J-C, 'De la richesse commerciale ou Principes d'économie politique appliqués à la législation du commerce' in P Bridel and others (eds), *Oeuvres économiques completes*, vol 2 (Economica 2012)
Sismondi (de) J-C, *Études sur les sciences sociales* in P Bridel and others (eds), *Œuvres économiques complètes* (Economica 2018)
Smith A, *The Wealth of Nations* (first published 1776, Penguin Classics 1999)
Stanziani A, *Bondage: Labor and Rights in Eurasia from the Sixteenth to the Early Twentieth Centuries* (Berghahn 2018)
Tomassetti J, 'Neoliberal Conceptions of the Individual in Labour Law' in Addabbo and others (eds), *The Collective Dimensions of Employment Relations: Interdisciplinary Perspectives on Workers' Voices and Changing Workplace Patterns* (Palgrave Macmillan 2021)
Vardi L, 'The Abolition of the Guilds during the French Revolution' (1988) 15(4) French Historical Studies 704
Weidel T, 'Moving Towards a Capability for Meaningful Labour' (2021) 19(1) Journal of Human Development and Capabilities 1
Wilson J, *Neoliberalism* (Routledge 2018)
Young A, *Political Essays Concerning the Present State of the British Empire* (Strahan and T Cadel 1772)

8

Labour Law and the Utopia of the Commons

*Paolo Tomassetti**

I. The State, the Market, and Beyond

Western capitalism has historically relied on the division between the state and the market.[1] In both civil and common law jurisdictions, this division has been fuelled by a separation between public and private law, with property rights being articulated accordingly.[2] Simon Deakin argues that Western law itself 'is premised on the separation of the spheres of the public and the private which is also an essential feature of a capitalist economic order'.[3] Such dichotomy, however, has proven to be unsustainable. Not only does the fracture of social life between public and private domains not fully account for the actual manifestation of human experience and, therefore, cannot adequately appreciate the real determinants of freedom.[4] But it also contributes to the current societal and environmental crisis as, echoing Elinor Ostrom, 'neither the state nor the market is uniformly successful in enabling individuals to sustain long-term, productive use of natural resource systems'.[5]

In parallel to the eclipse of the so-called welfare state and the colonization of the public by the private,[6] the 'tragedy of the commons'[7] materialized as a

* This chapter has received funding from the European Union's Horizon 2020 research and innovation programme under the Marie Skłodowska-Curie grant agreement no 101025998. The author is grateful to the editors, especially to Nicolas Bueno and Beryl ter Haar, and one anonymous referee for their suggestions and insightful comments on earlier versions of this chapter. The usual disclaimer applies.

[1] Wolfgang Streeck, *How Will Capitalism End? Essays on a Failing System* (Verso 2016).

[2] Hila Shamir, 'The Public/Private Distinction Now: The Challenges of Privatization and of the Regulatory State' [2014] Theoretical Inquiries in Law 1; Alain Supiot, 'The Public–Private Relation in the Context of Today's Refeudalization' [2013] International Journal of Constitutional Law 129; Alan Freeman and Elizabeth Mensch, 'The Public-Private Distinction in American Law and Life' [1987] Buffalo Law Review 237.

[3] Simon Deakin, 'The Law of the Anthropocene' in Samantha Besson and Samuel Jubé (eds), *Concerter les civilisations: mélanges en l'honneur d'Alain Supiot* (Seuil 2020) 114.

[4] Karl Klare, 'The Public/Private Distinction in Labor Law' [1982] University of Pennsylvania Law Review 1358.

[5] Elinor Ostrom, *Governing the Commons. The Evolution of Institution for Collective Action* (CUP 1990) 1.

[6] Shamir, 'The Public/Private Distinction' (n 2) 9.

[7] Garrett Hardin, 'The Tragedy of the Commons' [1968] Science 1243.

Paolo Tomassetti, *Labour Law and the Utopia of the Commons* In: *Labour Law Utopias.* Edited by: Nicolas Bueno, Beryl ter Haar, and Nuna Zekić, Oxford University Press.
DOI: 10.1093/oso/9780198889755.003.0008

metaphor for a contemporary 'social question', which rising inequalities, labour disempowerment, and ecological destruction have made severely manifest. What is essential to understanding tragedy as a metaphor, though, is not the mere occurrence of inegalitarian market outcomes as the erosion of the 'common good' took place. It is the *longue durée* sacralization of limitless growth as the solution to all societal problems—even the problems created by the growth itself.[8] Unsurprisingly, the irrationality of infinite growth on a finite planet was even inherent in John Locke's romanticized idea of private property. Locke argued that 'the same rule of propriety—viz., that every man should have as much as he could make use of, would hold still in the world, without straitening anybody, since there is land enough in the world to suffice double the inhabitants'.[9] This Lockean proviso 'reminds us that property entitlements are not absolute and that they must be subject to overriding concerns of public interest'.[10] An interest that, unfortunately, both the state and the market largely failed to protect.

The utopia of the commons provides a fascinating set of arguments to look beyond the state-market dichotomy and the multiple crises attached to it. It envisages any desirable society where the state and the market cleavage, and their institutional equivalents—state sovereignty and private property—are traced back to synthesis. Advocated by degrowth and post-growth scholars as an alternative to the *status quo*, collaborative commons are successful examples of 'real utopias'[11] that transcend the public-private divide and give value to collective action as a synthesis between the two spheres. The commons as a 'real utopia' reflect a variety of social practices of activists and communities that organize themselves for the protection and reproduction of social and natural resources while satisfying their fundamental needs outside of market exchange. From subsistence farming, the establishment of renewable energy communities, the re-municipalization of water, the self-management of cultural and urban spaces, to the co-housing experiences, and the free software and makers' movement, collaborative commons involve collective action that establishes

[8] Dennis Meadow and others, *Limits to Growth. The 30-Year Update* (Earthscan 2005).

[9] John Locke, *Two Treatises of Government* (Awnsham Churchill 1689) 120. Modern political thought is premised with similar naïve assumptions about abundance of land and natural resources; Pierre Charbonnier, *Abondance et liberté. Une histoire environnementale des idées politiques* (La Découverte 2021).

[10] Tonia Novitz, 'Locke's Property Rights: Pensions and Trade Unions' [2012] International Union Rights 6–7.

[11] Erik Wright, *Envisioning Real Utopias* (Verso 2010).

juridical spaces, institutions, and norms of polycentric governance of complex socioeconomic and ecological systems.[12]

After contextualizing the utopia of the commons and presenting collaborative commons as sociolegal institutions, this chapter contrasts their characteristics with the main common features of labour law and industrial relations frames of reference. Three broad claims are made and discussed in the following sections, drawing on legal and sociolegal literature on the commons. Firstly, classical labour law justifications and industrial relations frames of reference, based on the pluralistic assumption of a conflict of interest between capital and labour, are unfit to frame the idea of work in collaborative commons. Secondly, the ideal-typical function of the commons, which sees the corporation as a commons, is theoretically useful for many purposes. However, it lacks analytical capacity when it comes to assessing the structure of the employment relationship in the capitalistic corporation, which remains unchanged in contrast to the traditional shareholder conception of the firm. Thirdly, and most importantly, it is argued that although there is little scope for classical labour law to land in the non-place of the 'common good', the labour movement can learn a lot from the idea of work in collaborative commons. The commons, in fact, offer the possibility to rethink and question some of the basic assumptions of labour law and industrial relations institutions, to reflect on the role that these institutions can play to close the existing gap between the kind of society we have and the kind of society that current and future generations of workers might deserve.

II. Contextualizing the Utopia of the Commons

As a constitutive element of capitalism, the legal division between public and private domains assumes that the society and the market are two separate entities that the state—ideally, the so-called welfare state—should regulate to make them converge. In a welfare state regime, such convergence is achieved through the redistribution of wealth and power from the market to society. Redistribution is a key component of the idea of justice in a capitalist welfare state, to ensure that 'none should fall below a decent standard of life, and that all should receive certain protections against accident and misfortune—for

[12] Elinor Ostrom, 'Beyond Markets and States: Polycentric Governance of Complex Economic Systems' [2010] American Economic Review 644.

example, unemployment compensation and medical care'.[13] Yet redistribution is an ambivalent concept in capitalism.

Designed to keep social conflict under control by guaranteeing income stability through economic growth and distributive justice,[14] the welfare state institutions proved unable to achieve fair equality of opportunity in capitalist societies. Even in the liberal tradition of legal and political philosophy, there is consensus that the reason lies in the scale of background inequalities and concentration in the ownership of property.[15] Instead of addressing the root causes of the uneven distribution of wealth and power, welfare state regimes embraced the ideology of growth and productivism as foundational aspects of their socioeconomic model.[16] On the one hand, the rise of living standards and consumption possibilities in Western countries and newly industrialized economies has been traded-off as a form of social conflict mitigation, to sedate distributional conflicts over scarce resources. On the other hand, any inquiry about whether increased productivity or more efficient production is a good thing came to be stigmatized: to the extent that growth creates wealth and redistribution possibilities, 'it is, *per se*, a good thing'.[17] The goals of the market, though regularly presented as those of society, have progressively detached from them. And the market dimension of value has been increasingly decoupled from non-economic values, overlooking the human potential to create social (and natural) benefits beyond producing material goods and services.[18]

The erosion of the ecological limits to growth is a consequence of such an unnatural divide between the market and society. Allan Schnaiberg's theory of the 'Treadmill of Production' is illuminating in this respect. Schnaiberg argues that the more resources for economic growth are extracted, the more environmental degradation worsens, but uncontrolled depletion of limited resources also makes further social and economic development difficult, and distributive justice

[13] John Rawls, *A Theory of Justice* (Harvard UP 1999) xv.

[14] Tuuli Hirvilammi and others, 'Social Policy in a Climate Emergency Context: Towards an Ecosocial Research Agenda' [2023] Journal of Social Policy 1. Compare Béla Galgóczi and Philippe Pochet, 'Introduction. Welfare States Confronted by the Challenges of Climate Change: A Short Review of the Issues and Possible Impacts' [2022] Transfer 307, 309.

[15] John Rawls, *Justice as Fairness: A Restatement* (Harvard UP 2001) 137–38.

[16] Elise Dermine and Daniel Dumont, 'A Renewed Critical Perspective on Social Law: Disentangling Its Ambivalent Relationship with Productivism' [2022] International Journal of Comparative Labour Law and Industrial Relations 237, which define productivism as 'the ideology based on the belief that continually increasing production in a society is both possible and desirable, and that economic growth should be the central objective of all human organization' 239.

[17] John Galbraith, *The New Industrial State* (Princeton UP 2007) 425.

[18] Nicolas Bueno, 'From the Right to Work to Freedom from Work. Introduction to the Human Economy' [2017] International Journal of Comparative Labour Law and Industrial Relations 463.

impossible.[19] As a result, the nexus between the State and the economic power has been subverted, with the former no longer being able to sustain or protect the relatively broad distribution of wealth and power and therefore being no more effective at achieving social justice and sustainability.[20] Rather than ruling the economy, governments are controlled more and more by market forces while becoming increasingly exposed to the influence of those who contribute to and benefit the most from the spiral of growth.[21] Outside of any constitutional limit or judicial review, the polarization between the market and society extended to the point that, in most cases, the social utility of private property no longer coincides with its social function.

The intellectual and societal movement for the commons originates as a historical alternative to the fiction that the state and the market are mutually exclusive and exhaustive of humans' political possibilities.[22] The normative proposal of the commons questions the state-market polarity in favour of a collectivistic and participative reconfiguration of the relations between the two poles—one that is democratic, inclusive, and more effective at responding to current societal and environmental issues. As Raworth nicely puts it, the commons are 'shareable resources of nature or society that people choose to use and govern through self-organising, instead of relying on the state or market for doing so'.[23] The commons in this context become any non-place that is equidistant from the private and the public, involving direct civic participation and collective action as the new *pouvoir constituant*.[24]

The idea of the commons includes a variety of social practices and institutions. A major distinction is made between commons as resources or resource systems (named *common-pool resources*) and commons as a property-rights regime (named *common property*).[25] Also, experiences of commons vary

[19] Allan Schnaiberg, *The Environment: from Surplus to Scarcity* (OUP 1980). Schnaiberg's theory resonates with contemporary debates about degrowth and post-growth; see Tim Jackson, *Prosperity Without Growth: Foundations for the Economy of Tomorrow* (Routledge 2017).

[20] Ugo Mattei, 'The Rise and Fall of Law and Economics: An Essay for Judge Guido Calabresi' [2005] Maryland Law Review 220, 242, arguing that 'not only has the law been freed from the lethal hug of the state, but also the idea that the law is produced by market forces is now generally accepted'.

[21] Saki Bailey and Ugo Mattei, 'Social Movements as Constituent Power: The Italian Struggle for the Commons' [2013] Indiana Journal of Global Legal Studies 965, 974.

[22] Silvia Federici, *Re-Enchanting the World: Feminism and the Politics of the Commons* (PM Press 2018) 103.

[23] Kate Raworth, *Doughnut Economics: Seven Ways to Think Like a 21st-Century Economist* (Random House 2017) 82.

[24] Bailey and Mattei 'Social Movements' (n 21) 968; Fritjof Capra and Ugo Mattei, *The Ecology of Law: Toward a Legal System in Tune with Nature and Community* (Berrett-Koehler Publishers 2015); Ugo Mattei and Alessandra Quarta, *The Turning Point in Private Law. Ecology, Technology and the Commons* (Edward Elgar 2019).

[25] Charlotte Hess and Elinor Ostrom (eds), *Understanding Knowledge as a Commons: From Theory to Practice* (The MIT Press 2007).

in time and space. Although the traditional articulation of commons theory recalls ancient forms of collective ownership in rural communities, the concept has evolved to include all types of goods, resources, and collaborative work activities that aim to foster solidarity, social justice, and sustainability.[26] Examples of collaborative commons in real life refer to local communities in both advanced and developing economies resisting the expropriation of rural, urban, and cultural areas for market purposes, as well as to groups of self-organized workers undertaking the production of goods and services for the sake of sustainability.[27]

The utopian character of the commons lies in their radical critique of the existing socioeconomic model and its institutional infrastructure. Any critique of the public-private divide, in fact, involves a rejection, or at least a critical reconsideration, of the legal foundations of capitalism and the concurrent political and economic ideology of limitless growth. Yet, in contrast to classical utopian visions, there is no systemic programme to reform the overall organization of society. Although some aspects of the commons theory point in this direction, there is no comprehensive or general 'economic plan' implied in the normative idea of the commons, nor coordinative and redistributive roles attributed to central public authorities, nor private property nationalized and subjected to state planning. These characteristics distinguish the commons from communism, which 'consigned power to the state'.[28] The commons, instead, are not dependent on a supporting state. On the contrary, their legitimation is 'directly related to the crisis of the state form, which the failure of realized socialism and the internationalization of capital has made dramatically evident'.[29]

III. The Commons as Sociolegal Institutions

Besides differing from the socialist vision of a state-centric command economy, the commons also stand opposed to property.[30] Their reality manifests itself in

[26] Margherita Pieraccini, 'Taking Stock of Italian Commons: Un-common Grounds?' in Ting Xu and Alison Clarke (eds), *Legal Strategies for the Development and Protection of Communal Property* (OUP 2018) 38.

[27] Stefania Barca and Felipe Milanez, 'Labouring the Commons: Amazonia's "Extractive Reserves" and the Legacy of Chico Mendes' and Gustavo García-López, 'Commoning Labour, Labouring the Commons: Centring the Commons in Environmental Labour Studies' in Nora Räthzel, Dimitris Stevis, and David Uzzell (eds), *The Palgrave Handbook of Environmental Labour Studies* (Palgrave Macmillan 2021) 319 and 389, resp.

[28] Federici, *Re-Enchanting the World* (n 22) 95–96.

[29] ibid 167.

[30] Stefano Rodotà, *Il terribile diritto. Studi sulla proprietà privata e i beni comuni* (Il Mulino 2013).

a complex of characteristics that parallels those of collective forms of ownership: 'the priority of the group and the subordination of individuals and their ends to the group; the priority of objective ends, of the economic nature, destination and use of things, over subjective ends; the priority within the group of subjective situations of duty over those of power or right typical of the traditional *iura in re*'.[31] They are 'networks of relations, responsibilities, rights, and duties within organised groups' that seek to promote sustainable development of local communities and the reproduction of their material and immaterial resources.[32] These networks are so intermingled that any attempt to isolate the subjective dimension of the person from the group or the ecosystem in which she lives and within the limits of which she realizes herself socially is fruitless. Further characteristics of the commons, in fact, include their *contextual* and *relational* nature.[33] They cannot be divorced from the cultural, social, or environmental context in which they exist; they are an integral part of complex human-ecological systems. The demand for the commons is not transcendental but relational: it is the object of the struggle of communities attempting to defend them and structures of authority seeking to control them.[34]

The contextual and contingent character of the commons requires shifting the conceptualization of law from the positivistic and legalistic approach to pluralistic and anti-formalist ways of intending legal rationality and subjectivity. The movement for the commons has grown and developed in response to the crisis of the conceptual and institutional foundations of modern law: property and sovereignty; and the correlated state-centric legal categories grounded on positive law.[35] Instead, what emerges from the analysis of the commons as sociolegal institutions is precisely an idea of legal rationality intended as *living law*,[36] as an expression of autonomous and participatory processes of self-regulation and resistance by communities, local institutions, small firms, workers, and consumers.[37]

The commons' legal rationality is implicitly dismissive of the institutional foundations of capitalism, including positivism as a philosophical and legal

[31] Paolo Grossi, *An Alternative to Private Property: Collective Property in the Juridical Consciousness of the Nineteenth Century* (University of Chicago Press 1981) 23–24.

[32] ibid 155.

[33] Ugo Mattei, *The State, the Market, and some Preliminary Question about the Commons—IUC Research Commons* (International University College of Turin 2011) 1.

[34] Capra and Mattei, *The Ecology of Law* (n 24) 149–67.

[35] Paolo Grossi, *A History of European Law* (Wiley Blackwell 2010) 68–74.

[36] Eugen Ehrlich, *Fundamental Principles of Sociology of Law* ([1913]; Routledge 2001).

[37] Construed in this way, the movement for the commons parallels the characteristics of what Harry Arthurs has defined as 'the law of economic subordination and resistance'. See Harry Arthurs, 'Labor Law as the Law of Economic Subordination and Resistance: a Thought Experiment' [2013] *Comparative Labor Law & Policy Journal* 585.

doctrine. Critical scholars note that, in reproducing the radical dichotomy between private and public law, legal positivism contributes to the promotion and protection of the capitalistic logic of limitless growth and its inegalitarian outcomes.[38] On the contrary, the law that gains prominence in institutional analyses of the commons goes far beyond the law of the state. Collaborative commons comprise rules at different levels of decision-making. They are dynamic systems promoting legal learning and self-regulation.[39] These are normative patterns emerging from the 'laboratory of the real-life experience', to provide decentralized responses to forms of injustice, for the social reproduction of local communities and the sustainable use of natural resources over time and space.[40]

In this reading, Mattei and Quarta suggest rethinking Western law categories and regulation in light of the commons' non-property nature, as opposed to an extractive legal setting based on the supremacy of property rights meant to transform the commons into capital.[41] While this process of extraction was reasonable when the commons were abundant and capital scarce, Mattei and Quarta argue that the relation between the two factors is now reversed; thus, novel political and legal institutions are necessary to unfold the creative and transformative power of the commons. Instead of mandating new theoretical accounts of law, this might mean recognizing legal subjectivity to the commons and their grassroots normativity. This implies that private law should no longer be interpreted as the normative framework for competition, selfishness, and individualism. Private law should be construed as the juridical dimension to enforce the fundamental principles of dignity, freedom, and equality in society by empowering intermediate communities or specific networks of solidarity to direct action, participatory democracy, and self-regulation. Echoing Anna Grear, such networks are likely to be 'inherently responsive to lived realities—intrinsically more able, perhaps, to produce new, practical, organic and adaptive, self-governance responses emerging in non-state and commons-based initiatives—in turn, reconstituting agency in far more complex forms'.[42]

[38] Boaventura De Sousa Santos, *Towards a New Legal Common Sense: Law, Globalization and Modernity* (Sage 1990) 40.

[39] Margherita Pieraccini, 'A Politicized, Legal Pluralist Analysis of the Commons' Resilience: The Case of the Regole d'Ampezzo' [2013] Ecology and Society 1, 3.

[40] Capra and Mattei, *The Ecology of Law* (n 24) 160.

[41] Mattei and Quarta, *The Turning Point* (n 24).

[42] Anna Grear, 'Towards "Climate Justice"? A Critical Reflection on Legal Subjectivity and Climate Injustice: Warning Signals, Patterned Hierarchies, Directions for Future Law and Policy' [2014] Journal of Human Rights and the Environment 103, 132.

IV. Work in the Commons: From Subordination to Solidarity

For centuries, human labour was a way to transform natural resources into products and services to trade in the market.[43] Modern states justified the transformation of commons into capital as serving societal purposes. With the advent of industrial capitalism, labour law and industrial relations institutions became essential features for the sustainable development of this market mechanism.[44] However, the socially progressive goals of labour law, with their different articulations of means and objectives,[45] have only partially internalized the negative effects of such a market mechanism,[46] thus inadvertently contributing to the 'tragedy of the commons'.

In the field of labour law, it is true that 'none of the polarities expressed in general private law—subject and object, person and thing, status and contract, public and private—really make sense'.[47] But on closer inspection, both labour law and industrial relations frames of reference tend to reproduce the inconsistency of those cleavages when they embrace in their epistemic statute the normative function of redistribution of power and resources from capital to labour, and the consequential ideology of limitless and unpurposive growth.[48] While wage labour benefited from the share of welfare and economic resources redistributed from industrial growth, the social function of the business enterprise remained unquestioned in orthodox labour law scholarship, along with the invisible externalities of increasing productivity and consumption on social and environmental commons. The same goes for the field of industrial relations.

Another fundamental assumption of classical labour law and industrial relations epistemologies, which reflects the core feature of wage labour, contrasts with the essence of work in the commons: the existence of a conflict of interest between the employer and the worker.[49] Collaborative commons

[43] Alain Supiot, '*Homo faber*: continuità e rotture' in Axel Honneth, Richard Sennett, and Alain Supiot, *Perché lavoro? Narrative e diritti per lavoratrici e lavoratori del XXI secolo* (Fondazione Giangiacomo Feltrinelli 2020) 21.

[44] Simon Deakin, 'The Contribution of Labour Law to Economic and Human Development' in Guy Davidov and Brian Langille (eds), *The Idea of Labour Law* (OUP 2011) 156.

[45] Guy Davidov, *A Purposive Approach to Labour Law* (OUP 2016).

[46] Deakin, 'The Law of the Anthropocene' (n 3); Simon Deakin, 'Labour Law and the "Capitalocene": Law, Work and Nature in the Ecological *Long Durée*' (2023) International Journal of Comparative Labour Law and Industrial Relations 281.

[47] Deakin, 'The Law of the Anthropocene' (n 3) 121.

[48] For wider discussion on this aspect, see Dermine and Dumont, 'A Renewed Critical Perspective' (n 16). See also Elise Dermine, 'Towards a Sustainable Social Law: What Role for Legal Scholars?' (2023) International Journal of Comparative Labour Law and Industrial Relations 315.

[49] Otto Kahn-Freund, *Labour and the Law* (3rd edn, Stevens 1983) 26–28.

pose challenges to this pluralistic idea of labour law in both its individual and collective dimensions. Conflicts of interest underpinning the employment contract in wage labour fade away in work activities based on collaborative commons.[50] The same is true for the trade unions' logic of collective action in building solidarity to coordinate individual interests towards broader societal goals. Although positive developments are happening,[51] it is still common to find indifference among confederal unions towards forms of active citizenship promoted by individuals and organized groups in global cities, suburbs, and rural areas. This reveals the difficulty trade unions find when operating in contexts where the traditional forms of conflict between capital and labour yield to social and ecological reproductive activities based on cooperation and solidarity. In such activities, cooperation and solidarity are not goals to pursue; they are the assumed basis of social and work relationships.

This is evidenced by the nature of work in the commons. Literature concerned with collaborative commons hardly accounts for the specific jobs and tasks performed by the commoners. Some common elements can, nonetheless, be detected indirectly and show their irreducibility to classical labour law narratives. Further to the technical skills needed to perform commons-related activities, communing entails a set of soft skills, as well as relational and behavioural competencies. It involves different models of labour division outside of subordination, in which human time is freed up for proselytizing, organizing, and caring activities. Capra and Mattei, for example, note that the fundamental organizational principles of communing are 'caring, duty, reciprocity, and participation. It is about spending a lot of time together to care for something recognised as a common with high attention and patience.'[52] In the same vein, Federici observes that communing is 'the willingness to spend much time in the work of cooperation, discussing, negotiating, and learning to deal with conflicts and disagreement'.[53] To some extent, the universal services provided by the commoners 'are similar to household work, never noticed when the work is being done. Only when no one is there to do the dishes, you notice its value.'[54]

[50] Unsurprisingly, many forms of reproductive work have been marginalized by labour law rationality. See Ania Zbyszewska, 'Regulating Work with People and "Nature" in Mind: Feminist Reflections' (2018) Comparative Labor Law & Policy Journal 9.

[51] Besides the many examples in Räthzel, Stevis, and Uzzell, *Environmental Labour Studies* (n 27); see Ian MacDonald (ed), *Unions and the City. Negotiating Urban Change* (ILR Press 2017).

[52] Capra and Mattei, *The Ecology of Law* (n 24) 153–54.

[53] Federici, *Re-Enchanting the World* (n 22) 94.

[54] Mattei, *The State, the Market* (n 33) 3.

In the commons, labour is relational, associative, and solidarity-based. It is consistent with forms of non-market work in which social relations and values prevail over material interests.[55] Unlike a capitalistic division of labour, which occurs when the establishment of the employment relationship is formalized through a contract, the impulse that drives the parties in collective action aimed at protecting a common good is not based on conflicting economic interests; it is based on reciprocity, solidarity, and sociability. While the employment contract based on the exchange between wage and subordination presupposes a conflict of interest between employer and employee, activists involved in collaborative commons do not stand face to face but side by side. The working relationship in collaborative commons is horizontal. It relies on the existence of a common purpose of the commoners: the care of the commons. Such care activity involves a cooperation between parties who act in solidarity, as a band of parallel forces converging towards a common objective.

Even the more inclusive justifications of labour law, such as the legal construction of personal work relations, cannot entirely capture the essence of work in collaborative commons.[56] It comes with no surprise that Freedland and Kountouris exclude from their conceptualization some forms of socially valuable activities, such as care work, waste recycling, subsistence agriculture, and other activities comparable to work in collaborative commons.[57] Although the commoners engage personally in the performance of work activity, establishing relations with other persons, the type of social relation involved in the commons focuses on the *common good*. Work in collaborative commons is not performed to fulfil the personal interest of the worker or the employer. It is performed to serve the socially and environmentally progressive ends of care, preservation, and reproduction of a common good.

Cooperatives are instructive in further explaining the distance between wage labour and the reality of work in collaborative commons. The International Labour Organization (ILO) recommendation n. 193 defines the cooperative as 'an autonomous association of persons united voluntarily to meet their common economic, social and cultural needs and aspirations through a jointly owned and democratically controlled enterprise'.[58] Cooperatives might be one

[55] Noa Zatz, 'Working at the Boundaries of Markets: Prison Labor and the Economic Dimension of Employment Relationship' [2008] Vanderbilt Law Review 857.

[56] Mark Freedland and Nicola Kountouris, *The Legal Construction of Personal Work Relations* (OUP 2011) 351–52, 347–49, 354–56.

[57] This is noted by Supriya Routh, 'The Need to Become Fashionable' in Brian Langille (ed), *The Capability Approach to Labour Law* (OUP 2019) 113. On this issue, Routh cites Judy Fudge, 'Feminist Reflections on the Scope of Labour Law: Domestic Work, Social Reproduction, and Jurisdiction' [2014] Feminist Legal Studies 1, 12–16.

[58] ILO Recommendation on the Promotion of Cooperatives, 2002 (R.193), point 2.

of the institutional channels to give legal recognition to the commons, even if not all of the commons should necessarily be subsumed under the cooperative model. Collaborative commons, for example, can be organized and legally recognized through an association, a foundation, or even without any formal juridical status.[59]

Undoubtedly, both cooperatives and the commons emphasize social values and solidarity over economic interests. They both employ democratic forms of managing their activities, transcending the public-private divide.[60] However, while cooperatives are owned, the non-property nature of the commons remains an important feature that distinguishes the two models. This difference is accentuated when cooperatives focus on purposes and interests that are not coincident with the care and sustainability of the common good. When such institutional differences occur, the economic interests of the cooperative worker become relevant. Although the solidaristic dimension of the relationship may still be higher compared to work in capitalist corporations, it is not always the case that 'the employment in a cooperative blurs the division between the employer and the employee, de-constructing the main core of labour law scope'.[61] Instead, the existence of an economic interest of the worker, distinct from that of the cooperative as a legal person, shows that mutuality does not always imply the absence of conflict of interest in labour relationships.[62] This is evidenced by the fact that cooperative workers get a salary in exchange for their work and that trade unions in cooperatives continue to exist in many countries, even though their functions and purposes are pursued according to strategies that are not necessarily confrontational.

In short, if labour law and industrial relations institutions work to promote *organic solidarity*, social ties and work relationship in collaborative commons are based on *mechanical solidarity*.[63] In this context, the confrontational background of any property-based division of labour retrocedes, and solidarity rediscovers its function as the constitutive element of co-existence between the person, the community, and the common good that is to be protected.[64]

[59] Saki Bailey and Maria Edgarda Marcucci, 'Legalizing the Occupation: The Teatro Valle as a Cultural Commons' [2013] The South Atlantic Quarterly 396.

[60] For recent sociological and industrial relations research on cooperatives, Katherine Chen and Victor Tan Chen (eds), *Organizational Imaginaries: Tempering Capitalism and Tending to Communities through Cooperatives and Collectivist Democracy* (Emerald Publishing Limited 2021).

[61] Miriam Kullmann and Andrea Iossa, 'Subordination in Solidarity? The Labour Law of Workers' Cooperatives' [2020] *Global Workplace Law & Policy*.

[62] Marco Biagi, *Cooperative e rapporti di lavoro* (Franco Angeli 1983) 288, 301.

[63] Émile Durkheim, *De la division du travail social: étude sur l'organisation des sociétés supérieures* (Félix Alcan 1893).

[64] Rodotà, *Il terribile Diritto* (n 30) 498.

This way, labour (like natural resources) ceases to be a mere component of the market and regains its social and collective dimension of promoting the caring and sustainable development of those material and immaterial goods needed for the progress of humanity and the reproduction of social and natural ecosystems.

V. Beyond Utopias: The Ideal-Typical Function of the Commons

Academic interest in the commons has recently expanded from counter-hegemonic narratives to far less radical positions. While heterodox scholars articulate the idea of the commons in critical terms, even advocating it as a form of social unrest, the latter tend to construe the commons as an ideal type, emphasizing the transformative power that such an institution drives on traditional sociolegal categories. These categories include the classical articulation of property rights into separated public and private realms, as well as the conceptualization of the enterprise as the epitome of private property and shareholder primacy.

Drawing on the ideal-typical function of the commons, for example, Deakin sees the corporation 'as a collectively managed resource or "commons" which is subject to a number of multiple, overlapping and potentially conflicting property-type claims on the part of the different constituencies or stakeholders that provide value to the firm'.[65] He argues that viewing the corporation as a common is the first step towards a 'better understanding of the role that the corporate form can play in ensuring wider economic and social sustainability'.[66] Indeed, the overall sustainability of the corporation 'depends on ensuring proportionality of benefits and costs with respect to the inputs made to corporate resources, and on the participation of the different stakeholder groups in the formulation of the rules governing the management and use of those resources'.[67]

Deakin's conception of the corporation as commons parallels the main normative assumptions of the stakeholder theory, as well as the familiar narratives of the pluralist theory of industrial relations that sees the firm as a system of interests. Consider Ross' idea of the firm, for example. Ross looked

[65] Simon Deakin, 'The Corporation as Commons: Rethinking Property Rights, Governance and Sustainability in the Business Enterprise' [2012] Queen's Law Journal 339, 376.
[66] ibid 381.
[67] ibid 381.

at the corporation as a plural reality consisting of divergent but intermingled groups of interests, including those of consumers, suppliers, and organized workers.[68] In such a corporation, the management goal is to secure justice for all and unconditional maxima for none by balancing different interests with the aim to achieve 'the general interest of society'.[69] In this reading, management is not seen as the personification of capital interests opposed to those of salaried workers and other stakeholders, but as a rational agent of a higher collective interest, that is, what Deakin refers to as sustainability. Robert Dahl made a similar claim in his classical study of 1961.[70] Dahl depicted social organizations, including corporations, as pluralist communities with groups of competing interests that continually shift alliances and keep each other from monopolizing power. In a following study, he explicitly questioned the idea that shareholders should have priority in executive decision-making: 'Why should people who own shares be given the privilege of citizenship in the government of the firm when citizenship is denied to other people who also make vital contribution to the firm? The people I have in mind are, of course, employees and customers, without whom the firm could not exist, and the general public.'[71]

In line with Ross and Dahl's pluralist theory of the firm, scholars from the so-called 'Oxford school of industrial relations' emphasized the plurality of interests constituting the corporate structure. Fox, for example, looked at the enterprise as a 'stakeholder coalition', a 'democratic state in miniature' consisting of conflicting interest groups.[72] Similarly, Flanders argued that 'the business enterprise does not have a unitary structure of authority; in some degree it is always a pluralistic society composed of groups with divergent interests and values. Whether management appreciates this or not, it is invariably confronted with the problem of reconciling the impersonal aims of the enterprise with the personal aims of its many constituent groups.'[73] Like democratic participation in collaborative commons, industrial relations' pluralism assumes that the coordination and balancing of interests are achieved through a transaction, negotiation, and other mechanisms for conflict resolution. Although

[68] NS Ross, 'Organised Labour and Management: the UK' in Edward Maurice Hugh-Jones (ed), *Human Relations and Management* (North-Holland 1958) 101, 104.
[69] ibid 114.
[70] Robert Dahl, *Who Governs? Democracy and Power in an American City* (Yale UP 1961).
[71] Robert Dahl, *After the Revolution? Authority in the Good Society* (Yale UP 1970) 102.
[72] Alan Fox, *A Sociology of Work in Industry* (Collier-Macmillan 1971) 58.
[73] Allan Flanders, *Managements and Unions* (Faber and Faber 1970) 150.

there is no inherent common purpose in traditional capitalist firms, it is assumed that its constituent groups are dependent on each other to achieve their objectives.[74]

Two fundamental elements, though, distinguish the commons' system of governance from the pluralist idea of stakeholders' participation and negotiation with management in a business corporation. Firstly, shared governance in collaborative commons is connatural to the commons itself. Participation of the commoners is a truly democratic process, which extends to core decisions related, for example, to access and use of a common-pool resource. Secondly, such decisions are taken in a condition of substantial equality among the commons' constituents. This is a condition that, in principle, ensures fairness of the decision-making process and justice of the related outcomes. Even in the most participatory, horizontal, and democratized corporate structures, these two elements make the ideal-typical conception of the corporation as a commons hardly capable of achieving the egalitarian outcomes that the commons as a real utopia convey. John Rawls' idea of justice as fairness helps further clarify this.

Rawls derives principles for a just society from the agreement to a fair procedure: justice is the outcome of a decision-making process accepted as fair. According to Rawls, 'the primary subject of justice is the basic structure of society, or more exactly, the way in which the major social institutions distribute fundamental rights and duties and determine the division of advantages from social co-operation .... The justice of a social scheme depends essentially on how fundamental rights and duties are assigned and on the economic opportunities and social conditions in the various sectors of society.'[75] While justice is the outcome of fairness, the reverse is also true. The assessment of fairness in social relations requires consensus around an idea of justice based on shared values and fundamental principles of coexistence. These are the principles that 'free and rational persons concerned to further their own interests would accept in an *initial position of equality* as defining the fundamental terms of their association.'[76] It is only in a context where the justice of the prevailing definitions of 'fundamental rights and duties' can be taken for granted, as agreed by free and rational agents in a condition of substantial equality, that meaningful discussion on fairness is possible. Otherwise, the idea of fairness is arbitrary and subject to manipulation.[77]

[74] ibid.
[75] Rawls, *A Theory of Justice* (n 13) 6, 7.
[76] ibid 10 (emphasis added).
[77] Richard Hyman and Ian Brough, *Social Values and Industrial Relations* (Basil Blackwell 1975) 9.

The reality of work in capitalism is that the root causes of inequality within and beyond employment cannot be adequately addressed. It is not only unquestioned but even reflected in legal rationality that employers have the right to use labour (and natural resources) for less than its actual cost and for purposes that are not necessarily coincident with those of society, as much as workers (and natural resources) have the equivalent right not to be exploited excessively.[78] In this connection, the managerial attitude to consider labour as a cost to minimize mirrors the worker's and union's tendency to overlook non-materialistic values within and outside productive work.[79] This has the further consequence that, in principle, the voice of organized labour cannot extend the limit of workers' protection corresponding to the need to curb the worst implications of labour (and environmental) subordination to capital.[80] In conclusion, even in the inspiring view of corporations as commons, workers and their representatives can seek to expand democracy in firms and, perhaps, dampen the consequences of adverse managerial decisions. Nonetheless, they remain relatively powerless to alter the fundamental reality of management control over the strategy and direction of the enterprise, as well as the negative externalities of the division of labour in society.[81] Regardless of whether countervailing forces such as trade unions might be effectual in their role of stakeholders,[82] organized labour has no right to contrast the deepest sources of unsustainability.[83]

VI. Discussion and Conclusions

In this chapter, the commons have been considered real utopias and in their ideal-typical dimension. Consideration has been given to the extent to which mainstream and more progressive labour law justifications fit with the commons. Not surprisingly, one of the conclusions is that labour law scholarship is ill-fitted to frame the reality and the utopia of the commons. This is unsurprising as familiar categories of labour law refer to work relationships that—to a large extent—are incompatible with human activities in collaborative

[78] Richard Hyman, *Industrial Relations: A Marxist Introduction* (Macmillan 1975) 86.
[79] ibid 87.
[80] ibid.
[81] Karl Klare, 'The Labor-Management Cooperation Debate: A Workplace Democracy Perspective' [1988] Harvard Civil Rights-Civil Liberties Law Review 39, 71.
[82] Robert Michels, *Political Parties: A Sociological Study of the Oligarchical Tendencies of Modern Democracy* (Hearts International Library 1915); C Wright Mills, *The Power Elite* (OUP 1956).
[83] Hyman, *Industrial Relations* (n 78) 86, 87.

commons. The same goes for the dominant and pluralistic frame of reference in industrial relations.

Even though there is little scope for classical labour law to land in the non-place of the commons, some areas of such discipline can still be useful to protect and empower people involved in collaborative commons. Occupational health and safety is one of these areas, along with social security law, welfare provisions, and distribution norms that allow the commoners to actively participate in the life and reproduction of the common good. To the extent that the capability approach is functional to justify labour law beyond the assumption of inequality of bargaining power[84] and to disconnect income from the exchange value in the labour market,[85] this might contribute to rationalizing some aspects of the idea of work in collaborative commons. The expansion of human freedom to choose meaningful jobs within and beyond employment is certainly an area in which the capability approach might become relevant in the discourse about the commons. For example, active and passive labour market policies might contribute to support transitions from productive work to collaborative commons and vice versa. Indirect contributions from labour law could also stem from working time reductions in energy-intensive and polluting industries in order to free and empower people to engage in collaborative commons, political activism, and other social reproductive work.[86] Sabbatical leave, for example, would point in this direction.[87]

As with any utopia, the utopia of the commons is useful when it remains an ideal. When humans try to turn utopias into reality, they often fail miserably since real life is not the dimension of their existence. When applied to the utopia of the commons, for example, the fundamental principle of labour law—that is, *labour is not a commodity*—should not just imply that the worker is a subject worthy of protection—protection of his dignity, naked in the face of market and state strongholds, but rather, the worker should be protected as a person who actively participates in solidarity with the other commoners and with the life of the commons itself. However, in real life, solidarity can easily be manipulated for unethical purposes. It can be debased if solidarity efforts and commitments are not equally shared. The possibility that all successful institutions are also coercive, and the burden of coercion tends to fall unequally

[84] For a recent debate on the capability approach to labour law, see Brian Langille (ed), *The Capability Approach to Labour Law* (OUP 2019).

[85] Dermine and Dumont, 'A Renewed Critical' (n 16) 262, 265.

[86] Zbyszewska, 'Regulating Work' (n 50).

[87] Katerine Stone, 'Unions and On-demand Work in the United States' in Julia López (ed), *Collective Bargaining and Collective Action. Labour Agency and Governance in the 21st Century?* (Hart Publishing 2019).

on those who are less powerful, has been neglected in commons theory.[88] Likewise, the literature on new forms of collaborative commons documents internal problems of slack, opportunism, and other forms of non-cooperative behaviour. These problems result in a deterioration of the common good that is to be protected, in internal rent-seeking by commoners who have practical leverage over others, or in decreasing productivity of some of its members, who nevertheless demand their equal share in the outputs.[89]

In short, as long as the idealized resilience of the commons is vulnerable to the *iron law of oligarchy*,[90] classical labour law and industrial relations institutions regain importance to revive solidarity, regulating distributional conflicts and the asymmetry of power implicit in any type of organization. Putting this argument in Kahn-Freund's terms, it is 'sheer Utopia to postulate a common interest in the substance of labour relations. To dig up the roots of this Utopia of a "pre-established harmony" of management and labour would be a fascinating task for a sociologist: he would probably discover laissez-faire doctrines as well as a very crude type of Marxism and most certainly those (more or less bogus) ideological constructions which were used by Mussolini to bolster up the "*stato corporativo*", and he would also observe how the Utopia can degenerate into the sham romanticism of the feudalistic trappings used by Hitler for his labour laws.'[91]

Compared to utopias, ideal types can better reflect the imperfectness of real life, albeit this often happens at the cost of oversimplifying it. And an oversimplification of reality might involve disrespect for nature and human values. In this reading, the idea of corporations as commons should be taken as it is: a theoretical framework to analyse the legal structure of a business enterprise better than the shareholder primacy model does. But the temptation to expand the qualification of a commons to every good or service should be limited. Otherwise, the concept loses its specificity; if everything is a commons, nothing is a commons. Viewing the corporation as a commons, thus, would not necessarily help to deliver benefits for all its stakeholders and society as a whole. Instead, the 'tragedy of the commons' is still likely to materialize as long as the voices of employees, unions, and other stakeholders are excluded from or are unequally heard in core decisions concerned with property rights

[88] Compare Arun Agrawal, 'Sustainable Governance of Common-Pool Resources: Context, Methods and Politics' [2003] Annual Review of Anthropology 243, 257; Pieraccini, 'A Politicized, Legal Pluralist' (n 39).

[89] Amnon Lehavi, 'Re-romanticizing Commons and Community in Israeli Discourse: Social, Economic, and Political Motives' [2018] Theoretical Inquiries in Law 671, 699.

[90] Michels, *Political Parties* (n 82).

[91] Kahn-Freund, *Labour and the Law* (n 49) 28.

and the correlated economic freedom to choose *how*, *how much*, *where*, and above all *why* and *for whom* social and natural resources are used (for some, exploited) to produce value.

Regardless of the contribution of labour law and industrial relations institutions, the movement for commons will likely continue to expand and regain space for the sustainability of socioecological systems. Thousands of activists around the world have organized themselves in defence of the commons for current and future generations. Opposite to the unpurposive transformation of commons into capital, there is a flourishing progressive movement beyond the public-private fracture that retraces the early forms of solidarity and collective action that unions had promoted at the onset of industrial capitalism. These new forms of solidarity and collective action bring together humans that, irrespective of their status, share the purpose of defying 'the market-fundamentalism while also retaining the market space within the much broader socio-ecological one'.[92]

It is in this context that collaborative commons are emerging to lead a renewed, perhaps more effective, and therefore far more convincing twenty-first-century response to the parallel process of commodification of labour and nature. This is a response that originates out of formal legal institutions to confront superordinate public and private power. It flows from 'local struggles', from 'indigenous, implicit, and informal lawmaking', and from 'movements which have not become juridified but which actually draw their strength and sustenance from grass-roots involvement'.[93] Organized labour cannot ignore this. The *living law* of collective bargaining is an essential feature of the enduring idea of labour law.[94] Yet collective bargaining's contribution to achieving social justice and transformation in a post-industrial society has increasingly eroded. Despite a large part of labour being intrinsically mutualistic, cooperative, and relational, traditional segments of the market seek to expand the margins of competitiveness outside the boundaries of the market itself, multiplying the mechanisms of value extraction far beyond the paid working time. In times and places of post-industrial capitalism, where the scene of primitive accumulation revives, the capitalist illusion of an infinite growth on a finite planet is driving a process whose only end can be the destruction of the material conditions it needs to operate.[95]

[92] Supriya Routh, 'Embedding Work in Nature: The Anthropocene and Legal Imagination of Work as Human Activity' [2018] Comparative Labor Law and Policy Journal 29, 31.

[93] Harry Arthurs, 'Labour Law without the State?' [1996] The University of Toronto Law Journal 1, 45; Routh, 'Embedding Work in Nature' (n 92) 45.

[94] Ruth Dukes, *The Labour Constitution. The Enduring Idea of Labour Law* (OUP 2017).

[95] Deakin, 'Labour Law and the "Capitalocene"' (n 46) 290.

While nation-states seem powerless in front of this contemporary 'social question',[96] the language of public and private persists, both in legal discourse and in social life. Its enduring viability and power lie in its manipulability.[97] It can easily be turned inside out precisely because it has no logical content except for veiling the contradictions inherent in current economic and political institutions.[98] If legal rationality is still unable to reflect new forms of democratic self-governance and the full capacity of humans to experience freedom confronting existing patterns of domination,[99] collective action for the commons is, in conclusion, a reasonable utopia to creatively imagine a new model of sustainable coexistence between humans and nature; a model in which the fictitious polarities of the industrial social contract can definitely be deconstructed and traced back to synthesis. This could have important implications for democracy and progress, if it is true that freedom lies not in the option to choose between white and black but in the capability of humans to emancipate themselves from any prescribed choice.

Bibliography

Agrawal A, 'Sustainable Governance of Common-Pool Resources: Context, Methods and Politics' [2003] Annual Review of Anthropology 243

Arthurs H, 'Labour Law without the State?' [1996] The University of Toronto Law Journal 1

Arthurs H, 'Labor Law as the Law of Economic Subordination and Resistance: a Thought Experiment' [2013] Comparative Labor Law & Policy Journal 585

Bailey S and Edgarda Marcucci M, 'Legalizing the Occupation: The Teatro Valle as a Cultural Commons' [2013] The South Atlantic Quarterly 396

Bailey S and Mattei U, 'Social Movements as Constituent Power: The Italian Struggle for the Commons' [2013] Indiana Journal of Global Legal Studies 965

Barca S and Milanez F, 'Labouring the Commons: Amazonia's "Extractive Reserves" and the Legacy of Chico Mendes' in N Räthzel, D Stevis, and D Uzzell (eds), *The Palgrave Handbook of Environmental Labour Studies* (Palgrave Macmillan 2021)

Biagi M, *Cooperative e rapporti di lavoro* (Franco Angeli 1983)

Bueno N, 'From the Right to Work to Freedom from Work. Introduction to the Human Economy' [2017] International Journal of Comparative Labour Law and Industrial Relations 463

Capra F and Mattei U, *The Ecology of Law: Toward a Legal System in Tune with Nature and Community* (Berrett-Koehler Publishers 2015)

[96] Simon Deakin refers to the climate crisis in terms of modern 'social question'. ibid.

[97] Alan Freeman and Elizabeth Mensch, 'The Public-Private Distinction in American Law and Life' [1987] Buffalo Law Review 237, 248.

[98] Capra and Mattei, *The Ecology of Law* (n 24) 151.

[99] Klare, 'The Public/Private Distinction' (n 4) 1358.

Charbonnier P, *Abondance et liberté. Une histoire environnementale des idées politiques* (La Découverte 2021)
Chen K and Tan Chen V (eds), *Organizational Imaginaries: Tempering Capitalism and Tending to Communities through Cooperatives and Collectivist Democracy* (Emerald Publishing Limited 2021)
Davidov G, *A Purposive Approach to Labour Law* (OUP 2016)
Dahl R, *Who Governs? Democracy and Power in an American City* (Yale UP 1961)
Dahl R, *After the Revolution? Authority in the Good Society* (Yale UP 1970) 102
Deakin S, 'The Contribution of Labour Law to Economic and Human Development' in G Davidov and B Langille (eds), *The Idea of Labour Law* (OUP 2011)
Deakin S, 'The Corporation as Commons: Rethinking Property Rights, Governance and Sustainability in the Business Enterprise' [2012] Queen's Law Journal 339
Deakin S, 'The Law of the Anthropocene' in S Besson and S Jubé (eds), *Concerter les civilisations: mélanges en l'honneur d'Alain Supiot* (Seuil 2020)
Deakin S, 'Labour Law and the "Capitalocene": Law, Work and Nature in the Ecological *Long Durée*' [2023] International Journal of Comparative Labour Law and Industrial Relations 281
Dermine E and Dumont D, 'A Renewed Critical Perspective on Social Law: Disentangling Its Ambivalent Relationship with Productivism' [2022] International Journal of Comparative Labour Law and Industrial Relations 237
De Sousa Santos B, *Towards a New Legal Common Sense: Law, Globalization and Modernity* (Sage 1990)
Dukes R, *The Labour Constitution. The Enduring Idea of Labour Law* (OUP 2017)
Durkheim E, *De la division du travail social: étude sur l'organisation des sociétés supérieures* (Félix Alcan 1893)
Ehrlich E, *Fundamental Principles of Sociology of Law* (Routledge 2001)
Federici S, *Re-Enchanting the World: Feminism and the Politics of the Commons* (PM Press 2018)
Flanders A, *Managements and Unions* (Faber and Faber 1970)
Freedland M and Kountouris N, *The Legal Construction of Personal Work Relations* (OUP 2011)
Freeman A and Mensch E, 'The Public-Private Distinction in American Law and Life' [1987] Buffalo Law Review 237
Fox A, *A Sociology of Work in Industry* (Collier-Macmillan 1971)
Fudge J, 'Feminist Reflections on the Scope of Labour Law: Domestic Work, Social Reproduction, and Jurisdiction' [2014] Feminist Legal Studies 1
Galbraith J, *The New Industrial State* (Princeton UP 2007)
Galgóczi B and Pochet P, 'Introduction. Welfare States Confronted by the Challenges of Climate Change: A Short Review of the Issues and Possible Impacts' [2022] Transfer 307
García-López G, 'Commoning Labour, Labouring the Commons: Centring the Commons in Environmental Labour Studies' in Mendes' in N Räthzel, D Stevis, and D Uzzell (eds), *The Palgrave Handbook of Environmental Labour Studies* (Palgrave Macmillan 2021)
Grear A, 'Towards "Climate Justice"? A Critical Reflection on Legal Subjectivity and Climate Injustice: Warning Signals, Patterned Hierarchies, Directions for Future Law and Policy' [2014] Journal of Human Rights and the Environment 103
Grossi P, *An Alternative to Private Property: Collective Property in the Juridical Consciousness of the Nineteenth Century* (University of Chicago Press 1981)
Grossi P, *A History of European Law* (Wiley Blackwell 2010)
Hardin G, 'The Tragedy of the Commons' [1968] Science 1243

Hess C and Ostrom E (eds), *Understanding Knowledge as a Commons: From Theory to Practice* (The MIT Press 2007)
Hirvilammi T and others, 'Social Policy in a Climate Emergency Context: Towards an Ecosocial Research Agenda' [2023] Journal of Social Policy 1
Hyman R, *Industrial Relations: A Marxist Introduction* (Macmillan 1975)
Hyman R and Brough I, *Social Values and Industrial Relations* (Basil Blackwell 1975)
Jackson T, *Prosperity Without Growth: Foundations for the Economy of Tomorrow* (Routledge 2017)
Kahn-Freund O, *Labour and the Law* (3rd edn, Stevens 1983)
Klare K, 'The Public/Private Distinction in Labor Law' [1982] University of Pennsylvania Law Review 1358
Klare K, 'The Labor-Management Cooperation Debate: A Workplace Democracy Perspective' [1988] Harvard Civil Rights-Civil Liberties Law Review 39
Kullmann M and Iossa A, 'Subordination in Solidarity? The Labour Law of Workers' Cooperatives' [2020] Global Workplace Law & Policy
Langille B (ed), *The Capability Approach to Labour Law* (OUP 2019)
Lehavi A, 'Re-romanticizing Commons and Community in Israeli Discourse: Social, Economic, and Political Motives' [2018] Theoretical Inquiries in Law 671
Locke J, *Two Treatises of Government* (Awnsham Churchill 1689)
MacDonald I (ed), *Unions and the City. Negotiating Urban Change* (ILR Press 2017)
Mattei U, 'The Rise and Fall of Law and Economics: An Essay for Judge Guido Calabresi' [2005] Maryland Law Review 220
Mattei U, *The State, the Market, and some Preliminary Question about the Commons* (2011) *IUC Research Commons* (International University College of Turin)
Mattei U and Quarta A, *The Turning Point in Private Law*. Ecology, Technology and the Commons (Edward Elgar 2019)
Meadow D and others, *Limits to Growth. The 30-Year Update* (Earthscan 2005)
Michels R, *Political Parties: A Sociological Study of the Oligarchical Tendencies of Modern Democracy* (Hearts International Library 1915)
Novitz T, 'Locke's Property Rights: Pensions and Trade Unions' [2012] International Union Rights 6
Ostrom E, *Governing the Commons. The Evolution of Institution for Collective Action* (CUP 1990)
Ostrom E, 'Beyond Markets and States: Polycentric Governance of Complex Economic Systems' [2010] American Economic Review 644
Pieraccini M, 'A Politicized, Legal Pluralist Analysis of the Commons' Resilience: The Case of the Regole d'Ampezzo' [2013] Ecology and Society 1
Pieraccini M, 'Taking Stock of Italian Commons: Un-common Grounds?' in T Xu and, A Clarke (eds), *Legal Strategies for the Development and Protection of Communal Property* (OUP 2018)
Rawls J, *A Theory of Justice* (Harvard UP 1999)
Rawls J, *Justice as Fairness: A Restatement* (Harvard UP 2001)
Raworth K, *Doughnut Economics: Seven Ways to Think Like a 21st-Century Economist* (Random House 2017)
Rodotà S, *Il terribile diritto. Studi sulla proprietà privata e i beni comuni* (Il Mulino 2013)
Ross N, 'Organised Labour and Management: the UK' in Edward Maurice Hugh-Jones (ed), *Human Relations and Management* (North-Holland 1958)
Routh S, 'Embedding Work in Nature: The Anthropocene and Legal Imagination of Work as Human Activity' [2018] Comparative Labor Law and Policy Journal 29

Routh S, 'The Need to Become Fashionable' in B Langille (ed), *The Capability Approach to Labour Law* (OUP 2019)

Schnaiberg A, *The Environment: from Surplus to Scarcity* (OUP 1980)

Shamir H, 'The Public/Private Distinction Now: The Challenges of Privatization and of the Regulatory State' [2014] Theoretical Inquiries in Law 1

Stone K, 'Unions and On-demand Work in the United States' in J López (ed), *Collective Bargaining and Collective Action. Labour Agency and Governance in the 21st Century?* (Hart Publishing 2019)

Streeck W, *How Will Capitalism End? Essays on a Failing System* (Verso 2016)

Supiot A, 'The Public–Private Relation in the Context of Today's Refeudalization' [2013] International Journal of Constitutional Law 129

Supiot A, '*Homo faber*: continuità e rotture' in A Honneth, R Sennett, and A Supiot, *Perché lavoro? Narrative e diritti per lavoratrici e lavoratori del XXI secolo* (Fondazione Giangiacomo Feltrinelli 2020)

Wright E, *Envisioning Real Utopias* (Verso 2010)

Wright Mills C, *The Power Elite* (OUP 1956)

Zatz N, 'Working at the Boundaries of Markets: Prison Labor and the Economic Dimension of Employment Relationship' [2008] Vanderbilt Law Review 857

Zbyszewska A, 'Regulating Work with People and "Nature" in Mind: Feminist Reflections' [2018] Comparative Labor Law & Policy Journal 9

9

Labour Law for Care and Wellbeing

Rafael Encinas de Muñagorri

I. Introduction

A. Global Care as a Utopian Programme

Let us imagine it is 2054, and the members of the United Nations (UN) have just adopted the *Globalcare* framework programme. Sceptics and opponents have mocked its name for its evocation of proximity with the global, transnational chains of care workers providing care in Western countries. Yet the same critics had recognized the quality of the participative democratic process before its adoption. *Globalcare* is an ambitious programme, presented by its promoters as a 'turning point in civilisation'. During the debate that preceded the adoption of *Globalcare*, its promoters insisted on—and sometimes dramatized—the current emergency facing the world in the context of decades of challenges (eg global warming, economic depressions, mass migrations, growing inequalities and poverty, and the intensification of modern slavery). The old capitalist economic system based on productivity had to give way to new alternatives. *Globalcare* was conceived as the best political and social solution, driven by the simple idea that our society has to prioritize care and wellbeing over other considerations.

In 2050, governments produced a report in which the *Globalcare* programme was prepared, with contributions from experts, scientists, and ordinary citizens. The report was based on the three guiding principles of Utility, Equity, and Liberty. Let's briefly examine these principles in broad terms. Firstly, care work is the most useful and valuable factor for ensuring social continuity, and caregivers must be protected, recognized, and accorded appropriate status. Secondly, all citizens have equal rights and obligations as care beneficiaries and caregivers. Thirdly, each individual has the freedom to choose whether or not to provide care at different periods in their lives to find a balance between care work and other activities.

Rafael Encinas de Muñagorri, *Labour Law for Care and Wellbeing* In: *Labour Law Utopias*. Edited by: Nicolas Bueno, Beryl ter Haar, and Nuna Zekić, Oxford University Press. © Oxford University Press 2024.
DOI: 10.1093/oso/9780198889755.003.0009

General formulations are always a bit vague, and real-life case studies can help to clarify them. Of the many case studies cited in the Report, one is that of Camille, a man caring for his dying partner. He is exhausted by the effort of trying to hold down a full-time job while providing appropriate care to his partner. He has been unable to find sufficient support to cope with the situation. His employer feels sorry for him but has done nothing to help with Camille's 'personal tragedy'. The public health system and his private medical insurance company have only provided minimal support while following their 'home healthcare autonomy' protocols. The implementation of *Globalcare* will, by contrast, allow Camille to prioritize his care work over his other activities, meaning he could reduce or even interrupt his paid employment without prejudice or loss of income. He will also be able to request the assistance of professional care workers at home or to use appropriate care services for him and his partner. Other case studies in the Report include those of Nancy, a woman who wants to stay at home to care for her children and her elderly parents instead of working in paid employment, and Anita, who gets paid to do domestic work in other households who then comes home and cares for her own family. The *Globalcare* framework programme suggests models for the reform of national labour and welfare laws governed by public and private institutions. Substantially funded and coordinated at different operational levels, *Globalcare* is a worldwide project that has made an end-of-the-century utopia come true.

B. Care, Wellbeing, and New Welfare Economics

However, we are now in 2022, not 2054, and my contribution to this book will examine a puzzling and somewhat obsessive question: why are there so few utopian visions related to care work? It is hard to give an answer, perhaps because the tasks involved in care work are deeply rooted in our day-to-day lives or the challenge of universal care is too daunting.[1] People have to be cared for as a matter of routine, and even if new technologies (eg robots) could sometimes help, the bulk of the work will always have to be done by human beings. Our sense of wellbeing depends on how much care work is available. And it is probably easier to imagine reconstructing a brave new world after an attack by extra-terrestrials than profoundly rethink our daily lives. That said, care work has received plenty of attention from social scientists, leading to many

[1] The Care Collective of Others (eds), *The Care Manifesto: The Politics of Interdependence* (Verso Books 2020).

written contributions,[2] especially from feminist thinkers. As a white European male academic law professor in his fifties, and a relative newcomer to this field, I cannot claim any specific expertise, experience, or legitimacy. Nevertheless, in this chapter, I will try to bring together the research and contributions of others with my hazardous methodology of eclecticism.

Many definitions and conceptions of care have been given from different disciplines and standpoints. One of the most famous is 'everything we do to continue, repair, and maintain ourselves so that we can live in the world as well as possible'.[3] More recently, care work has been defined as 'activities and relations involved in meeting the physical, psychological and emotional needs of adult and children, old and young, frail and able-bodied'.[4] This broad definition includes both paid and unpaid care work. It is in line with the 'conceptually revolutionary definition of work' adopted in 2013 by the 19th International Conference of Labour Statisticians.[5] From a labour law perspective, it could seem curious to include unpaid care work, but the idea of expanding labour law to include unpaid care work is precisely one of the important points at stake.[6]

In this chapter, I will focus on both paid and unpaid care work and its assumed contribution to the wellbeing of society. Care work is frequently associated with larger notions, such as reproductive labour or social reproduction.[7] I will pay special attention to care activities in the home, where the boundaries between direct (face-to-face) and indirect care are often blurred in practice. Domestic and care work have been studied together.[8] The best specialist studies of domestic workers use the terminology with nuances, avoiding implicit hierarchies between 'noble' activities (direct care work) and 'less noble' activities (indirect care work as household work).[9] In this chapter, I will use 'care work' as a general term, giving more precision when necessary.

What branch of economics could be of interest when rethinking the importance of care work in our society? Traditional approaches, which analyse economies through capitalism, markets, and productivity, are not appropriate here.

[2] Raffaella Sarti, 'Historians, Social Scientists, Servants, and Domestic Workers: Fifty Years of Research on Domestic and Care Work' (2014) 59 International Review of Social History 279.

[3] Joan Tronto and Berenice Fisher, 'Toward a Feminist Theory of Caring' in Emily Abel and Margaret Nelson (eds), *Circles of Care* (SUNY Press 1990).

[4] ILO, *Care Work and Care Jobs for the Future of Decent Work* (Report ILO 2018) 6.

[5] ibid 10.

[6] Judy Fudge, 'Feminist Reflections on the Scope of Labour Law: Domestic Work, Social Reproduction, and Jurisdiction' (2014) 22 Feminist Legal Studies 1.

[7] Judy Fudge, 'Labour as a "Fictive Commodity": Radically Reconceptualizing Labour Law' in Guy Davidov and Brian Langille (eds), *The Idea of Labour Law* (OUP 2011) 130.

[8] Sarti, 'Historians, Social Scientists, Servants, and Domestic Workers' (n 2).

[9] Adelle Blackett, *Everyday Transgressions: Domestic Workers' Transnational Challenge to International Labor Law* (Cornell UP 2019) 181, app 1.

Moreover, they have been accused, particularly by feminist political economists, of neglecting, or even ignoring, the importance of care work. Alternative currents of non-conventional economics have flourished in the last two decades. Post-growth theories are one of the more promising of these currents.[10] Not surprisingly, care work is considered a meaningful activity at the core of prosperity.[11] Its future is envisioned both as paid and unpaid, or, more precisely, as a combination of both: 'For a post-growth society strongly characterized by work on and with people, in which formal employment would become less important for all citizens and there would more time for personal initiatives and unpaid care work due to the reduction of working hours, care activities brought together in a hybrid way—a resource system in which formal and informal care work co-operate—could become a distinguishing feature'.[12] Such a prediction would appear fragile without strong institutional support. And in his conclusion, the author recognizes the importance of public infrastructure to make possible the combination of benevolent care with formal social services: 'the state may, must and can—oblige all citizens to contribute to the financing of formal and informal work through social security contributions and taxes'.[13]

Current developments in *new welfare economics* are able to support a fruitful and pragmatic dialogue with the rethinking of labour law from a care work perspective. There are two main reasons for this. The first relates to the definition of welfare economics as 'the part of economics that deals with evaluating the state of the world and formulating recommendations for policies that would improve the wellbeing of society as a whole'.[14] Care work is intrinsically linked to the wellbeing of individuals and society in general. This strong connection suggests that welfare economics could accurately design or influence policies promoting a care-orientated society. The second reason is methodological: new welfare economics has assumed its normative dimension as a moral science and criticizes 'welfarism', the tendency—denounced by Amartya Sen—to reduce welfare economics to merely what can be counted and measured for individuals, ignoring other types of information and other considerations, such as justice, freedom, or rights. Welfare economics is 'first required

[10] Tim Jackson, *Post-Growth: Life After Capitalism* (Polity Press 2021); Lorenzo Fioramonti, *Wellbeing Economy: Success in a World Without Growth* (Macmillan 2017).

[11] Jackson (n 10) chs 4 and 7.

[12] Jonas Hagedorn, 'Formal and Informal Care Work' in Irmi Seidl, Angelika Zahrnt, and Ray Cunningham (eds), *Post-Growth Work: Employment and Meaningful Activities within Planetary Boundaries* (Routledge 2021).

[13] ibid 118.

[14] Roger Backhouse, Antoinette Baujard, and Tamotsu Nishizawa (eds), *Welfare Theory, Public Action, and Ethical Values: Revisiting the History of Welfare Economics* (Cambridge UP 2021).

to define or decide what social welfare depends on, and which values should be considered as legitimate in this process'.[15] This position is epistemologically coherent and allows us to imagine how welfare economics could support both care work-orientated policies at the state level and care work attitudes among individuals.

In the framework of this collective book, this chapter aims to explore and assess the implications of the utopian perspective of promoting care and wellbeing for work and labour law. In this introductory Section I, the three principles mentioned above (Utility, Equity, and Liberty) have been briefly presented in line with the normative values of new welfare economics. In Section II, I will show why care work is economically useful and can no longer be considered unproductive. In Section III, I will explain the importance of gender equity promoted by feminist theories. Finally, in Section IV, I will examine the frequent dilemma of combining the duty to care with the freedom to choose not to do care work.

II. Care Work and Its Utility

Even if it seems obvious today that care work is useful to our society, this was not the case in the traditional economic analysis of capitalism. It is necessary to understand why before we go forward.

A. Care Work as Unproductive in an Analysis of Capitalism

In his famous *An Inquiry into the Nature and Causes of the Wealth of Nations*, Adam Smith established a clear dichotomy between 'productive' and 'unproductive' labour. He compared the labour of a manufacturer producing goods with that of a menial domestic servant caring for his employer. While the manufacturer adds to the value of the raw materials he transforms into goods, 'the menial servant, on the contrary, adds to the value of nothing'.[16] Smith did not deny the value of the work done by the menial servant: 'The labour of the latter [the menial servant], however, has its value, and deserves its reward as well as that of the former [the manufacturer]', but this value has less economic

[15] Antoinette Baujard, 'Values in Welfare Economics' in Conrad Heilmann and Julian Reiss (eds), *The Routledge Handbook of the Philosophy of Economics* (Routledge 2021) 23.

[16] Adam Smith, *An Inquiry into the Nature and Causes of the Wealth of Nations* (first published 1776, Penguin 1999), Book II, ch III.

importance in a capitalist society. The services that the menial servant performs 'perish in the very instant of their performance, and seldom leave any trace of value behind them for which an equal quantity of service could afterwards be produced'. Not being embodied in material goods, this work cannot be stocked, stored, and put into circulation.

Domestic servants are not the only category of 'unproductive' workers for Smith. He includes other occupations: civil servants, lawyers, physicians, men of letters of all kinds, and more frivolous occupations such as 'buffoons', musicians, and actors. The work done by these individuals has a certain value, but 'the work of all of them perishes in the very instant of their production'.[17] For this reason, and even when they receive a wage, these workers are considered 'unproductive' in a capitalist society. Besides domestic servants, Smith did not explicitly refer to care workers, but they obviously fall into the same category as all kinds of care work are 'unproductive' work. But, as John Stuart Mill observes: 'The labour of saving a friend's life is not productive, unless the friend is a productive labourer'.[18]

Karl Marx refined Smith's distinction[19] in two ways. Firstly, he insists on the importance of the distinction *from a capitalist economic standpoint*. Work could be productive and useful *in general* without being considered so from a capitalist point of view. For example, consider peasants producing goods for themselves or selling such goods as self-employed artisans. Their labour is productive and useful in general, but not to the capitalist system, or as Marx states several times: 'Only labour *which is directly transformed into capital is productive*'[20] or, more explicitly: 'From the capitalist standpoint only that labour is productive which creates a surplus-value; and in fact not a surplus-value for itself, but for the owner of conditions of production'.[21] A simple purchase of labour services with money is not enough to make it productive labour because it needs to create a surplus value for the capitalist system.

Secondly, Marx states that 'the designation of labour as *productive labour* has absolutely nothing to do with the determinate content of that labour, its special utility, or the particular use-value in which it manifests itself. *The same* kind of labour may be *productive* or *unproductive*.'[22] In particular, it has nothing to do

[17] ibid.

[18] Nicolas Bueno, 'From Productive Work to Capability-Enhancing Work: Implications for Labour Law and Policy' (2022) 23 Journal of Human Development and Capabilities 354–56.

[19] Ian Gough, 'Marx's Theory of Productive and Unproductive Labour' (December 1972) I/76 New Left Review 47

[20] Karl Marx, *Theories of Surplus Value* (1862 Lawrence & Wishart 1969) 393 <https://archive.org/details/marxtsvpart1/page/392/mode/2up?view=theater> accessed 6 January 2023 (emphasis original).

[21] ibid 153.

[22] ibid 401 (emphasis original).

with producing or transforming material things. Marx compares the example of an actor or a clown employed by a capitalist entrepreneur to whom he returns more labour than he receives in the form of wages ('productive' labour) with that of a jobbing tailor who comes to the capitalist's house to repair his trousers for him ('unproductive' labour). Marx always vigorously denounced the tendency—attributed to Smith and his disciples—of only taking 'productive' work, embodied in materiality, into account.

Care work as a form of reproductive labour fits more easily into Marx's analysis than Smith's. Care work is productive and useful work from a general standpoint that is not merely capitalist, and therefore is legitimate in a non-capitalist society. This is why the Soviet economist SG Strumiling included housework as 'productive' labour in his 1926 writing.[23] For him, 'all social forms of labour that promote the welfare of the whole society are seen as productive'.[24] However, the Soviet Union government in the 1930s, for whom more traditionally 'productive work' was assimilated with labour embodied in material goods, did not uphold this position. This is one of many examples of the gap between the Marxist legacy and Marx's original doctrine.

Marx added a thoughtful statement when he observed that, even in the capitalist system, a job could be considered both 'productive' and 'unproductive', depending on the super-value it generates. Reproductive labour is not an exception. While most of it is still performed outside the realm of a capitalist market economy, another part of it has been progressively organized as a market.[25] At least in Western Europe, a market sector for care and wellbeing services has emerged, partly encouraged by government policies; employers have designed capitalist strategies to offer services adapted to consumers. Our wellbeing is their 'product', and this sector of the economy is based almost entirely on a workforce of employees.

At this point, it is important to recall that the distinction between 'productive' and 'unproductive' labour is an outcome of capitalist economics. Care work is 'unproductive' in the traditional economic sense because it is not a commodity with an exchange value. But it could also be 'productive' if it is commoditized as a paid-for service provided by capitalist entrepreneurs.

[23] Alena Heitlinger, *Women and State Socialism* (Palgrave Macmillan 1979) 25.
[24] ibid.
[25] Clémence Ledoux, Karen Shire, and Franca van Hooren, *The Dynamics of Welfare Markets: Private Pensions and Domestic-Care Services in Europe* (Palgrave Macmillan 2021).

B. Care Work as Crucial for any Economic System

Even though it is considered 'unproductive' and/or 'unpaid', nobody would deny that care work is necessary, even indispensable, for capitalist economies. The idea that capitalism could not sustain itself without care work is a commonly held view. Reproductive labour is essential for maintaining the strength of the workforce and, in the long term, for producing new generations of workers to perpetuate the productive workforce.

The value of reproductive labour can also be assessed from another perspective. An anthropological study based on empirical research has demonstrated that 'contrary to many characterizations of reproductive labour, reproductive and productive labour add value to one another and, in the process, serve as sources of happiness, dignity, and social legitimacy to women and men working in jobs that many consider onerous, dirty, smelly, undignified, and poorly remunerated'.[26] Yet, even if clearly articulated, the value of productive and reproductive activities is not equally important for individuals. Reproductive labour is a source of happiness and satisfaction when performed in informal settings, such as family homes, but is less valued when performed for others in the formal economy.

This dichotomy highlights what is considered 'useful' and for whom. 'Utility' has no meaning in itself, disconnected from the points of view of individuals, entrepreneurs, or governments. What is 'useful' for some could be considered useless, futile, or even harmful for others. The utilitarian concept inherited from Bentham, which continues to influence many economic analyses, is too narrow to grasp the complexity of the wellbeing of individuals taken as such or collectively. New welfare economics has criticized the flaw of considering only individual preferences to evaluate social wellbeing. The weakness of utilitarianism is its focus on individual preferences. The challenge of new welfare economics is based on axioms derived from theories of justice, such as that proposed by Amartya Sen, that give analytical tools to objectively compare one situation to another to decide which is better for society. What could be seen as more productive *or* just in the economy? This question points towards different values and political choices. That is why feminist thinkers about care work, for example, have pointed out the lack of equity between men and women.

[26] David Griffith, Kerry Preibisch, and Ricardo Contreras, 'The Value of Reproductive Labor' (2018) 120 American Anthropologist 224.

III. Care Work and Gender Equity

Who are the carers contributing to the wellbeing of others? Intuitively, we think of a nurse looking after patients or a mother caring for her children, partner, or elderly relatives rather than a soldier fighting to defend his compatriots against their enemies. Of course, this representation is traditional, but it corresponds to a long-established reality: the people performing care work are predominantly women. The productive and reproductive labour dichotomy was not conceptually institutionalized in feudal societies and only became more pronounced during the transition to industrial capitalism.[27] In a gendered complementarity, men and women have been cast respectively as paid professional workers (male breadwinners) and unpaid non-professional housekeepers (female caregivers). But, as has been widely demonstrated, this division is unfair and creates barriers to transforming modern societies.

Women suffer from gender inequalities *both* in their professional lives and their family lives (by taking care of others). The professional and familial spheres are separate in our current institutions, but they interact in our daily lives. And it is barely possible to be fully engaged in one sphere without detrimental consequences for the other. The best professional careers are not fully compatible with family obligations (and vice versa). How can we solve what could be called 'the unpaid care/work conflict'?[28] Is it possible to reconcile unpaid care work with paid work? Among feminist scholars, this question has received different answers depending on welfare traditions: some national policies are more gender-orientated than others.[29] Yet this problem is also theoretical and grounded in a plurality of feminist approaches: some stress the specificity of women (*differentialist*), while others insist on equality with men (*universalist*).

The challenge is deeply cultural: 'in many cultures, being female is associated with care for others'.[30] And this representation of women's 'natural altruism' explains why economists have considered care work a free-of-charge contribution, separate from the market economy. Even economic theories of justice focus more, in their examples, on resources, opportunities, and allocations than on burdens. However, the burden of taking care of others is inescapable. How

[27] Joanne Conaghan, 'Gender and the Labour of Law' in Hugh Collins, Gillian Lester, and Virginia Mantouvalou (eds), *Philosophical Foundations of Labour Law* (OUP 2018).

[28] Nicole Busby, *A Right to Care? Unpaid Care Work in European Employment Law* (OUP 2011) ch 1.

[29] Jane Lewis, 'Gender and the Development of Welfare Regimes' (1992) 2(3) Journal of European Social Policy 159.

[30] MV Lee Badgett and Nancy Folbre, 'Assigning Care: Gender Norms and Economic Outcomes' (1999) 38(3) International Labour Review 311.

can men and women share care responsibilities? This major issue is not new and has many dimensions: 'social norms that closely link being female to care of others have significant economic consequences that contribute to gender inequality within both the household and the labour market'.[31] It also has political and legal dimensions that feminists and legal scholars have examined.

A. Feminist Movements Demanding Equity and Pay for Care

The first wave of the feminist movement was particularly active in France and has been called 'maternal feminism' by historians.[32] Feminist women claimed pay for stay-at-home mothers, initially just for poor mothers and then for all mothers. They campaigned for a kind of citizenship and welfare state that recognizes their contributions to society as mothers. The International Congress for the Rights of Women held in 1892 was the first explicitly feminist call for 'social protection for all mothers'. Hubertine Auclert proposed state maternity benefits, funded by a new tax on fathers to reward women for their 'indispensable services to the state'. Käthe Schirmacher, in France and then in Germany, criticized economists for ignoring the work done by women. She argued that domestic work performed by women was 'real work' and 'work creating value', adding, 'there is no work more productive than that done by mothers'. Therefore, this work deserved pay. Why should women have to do house and care work for free, when they knew that other domestic workers got paid to do it? Moreover, Schirmacher argued that housework performed in the home by women is the '*sine qua non* condition' of the paid work performed outside the home by men and that 'employers and men's work is dependent on women'. Society should recognize domestic work's political and economic value by paying for it. In the same period, other feminists made similar arguments, for example, Léonie Rouzade on the 'social function' of maternity; Marguerite Durand on the necessity of remunerating housework and establishing a social insurance maternity fund; and Nelly Roussel on a 'fair wage for the noble maternal work', threatening a 'womb strike' to get it. Similar ideas and propositions bloomed in other Western countries at the beginning of the twentieth century. It is important to remember these claims, not only because they are at

[31] ibid 323.

[32] Gisela Bock and Pat Thane (eds), *Maternity and Gender Policies: Women and the Rise of the European Welfare States, 1880s–1950s* (Routledge 1991); Gisela Bock, 'Pauvreté féminine, droits des mères et Etats-Providence' in Georges Duby and Michelle Perrot (eds), *Histoire des Femmes en Occident* (Tempus 2002).

the origin of the feminist movement but also because they could be forgotten or undermined by what later became the dominant idea identified with social progress for women: gaining access to the labour market on an equal footing with men.

A century after the beginning of the feminist movement, it is clear that women have gained emancipation by working outside the home in the same way as men. However, care and reproductive work must still be done, whether it be by paid domestic workers, by other members of the household, by the working women themselves, or shared with their male partners. The idea of sharing this work became a permanent source of frustration and tension, particularly in the seventies, in the context of rapid changes in values and family structures in Western countries.

Strategic questions have been raised in controversial ways, such as: 'How can we attack the unequal sharing of unpaid domestic work?'[33] a paper in which the sociologist and feminist Christine Delphy analyses the exploitation of unpaid domestic work performed by women for the benefit of men. She generally takes a critical approach to the patriarchal mode of production based on the exploitation of the female workforce. Her objective is abolitionist: nobody should work for others for free. Domestic work does not so much benefit capitalism as it benefits men as a dominant group. She denounces welfare state regimes that support such inequalities between women and men and suggests ways to eradicate or at least reduce this injustice in our society. Her main proposal is to withdraw the fiscal and social advantages men could have by exploiting their female domestic partners. She argues that it should become normal for men to pay wages to their female partners who stay at home and also that society should give such women all the rights and social protections associated with paid work (eg sick pay, paid holidays, and retirement pension). That would mean that the women who work at home and contribute to the wellbeing of others would become paid domestic workers protected by labour law and social security law.

Nancy Fraser, the famous feminist thinker, tackled the problem in an article[34] reproduced as a book chapter[35] with the evocative title: 'After the Family Wage. A Post-industrial Thought Experiment'. It is probably one of the most

[33] Christine Delphy, 'Par où attaquer le "partage inégal" du "travail ménager"?' (2003) 22(3) Nouvelles Questions Féministes 47; Christine Delphy, *Close to Home: A Materialist Analysis of Women's Oppression* (Verso 2016).

[34] Nancy Fraser, 'After The Family Wage: Gender Equity and the Welfare State' (1994) 22(4) Political Theory 591.

[35] Ngaire Naffine (ed), *Gender and Justice* (Routledge 2002).

well-known attempts to assess utopian conceptions of gender equity in social welfare. One of its crucial elements is care work and how it could ideally be assigned to institutions such as the family, the market, civil society, or the state. Fraser contrasts and compares two models of social welfare for gender equity: the 'Universal Breadwinner' model and the 'Caregiver Parity' model. In the Universal Breadwinner model, 'the bulk of such work would be shifted from the family to the market and the state, where it would be performed by employees for pay. Who, then, are these employees likely to be? In many countries today, including the United States, paid institutional care work is poorly remunerated, feminized, and largely racialized and/or performed by immigrants'.[36] Giving weight to the Universal Breadwinner model for all women would require us to 'upgrade the status and pay attached to care work employment, making it, too, into primary-labor-force work'.[37] In the Caregiver Parity model, which is more in line with European social democratic policies, the aim is to 'promote gender equity principally by supporting informal care work. The point is to enable women with significant domestic responsibilities to support themselves and their families either through care work alone or through care work plus part-time employment.'[38] With the support of public funds, 'care work would be counted on a par with years of employment' with the rights and protections associated with employment, such as unemployment benefits and pensions. For Fraser, both models are utopian, but neither is utopian enough. Therefore, she proposes a third model, the Universal Caregiver model, 'to *induce men to become more like most women are now*, namely, people who do primary care work'.[39] In this model, 'all jobs would be designed for workers who are caregivers too.... Some informal care work would be publicly supported and integrated on a par with paid work in a single social-insurance system. Some would be performed in households by relatives and friends, but such households would not necessarily be heterosexual nuclear families. Other supported care work would be located outside households altogether—in civil society.'[40] This reference to civil society and self-managed care work activities 'would overcome the "workerism" of Universal Breadwinner and the domestic privatism of Caregiver Parity'.[41] The aim is to discourage freeriders: 'men of all

[36] ibid 52.
[37] ibid 52.
[38] ibid 55.
[39] ibid 60 (emphasis original).
[40] ibid 61.
[41] ibid 62.

classes who shirk care work and domestic labor, as well as corporations who free-ride on the labor of working people, both underpaid and unpaid'.

Such feminist ideas must be taken seriously and have made stimulating contributions to rethinking the social status of caregivers who contribute to the wellbeing of others. Feminist utopias have strong implications for the meaning of 'work' in our societies and the definition of who should be identified as workers.

B. Feminist Legal Thinkers' Proposed Enlarged Scope of Labour Law

Feminist legal thinkers have suggested enlarging the scope of labour law to include home-based care and domestic work.[42] The main problem with this proposal has been, and still is, how to account for the so-called *invisible* work, performed mostly by women, in homes. This ongoing challenge can be considered at different levels, and it deserves a general overview, from a historical and cultural perspective.[43]

As Judy Fudge notes: 'traditional accounts of work and labour law have ignored all the unpaid domestic work, overwhelmingly performed by women'.[44] Joanne Conaghan observes similarly that: 'feminist exhortations to expand the reach of labour law to encompass unpaid domestic labour are generally met with polite bewilderment'.[45] They both advocate change to this situation by reconceptualizing labour law in a broader sense. Scholarly feminists want to 'extend the boundaries of the field beyond paid work to unpaid care and domestic labour' and to 'revitalize our thinking about law for a post-industrial and globalized world'.[46] These ambitious changes would not only recognize unpaid, non-professional care and domestic tasks as work but would, more precisely, make such work covered by labour law. There are two main objectives for such a change.

First, it aims to achieve *equality between women and men in society*. The traditional gendered division of labour (male breadwinner and female caregiver) is unequal and must be changed.[47] The structural and legal separation of labour

[42] Fudge, 'Labour as a "Fictive Commodity"' (n 7); Fudge, 'Feminist Reflections on the Scope of Labour Law' (n 6); Conaghan, 'Gender and the Labour of Law' (n 27).

[43] Raffaella Sarti, Anna Bellavitis, and Manuela Martini, *What Is Work?: Gender at the Crossroads of Home, Family, and Business from the Early Modern Era to the Present* (Berghahn Books 2018).

[44] Fudge, 'Labour as a "Fictive Commodity"' (n 7).

[45] Conaghan, 'Gender and the Labour of Law' (n 27) 271.

[46] Fudge, 'Feminist Reflections on the Scope of Labour Law' (n 6) 2.

[47] Fudge, 'Labour as a "Fictive Commodity"' (n 7) 131.

and family domains perpetuates that division. 'In societies that value paid employment as the primary path to "citizenship", treating unpaid care work, predominantly performed by women, as a matter of family law, and not labour law, reinforces the idea that such work is not only a woman's natural role, but also that in the social hierarchy it is of lower value than paid employment.'[48] To avoid this tendency, the proposal is to consider all kinds of work under the same labour law umbrella. That would confer the same symbolic status on care and domestic work as on other work. 'There is no *a priori* conceptual reason why such work should fall outside the boundaries of labour law.'[49]

The second objective is for labour law to cover *unpaid and paid work*. Proposing that 'unpaid care work be located within the personal scope of labour law is designed to provide a critical perspective on the process of legal characterization and the concept of legal jurisdiction'.[50] This ambition goes beyond feminism: 'it is a recurrent misapprehension of labour-law scholars to assume that the feminist focus on unpaid work is animated solely by egalitarian or justice-seeking aspirations. In fact, the feminist foregrounding of empirical work is equally driven by concerns to value the utility of the analytical and conceptual frames through which labour is commonly apprehended.'[51]

Yet, the idea of enlarging the scope of labour law has to confront serious obstacles. It threatens the identity of labour law in its usual conception. That is why those who propose it devote time to studying the ideas of potential allies. For example, Judy Fudge examines Mark Freeland and Nicola Kontouris's conception of 'personal work relations' and their efforts to move on from traditional labour law categories based on formal paid contracts to include categories of workers such as volunteers and trainees. However, Fudge reproaches them for not being fully coherent with their criteria: care and domestic work for the benefit of the household is not on their list, even if 'care work performed by a member of a household for a dependent is both relational and personal'.[52] Fudge considers that Freeland and Kontouris retain a conventional understanding of labour law.

Is there any conceptual opening for unpaid care work to become covered by labour law? Pessimistic opinions about 'work law' as a large domain of regulations encompassing many forms of market and non-market work have been

48 ibid 136.
49 ibid 132.
50 Fudge, 'Feminist Reflections on the Scope of Labour Law' (n 6) 3.
51 Conaghan, 'Gender and the Labour of Law' (n 27) 272.
52 Fudge, 'Feminist Reflections on the Scope of Labour Law' (n 6) 16.

expressed.[53] Domestic housework and care work within families provides the 'principal example' of non-market work, which differs from employment, as it obviously lacks an 'employer' and a clear 'exchange dimension'.[54] Women working in their homes have no contract, salary, or professional activity, even as independent workers. But these elements of the classical definition of labour law are also flexible and are precisely what is at stake. Currently, or at least in Europe, the general trend is to expand the scope of labour law in two main directions: one to broaden the definition of employee and the other to extend the protection of labour law to non-employees.[55] Each of these has been legally explored for caregivers contributing to the wellbeing of others.[56]

What should the boundaries of labour law, as an academic domain and as a set of conceptually forged and constructed categories and institutions, be? Who should be considered a worker and why? These questions are not new, but interest in them has been renewed by the ongoing dynamic of paid and unpaid care work. The scope of labour law is pragmatically and epistemically flexible. Another perspective is needed. 'A new imagining would require us to go beyond analogizing household and familial relationships to employment and would put a greater emphasis on public provision and social responsibilities.' For that reason, Fudge supports basic income strategies over wages-for-housework policies.[57] Her opinion is fully coherent. Enlarging the scope of labour law to include unpaid domestic workers and carers seems possible. It would bring us back to the original, broad concept of labour law as proposed by its founders, such as Sinzheimer, who encapsulates social welfare within it.[58] Perhaps more radically, labour law could nowadays be conceived as an addition to a new welfare paradigm, and not the other way around.

Bringing together the forces of the feminist movement and critical thinking is welcome. There is a long road ahead for solving the gender equity problem in care work. In a utopian future, it would not be necessary to distinguish care work and reproductive labour from productive labour because they would be

[53] Noah Zatz, 'The Impossibility of Work Law' in Guy Davidov and Brian Langille (eds), *The Idea of Labour Law* (OUP 2011).

[54] ibid 235.

[55] Adalberto Perulli, 'The Legal and Jurisprudential Evolution of the Notion of Employee' (2020) 11(2) European Labour Law Journal 117.

[56] See eg the French Law of 28 December of 2015 concerning the adaptation of an ageing society and the status of '*proche aidant*' (close helper/carer of a dependant elder in the household). Under certain conditions, he could become the employee of the dependent person. Even without this qualification, a system of respite leave has been implemented to allow caregivers to rest to avoid the risk of exhaustion caused by taking care of a dependent person.

[57] Fudge, 'Labour as a "Fictive Commodity"' (n 7) 136 n 96.

[58] Ruth Dukes, *The Labour Constitution: The Enduring Idea of Labour Law* (OUP 2014) 15. The founders of the discipline had such a broad conception in mind yet restricted it to dependent labour.

shared by men and women and considered equal in value and dignity. An integrated welfare and labour law system could better achieve this aim than separate systems.

IV. Care Work as Freely Chosen

Giving care to others is time-consuming and could be considered real work. However, in societies dominated by traditional conceptions of employment, it is difficult to imagine a framework that would include unpaid and paid work under the same umbrella. This situation creates a sort of paradox: care work is only considered work when it is paid. This institutionalized prevalence is not justified. A new, utopian perspective considers care work as real work, whether paid or unpaid.

That said, it is important to consider fundamental questions: is care work an obligation? How is it related to the right to work or the freedom not to work? Declarations of human rights have stressed the right to work as both a positive and a negative obligation.[59] Positively, the right to work has been considered the right to access a (paid) job and, in a broader perspective, the right to a free choice of employment and the right to develop at work. Negatively, it refers to the prohibition of forced or compulsory labour. This sheds light on a consequence that is not always socially recognized: prohibiting forced or compulsory labour implies, logically, the freedom *not* to work.[60] Moreover, in a human economy, this end is desirable: freedom from work could be considered a new motivating force that promotes human potential and creativity.[61]

Amartya Sen's theory of justice has also stressed the positive meaning of liberty rather than the negative one. The capability approach has been examined widely, even in the field of labour law.[62] But care work is not only a question of individual choice: it is also a burden, a moral and social responsibility that is unavoidable at the collective level. Care work is required for a society to survive and for the wellbeing of its members. Therefore, institutions have to promote care work, both paid and unpaid.

[59] See Chapter 11 by De Becker and Claus in this book.

[60] Rafael Encinas de Muñagorri, 'Existe-t-il une liberté de ne pas travailler?' (2020) Droit social 416.

[61] Nicolas Bueno, 'From the Right to Work to Freedom from Work. Introduction to the Human Economy' (2017) 33(4) International Journal of Comparative Law and Industrial Relations 463.

[62] Brian Langille, *The Capability Approach to Labour Law* (OUP 2019); Bueno, 'From Productive Work' (n 18) 362–65, introduces the dichotomy between capability-enhancing and capability-reducing work; care work, paid or unpaid, being part of the former.

Applying the freedom from work to care leads to an uncomfortable conclusion: everyone has the option between whether or not to take care of others. Although this is coherent in an individualistic concept of freedom, it is understandable that it is economically and socially better for society to encourage individuals to care for others.

This problem is not abstract and can become prominent when individuals are workers for an employer, on top of being carers for their relatives. Many Western countries have adopted policies that reconcile paid employment and unpaid care.[63] 'Rather than resulting from a new political awareness of the needs of workers-carers, such recent additions to the law and policy mix are part of the slow, incremental movement towards targeted state support for the management of unpaid care and paid employment within a social welfare framework.'[64] Welfare is the appropriate framework for rethinking the status of carers who contribute to the wellbeing of others because of its ability to grasp the professional and non-professional aspects of our lives simultaneously. But how is it possible to reconcile unpaid care work with paid employment?

Supiot's report deserves special attention here. One of its main proposals is to go *beyond employment* and accommodate a greater diversity of work. The report proposed the delineation of a *professional status* that encompasses all the forms of work that individuals could perform in their lifetimes, from initial training to retirement, including employed or self-employed work in the market, work to acquire or improve knowledge, work for the benefit of others in the public sphere, voluntary work, and 'even work performed in the domestic sphere'.[65] Basically, each individual should be able to use their freedom to choose between different kinds of work activities, considered socially valuable at different stages of their lives. This proposal implies creating a new welfare system in which domestic and care work could be integrated into other work activities. However, although this would be an improvement, unpaid care work will remain at the margin, eclipsed by paid employment. More ideally, the status of caregivers who contribute to the wellbeing of others would be detached from the classical representation of work as paid employment.

It would be a paradigm shift to transfer this problem away from employment (or even *beyond* employment) to the realm of social welfare. Pascale Vielle has taken such direction, and she raises interesting questions: what kind of needs

[63] Example from the European Union (EU): Directive (EU) 2019/1158 of 20 June 2019 on work-life balance for parents and carers.

[64] Busby, *A Right to Care?* (n 28) 1.

[65] Alain Supiot, *Au-delà de l'emploi: les voies d'une vraie réforme du droit du travail* (2nd edn, Flammarion 2016) xxvii.

do individuals freed from benefits related to care activities have? What types of actions and solidarity are required to satisfy such needs? Various techniques, including integrating paid employment with unpaid care work, have been used in some state social security systems to protect individuals who care for others in their households (eg children, elderly relatives, and partners). Vielle's comparative study reviewed the different legal criteria that give access to state benefits, but neither those derived from paid employment nor their extension to care work seemed appropriate.[66] Therefore, social security systems should account for a new risk of conflict for individual paid employees with obligations to care for others. Yet Vielle's proposed system is still based on the idea that individuals have paid jobs alongside their unpaid care work, it does not claim to include all the individuals who are not in paid employment and is limited to fixed time periods, for example when children are in full-time education. The typical individual in the proposed system works both outside and inside the home. Nevertheless, it opens the door to reconsidering the status of unpaid carers who contribute to the wellbeing of others, for example, in 'parental activities'.[67]

To go further would abolish the advantage of paid work for an employer over unpaid care work for the wellbeing of others. Because a utopian society is not necessarily based on the obligation to care for others, it should make it possible, when desired or required, to find care workers instead of having to provide the care oneself. But who would these workers be, and who would set their conditions of work?

Domestic workers are here a specific example. Despite there being large obstacles to overcome (eg risk of modern slavery, exploitation of immigrants in global care chains, difficulty of effective collective action, and additional public health precautions required during pandemics), a realignment of the status of domestic and care workers seems to be taking place at the moment. The most normative improvement at the international level was the adoption of ILO Convention 189 in 2011. All domestic workers—representing approximately 8 per cent of all working women—should be treated the same as paid employees, even if, in reality, many of them are currently undeclared or unofficial. Moreover, ensuring the decent treatment of care workers is essential.[68]

[66] Pascale Vielle, *La sécurité sociale et le coût indirect des responsabilités familiales: une approche de genre* (Bruylant 2001) 126–29.

[67] ibid 408.

[68] ILO, *Securing Decent Work for Nursing Personnel and Domestic Workers: Key Actors in the Care Economy* (Reports of the CEACR, ILC 110th Session ILO 2022).

Ideally, 'nobody should be reduced to an inferior status because they fulfil obligations to care for others',[69] so improving the status of individuals who contribute to the wellbeing of others is a desirable objective. Yet, the status of paid care workers is currently low, and not only in Western societies. Market forces control the care work sector almost everywhere and have created a dynamic that has commodified care work, as illustrated by the emergence of big, for-profit firms that have structured and formalized the market for care work or by the generalization of poor working conditions and terms of employment in the care work sector. More generally, there is 'a theoretical continuation of the care economy between unpaid care and care that has been marketized'.[70]

But the emancipation of paid and unpaid care workers is still an objective that could one day be envisioned in a utopian *Globalcare* framework programme. Of utility to any economic system, care work is particularly desirable in a post-growth society that aims to sustain and develop wellbeing among its members. Care work should no longer be assigned solely to women or abandoned to the goodwill of benevolent individuals. It should be distributed equally to men and women by the policies supporting social welfare and labour law systems.

Bibliography

Addati L and others, *Care Work and Care Jobs for the Future of Decent Work* (ILO 2018)

Backhouse R, Baujard A, and Nishizawa T (eds), *Welfare Theory, Public Action, and Ethical Values: Revisiting the History of Welfare Economics* (Cambridge UP 2021)

Badgett M and Folbre N, 'Assigning Care: Gender Norms and Economic Outcomes' (1999) 138(3) International Labour Review 311

Baujard A, 'Values in Welfare Economics"' in C Heilmann and J Reiss (eds), *The Routledge Handbook of the Philosophy of Economics* (Routledge 2021)

Blackett A, 'Emancipation in the Idea of Labour Law' in G Davidov and B Langille (eds), *The Idea of Labour Law* (OUP 2011)

Blackett A, *Everyday Transgressions: Domestic Workers' Transnational Challenge to International Labor Law* (Cornell UP 2019)

Bock G, 'Pauvreté féminine, droits des mères et États-Providence' in G Duby and M Perrot (eds), *Histoire des Femmes en Occident* (Tempus 2002)

Bock G and Thane P (eds), *Maternity and Gender Policies: Women and the Rise of the European Welfare States, 1880s–1950s* (Routledge 1991)

[69] Fudge, 'Labour as a "Fictive Commodity"' (n 7) 135, quoting Elizabeth Anderson's idea of equality.

[70] Adelle Blackett, 'Emancipation in the Idea of Labour Law' in Guy Davidov and Brian Langille (eds), *The Idea of Labour Law* (OUP 2011) 429–30.

Bueno N, 'From the Right to Work to Freedom from Work. Introduction to the Human Economy (2017) 33(4) International Journal of Comparative Law and Industrial Relations 463

Bueno N, 'From Productive Work to Capability-Enhancing Work: Implications for Labour Law and Policy' (2022) 23 Journal of Human Development and Capabilities 354

Busby N, *A Right to Care? Unpaid Care Work in European Employment Law* (OUP 2011)

Conaghan J, 'Gender and the Labour of Law' in H Collins, G Lester, and V Mantouvalou (eds), *Philosophical Foundations of Labour Law* (OUP 2018)

Delphy C, 'Par où attaquer le "partage inégal" du "travail ménager"?' (2003) 22(3) Nouvelles Questions Féministes 47

Delphy C, *Close to Home: A Materialist Analysis of Women's Oppression* (Verso 2016)

Dukes R, *The Labour Constitution: The Enduring Idea of Labour Law* (OUP 2014)

Encinas de Muñagorri R, 'Existe-t-il une liberté de ne pas travailler?' (2020) 5 Droit social 416

Fioramonti L, *Wellbeing Economy: Success in a World Without Growth* (Macmillan 2017)

Fraser N, 'After The Family Wage: Gender Equity and the Welfare State' (1994) 22(4) Political Theory 591

Fudge J, 'Labour as a "Fictive Commodity": Radically Reconceptualizing Labour Law' in G Davidov and B Langille (eds), *The Idea of Labour Law* (OUP 2011)

Fudge J, 'Feminist Reflections on the Scope of Labour Law: Domestic Work, Social Reproduction, and Jurisdiction' (2014) 22 Feminist Legal Studies 1

Gough I, 'Marx's Theory of Productive and Unproductive Labour' (1972) I(76) New Left Review 47

Griffith D, Preibisch K, and Contreras R, 'The Value of Reproductive Labor' (2018) 120(2) American Anthropologist 224

Hagedorn J, 'Formal and Informal Care Work' in I Seidl, A Zahrnt, and R Cunningham (eds), *Post-Growth Work: Employment and Meaningful Activities within Planetary Boundaries* (Routledge 2021)

Heitlinger A, *Women and State Socialism* (Palgrave Macmillan 1979)

ILO, *Securing Decent Work for Nursing Personnel and Domestic Workers: Key Actors in the Care Economy* (Reports of the CEACR, ILC 110th Session ILO 2022)

Jackson T, *Post-Growth: Life After Capitalism* (Polity Press 2021)

Langille B, *The Capability Approach to Labour Law* (OUP 2019)

Ledoux C, Shire K, and van Hooren F, *The Dynamics of Welfare Markets: Private Pensions and Domestic-Care Services in Europe* (Palgrave Macmillan 2021)

Lewis J, 'Gender and the Development of Welfare Regimes' (1992) 2(3) Journal of European Social Policy 159

Marx K, T*heories of Surplus Value* ([1862] Lawrence & Wishart 1969) <https://archive.org/details/marxtsvpart1/page/392/mode/2up?view=theater>

Naffine N (ed), *Gender and Justice* (Routledge 2002)

Perulli A, 'The Legal and Jurisprudential Evolution of the Notion of Employee' (2020) 11(2) European Labour Law Journal 117

Sarti R, 'Historians, Social Scientists, Servants, and Domestic Workers: Fifty Years of Research on Domestic and Care Work' (2014) 59 International Review of Social History 279

Sarti R, Bellavitis A, and Martini M, *What Is Work?: Gender at the Crossroads of Home, Family and Business from the Early Modern Era to the Present* (Berghahn Books 2018)

Smith A, *An Inquiry into the Nature and Causes of the Wealth of Nations* (first published 1776, Penguin 1999)

Supiot A, *Au-delà de l'emploi: les voies d'une vraie réforme du droit du travail* (2nd edn, Flammarion 2016)

The Care Collective of Others (ed), *The Care Manifesto: The Politics of Independence* (Verso Books 2020)

Tronto J and Fisher B, 'Toward a Feminist Theory of Caring' in E Abel and M Nelson (eds), *Circles of Care* (SUNY Press 1990)

Vielle P, *La sécurité sociale et le coût indirect des responsabilités familiales: une approche de genre* (Bruylant 2001)

Zatz N, 'The Impossibility of Work Law' in G Davidov and B Langille (eds), *The Idea of Labour Law* (OUP 2011)

10

Channelling Technologies to Benefit Employees via Labour Law

Einat Albin

I. Introduction

Since childhood, I have loved watching the *Star Wars* movies. The films portray a futuristic vision of robots (called 'droids') and other life forms, often anthropomorphic in appearance, supporting humans to protect and promote moral values of the good. On many levels, *Star Wars* represents the utopian vision of cooperation between humans and technologies for the greater good—a vision that seems quite removed from our current realities. Nevertheless, it might be that this vision is not, in fact, that far from what characterizes our labour markets—or, more importantly, is not that far from what *should* characterize them.

In contemporary labour markets, technologies cooperate with workers in their daily work. However, the law does not see them as protecting and promoting the moral values of the workers but rather as endorsing the interests of the employers. While values such as wellbeing (including parental rights and leisure time), health, equality, and other social and welfare ideals are central goals of labour law,[1] technologies are not seen as parties to these values but are rather developed, designed, and deployed towards workplace growth, efficiency, and productivity. I will claim in this chapter that this is due in part to the paradigm adopted by labour law towards technologies, which is, in fact, pro-capitalist. The existing paradigm sees technologies as commodities of the employer and subject to their almost unlimited prerogative, with their main purpose being to further its growth. Studies in the field of labour law show that technologies enhance managerial prerogative and the employer's authoritative power[2] and that labour law authorizes employers to insert any technology they

[1] Guy Davidov, *A Purposive Approach to Labour Law* (OUP 2017).

[2] Valerio De Stefano, 'Negotiating the Algorithm: Automation, Artificial Intelligence and Labour Protection' (2018) International Labour Office, Working Paper 246; Jeremias Adams-Prassl, 'What

Einat Albin, *Channelling Technologies to Benefit Employees via Labour Law* In: *Labour Law Utopias*. Edited by: Nicolas Bueno, Beryl ter Haar, and Nuna Zekić, Oxford University Press.
DOI: 10.1093/oso/9780198889755.003.0010

see fit into the workplace, including those based on the collection of employees' personal data.[3] They also exhibit how the use of technologies can contribute to infringing basic labour rights, such as the right to privacy, equality, unionization, and so on.[4] Under the existing legal paradigm, technologies have become the new venue through which capitalist goals are promoted and enhanced. Workers' rights, and their social and welfare interests, are ancillary to the main goals of capitalism.

But technologies are market-driven, and what shapes these markets are, among other things, laws. Hence, what if labour law were to adopt a different logic? What would labour law look like if it embraced a post-work perspective towards technologies while shifting its pro-capitalist bias to one that tilts towards humanity, wellbeing, and other social and welfare values? Technologies can be useful in pursuing these aims, and labour laws can easily frame their role and function through this lens. This chapter sets out a challenge to the pro-capitalist paradigm of labour law concerning the use of technologies in the workplace, proposing an alternative post-work utopia. It argues that if seen through a post-work perspective, workplace technologies should be viewed primarily as 'accommodations' to workers rather than as the employer's commodity or as 'algorithmic bosses'.[5] If viewed as 'accommodations', technological development, design, and use would be based on functions needed to protect and promote the social and welfare values of the workforce. This perspective, I argue, will ultimately positively impact labour relations and workers' rights—and will also be profitable for employers.

Post-work theories invite us to re-think the supremacy of formal employment, offering a broad understanding of work and scaling back the emphasis placed on human work as a tradable good.[6] These theories, elaborated in

if Your Boss Was an Algorithm? Economic Incentives, Legal Challenges, and the Rise of Artificial Intelligence at Work' (2019) 41(1) Comparative Labor Law and Policy Journal 123.

[3] Brishen Rogers, 'The Law & Political Economy of Workplace Technological Change' (2020) 55 Harvard Civil Rights- Civil Liberties Law 531.

[4] Matthew Bodie, 'The Law and Politics of People Analytics' (2017) 88(4) Colorado Law Review 961; Allan King and Marko Mrkonich, '"Big Data" and the Risk of Employment Discrimination' (2016) 68 Oklahoma Law Review 555; Arianne Renan-Barzilai, 'Platform Inequality: Gender in the Gig-Economy' (2017) 47 Seton Hall Law Review 393; Antonio Aloisi and Elena Gramano, 'Artificial Intelligence Is Watching You at Work: Digital Surveillance, Employee Monitoring, and Regulatory Issues in the EU Context' (2019) 41 Comparative Labor Law & Policy Journal 95; Tammy Katsabian, 'Employees' Privacy in the Internet Age' (2019) 40(2) Berkley Journal of Employment and Labour Law 203; Tammy Katsabian, 'The Telework Virus: How COVID-19 Has Affected Telework and Exposed Its Implications for Privacy' (2023) 44 Berkeley Journal of Employment and Labor Law 141.

[5] On algorithmic bosses, see Adams-Prassl, 'What if your Boss' (n 2).

[6] Linda Nierling and Bettina Krings, 'Digitalisation and Concepts of Extended Work' in Irmi Seidl and Angelika Zahrnt (eds), *Post-Growth Work: Employment and Meaningful Activities within Planetary Boundaries* (Routledge 2021).

previous chapters,[7] are linked to the idea that a wide range of activities promote a self-determined lifestyle and sustainable working and living conditions encompassing the whole worker and his or her social environment. These theories also adopt the view that workers should not be viewed as a tradable good, stressing social and welfare goals as the aspired central factor in the economic arrangements of employment. Work should be fulfilling, enriching, and of value to humans. Through that perspective, 'value neutral' technologies, as Lobel recently wrote,[8] can be developed, designed, and used within the workplace. Labour law, too, can follow such a paradigm because, as Racabi said, 'workplace power is not a static object'.[9]

The emphasis that our societies place on growth, and from this, the view of humans as tradable goods, plays an active role in shaping dystopias about the role of technologies in the workplace.[10] Anxieties about this dystopic future include fears that technologies will replace humans at work;[11] that humans will require reskilling;[12] that technologies will prove to be superior to human labourers and will ultimately govern them;[13] and that technologies will strip humans of their autonomous decision-making capabilities,[14] subordinating them to the authoritative power of the technology. All these have been widely expressed in the literature and by the International Labour Organization (ILO).[15] The post-work perspective can help to address anxieties about dystopias of this nature, offering an alternative conception of the place of technologies in the workplace, while also making it possible to envision how technologies can contribute to achieving post-work utopias by, for example, offering humans more valuable and enriching work.

The chapter is structured as follows: Section II introduces the current paradigm that labour law upholds, of technologies as commodities of the employer, deployed to further efficiency and productivity goals. The section also demonstrates how these conceptions strengthen the prerogative and authority of the employer within the workplace—in other words, the pro-capitalist paradigm

[7] See Chapter 3 by ter Haar and Chapter 4 by Zekić in this book.

[8] Orly Lobel, *The Equality Machine: Harnessing Digital Technology for a Brighter, More Inclusive Future* (Public Affairs 2022) 5.

[9] Gali Racabi, 'Abolish the Employer Prerogative, Unleash Work Law' (2021) 43 Berkley Journal of Labor & Employment Law 4.

[10] On technological dystopias, see Section V.

[11] Cynthia Estlund, 'What Should We Do After Work: Automation and Employment Law' (2018) 128 Yale Law Journal 245.

[12] ILO Global Commission on the Future of Work, *Work for a Brighter Future*, 43.

[13] This is very much evident in the idea of the algorithmic boss, Adams-Prassl, 'What if your Boss' (n 2).

[14] ILO, *Work for a Brighter Future* (n 12) 43.

[15] ibid.

concerning technologies. Section III discusses the role of technologies in the market today as actually being in cooperation with and in support of workers, pointing out that the deployment of technologies in the workplace is very similar to that of workplace accommodations. It shows this by discussing regulations regarding workplace accommodations for workers with disabilities. In following the model and basic idea of accommodations, Section IV presents the *technologies as accommodations* utopia as an alternative to the *pro-capitalist* paradigm; this leans on the functions of technologies and the possibilities created thus for support and assistance to the workforce by technologies. This section sets out the advantages that this perspective affords labour law and puts forth four justifications for the adoption of this paradigm. Following this, Section V discusses how the *technologies as accommodations* utopia can address some current dystopias concerning the place of technologies in the workplace. Section VI concludes.

II. The Pro-Capitalist Paradigm of Technologies

An analysis of the literature on technologies at work, and court judgments related to this interface, clearly reveals that labour law entails the following paradigm in relation to technologies: They are (1) commodities; (2) purchased or otherwise acquired by the employer for the business, including the fulfilment of legal obligations, organizational functions, and production and service benefits; (3) are the property of the business and the employer (or the subject of a licence acquired for their use). Consequently, technologies are being manufactured, designed, and redesigned according to the employer's interests; decisions on how to use the technology are seen as the employer's prerogative (within (limited) restrictions set by law). As a result, this paradigm strengthens the authority of the employer. Under this paradigm, the employer is seen as responsible for the protection of labour rights generally if these are infringed due to the use of new technologies.[16] This is what I term the *pro-capitalist paradigm of technologies* because it rests on the view of technologies as 'owned' or 'purchased' by the employer and subject to the employer's almost unlimited prerogative with regard to their use. In some jurisdictions, unions and other workers' representatives have a voice in negotiations about introducing such technologies into the workplace and their use. This is, however, quite rare.[17]

[16] De Stefano, 'Negotiating the Algorithm' (n 2); King and Mrkonich, '"Big Data"' (n 4).

[17] Emanuele Dagnino and Ilaria Armaroli, 'A Seat at the Table: Negotiating Data Processing in the Workplace. A National Case Study and Comparative Insights' (2019) 41 Comparative Labor Law

The pro-capitalist paradigm not only rests on the employer's almost unbounded prerogative but also leads to the ultimate increase of such prerogative and, consequently, the employer's authority. Once viewed as commodities and as serving the employer's prerogative, technologies constitute an economic good and a resource that can be purchased, used, or replaced: a resource autonomously deployed by the employer. As a customer of technologies, the employer purchases technologies, or the requisite licences for their use, for any number of reasons: legal obligations (like data protection[18] or health protection requirements[19]); human resource management (people analytics,[20] surveillance technologies,[21] biometric identification[22]); to increase workplace productivity (databases, file management, accounting algorithms); and much more. Given that the employer has both the capital and the commercial motivation to acquire such technologies and given that they are viewed as serving the organization, these technologies are manufactured and designed according to the organizational interest. Additionally, technology vendors may explicitly discuss redesign and adaptation requirements with the employer-purchaser before such technologies are integrated into the workplace.[23] Until now, these vendors have had no legal duties to uphold workers' rights.

& Policy Journal 173. See also the framework agreement, EU Regulation 2016/679 of the European Parliament and of the Council of 27 April 2016 on the Protection of Natural Persons with Regard to the Processing of Personal Data and on the Free Movement of such Data, and repealing Directive of General Data Protection Regulation [2016] 95/46/EC.

[18] ibid, EU Regulation 2016/679.

[19] On the use of technologies during the Covid-19 pandemic, see Katsabian, *The Telework Virus* (n 4); Daniel Ravid, Jerod White, and Tara Behrend, *Implications of COVID-19 for Privacy at Work, Industrial and Organizational Psychology: Perspectives on Science and Practice* (CUP 2021).

[20] Bodie, 'The Law and Politics' (n 4).

[21] Ifeoma Ajunwa, 'Algorithms at Work: Productivity Monitoring Applications and Wearable Technology as the New Data-Centric Research Agenda for Employment and Labor Law' (2018) 63 St. Louis University Law Journal 21; Richard Bales and Katherine Stone, 'The Invisible Web at Work: Artificial Intelligence and Electronic Surveillance in the Workplace' (2020) 41 Berkeley Journal of Employment & Labor Law 1; Jerry Kang and others, 'Self-Surveillance Privacy' (2012) 97 Iowa Law Review 809.

[22] William Herbert and Amelia Tuminaro, 'The Impact of Emerging Technologies in the Workplace: Who's Watching the Man (Who's Watching Me)' (2008) 25 Hofstra Labor & Employment Law Journal 35; Carra Pope, 'Biometric Data Collection in an Unprotected World: Exploring the Need for Federal Legislation Protecting Biometric Data' (2018) 26 Journal of Law & Policy 769; Case 7541-04-14 *Qalansawe Municipality v General Workers Union*, Israel National Labor Court (Delivered 15 March 2017).

[23] Information pamphlets of tech companies present this as part of their service. See Roee Abaiov, 'Business Critical Applications' (*CyberArk* 2019) <https://www.infocomsecurity.gr/presentations/2019/day2/abaiov.pdf> accessed 13 March 2022; FireEye, 'FireEye Security Suite' (*FireEye* 2019) <https://www.fireeye.com/content/dam/fireeye-www/products/pdfs/pf/suite/ds-security-suite.pdf> accessed 13 March 2022; Symantec, 'Internet Security Threat Report' (*ISTR* vol 24 2019) <https://docs.broadcom.com/doc/istr-24-2019-en> accessed 13 March 2022.

Technologies, thus, become part of the organizational structure at work: governed by the employer as part of its prerogative. Employer prerogative refers to a workplace management's authority to make unilateral decisions in the workplace.[24] This is the basic rule of work governance, except when limited by contract or any other law (legislation, regulation, case law, etc). In the case of technologies, most of the limitations on their design and use have been set by labour protection laws. But, as research has shown, these rights are not necessarily protected in the technological era, presenting significant and multiple challenges.[25] More significantly, and as noted by Racabi, the managerial prerogative sets a rebuttable presumption against workplace intervention of any sort. The power disparities between employers and workers make contractual limitations on this prerogative unattainable for most workers.[26] This is particularly true in the case of technologies of which workers have very limited knowledge and very minimal protections. Therefore, it is no surprise that the use of technologies in the workplace is a way to strengthen the employer's authority.

The conception that the law upholds is very much associated with theories of economic growth, which encompass the view of human work as a tradable good. It focuses on the relative productivity of workers, identifying where technology can enhance the productivity and growth of the employer. Under this paradigm, workers are outsiders in determining what technologies to introduce into the workplace and how these should be used; the narrow interest of maximizing profits comes before all.[27] Consequently, the employer is automatically viewed as controlling the technology in question—a productivity algorithm, for example; and algorithms are designed to be 'algorithmic bosses'. Under the logic of the algorithmic boss, the unique characteristics of artificial intelligence (AI) technologies, along with the automated decision-making that exists across the lifecycle of the employment relationship, are automatically associated with interests of the employer.[28] This has been demonstrated, bluntly, in labour law scholarship.[29]

Under this regime, workers' rights, wellbeing, and social and welfare interests become ancillary to the main goal of technologies, pale in comparison to their declared purpose. Therefore, it is no wonder that labour rights are

[24] Racabi, 'Abolish the Employer Prerogative' (n 9); Henry Chambers, 'Employer Prerogative and Employee Rights: The Never-Ending Tug-of-War' (2000) 65 Missouri Law Review 877.

[25] See references in n 4.

[26] Racabi, 'Abolish the Employer Prerogative' (n 9).

[27] See similar discussion in Kate Raworth, *Doughnut Economics: Seven Ways to Think Like a 21st-Century Economist* (Randon House 2017) 191–95.

[28] Adams-Prassl, 'What if your Boss' (n 2).

[29] De Stefano, 'Negotiating the Algorithm' (n 2); Adams-Prassl, 'What if your Boss' (n 2); Rogers, 'The Law and Political' (n 3).

constantly being infringed. Clearly, the potential of technologies to protect and promote employees' (or other worker categories) rights, wellbeing, and welfare is being missed. Such a waste of potential is unfortunate, given that it has been an aim of various bodies, including the ILO, and given that technologies can fulfil such goals since they are neutral. Technologies can be developed to protect privacy, enhance equality within the workplace, and promote unionization. In its *Work for a Brighter Future* report,[30] the ILO acknowledges the potential of technologies to free workers from arduous labour and dangerous work and how they can reduce the incidence of work-related stress and injuries.[31] However, the main concern of this report is on technologies deployed by an employer and the infringement of rights. The report proposes steps to 'actively' manage 'technology to ensure decent work'[32] and to ensure 'human in command' and puts forth other mechanisms, such as union involvement, to counteract the sole management of technologies by employers. Even so, it does not offer any alternative paradigm to that of 'employer control' of technologies, that is, an alternative to the pro-capitalist paradigm.

III. The Actual Role of Technologies at Work: Accommodations

Despite the law's conceptualization of technologies as presented above, a close look at new technologies, specifically those enabled by AI, reveals the value of technologies in supplementing human activities and actions. The sophistication and autonomous decision-making of technologies can support, and indeed enhance, the performance of routine tasks, including tasks in the workplace; free workers from arduous labour and dangerous work; reduce incidents of work-related stress and injuries; promote equality in the workplace; protect workers' privacy; and enhance possibilities for collective organization and unionization. The capabilities of some of these technologies match, and may even surpass, those of humans and, therefore, can be tailored towards fulfilling such aims; examples already exist in the market. Technologies with visual senses, cognition, and caring capabilities can replace some of the 'dirty' work undertaken by human workers. Technologies that, for example, automatically generate the minutes and official transcripts of meetings would discharge

[30] ILO, *Work for a Brighter Future* (n 12).
[31] ibid 43.
[32] ibid.

workers—mainly women—from these tasks. Humans and their work performance are the sources of inspiration for technological developments; attempts have also been made to 'humanise technology', 'rehumanise technology', and promote 'digital humanism', as termed in the literature.[33] Examples of humanized technologies include chatbots and bots providing call centre services. Technologies that exhibit human-like facial expressions, and technologies able to provide elderly care are two other examples.[34] Visual technologies taking their inspiration from the functioning of the biological eye can gather information for automated cars and for medical, security, and military functions, and more.[35] Additionally, the capacity of smart technologies to reach independent conclusions based on database sets and self-learning abilities is better placed to address discrimination than the biased human.[36] The intent of developments such as this is not necessarily to replace humans but to enable the use of technology in everyday human life.[37] People refer to technology as smart, friendly, and even as funny[38]—despite questions regarding whether algorithms or trained systems can reflect the human values of fairness, accountability, and transparency.[39]

Despite dystopian predictions regarding technologies replacing humans in the workplace,[40] studies show that, in most instances, humans continue to work alongside technologies. Several recent studies have found that earlier concerns regarding the possibility of widespread AI adoption leading to mass unemployment are unlikely to be realized. Much to the contrary, AI enables new industries to grow and will generate more innovative jobs than those it erases.[41] Moreover, studies have shown how technology works to supplement

[33] PageUp, 'Five Ways Technology Is Becoming More Human' (*PageUp* 29 November 2017) <https://www.pageuppeople.com/resource/five-ways-technology-is-becoming-more-human/> accessed 13 March 2022.

[34] Jane Bambauer, 'Dr. Robot' (2017) 51 University of California, Davis Law Review 383; Engineered Arts, 'Ameca The Future Face Of Robotics' <https://www.engineeredarts.co.uk/robot/ameca/> accessed 9 March 2022; Corinne Purtill, 'Stop Me if You've Heard This One: A Robot and a Team of Irish Scientists Walk into a Senior Living Home' (2019) <https://time.com/longform/senior-care-robot/> accessed 9 March 2022.

[35] Gil Ju Lee and others, 'Bioinspired Artificial Eyes: Optic Components, Digital Cameras, and Visual Prostheses' (2017) 28 Advanced Functional Materials 24.

[36] Lobel, *The Equality Machine* (n 8).

[37] Of course, this does not mean that some of these technological developments are not concerning. eg tricking people into believing that a technology interface is human might be extremely problematic, creating both ethical legal problems. Hence the need to regulate such situations, as suggested by the proposed EU AI Act, art 52(1).

[38] PageUp, 'Five Ways' (n 33).

[39] Ryan Calo, 'Artificial Intelligence Policy: A Primer and Roadmap' (2017) 51 University of California, Davis Law Review 399; see also the webpage of the organization: 'Fairness, Accountability and Transparency in Machine Learning' <http://www.fatml.org> accessed 9 March 2022.

[40] See Section V.

[41] Thomas Malone, Daniela Ras, and Robert Laubacher, 'Artificial Intelligence and the Future of Work' (2022) MIT Sloan <https://mitsloan.mit.edu/ideas-made-to-matter/why-future-ai-fut

human labour while changing the functions of the human worker. Daugherty and Wilson, for example, show that AI can transform business processes within an organization, with humans and smart machines collaborating more closely than before.[42] Consequently, work processes become more fluid and adaptive.[43]

Indeed, within the labour market, human labour interacts with technologies of all sorts every day, the two supporting and complementing one another. Workers have smartphones, computers, and the support of various algorithms for conducting basic daily activities at work. These technology-enabled devices have transformed work by reformulating subjectivity and complementing the worker in his or her work. Studies show the power and politics of technologies, stressing their lack of neutrality and highlighting their agency and impact on human norms and behaviours.[44] Through interrelations with new technologies, humans are evolving. Consider, for example, an artificial heart transplant or a bionic hand. One excellent example of such evolution in the workplace is the introduction of smartphones. In facilitating communication and enhanced access to various technologies for improving worker performance, such as emails, social media, and WhatsApp,[45] these technologies interrelate with the human, changing workers' behaviour as they support work practices.[46]

The unique characteristics of smart and new technologies have motivated legal authors in various disciplines to consider how to address these technologies from a legal perspective. While some writers argue that there is nothing necessarily new in AI and, therefore, that it should be treated the same way as other goods,[47] others argue that AI is unique and thus warrants a different legal approach. Some even call for bestowing the rights—and responsibilities—of a

ure-work> accessed 13 March 2022; Philippe Aghion, Benjamin Jones, and Charles Jones, 'Artificial Intelligence and Economic Growth' in *The Economics of Artificial Intelligence: An Agenda* (University of Chicago Press 2019); Jason Furman and Robert Seamans, 'AI and the Economy' (2019) National Bureau of Economic Research, Working Paper 24689; David Kiron and Gregory Unruh, 'How AI Will Define New Industries' [2018] MIT Sloan Management Review <https://sloanreview.mit.edu/article/how-ai-will-define-new-industries/> accessed 9 March 2022.

[42] Paul Daugherty and James Wilson, *Human + Machine. Reimagining Work in the Age of AI* (Harvard Business Review Press 2018).

[43] ibid.

[44] Sheila Jasanoff, *States of Knowledge: The Co-production of Science and Social Order* (Routledge 2004).

[45] Tarafdar and others, 'Technostress: Negative Effect on Performance and Possible Mitigations' (2015) 25(2) Information Systems Journal 103.

[46] This does not mean there are no problems with such technologies. One example is technostress, the pressure to multitask rapidly with reference to multiple streams of information. On such disadvantages, see Yu-Kang Lee and others, 'The Dark Side of Smart-Phone Usage: Psychological Traits, Compulsive Behaviour and Technostress' (2014) 31 Computers in Human Behavior 373.

[47] This can be said to be the current approach of the proposed EU Regulation on AI. In that proposal there is only regulation of what are seen as 'high-risk' AI systems and not all the others.

formal legal persona on technologies;[48] there are even (rare) voices who argue that AI robots should be granted legal rights.[49] I believe, however, that these proposals miss the point; the point is that while technology can be used to better the lives of workers and to protect and promote their rights, wellbeing, and social and welfare interests, in practice, they do much the opposite. Moreover, I argue that the approach towards technologies does not acknowledge *what technologies do*—that is, supporting workers' daily tasks—which is in fact providing forms of accommodations for human workers.

Interestingly, the law regarding accommodations is, theoretically and practically, an alternative to the pro-capitalist paradigm, with an excellent example being the regulation of accommodations for workers with disabilities. The legal requirement—that accommodations must be provided for workers with disabilities and for work performance and ability evaluations to be conducted only after such accommodations have been made—reflects part of how technologies can be tailored for the good. It also emphasizes the interrelations between humans and technologies and the support technologies can offer people to conduct valuable and meaningful work. This perspective shifts the focus from the question of who manages the technology to the issue of the functions of the technology or technologies under consideration and to providing support and assistance to workers while fulfilling overarching goals such as social inclusion and equality. Such a perspective entails an appreciation of the agency that technologies can have in modifying and making adjustments for individual needs.

This approach is to the fore in the Convention on the Rights of Persons with Disabilities (CRPD) 2008. Article 27 CRPD on the right to work lays out in sub-article (i) that 'reasonable accommodation is provided to persons with disabilities in the workplace'.[50] 'Reasonable accommodation' is defined in the CRPD as 'necessary and appropriate modification and adjustments ... to ensure to persons with disabilities the enjoyment of exercise on an equal basis with others of all human rights and fundamental freedoms'.[51] According to the Convention, not providing reasonable accommodations is construed as discrimination based on disability.[52] Indeed, the idea of accommodations, as I have written elsewhere, is to further structural-institutional equality by

[48] SN Lehman-Wilzig, 'Frankenstein Unbound: Towards a Legal Definition of Artificial Intelligence' (1981) Futures 442, 447; European Parliament Doc 2015/2103(INL) *Draft Report with recommendations to the Commission on Civil Law Rules on Robotics* (2016).

[49] BJ Murphy, 'Do Robots Deserve the Right to Unionize?' (*Medium* 2019) <https://medium.com/@BJ_Murphy/do-robots-deserve-the-right-to-unionize-6a683d4dc999> accessed 8 March 2022.

[50] Article 27(i) CRPD.

[51] Article 2 CRPD.

[52] See the definition of 'discrimination on the basis of disability' in art 2 CRPD.

requiring that relevant actors unpick the factors that increase or maintain the disadvantage experienced by persons with disabilities, placing a duty on these actors to restructure the workplace so as to address these factors.[53] Hence, in providing accommodations, the focus is on two central issues: the first is the functions that will aid people at work, and the second is that it does so while addressing hurdles preventing their inclusion in the market while promoting such inclusion and their right to equality.

Similar rules of accommodation have been adopted in other countries,[54] some extending the requirements even further than the CRPD. For example, an Israeli Supreme Court decision stated that when assessing whether a work candidate with a disability is suitable for a particular job, his traits and abilities should be reviewed *after* relevant accommodations have been considered[55]—thus accepting the significant transformative potential offered by various accommodations, including technologies. This approach towards accommodations has impacted the design and manufacture of technologies directed towards such purposes. The law has created a market for technologies that support workers and their inclusion, enhancing social and welfare values. By aiming to support workers with disabilities and enable their workplace participation with the assistance of technologies, the worker becomes the focus of attention. Accordingly, companies involved in the manufacture, design, and adaptation of technology for the workplace acknowledge the interests and needs of the worker, with the technology conceptualized and actualized towards that end.[56] *Reasonable* accommodations are thus not seen as a burden but rather as an asset that can modify and adjust the workplace to the needs of persons with disabilities. Usually, the employer is the one who purchases the technology or acquires the required user licence.

[53] Einat Albin, 'Universalizing the Right to Work of Persons with Disabilities' in Virginia Mantouvalou (ed), *The Right to Work* (OUP 2015).

[54] See eg the Equal Rights for People with Disabilities Act, Israel 1998, s 8; the UK's Equality Act 2010, s 60; Americans with Disabilities Act 1990, ss 12101(a)(5), 12201(h).

[55] Case 6069/10 *Mahmeli v Prison Service*, High Court (Delivered 5 May 2014).

[56] See eg pamphlets produced by the following companies, which all design and manufacture technologies to support persons with disabilities: Ava, 'Introducing Ava: 24/7 accessible conversations with deaf & hard-of-hearing people' (2016) YouTube <https://www.youtube.com/watch?v=GJSWTJDxn5k> accessed 8 March 2022; ZoomText, 'ZoomText Magnifier/Reader' <https://www.zoomtext.com/products/zoomtext-magnifierreader/> accessed 8 March 2022

IV. The Technologies as Accommodations Paradigm

Is it justifiable that labour law adopts the accommodations paradigm to technologies, not only regarding technologies developed for persons with disabilities but for the entire workforce? One can envision a similar rule to the one established by article 27 CRPD that will say: 'the introduction, re-design and use of technologies within the workplace will be done by addressing all necessary and appropriate modification and adjustments to ensure persons the enjoyment and exercise of their labour rights and fundamental freedoms'. But is such a rule justifiable? I will argue that it is and propose four reasons for its adoption.[57]

The first reason is that this is the actual role of technologies at work. Technologies are more like co-workers, supporting and supplementing the work of workers while altering their behaviours for the good than they are algorithmic bosses. The second justification is that the employer prerogative is already a powerful force in labour relations; there is no need to strengthen it with the pro-capitalist paradigm with regard to technologies. The third reason comes from labour law ideas of dignity, distributive justice, inequality of bargaining power, and human rights, particularly equality, privacy, and the right to unionize. The paradigm of technologies as accommodations furthers these exact ideas. The fourth and final reason comes from economic theories arguing that accommodations enable an improved, participative economic and social environment for all members of society. Moreover, and as described in Section V, the paradigm of technologies as accommodations addresses some central dystopias attached to the introduction of technologies and ensures the promotion of further utopias, such as offering humans more valuable and enriching work.

A. Technologies as Co-Workers

In order to clarify that most technologies at work are, in fact, more like co-workers than algorithmic bosses, I will use the functional approach found in labour law practice and theory. The functional approach has been proposed as an answer to the question: Who is an employer when employing

[57] A possible alternative argument is to universalize workers' rights with disabilities to all workers. For such an approach, see Albin, 'Universalizing the Right to Work' (n 53); Guy Davidov and Guy Mundlak, 'Accommodating All? (or: "ask Not What You Can Do for the Labour Market; Ask What the Labour Market Can Do for You")' (2016) 93 Bulletin of Comparative Labour Relations 191.

functions are distributed among several entities, especially in subcontracting and agency work?[58] This is a suitable approach since, according to Adams-Prassl, 'the current concept of the employer is a riddle with internal contradictions'.[59] Adams-Prassl continues: 'These problems can only be addressed by a careful reconceptualisation and the development of a more openly functional concept.'[60] Other studies have proposed a functional approach for addressing scenarios in which additional parties take part in the employment of workers, as in the case of customers[61] and shareholders.[62] Freedland was the first scholar to identify and distinguish employers' functions. His taxonomy included: (1) engaging workers for employment and terminating employment; (2) remunerating and providing workers with additional benefits of employment; (3) managing the employment relationship and the work process; and (4) using workers' services in the process of production or service provision.[63] According to Freedland, these functions may be exercised by a single entity or various employing entities. Building on Freedland's work, Adams-Prassl proposed additional functions, arguing that legal responsibility should be more flexible and not applied as a matter of course to anything that carries out employer functions. He observed: 'Just as employer functions can be divided up in different ways, so can different obligations be placed on entities exercising them.'[64]

In applying the functional approach, one should be careful when distinguishing employer functions from the functions of employees or other worker categories. That is because, at times, employees, such as human resource workers, are the ones who perform some of the functions presented above. And while such employees could be considered semi-employers,[65] they are still employees under the law.[66] Therefore, in addition to developing the functional approach to ask 'who is the employer', it is also highly significant to develop one concerning the category of employees before assessing how

[58] Mark Freedland, *The Personal Employment Contract* (OUP 2005) 40–45; Jeremias Adams-Prassl, *The Concept of the Employer* (OUP 2015).

[59] Adams-Prassl, *The Concept of the Employer* (n 58) 5.

[60] ibid 5, 6.

[61] Einat Albin, 'Labour Law in a Service World' (2010) 73(6) Modern Law Review 959; Einat Albin, 'A Worker-Employer-Customer Triangle: The Case of Tips' (2011) 40(2) Industrial Law Journal 181.

[62] Adams-Prassl, *The Concept of the Employer* (n 58) ch 4.

[63] Freedland, *The Personal Employment Contract* (n 58) 40.

[64] Adams-Prassl, *The Concept of the Employer* (n 58) 185.

[65] Paul Davies and Mark Freedland, 'Who Is the Employer?' in Brian Langille and Guy Davidov (eds), *Boundaries and Frontiers of Labour Law* (Bloomsbury Publishing 2006).

[66] For a justification of such an approach, see Guy Davidov, 'The Three Axes of Employment Relationships: A Characterization of Workers in Need of Protection' (2004) 58 University of Toronto Law Journal 357.

the two work together. My intention is not to do so within the scope of this chapter. Nevertheless, I believe that technologies should be seen as performing employer functions only when they exhibit an independent managerial prerogative—or, in other words, when they are *clearly* algorithmic bosses. In all other situations, technologies' functions are actually those of workers.

For example, conducting work and working side-by-side with workers are usually employee functions. Replacing roles done previously by employees also underlines the fact that technology is indeed carrying out employee functions. Moreover, the available legal tests for determining an employment relationship and determining who is an employee (as opposed to being self-employed) can be helpful. While these tests vary from one national context to another, they share the existence of a power disparity, subordination, or dependency between the parties to the relationship.[67] From this perspective, there may be some justification for the approach of technologies as being similar to employees due to the ability of the employer to control and even redesign them.

One example of technologies conducting employee functions is that of the technologies replacing or supplementing the work of human resources sections—collecting and holding personal information about workers, reviewing their workplace activities, and conducting investigations. People analytics is the term used to discuss such technologies.[68] In people analytics, human resource activities rely upon data analysis rather than the vagaries of human subjectivity.[69] These technologies do not work alone but rather as 'co-workers' of the human workers in human resources departments that depend on their input. Hence, at all levels, technologies support *and* benefit human resource workers. They are a form of functional accommodation for these workers.

Accommodations are also very similar to co-workers. They aim to assist the worker with a disability in his or her inclusion into the workplace. Once seen as co-workers, one can argue that technologies have co-worker obligations—including solidarity with their co-workers. That has substantial meaning, which I will explain by providing an example: an employee with a visual disability receives natural reader technology when hired to a position, and two years on, the technology has developed to conduct 90 per cent of the work itself—for example, doing calculations or writing texts; no one will think that the expanded capabilities of this technology—originally purchased to include

[67] ibid.
[68] Bodie, 'The Law and Politics' (n 4).
[69] ibid.

workers with disabilities in the labour market and promote their equality—should lead to the worker's dismissal. Technologies will continue in the co-worker position, even if the worker's tasks change accordingly. Through this lens, solidarity is inherent to the idea of accommodations. Given the examples provided in this subsection and the studies presented in Section II above, it seems clear that most technologies are closer to accommodations in their character than 'algo-bosses'.

B. There Is No Need to Further Strengthen Employer Prerogative

Under current labour laws, employer prerogative is very strong. Anderson argued that the employer prerogative is so strong that it mirrors the authority of a state.[70] Such an argument had already been made forty years ago by Freedland and Davies.[71] In discussing the employer prerogative, Racabi exhibited how it is the default governance rule in the workplace, and accordingly, all workplace-related decisions fall within its discretion.[72] He detailed the 'sticky' nature of the employer prerogative—which is to say it is very difficult to detach from it. Courts have upheld the employer prerogative on numerous occasions. Most workers face a significant market power disadvantage in comparison to their employer, making contractual limitations unattainable for a vast majority of people; there are work enforcement gaps, which limit the scope of protections for employees and other worker categories from such a prerogative; employers use their prerogative to find permissible workarounds to redistributive policies and actions; and also, the use that employers make of their prerogative to change organizational structures (including outsourcing and the use of technologies) to 'punish' workers, customers, and others who pursue business-adverse policies and actions.[73] Indeed, both Anderson and Racabi are researchers of the US legal system, where the employer prerogative is very strong. But as noted above, similar understandings have previously been made regarding the English legal system and others.[74] In most legal systems, the employer prerogative is the 'default rule' of labour laws.

[70] Elizabeth Anderson, *Private Government* (Princeton UP 2018).
[71] Paul Davies and Mark Freedland, *Kahn-Freund's Labour and the Law* (Stevens 1984).
[72] Racabi, 'Abolish the Employer Prerogative' (n 9) 10–16.
[73] ibid 8, 9, 16–33, 36–44.
[74] Davies and Freedland, *Kahn-Freund's Labour* (n 71).

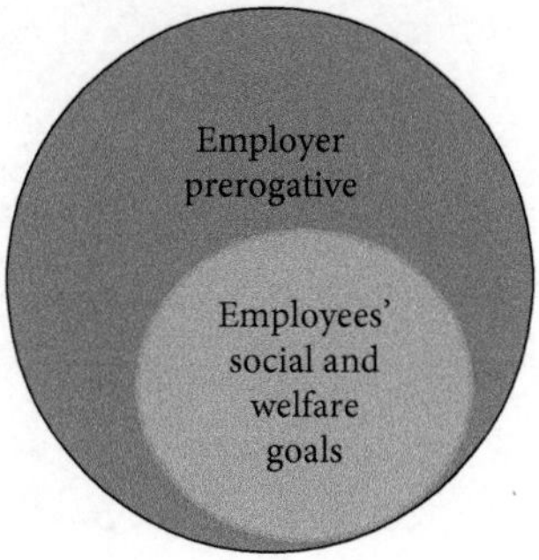

Figure 10.1 Employer prerogative to technologies in positive labour law

Employer prerogative covers various aspects of working life, starting from decisions on hiring and firing to determining the workers' wage rate and deciding and changing of the workplace organizational structure. Employers can define what employees wear and how they look; they can track workers' activities at and outside work due to the increasingly blurred boundaries separating work and private life; control their work environment, their work routine, hours of work, requests for working at home, and, hence impact on employees' work-life balance, etc. That is a partial list of all the things employers can do under their prerogative, but from the extent of this list, it is hard to find any justification for further strengthening such prerogative.

On the contrary: at the beginning of the last century, long before technology had the transformative powers we are experiencing today, Kahn-Freund argued that counterbalancing the employer's social and economic powers would protect employees.[75] Providing employers with more power than they already have, or tailoring technological abilities and strengths to promote employers' economic goals and growth, would contradict such aspirations. Hence, the pro-capitalist paradigm of technologies does the exact opposite of what Kahn-Freund suggested; it increases power disparities among the parties to the employment relationship, as numerous studies have demonstrated, contradicting the call to countervail them. The opposite will occur if one follows the paradigm of technologies as accommodations.

I will try to show this via the following figures. Figure 10.1 shows the employer prerogative in relation to technologies today under labour law with the scope of protection given to workers. Figure 10.2 shows what the alternative technologies as accommodations paradigm offers.

[75] ibid.

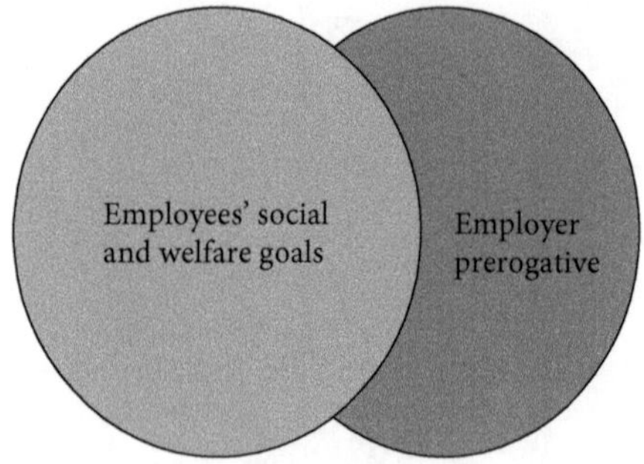

Figure 10.2 Prerogative to technologies as accommodations

C. Furthering the Ideas of Labour Law

The ideas of labour law have extended in recent years, most of these addressing the protection of employees' social and welfare goals, alongside protecting market activity.[76] In summarizing the various ideas of labour law, Davidov divided these goals into three main categories.[77] The first is ideas that address concrete vulnerabilities of workers, including organizational, social and psychological, and economic vulnerabilities; the second is ideas addressing market problems, like systematic market failures and inequality in bargaining power; and the third is other values and interests advanced by labour law, like democracy, distribution, human rights, dignity, social inclusion, human freedom, capabilities, etc.

The problem, however, is that even though these ideas are at the heart of labour law, they are not the default other than in relatively few legal systems. These ideas become more marginal in legal systems where the employer prerogative is the default rule, realized by providing space and freedom to employers' decisions and actions. They are only there to protect workers, not as the basic idea that lead the regulation of the market. The pro-capitalist paradigm for technologies, and the numerous studies examining its application to workers, clearly illustrate the marginalization of such ideas, whereby workers' rights are minimally protected. The paradigm of technologies as accommodations does the opposite. As Figure 10.2 shows, it foregrounds social and welfare goals, and thus the employee's wellbeing and rights, as the goal of labour law—in other words, as a shared default rule, alongside the employer prerogative.

[76] Hugh Collins, *Employment Law* (OUP 2003) Part I.
[77] Guy Davidov, *A Purposive Approach* (n 1).

In the following subsection, I will elaborate on why this does not necessarily contradict commercial growth and development objectives but rather the opposite.

D. Enabling an Improved Economic and Social Environment

Studies have shown how accommodations can enable an improved, participative economic and social environment for all members of society. There are a few studies that have evaluated the cost-effectiveness of accommodations.[78] One of these studies, assessing an online survey of 128 employers (including small and large employers), found direct and indirect benefits from implementing workplace accommodations.[79] The direct benefits were: retaining a qualified employee, increasing worker productivity, and eliminating the cost of training a new employee; the most noted indirect benefits were improving interactions with co-workers, increasing overall company morale, and overall company productivity.[80] Most respondents estimated the direct benefits of having made an accommodation at over USD1000.[81] Most clearly, the inclusion of persons with disabilities is a central part of the UN's Agenda for Sustainable Development, recognizing that tools used to enhance such inclusion are vital for development and economic growth.[82] Likewise, numerous studies have highlighted how protecting and promoting workers' rights and wellbeing can boost economic growth.[83]

Thus, there is no reason to think that conceptualizing technologies as accommodation for all workers would impact growth and development. Various technological developments complement the accommodations paradigm and could contribute to further economic gains. These gains include the promotion of innovation and growth, resulting from the protection of privacy;[84]

[78] For a survey of articles on the subject and the finding that there is a very small number of studies doing such work, see Kathy Padkapayeva and others, 'Workplace Accommodations for Persons with Physical Disabilities: Evidence Synthesis of the Peer-Reviewed Literature' (2016) 39(21) Disability and Rehabilitation 2134, 2143.

[79] Tatiana Solovieva, Denetta Dowler, and Richard Walls, 'Employer Benefits from Making Workplace Accommodations' (2011) 4 Disability and Health Journal 39.

[80] ibid.

[81] ibid.

[82] See UN Resolution adopted by the General Assembly on 25 September 2015 on the 2030 Agenda for Sustainable Development, at <https://documents-dds-ny.un.org/doc/UNDOC/GEN/N15/291/89/PDF/N1529189.pdf?OpenElement> accessed 29 January 2023.

[83] Simon Deakin, 'The Contribution of Labour Law to Economic Development and Growth' (2017) Working Paper 478, Centre for Business Research, University of Cambridge.

[84] Jolie Cohen, 'What Privacy Is For' (2013) 126(7) Harvard Law Review 1904; Carrisa Veliz, 'Privacy Is Power: Why and How You Should Take Back Control of Your Data' (2022) 12(3) International Data Privacy Law Journal 255; Valerie Steeves, 'Reclaiming the Social Value of Privacy' in Ian Kerr, Valerie

technologies that foster equality at work, acknowledging that equality enhances productivity and gains for companies;[85] and technologies enabling collective organization and action. Developing legal tools is a way to safeguard such a regime—not only the proposed rule of accommodation but also the establishment of collective rights with regard to technologies.[86]

In sum, the notion of *technologies as accommodation* can alter how technologies are conceptualized by the law, consequently impacting the market. This would be the case even when technologies are considered commodities, purchased or acquired by the employer to fulfil legal obligations, organizational functions, and production and service benefits; their development, design, and use should mainly be for fulfilling the social and welfare goals of workers. In other words, even if viewed as the employer's property, their licences and design should reflect their role as accommodations to workers meant to ensure for workers the enjoyment and exercise of their labour rights and fundamental freedoms. Consequently, workers would be seen as having legitimacy in taking part in governing the technologies; technologies will be manufactured and designed with the social and welfare interests of workers in mind (with limitations as set by the law); and balance the interests of both sides of the employment relationship while limiting the employer's prerogative. Under this paradigm, the employer will still be responsible for safeguarding workers' labour rights when these are infringed; unions and workers will have a leading voice in designing, planning, and deciding on whether to introduce technology into the workplace and will be part of its 'job crafting' and usage, ensuring that the technology indeed supports workers' rights and wellbeing.[87]

Steeves, and Carole Lucock (eds), *Lessons from the Identity Trail: Anonymity, Privacy and Identity in a Networked Society* (OUP 2009) 191.

[85] Lobel, *The Equality Machine* (n 8).

[86] The German example is excellent in this respect; see the analysis in Dagnino and Armaroli (n 17). OECD reports show that Germany has a higher-than-average Gross National Income. See <https://data.oecd.org/natincome/gross-national-income.htm> accessed 7 February 2023.

[87] A document that can be interpreted as adopting a paradigm similar to the technologies as accommodation paradigm is the European Social Partners Framework Agreement on Digitalization, which proposes the shared commitment of employers, workers, and their representatives to make most of the opportunities that technologies offer, stressing that the use of technologies should be mutually beneficial for employers and workers.

V. Adopting the *Technologies as Accommodations* Utopia and Addressing Existing Dystopia

The *technologies as accommodations* utopia can also address some of the most pressing dystopian visions concerning the presence of technologies in the workplace. One such dystopia is automation—the replacement of workers by technologies. That was one of the first pressing fears of the new technological era; studies from that time predicted that technologies would ultimately replace anything from 20 to 80 per cent of the human workforce, leading to a world without work.[88] More recent studies, however, have shown that these fears are now less realistic than they once were. In fact, in most instances, introducing technologies into the workplace has generally changed the roles and functions of the employees who work side-by-side with the technology in question,[89] as the examples provided in Sections II and III have emphasized. Hence, the *technologies as accommodations* utopia is more realistic and relevant today than the automation dystopia.

Another dystopian prediction is that some occupations and sectors will be eroded or disappear altogether, thanks to the march of technology.[90] While this might indeed be a part of our future, it is not necessarily problematic in the eyes of the *technologies as accommodations* utopia. The fact that some occupations and sectors may become obsolete is not necessarily bad, particularly in the case of unsanitary, precarious, or low-paying jobs. The ILO has noted that technologies can also promote dignified work and working conditions by freeing workers from arduous labour or dirty and dangerous jobs.[91] This shift has occurred throughout history for many reasons other than technological advancements; it can lead to workers developing new traits and abilities and benefitting from more leisure time.[92] One main concern regards financial support (or lack thereof) when needed; in the *technologies as accommodations* utopia and post-work theories, it appears such financial support becomes more justified for several reasons. This paradigm aims to promote social and welfare ideas, such as workers' rights, including those established in welfare law.[93]

[88] A summary of some of these studies can be found in Estlund, 'What Should We Do After Work' (n 11).

[89] Daugherty and Wilson, *Human + Machine* (n 42).

[90] ILO, *Work for a Brighter Future* (n 12) 43.

[91] ibid.

[92] Estlund discussed such possibilities as advantages; 'What Should We Do After Work' (n 11).

[93] Emile Durkheim, *The Division of Labor in Society* (The Free Press of Glencoe Illinois 1960); Kurt Bayertz, 'Four Uses of "Solidarity"' in Kurt Bayertz (ed), *Solidarity* (Springer 1999) 3, 4, 25; Roberto Frega, 'Solidarity as Social Involvement' (2019) 8(2) Moral Philosophy and Politics 179; Margaret Kohn, 'Solidarity and Social Rights' (2018) 21(5) Critical Review of International Social & Political Philosophy 616.

Moreover, given the idea of 'co-workers', the obligation of solidarity also pushes towards the finding of avenues for financial support for those in need. It might also be that the obligation of solidarity would lead to a push for tax payments by 'algo co-workers', not dissimilar to Bill Gates' idea of a tax on robots.[94]

A further dystopia evoked in the introduction of new and smart technologies into the workplace was that they would become superior to human labourers and would, ultimately, come to govern them, stripping humans of their capacity for autonomous decision-making and subordinating them to the authoritative power of the technology. The car hire platform Uber is a prominent example of this particular dystopia. However, this state of affairs is a consequence of the existing *pro-capitalist* paradigm, underscored by a managerial prerogative allowing management to structure work relations in such a way as to avoid the 'burden' of labour laws. It is debatable whether this would have been the outcome if the *technologies as accommodation* utopia had been adopted, given the history of collective strikes and other actions by Uber drivers against their 'algo-boss'[95]—activities where, incidentally, the human labourers used technologies to connect with one another and to advance their cause.[96] Moreover, had technological manufacturing, design, and re-design been carried out according to the interests of championing the social and welfare goals of workers, including solidarity and respect for labour laws (or at least some of them), the Uber technology would not have been developed and designed as an algo-boss from the start. As Gidari wrote: 'As with all technological advances, not everyone shares equally in the gains or benefits in the same way, and some may even experience disproportionately negative impacts, but that does not diminish the overall societal value of the advancements. Instead, it should motivate society to extend those benefits to all, to find equity and reduce the negative impacts.'[97]

[94] *Quartz*, 'Bill Gates thinks we should tax the robot that takes your job' (*YouTube* 2017) <https://www.youtube.com/watch?v=nccryZOcrUg> accessed 13 March 2022.

[95] Annie Nova, 'Uber drivers block traffic in Manhattan, protesting low pay and poor working conditions' (2019) CNBC <https://www.cnbc.com/2019/09/17/uber-drivers-are-protesting-again-heres-what-the-job-is-really-like.html> accessed 10 March 2022; Kate Conger, Vicky Xiuzhong Xu, and Zach Wichter, 'Uber Drivers' Day of Strikes Circles the Globe Before the Company's I.P.O.' (*The New York Times* 2019) <https://www.nytimes.com/2019/05/08/technology/uber-strike.html> accessed 10 March 2022.

[96] Gali Racabi, 'Despite The Binary: Looking for Power outside the Employee Status' (2021) 95 Tulane Law Review 1167

[97] Albert Gidari, 'Are We Already Living in a Tech Dystopia' (2020) <https://cyberlaw.stanford.edu/publications/are-we-already-living-tech-dystopia> accessed 13 March 2022.

VI. Conclusion

As a veteran fan of the *Star War* movies, I have long been inspired by their spirit. What might seem a far-reaching utopia at first is characterizing our world more than we consciously acknowledge. Workers and technologies co-work together, but under a pro-capitalist regime, their co-work and support are unnoticed and are not captured by the law. Clearly, the turn from the pro-capitalist paradigm of technologies to the paradigm of technologies as accommodations is timely and justifiable. This is not only because serious engagement with the line of thought presented here represents the more real, correct, and defining prism for the use of technologies in the workplace today; the strong justifications presented in the chapter are equally influential. By being value-neutral, technologies can become less threatening, more accepting, less hierarchical, more horizontal, and less focused on the goal of productivity (even though the proposed prism is also based on the recognition of the paradigm as ultimately enhancing growth and development). Technologies can uphold a vision more interested in connections and support of workers and in protecting and promoting their rights and wellbeing. If labour law can transform itself to grasp this paradigm, we might eventually see the world of humans and technologies at work in a brighter light, as part of our reality, not merely as a utopia.

Bibliography

Abaiov R, 'Business Critical Applications' (*CyberArk* 2019) <https://www.infocomsecurity.gr/presentations/2019/day2/abaiov.pdf>

Adams-Prassl J, *The Concept of the Employer* (OUP 2015)

Adams-Prassl J, 'What if Your Boss was an Algorithm? Economic Incentives, Legal Challenges, and the Rise of Artificial Intelligence at Work' (2019) 41(1) Comparative Labor Law and Policy Journal 123

Aghion P, Jones B, and Jones C, 'Artificial Intelligence and Economic Growth' in *The Economics of Artificial Intelligence: An Agenda* (University of Chicago Press 2019)

Ajunwa I, 'Algorithms at Work: Productivity Monitoring Applications and Wearable Technology as the New Data-Centric Research Agenda for Employment and Labor Law' (2018) 63 St. Louis University Law Journal 21

Albin E, 'Labour Law in a Service World' (2010) 73(6) Modern Law Review 959

Albin E, 'A Worker-Employer-Customer Triangle: The Case of Tips' (2011) 40(2) Industrial Law Journal 181

Albin E, 'Universalizing the Right to Work of Persons with Disabilities' in V Mantouvalou (ed) *The Right to Work* (OUP 2015)

Aloisi A and Gramano E, 'Artificial Intelligence Is Watching You at Work: Digital Surveillance, Employee Monitoring, and Regulatory Issues in the EU Context' (2019) 41 Comparative Labor Law & Policy Journal 95

Anderson E, *Private Government* (Princeton UP 2018)
Bales R and Stone K, 'The Invisible Web at Work: Artificial Intelligence and Electronic Surveillance in the Workplace' (2020) 41 Berkeley Journal of Employment & Labor Law 1
Bambauer J, 'Dr. Robot' (2017) 51 University of California, Davis Law Review 383
Bayertz K, 'Four Uses of "Solidarity"' in K Bayertz (ed), *Solidarity* (Springer 1999)
Bodie M, 'The Law and Politics of People Analytics' (2017) 88(4) Colorado Law Review 961
Calo R, 'Artificial Intelligence Policy: A Primer and Roadmap' (2017) 51 University of California, Davis Law Review 399
Chambers H, 'Employer Prerogative and Employee Rights: The Never-Ending Tug-of-War' (2000) 65 Missouri Law Review 877
Cohen J, 'What Privacy Is For' (2013) 126(7) Harvard Law Review 1904
Collins H, *Employment Law* (OUP 2003)
Conger K, Xiuzhong Xu V, and Wichter Z, 'Uber Drivers' Day of Strikes Circles the Globe Before the Company's I.P.O.' (*The New York Times* 2019) <https://www.nytimes.com/2019/05/08/technology/uber-strike.html>
Dagnino E and Armaroli I, 'A Seat at the Table: Negotiating Data Processing in the Workplace. A National Case Study and Comparative Insights' (2019) 41 Comparative Labor Law & Policy Journal 173
Daugherty P and Wilson J, *Human + Machine. Reimagining Work in the Age of AI* (Harvard Business Review Press 2018)
Davidov G, 'The Three Axes of Employment Relationships: A Characterization of Workers in Need of Protection' (2004) 58 University of Toronto Law Journal 357
Davidov G, *A Purposive Approach to Labour Law* (OUP 2017)
Davidov G and Mundlak G, 'Accommodating All? (or: "Ask Not What You Can Do for the Labour Market; Ask What the Labour Market Can Do For You")' (2016) 93 Bulletin of Comparative Labour Relations 191
Davies P and Freedland M, *Kahn-Freund's Labour and the Law* (Stevens 1984)
Davies P and Freedland M, 'Who Is the Employer?' in B Langille and G Davidov (eds), *Boundaries and Frontiers of Labour Law* (Bloomsbury Publishing 2006)
Deakin D, 'The Contribution of Labour Law to Economic Development and Growth' (2017) Working Paper 478, Centre for Business Research, University of Cambridge
De Stefano V, 'Negotiating the Algorithm: Automation, Artificial Intelligence and Labour Protection' (2018) International Labour Office, Working Paper 246
Durkheim E, *The Division of Labor in Society* (The Free Press of Glencoe Illinois 1960)
Engineered Arts, 'Ameca The Future Face Of Robotics' <https://www.engineeredarts.co.uk/robot/ameca/>
Estlund C, 'What Should We Do After Work: Automation and Employment Law' (2018) 128 Yale Law Journal 245
FireEye, 'FireEye Security Suite' (*FireEye* 2019) <https://www.fireeye.com/content/dam/fireeye-www/products/pdfs/pf/suite/ds-security-suite.pdf>
Freedland M, *The Personal Employment Contract* (OUP 2005)
Frega R, 'Solidarity as Social Involvement' (2019) 8(2) Moral Philosophy and Politics 179
Furman J and Seamans R, 'AI and the Economy' (2019) National Bureau of Economic Research, Working Paper 24689
Gidari A, 'Are We Already Living in a Tech Dystopia' (2020) <http://cyberlaw.stanford.edu/publications/are-we-already-living-tech-dystopia>
Herbert W and Tuminaro A, 'The Impact of Emerging Technologies in the Workplace: Who's Watching the Man (Who's Watching Me)' (2008) 25 Hofstra Labor & Employment Law Journal 35

Jasanoff S, *States of Knowledge: The Co-production of Science and Social Order* (Routledge 2004)

Ju Lee G and others, 'Bioinspired Artificial Eyes: Optic Components, Digital Cameras, and Visual Prostheses' (2017) 28 Advanced Functional Materials 24

Kang J and others, 'Self-Surveillance Privacy' (2012) 97 Iowa Law Review 809

Katsabian T, Employees' Privacy in the Internet Age' (2019) 40(2) Berkley Journal of Employment and Labour Law 203

Katsabian T, 'The Telework Virus: How COVID-19 has Affected Telework and Exposed its Implications for Privacy' (2023) 44 Berkeley Journal of Employment and Labor Law 141

King A and Mrkonich M, '"Big Data" and the Risk of Employment Discrimination' (2016) 68 Oklahoma Law Review 555

Kiron D and Unruh G, 'How AI Will Define New Industries' [2018] MIT Sloan Management Review <https://sloanreview.mit.edu/article/how-ai-will-define-new-industries/>

Kohn M, 'Solidarity and Social Rights' (2018) 21(5) Critical Review of International Social & Political Philosophy 616

Lee Y and others, 'The Dark Side of Smart-Phone Usage: Psychological Traits, Compulsive Behaviour and Technostress' (2014) 31 Computers in Human Behavior 373

Lehman-Wilzig S, 'Frankenstein Unbound: Towards a Legal Definition of Artificial Intelligence' (1981) Futures 442

Lobel O, *The Equality Machine: Harnessing Digital Technology for a Brighter, More Inclusive Future* (Public Affairs 2022)

Malone T, Ras D, and Laubacher R, 'Artificial Intelligence and the Future of Work' [2022] MIT Sloan <https://mitsloan.mit.edu/ideas-made-to-matter/why-future-ai-future-work>

Murphy B, 'Do Robots Deserve the Right to Unionize?' (*Medium* 2019) <https://medium.com/@BJ_Murphy/do-robots-deserve-the-right-to-unionize-6a683d4dc999>

Nierling L and Krings B, 'Digitalisation and Concepts of Extended Work' in I Seidl and A Zahrnt (eds), *Post-Growth Work: Employment and Meaningful Activities within Planetary Boundaries* (Routledge 2021)

Nova A, 'Uber drivers block traffic in Manhattan, protesting low pay and poor working conditions' (2019) CNBC <https://www.cnbc.com/2019/09/17/uber-drivers-are-protesting-again-heres-what-the-job-is-really-like.html>

Padkapayeva K and others, 'Workplace Accommodations for Persons with Physical Disabilities: Evidence Synthesis of the Peer-Reviewed Literature' (2016) 39(21) Disability and Rehabilitation 2134

Pope C, 'Biometric Data Collection in an Unprotected World: Exploring the Need for Federal Legislation Protecting Biometric Data' (2018) 26 Journal of Law & Policy 769

Racabi G, 'Abolish the Employer Prerogative, Unleash Work Law' (2021) 43 Berkley Journal of Labor & Employment Law

Racabi G, 'Despite The Binary: Looking for Power outside the Employee Status' (2021) 95 Tulane Law Review 1167

Ravid D, White J, and Behrend T, *Implications of COVID-19 for Privacy at Work, Industrial and Organizational Psychology: Perspectives on Science and Practice* (CUP 2021)

Raworth K, *Doughnut Economics: Seven Ways to Think Like a 21st-Century Economist* (Randon House 2017)

Renan-Barzilai A, 'Platform Inequality: Gender in the Gig-Economy' (2017) 47 Seton Hall Law Review 393

Rogers B, 'The Law & Political Economy of Workplace Technological Change' (2020) 55 Harvard Civil Rights- Civil Liberties Law 531

Solovieva T, Dowler D, and Walls R, 'Employer Benefits from Making Workplace Accommodations' (2011) 4 Disability and Health Journal 39

Steeves V, 'Reclaiming the Social Value of Privacy' in Ian Kerr, Valerie Steeves, and Carole Lucock (eds), *Lessons from the Identity Trail: Anonymity, Privacy and Identity in a Networked Society* (OUP 2009)

Veliz C, 'Privacy is Power: Why and How You Should Take Back Control of Your Data' (2022) 12(3) International Data Privacy Law Journal 255

11

Social Security and the Right to Laziness Beyond just Basic Income

Alexander De Becker and Flore Claus

I. Introduction

The idea of a basic income dates back centuries; the first to mention the idea was Thomas More in his book *Utopia*.[1] The concept of a basic income was further explicitly discussed in the work of Juan Luis Vives, *De Subventione Pauperum* (*On the Assistance to the Poor*), where he proposed the notion of a subsistence minimum for the poorest inhabitants of a municipality.[2]

Although the idea was often discussed in the eighteenth and nineteenth centuries, it fell out of sight in most European countries in the second half of the twentieth century. The reason for this was because of the development of social security and social welfare systems.[3] It resurfaced in the 1980s and is now founded in a larger quest for discussions in the post-growth debate.[4] The idea of a basic income within a post-growth debate includes a transition towards a more sustainable and ecological model of social welfare and social security systems.

The number of real initiatives concerning the introduction of the right to a basic income remained very limited. In Finland, an initiative to introduce a basic income was organized. Nevertheless, the Finnish authorities installed a very limited regulation that provided for a small number of unemployed persons to receive a basic income of 560 euros without any associated control mechanism. The experiment included minor and temporary modifications of Finnish regulations regarding a basic income for jobless persons looking for a

[1] Thomas More, *De optimo statu reipublicae deque nova insula Utopia* (Dirk Martens 1516).
[2] Juan Luis Vives, *De subventione pauperum* (De Crook 1526).
[3] Jef Van Langendonck and others, *Handboek Socialezekerheidsrecht* (10th edn, Intersentia 2020) 20–32.
[4] Kate Raworth, *Doughnut Economics: Seven Ways to Think like a 21st-Century Economist* (Random House 2018) 200, in particular. See also Chapter 5 by Carelli in this book.

Alexander De Becker and Flore Claus, *Social Security and the Right to Laziness Beyond just Basic Income* In: *Labour Law Utopias*. Edited by: Nicolas Bueno, Beryl ter Haar, and Nuna Zekić, Oxford University Press. © Oxford University Press 2024.
DOI: 10.1093/oso/9780198889755.003.0011

job. Without going into further detail on the conditions of the Finnish right to a basic income,[5] the modification did not include an adaptation of the general social security system. No fundamental legal basis was established concerning basic income in Finland.[6] In Switzerland, a referendum rejected the introduction of a basic income.[7]

The main weakness in the scholarship defending the right to a basic income remains the legal foundations of positive law. However, those foundations are very important in underpinning the development of the idea of a basic income. This element will be addressed in this contribution.

First, we will discuss the role of social rights in the current framework. How have social rights (particularly the right to work and the right to social security) developed since their foundations? What are the current problems regarding the right to work and the right to social security? The focus will then be on the missing link in the current legal framework: the absence of the possibility not to work. In Western Europe, the right to work has evolved from a right to a duty for most citizens who can work. Alongside the development of the right to laziness, the right to work should also become freedom to work. The freedom to work includes the provision that, where somebody does not work, they are not to be penalized by being excluded from social security schemes. One may work as a form of personal development, but no one is obliged to do so. The shift from the obligation to work to the freedom to work offers new opportunities. However, the establishment of such a fundamental freedom, which may or may not be exercised, raises a new fundamental issue: how to ensure that the fundamental right to social security gets funded. The right to work, without an actual duty to work, weakens the link between labour and social security. In the current framework, the existing fundamental right to social security puts pressure on the existing fundamental right to work. Albeit, one must work to contribute to the realization of the right to social security.

This chapter attempts to overcome this connection. The shift from a right to work to a freedom to work, coupled with a right to laziness, introduces a real right not to work.[8] These innovations include an opportunity to change

[5] The right to basic income was limited to jobless persons between 29 and 58 years of age. The main reason was to lower the unemployment rate in Finland (which was historically high: Simon Birnbaum, Jurgen de Wispelaere, and Robert van der Veen, *Basinkomstens nya vaag* (IFF 2020) 32).

[6] Act on the Basic Income (Lag om försök med basinkomst fra 13 December 2016) – unemployed persons between 29 and 58 years could opt for a basic income of 580 euros which was a very limited amount for a limited group within the larger scope of the safeguard of social security as a right.

[7] Swiss Federal Council, 'Unconditional Basic Income' Popular Initiative <https://www.admin.ch/gov/en/start/documentation/votes/20160605/unconditional-basic-income.html> accessed 5 July 2023.

[8] Some may indicate this a freedom from work but this is a too negative approach to positive rights, according to us.

existing balances. The idea will therefore be further developed within the context of post-growth strategies and indicate which new fundamental right should be created and how this right should be legally embedded.

II. The Current Right to Social Protection

A. The Right to Social Security at the International Level

Social security became an important issue in the nineteenth century with the development of industrialization. The concentration of large groups of workers in towns and cities with high poverty rates was accompanied by a growing social backlash for a category of people (mainly family members) depending on the limited income of factory workers.[9]

After the Second World War, the right to social security was incorporated into several international conventions. The right to social security was actually considered to be the foundation for a right to a basic income. Articles 22 and 25 of the Universal Declaration of Human Rights (UDHR) recognize the right to social security and social welfare. The inclusion of the right to social security within the UDHR was seen as a significant milestone towards establishing the right to a basic income. The preparatory documents include the following:

> 'The extension of social security measures to provide a basic income to all in need of such protection and comprehensive medical care', as well as 'provision for child welfare and maternity protection'[10]

The International Labour Organization (ILO) has taken significant steps in the development of the right to social security. Through Convention No 102 Social Security (Minimum Standards) of 1952, the ILO has had a major influence on defining the substance of the fundamental right to social security. Convention No 102 outlines the nine parts of social security: medical care, sickness benefits, unemployment benefits, old-age benefits, employment injury benefits, family benefits, maternity benefits, invalidity benefits, and survivor benefits. According to article 3, the duty of the state is nevertheless limited as it

[9] Andreas Gestrich, Elisabeth Grüner, and Susanne Hahn (eds), *Poverty in Modern Europe* (OUP 1986).

[10] ILO: Declaration concerning the aims and purposes of the International Labour Organisation (Declaration of Philadelphia), adopted by the International Labour Conference at its 26th Session, held in Philadelphia, on 10 May 1944, arts III(f) and (h).

stipulates that only three branches of the nine mentioned in the Convention must be included. These branches are medical care, sickness, unemployment, old age, employment injury, family, maternity, invalidity, and survivors' benefits. Consequently, the legal impact of ILO Convention No 102 remains limited.

The right to social security is further guaranteed at the international level in article 9 of the International Convention on Economic, Social and Cultural Rights (ICESCR) and within the European context, by the European Code of Social Security, which has been established under the framework of the Council of Europe. Additionally, the recently introduced Pillar of Social Rights of the European Union (EU) also includes the right to social protection (Principle No 12).

Within this framework, two distinct models of social security systems were developed. The Bismarck model (launched in 1889)[11] was based on an existing professional bond. Social security in the Bismarck model is commutative, meaning that the contribution of individuals through labour leads to the opening of social security and/or social welfare rights for the same persons. In contrast, the Beveridge model (originating from a report on social insurance submitted by the English economist William Beveridge to the UK government in 1942) adopts a universal health care approach for citizens, with a National Health Service (NHS) paid for by taxpayers.[12] The idea of healthcare for all citizens is a universal and distributive concept. Everyone in need is entitled to free healthcare, whether the citizen concerned is working or not.[13]

The Bismarck model primarily encompassed countries in Central Europe (Austria, Belgium, Bulgaria, France, and Germany). In contrast, the Beveridge model was mainly developed in Northern European countries (the UK, Denmark, and Sweden).

However, harmonization of social security models at international and EU levels remains limited.[14] The EU has taken one significant step towards harmonizing social security systems through Council Recommendation 92/442/

[11] Timothy W Guinanne, Tobias A Job, and Jochen Strep, 'Bismarcks Sozialversicherung und ihr Einfluss auf Deutschlands demografischen Wandel' (2021) 101(4) Zeitschrift für Wirtschaftspolitik 246.

[12] The Beveridge report of 1 December 1942, often discussed but very well described, in Gwyn Bevan, Jan-Kees Helderman, and David Wilsford, 'Changing Choices in Health Care: Implications for Equity, Efficiency and Cost' (2010) 5(3) Health Economics, Policy and Law 251.

[13] The right to social security is recognized in art 22 UDHR and in arts 9 and 10 ICESCR. Furthermore, art 11 of the Convention on the Elimination of All forms of Discrimination against Women (CEDAW) recognizes the right to social security for women. Article 26 of the Convention on the Rights of the Child (CRC) also specifically guarantees the right of the child to social security and social insurance.

[14] We should point out the importance of Council Regulation (EC) 1408/71 on the application of social security schemes to employed persons and their families moving within the Community [1971] OJ L149/7 as this Regulation granted an important content to free movement of persons in the EU while keeping social protection.

EEC of 27 July 1992 on the convergence of social protection objectives and policies, which provides five criteria that combine the Bismarck and Beveridge models: (1) to guarantee a level of resources in keeping with human dignity; (2) the chance to benefit from the system for the protection of human health existing in the Member State; (3) to help to further the social integration of all persons legally residing within the territory of the Member State and the integration into the labour market of those who are in a position to exercise a lucrative activity; (4) to provide a replacement income for employed workers who cease work at the end of their working lives or are forced to interrupt their careers owing to sickness, accident, maternity, invalidity, or unemployment; and (5) to examine the possibility of introducing and/or developing appropriate social protection for self-employed persons.

Within the framework of the Council of Europe, the European Court of Human Rights (ECtHR) has ruled in a few cases that certain elements of social security can be linked to a fundamental right with direct effect.

This direct effect has the potential to harmonize the two social security models. Despite the significance of these judgments, the harmonizing effect of the judgments remains rather limited as they primarily focus on procedural guarantees and the right to property. Furthermore, the case law only focuses on pensions.[15]

That leads to the conclusion that social security law is primarily developed within national frameworks, which means that the recognition of a fundamental right is only the starting point. Further development lies in the hands of the Member States which have signed the conventions.

As a result of the EU initiatives, countries following the Bismarck model are no longer exclusively financed by social contributions paid by employers and workers.[16] Contributions paid by taxes grew in countries that initially followed the Bismarck model.[17] Conversely, some countries that initially adopted the Beveridge model have also introduced other forms of funding, such as contributions by employers and employees.[18]

[15] Ana Gómez Heredero, *Social Security as a Human Right* (Council of Europe Publishing 2007).

[16] Anja Rohwer, 'Bismarck versus Beveridge: ein Vergleich von Sozialversicherungssystemen in Europa' (2008) 61(21) ifo Schnelldienst 26, 28.

[17] Laurence J Kotlikoff, 'Fixing Social Security: What Would Bismarck Do?' (2011) 64(2.1) National Tax Journal 415.

[18] Twenty per cent of the UK budget for health service is paid by employers and employees, to be found on 'The Right to Social Security in National Law' <https://www.commonwealthfund.org/international-health-policy-center/countries/england> accessed 11 April 2023.

B. The Right to Social Security in National Law

Besides a limited harmonizing effect on national social security systems, none of the international and European human rights instruments grant individuals a direct right to social security. Therefore, social security remains a predominantly national subject.[19] No direct right to social security exists in any EU Member State. In fact, the wording of the articles of all the EU Member State constitutions confirms the non-direct effect of the right to social security (Table 11.1).

In conclusion, it is evident that the recognition of the right to social security as a fundamental constitutional right in all EU constitutions necessitates an active role of the state in establishing an adequate system.

C. The Impact of National Regulation on the Existing Models in the EU

Several countries in Middle Europe, for example Austria, Belgium, the Czech Republic, Estonia, France, Germany, and Slovakia, adhere to the Bismarck model, meaning that they have opted for a system where social security is funded by the contributions of employers and employees.[20] This funding accounts for over 65 per cent of the financing of the social security system. However, there is a growing trend among EU Member States to fund their social security schemes through increased governmental intervention on top of contributions from workers, employers, and employees. This shift indicates a convergence of funding methods.[21]

One of the major drawbacks of the Bismarck model is its reliance on a societal structure where the number of workers must be larger than the number of individuals requiring support.[22] This makes the model sensitive to demographical

[19] Article 1 First Protocol ECvHR: 'Every natural or legal person is entitled to the peaceful enjoyment of his possessions. No one shall be deprived of his possessions except in the public interest and subject to the conditions provided for by law and by the general principles of international law. The preceding provisions shall not, however, in any way impair the right of a state to enforce such laws as it deems necessary to control the use of property in the general interest or to secure the payment of taxes or other contributions or penalties.' This article is often invoked in litigation on pensions: Heredero, *Social Security as a Human Right* (n 15) 23–30.

[20] Rohwer, 'Bismarck versus Beveridge' (n 16) 26–29.

[21] France, Italy, Spain, and Portugal have increasingly used taxes to fund their social security schemes. See ibid for more on this.

[22] José Ignacio Condé-Ruiz and Clara I Gonzalez, 'From Bismarck to Beveridge: The Other Pension Reform in Spain' (2016) 7 SERIEs 461, 482–83.

Table 11.1 Right to social security in constitutions in Europe

Constitution	Article	Content
Austria	-	-
Belgium	23	The right to social security shall be established by the state: to this end, the laws, federate laws, and rules referred to in article 134 guarantee economic, social, and cultural rights, taking into account corresponding obligations, and determine the conditions for exercising them.
Bulgaria	51	The right to social security to be established by the state: (1) Citizens shall have the right to social security and social assistance. (2) The state shall provide social security for the temporarily unemployed in accordance with conditions and procedures established by law. (3) The aged without relatives and unable to support themselves, as well as persons with physical and mental disabilities shall receive special protection from the state and society.
Croatia	57	The right of employees and their family members to social security and social insurance shall be regulated by law and collective agreements.
Cyprus	9	Every person has the right to a decent existence and to social security. A law shall provide for the protection of the workers, assistance to the poor, and for a system of social insurance.
Czech Republic	30	Act of Parliament deals with how the right is provided.
Denmark	75	The right to social assistance to the extent that someone fulfills the legal conditions to receive them.
Estonia	28	Every citizen of Estonia is entitled to government assistance in the case of old age, incapacity for work, loss of provider, or need. The categories and extent of the assistance, and the conditions and procedure for its allocation are provided by law.
Finland	19	Everyone shall be guaranteed by an Act the right to basic subsistence in the event of unemployment, illness, and disability and during old age as well as at the birth of a child or the loss of a provider. The public authorities shall guarantee for everyone, as provided in more detail by an Act, adequate social, health, and medical services and promote the health of the population.
France	11 and 22(5)	The French Republic shall guarantee to all people who, by virtue of their age, physical or mental condition, or economic situation, are incapable of working shall have the right to receive suitable means of existence from society. Article 22(5) provides a right to social security taken care of by the state.

(*continued*)

Table 11.1 Continued

Constitution	Article	Content
Hungary	70	A right to social security which will be implemented by the Hungarian Republic.
Ireland	45	A right to distribution of common goods to protect the weaker better.
Italy	38	The right to social security but without direct effect before the judiciary.
Latvia	109	The right to social security for citizens of Latvia.
Lithuania	52	The state shall guarantee social security rights.
Luxemburg	11.5	A right to social security regulated by law.
Malta	17	A right to social protection but without any direct effect.
The Netherlands	20	1. It shall be the concern of the authorities to secure the means of subsistence of the population and to achieve the distribution of wealth. 2. Rules concerning entitlement to social security shall be laid down by Act of Parliament. 3. Dutch nationals resident in the Netherlands who are unable to provide for themselves shall have a right, to be regulated by Act of Parliament, to aid from authorities.
Poland	68.1	Public authorities shall ensure equal access to health care services, financed from public funds.
Portugal	63	Public authorities shall ensure equal access to health care services, financed from public funds.
Romania	47	The law stipulates how social security rights shall be secured.
Slovakia	39	Details concerning the rights shall be established by Parliament.
Slovenia	50	Task to provide a social security system on the shoulders of the state.
Spain	41	The right to social security contains a task for the state.
Sweden	2 (Instrument of Government)	The right to social security is an aim of government.

developments.[23] Data show that the number of social security-dependent elderly persons (who are over 65 years of age) is increasing from around 25 per cent of the population in 2000 towards 50 per cent of the population in 2050.[24]

These demographic changes place a strain on the funding basis of social security systems. Consequently, the social contributions will become insufficient

[23] EUROSTAT indicates that only 20 per cent of the population is younger than 20 years while 21 per cent of people in the EU are older than 65 to be consulted at <europa.eu.int>.

[24] Rohwer, 'Bismarck versus Beveridge' (n 16) 28.

to fund the existing social security schemes. In that context, a shift to the Beveridge model based on general tax payments could be considered a solution. Nonetheless, such a shift is not easy, nor will it be fully effective in addressing the issue, as demonstrated by Spain's attempt to make the necessary changes in the pension schemes. The pensions granted under the Bismarck model were significantly higher than the general (minimum) pensions provided under the Beveridge model.[25]

In addition, employment relations shift in the EU. More and more self-employed persons count only one client or a very dominant client.[26] The Netherlands has the biggest problem because 31.3 per cent of self-employed persons confirm that their client controlled their working process.[27] This evolution is linked to the rise in the number of self-employed persons without employees.[28] Even if not all the EU Member States share the problem in the same manner, it does indicate that shifting work relations imply more uncertainty over contributions to fund the social security systems. This is mainly significant for countries following the Bismarck model. Bogus self-employed persons whose work is dominated by one client are no longer considered employees in countries such as the Netherlands, France, Italy, and Spain.[29] The group of contributors decreases, which leads to a problem of funding the Bismarck model.

Some authors, therefore, prefer the Beveridge model.[30] That model is also under pressure because a similar problem arises due to demographic evolutions. If the group relying on the taxes of others for their income is at least as large as the group responsible for providing the funding through taxes, it becomes evident that the existing regime is no longer sustainable. This observation applies particularly to the Beveridge model, where the majority of the taxes are income taxes. When considering the division of taxes, it becomes clear that, in the long run, the Beveridge model is also not sustainable.[31] Therefore, a shift towards another model to fund the right to social security is necessary.

[25] Condé-Ruiz and Gonzalez, 'From Bismarck to Beveridge' (n 22) 482–83.

[26] This statement is confirmed by 18 per cent of the self-employed persons in the EU, to be found at Eurostat statistics explained at Self-employment statistics – Statistics Explained (europa.eu).

[27] To be found at Eurostat statistics explained at Self-employment statistics – Statistics Explained (europa.eu).

[28] Eurofound, 'Exploring self-employment in the European Union' (Publications Office of the European Union, Luxembourg 2017) 7, to be found at Exploring self-employment in the European Union (european-microfinance.org).

[29] ibid 45.

[30] Condé-Ruiz and Gonzalez, 'From Bismarck to Beveridge' (n 22) 482–83.

[31] Sweden and Denmark figure among the countries with the highest income taxes <https://stats.oecd.org/index.aspx?DataSetCode=TABLE_I7> (accessed on 11 May 2024) while the UK did not provide a full possibility for a pension for many citizens. See Traute Meyer and Paul Bridgen, 'Towards German Liberalism and British Social Democracy: The Evolution of Two Public Occupational Pension

Analysis of the tax reform required in different countries is a matter that requires the expertise of economists and public administration specialists.[32] When it comes to the fundamental right to social security though (in case it is retained as it was established in ILO Convention No102 but also in art 34 of the EU Charter of Fundamental Rights), a different approach is needed. The fundamental right cannot be granted under the same conditions as in the past. Neither the Bismarck model nor the Beveridge model is sustainable through the demographic evolution. Specifically for the Bismarck model, the shift in employment relations will further affect the funding of the model. That applies particularly to countries such as the Netherlands, Spain, Italy, and Greece.[33]

Consequently, the financing model of most social security systems, which has relied on economic growth and contributions from employed individuals, is facing significant pressure.

III. The Right to Social Security in a Novel Framework

The right to social security is mentioned in major international treaties. Nevertheless, this fundamental right is not sufficiently enforced in practice. Many EU constitutions explicitly recognize the fundamental right to social security or, at the very least, impose a duty on the state to provide social security.[34] This duty entails the development of policies that grant social security, including healthcare, in most cases.

Therefore, maintaining this right requires an important reform of the existing systems. The concept of a basic income, in conjunction with the idea of a post-growth societal model, provides a new foundation for such reforms.

Regimes from 1945 to 2009' in Jochen Clasen (ed), *Converging Worlds of Welfare? British and German Social Policy in the 21st Century* (OUP 2011) 157.

[32] Kate Raworth, *Doughnut Economics: Seven Ways to Think Like a 21st-Century Economist* (Chelsea Green Publishing 2017) 140–70 where she pleads for a distributive economy and Thomas Piketty, *Le Capital au XXI siècle* (Editions du Seuil 2013), where he pleas for taxation based on wealth and not on income.

[33] Eurofound (2017) (n 28) 45.

[34] Article 38 of the Austrian Constitution; art 23 of the Belgian Constitution; art 57 of the Croatian Constitution; art 9 of the Cypriot Constitution; art 75, para 2 of the Danish Constitution; art 19 of the Finnish Constitution; art 22 of the Greek Constitution; art XIX of the Hungarian Constitution; art 109 of the Latvian Constitution; art 48 of the Lithuanian Constitution; art 11 of the Luxembourgian Constitution; art 20 of the Dutch Constitution; art 67 of the Polish Constitution; art 63 of the Portuguese Constitution; art 34 of the Romanian Constitution; art 50 of the Slovenian Constitution; art 41 of the Spanish Constitution; art 2(2) of the Swedish Instrument of Government.

To reaffirm the right to social security, it must be separated from the right to work. As Bueno correctly pointed out, labour law aims to protect the weaker against the risks linked to the execution of labour.[35]

The problem is that in most EU countries that adopt a primarily Bismarck model, the right to work has evolved almost towards a duty to work in order to ensure enough contributions to afford social security. This approach can lead to potential income losses for unemployed individuals who are unable to find employment.[36] It is unrealistic to place this burden solely on a shrinking group of workers and employers. The right to work, as currently conceived, does not adequately support the idea of individual growth, and it does not ensure, in practice, a reasonable income in order to afford a reasonable life to provide you and your family with.[37] Moreover, work serves as an important means to generate social security for others.

The predictable outcome of the current model is that as the numbers of elderly persons grow in comparison to the working-age population, there will be a need for cost-saving measures in social security. That is exactly what is happening in those EU Member States. Several EU Member States, such as Belgium, France, Italy, and Portugal, are already undergoing significant reforms to their social security systems. The reasons behind those reforms are always similar: governments and parliaments decide to cut into the funding of social security schemes. Still, at the same time, they decide to keep the social security model as they are obliged to do so within the international legal framework.

In the long run, these reforms will not stand the heat. The major concern remains the funding of the model. An economy not based on growth still needs sufficient resources to ensure this fundamental right. Alongside the idea of a post-growth economy which may lead to a reversal of priorities, where leisure and free development become more important than the right to work. The right to work remains of the utmost interest given its role in productivity.

Productivity is no longer the sole aim of the economic model. The non-domination approach, which has received significant attention in recent years, allows workers to make employment choices that are not driven by economic necessity or the fear of income loss.[38] This approach emphasizes that work

[35] Nicolas Bueno, 'Freedom *at*, *through* and *from* Work: Rethinking Labour Rights' (2021) 160(2) International Labour Review 311, 325.

[36] Belgium, Acts of 28 December 2011; France, the Act is pending before the Constitutional Council which will decide on 14 April; Italy, Act of 28 January 2019; Portugal, Act of 9 December 2022.

[37] Paul Schoukens, Alberto Barrio, and Eleni De Becker, 'Platform Economy and the Risk of in-Work Poverty: A Research Agenda for Social Security Lawyers' in Valerio Di Stefano and others (eds), *A Research Agenda for the Gig Economy and Society* (Edward Elgar 2022) 93, 93–95.

[38] Bueno, 'Freedom *at*, *through* and *from* Work' (n 35) 317–19.

decisions should be based on the capacity of individuals to find fulfilment in their lives rather than being driven by anxiety.[39]

Within this framework, two major shifts need to take place regarding fundamental labour rights:

(1) To develop a crucial right to laziness: the right to receive social security should no longer be based on the duty to work but on human existence without conditions;
(2) To establish true freedom to work that truly ensures free human development rather than the duty to work as it is currently shaped.[40]

A. The Right to Laziness: Not Enough as a Legal Basis

The right to leisure, as outlined in article 24 UDHR, does not suffice as the legal basis for a fundamental right as it is still linked to work and the right to work (including reasonable working time, holiday, and resting time). 'Reasonable limitation of working hours' and 'periodic holidays with pay' are the constitutive elements. What is required here is a right not to engage in work rather than simply a right to recover from work.

The concept of a right to laziness becomes crucial when the aim is to adapt to a new societal conception or utopia. The fear traditionally associated with the idea of creating a right to laziness needs to be dispelled. Self-development becomes essential for shaping a new vision of society and reimagining social security and the freedom to live one's life.

The right to laziness has to be recognized besides the freedom to work. Working should no longer be the basis for financial resources. Labour rights currently focus on the creation of a financial income. Many authors actually support this idea. Bueno highlights a significant challenge in developing the idea that a basic income would liberate people when their income needs to be provided by adequate funding.[41] Dumont and Dermine state

[39] Virginia Mantouvalou, 'Legal Construction of Structures of Exploitation' in Hugh Collins, Gillian Lester, and Virginia Mantouvalou (eds), *Philosophical Foundations of Labour Law* (OUP 2012) 188, 188–92.

[40] Elise Dermine, 'Activation Policies for the Unemployed and the International Human Rights Case Law on the Right to a Freely Chosen Work' in Elise Dermine and Daniel Dumont (eds), *Activation Policies for the Unemployed, the Right to Work and the Duty to Work* (Peter Lang 2014) 139.

[41] Bueno, 'Freedom *at*, *through* and *from* Work' (n 35) 322.

that, currently, fundamental labour rights do not address the social utility of work.[42]

From a legal standpoint, the term 'duty to work' provides a better description than the right to work. It is legally recognized that the right to work exists in order to allow people to develop a decent life. This necessitates a reasonable and fair wage. Therefore, the right to work should encompass the ability to live a decent life. Nonetheless, recent research reveals that the possibility of ending up in poverty significantly increases when a (single) individual relies on social security revenue.[43] Living for an income which is based on the incapacity to work or living for a pension seems inadequate for the development of a decent life.[44]

In fact, the basic right to social security also includes an implicit duty to work.[45] The activation policies in different EU countries involve the state actively intervening to promote forms of employment. Jobless individuals are encouraged to respond to job vacancies, participate in unpaid training periods, or consider internship opportunities, as highlighted by Dermine, Dumont, and Adkins.[46] As mentioned earlier, the current understanding of the right to work is closely tied to productivity. Dermine and Dumont have already pointed out that most international standards also include (alongside supporting some aspects of decommodification) the support of a productivity model.[47] Productivity is crucial for financing existing social security models. Given that most EU countries combine features of both the Bismarck and Beveridge models, it is, at this stage, inconvenient to combine both.

Social security law and basic social security rights are not solely based on work itself, but accessibility becomes linked to the execution of work. However, authors such as Cholbi underestimate this necessary link by claiming that there

[42] Elise Dermine and Daniel Dumont, 'A Renewed Critical Perspective on Social Law: Disentangling Its Ambivalent Relationship with Productivism' (2022) 38(3) International Journal of Comparative Labour Law and Industrial Relations 237, 254.

[43] <https://ec.europa.eu/eurostat/statistics-explained/index.php?title=EU_statistics_on_income_and_living_conditions_(EU-SILC)_methodology_-_people_at_risk_of_poverty_or_social_exclusion#Description> consulted on 11 May 2024. Even for people in employment the risk is rising, see Christina Hiessl, 'Working, Yet Poor: A Comparative Appraisal' in Luca Ratti (ed), *In Work Poverty in Europe: Vulnerable and Under-Represented Persons in a Comparative Perspective* (Kluwer 2022) 313.

[44] <https://ec.europa.eu/eurostat/statistics-explained/index.php?title=EU_statistics_on_income_and_living_conditions_(EU-SILC)_methodology_-_people_at_risk_of_poverty_or_social_exclusion#Description> accessed on 11 May 2024.

[45] Amir Paz-Fuchs, 'The Right to Work and the Duty to Work' in Virginia Mantouvalou (ed), *The Right to Work. Legal and Philosophical Perspectives* (Hart Publishing 2015) 177. See also Dermine and Dumont, 'A Renewed Critical Perspective' (n 42) 253.

[46] Lisa Adkins, 'Out of Work or Out of Time? Rethinking Labor After the Financial Crisis' (2012) 111(4) South Atlantic Quarterly 621; Dermine and Dumont, 'A Renewed Critical Perspective' (n 42) 253.

[47] Dermine and Dumont, 'A Renewed Critical Perspective' (n 42) 262.

is no duty to work because there exists only limited reciprocity.[48] The duty to work is, to a certain extent, linked to the possibility of enjoying some social security benefits (benefits for the unemployed or entitlement to a pension). Despite this existing link, the duty to work may not be counterbalanced on an individual level with regard to the productivity of the function executed. Therefore, in our approach, it needs to be considered within a broader context, focusing on the duty to work to ensure the solvability of the existing system.[49]

Reforms of current social security systems increasingly emphasize the importance of work. The expectation is that every adult should work, and continue working longer, to ensure the affordability of the social security system. However, without major modifications in the demography of European countries, these reforms may not be enough to overcome the crisis.

Given the financial unsustainability of the current system, this chapter seeks to explore a utopian solution. This utopian solution involves shifting the focus away from the productivity of work as a means to contribute to the social security systems. Instead, the focus should revolve around how society can afford a reasonable quality of life for everyone without placing excessive pressure on all participating citizens. The focus should no longer be on the productivity of work to contribute to social security systems but on how society can afford a reasonable life for everyone without putting too much pressure on all citizens participating in that society.

In our opinion, the most fundamental shift in thinking lies in developing a comprehensive and individual right to laziness. The right to laziness encompasses the choice not to work (the negative freedom to work)[50] but goes beyond that because the right to a decent life as a fundamental right needs to be combined with the right to laziness. That implies a fundamental shift in the existing recognition of human rights (including socioeconomic rights).

Based on this right to laziness, a new model can be developed to guarantee a fundamental right to social security.

B. Right to Work Interpreted as a Freedom

Article 6 ICESCR defines the right to work as 'the right of everyone to the opportunity to gain his living by work which he freely chooses or accepts, and will

[48] Michael Cholbi, 'The Duty to Work' (2018) 21(5) Ethical Theory and Moral Practice 1119, 1131–33.
[49] Rohwer, 'Bismarck versus Beveridge' (n 16) 28.
[50] Nicolas Bueno, 'From the Right to Work to Freedom from Work' (2017) 33(4) International Journal of Comparative Labour Law and Industrial Relations 463.

take appropriate steps to safeguard this right'.[51] It has a more profound interpretation than the European Convention on Human Rights (ECHR), which prohibits forced labour and establishes a positive right to be employed, but not a factual duty to work to fund the right to social security.[52]

Previously, the right to work sparked a similar discussion during the drafting of article 23 UDHR. René Cassin, a French lawyer, professor, and former French representative for the League of Nations, introduced an important element by stating that 'everyone has the right and duty to perform socially useful work to the full development of his personality'. He derived this from the French Constitution of 1946.[53] Despite his efforts, the US vetoed his proposal because the phrase 'duty of work' could be interpreted as 'forced labour in some countries'.[54] Additionally, the reference to the 'development of his personality' never made it to the final version of the right to work because some parties, such as the UK and Chile, felt that one could already read this into article 29 UDHR. Consequently, to distinguish the core principles from the further interpretation or details, that part of the article was removed.[55]

In the current framework, work is considered a safeguard against poverty. That is also the approach taken by the ECtHR. However, the approach of imposing a duty to accept work in case of unemployment needs to be revisited.

Nevertheless, this approach is prevalent in many Treaties. Article 1 of the European Social Charter, for example, emphasizes states' ability to provide employment opportunities to address social security issues.

The right to work has never been fully established as a positive right for citizens of the signatory parties. Furthermore, many Member States consider it a duty to develop policies aimed at providing employment for their citizens.[56] This obligation extends to achieving the highest possible employment rate, to the extent that the EU publishes figures on the employment rates in each

[51] International Covenant on Economic, Social and Cultural Rights (Adopted 16 December 1966, entered into force 3 January 1976) 993 UNTS 3.

[52] Philip Harvey, 'Human Rights and Economic Policy Discourse: Taking Economic and Social Rights Seriously' (2002) 33(2) Columbia Human Rights Law Review 363, 380.

[53] United Nations Secretariat, Plan of the draft outline of an International Bill of Rights (1947) UN Doc E/CN.4/AC.1/3/Add.2.

[54] UNCHR, Summary record of the 9th meeting (1947) UN Doc E./CN.4/AC.1/SR.9, 11. Mary Ann Geldon, 'John P. Humphrey and the Drafting of the Universal Declaration of Human Rights' (2000) 2 Journal of the History of International Law 250, 257. A possible explanation could be the economic crisis after the Second World War, where the US and several other states were confronted with high unemployment rates. See also Johannes Morsink, *The Universal Declaration of Human Rights: Origins, Drafting, and Intent* (Pennsylvania Press 1999) 162.

[55] UNCHR, Summary record of the 9th meeting (n 54). UNCHR, Summary record of the 14th meeting UN Doc E/CN.4/AC.1/SR.14, 6.

[56] Article 23 of the Belgian Constitution or art 30 of the Dutch Constitution, eg.

Member State.[57] In reality, that means that the state has to make as much effort as possible to provide a job for each citizen in the country.[58] The natural consequence is that the states do not really develop a right to work but a duty to work to finance their Bismarck or Beveridge model.

Currently, the right to work is often exploited to ensure the fulfilment of another right, namely the right to social security. Each state requires a workforce which is large enough to provide social security for all of its citizens.

Bueno, Dermine, and Dumont propose an alternative idea where work should not be solely linked to increased productivity but also personal development.[59] These theories promise an interesting different approach towards the right to work. The realization of the right to work depends on the individual. One may choose to work for personal development, but it remains a free choice. There is no obligation to work. You can choose to work or not to work.

C. End of the Current Duty to Work

The right to work has evolved towards a duty to work due to the development of the right to social security.[60] The legal obligation to provide a fundamental right to social security also implies that the right to social security needs to be financed. Therefore, the right to work needs to guarantee the payments of social contributions, primarily paid by employers and, to a lesser extent, by employees within the EU. However, demographic changes, such as the ageing population, the declining younger generations, and shifting employment relations, pose challenges to the sustainability of the current social security system. The system places constant pressure on the working population to provide sufficient means for those not in the workforce, creating a self-perpetuating cycle.

To maintain the affordability of social security, many EU Member States are evolving towards a strict regulatory framework on unemployment and sickness. Examples of that behaviour include the higher retirement age in several EU Member States like Belgium, Denmark, Ireland, the Netherlands, Germany, and France. These developments highlight the inconsistency in the evolution of social security policies across different countries.

[57] This fits the human capital theory as developed by Gary Becker. See A Coppin, *The Human Capital Imperative* (Springer 2017).

[58] Dermine and Dumont, 'A Renewed Critical Perspective' (n 42) 266.

[59] Nicolas Bueno, 'From Productive Work to Capability-Enhancing Work: Implications for Labour Law and Policy' (2022) 23(3) Journal of Human Development and Capabilities 354, 362; Dermine and Dumont, 'A Renewed Critical Perspective' (n 42) 262.

[60] Heredero, *Social Security as a Human Right* (n 15) 23–29.

A basic income has the potential to fundamentally change this approach, despite being raised in the recent past.[61] Under a basic income system, the state provides sufficient income to guarantee a decent life for all individuals. That would require a complete rethinking of the legal concept of social protection, as pointed out by Dumont,[62] but also of the financing models of social protection. In this system, individuals have the freedom to work for personal or financial development, but no one is obliged to do so. Legally, anyone has the freedom not to work or, better yet, the right to stay lazy. One may shift from one's freedom to work towards one's right to laziness.

Obviously, questions will arise regarding how the right to social security should be financed. It is certainly challenging for legal experts to determine the best approach to funding. Many ideas have been proposed. For example, a tax on consumption or wealth rather than income.[63] To some extent, this may help to overcome the current dysfunctional approach where working individuals bear the burden of supporting those living off a basic income. On the other hand, some businesses may have doubts about developing their products due to the inclusion of taxes in their pricing. The feasibility and implications of such financing models remain to be seen.

The introduction of consumption taxes has delivered positive economic outcomes in EU Member States with high vaccination rates. Consumption has proven to be a human necessity and a driving force behind economic growth.[64] Therefore, taxation on consumption rather than on labour is a very important shift to establish freedom to work and a right to laziness.

IV. Conclusion

The current legal framework is not conducive to the sustainable development of social security. Alternative forms of financing our social security models will be necessary to ensure the continuity of our welfare states.

When analysing recent and ongoing reforms in different EU Member States, it becomes apparent that the focus is primarily on increasing efforts of the working population to sustain social security in the future. Nonetheless,

[61] Daniel Dumont, 'Universal Basic Income as a Source of Inspiration for the Future of Social Protection Systems? A Counter-Agenda' (2022) 24(4) European Journal for Social Security Law 299.

[62] ibid 301–02.

[63] Piketty, *Le Capital au XXI siècle* (n 32), where he argues for taxation based on wealth and not on income.

[64] Jonathan Cylus and others, 'Consumption and Tax Gains Attributable to Covid-19 Vaccinations in 12 EU Countries with Low Vaccination Rates' (2023) 33(2) European Journal of Public Health 228.

demographic studies indicate that this is not a viable long-term solution. In all EU Member States, the population is ageing, and the ratio between the working population and those dependent on social security is shifting from a pyramid shape to one with a narrower base and a larger top. Many EU countries, especially those following the Bismarck model, are transitioning from a right to work towards a duty to work in order to increase the number of workers. Having a significant number of workers is crucial to maintain affordable social security systems. Not working when one is capable of doing so is considered inappropriate and often results in punishment. In reality, the right to work has evolved into a duty to work.

Regardless of whether the Bismarck or Beveridge model is applied, the consequence is that current reforms are inadequate for dealing with the existing challenges and changes. A major shift needs to occur. The right to work should evolve into the freedom to work without any obligations. And to ensure the right to social security, a basic income should be provided to individuals who choose not to work. They should be able to afford a decent life. Legally, this transformation would establish a new fundamental right: the right to laziness. No one would be obligated to work or to accept any job offers. Everyone would have the freedom to choose.

Once everyone is free to decide whether to work or not to work, taxes on labour and income should no longer serve as the primary means of funding social security systems. Instead, social security should be funded through consumption-based taxes.

In an ideal world, we would support each other by purchasing the goods and services we desire without the pressure of having to work solely for them. We could choose to work for them if we wish or opt not to work for them. We would have the freedom to organize our lives and prioritize our desired goals. This concept represents a significant leap towards a utopian society.

Bibliography

Adkins L, 'Out of Work or Out of Time? Rethinking Labor After the Financial Crisis' (2012) 111(4) South Atlantic Quarterly. 621

Bevan G, Helderman J-K, and Wilsford D, 'Changing Choices in Health Care: Implications for Equity, Efficiency and Cost' (2010) 5(3) Health Economics, Policy and Law 251

Birnbaum S, De Wispelaere J, and Van der Veen R, *Basinkomstens nya vaag* (IFF 2020) 32

Bueno N, 'From the Right to Work to Freedom from Work' (2017) 33(4) International Journal of Comparative Labour Law and Industrial Relations 463

Bueno N, 'Freedom *at, through* and *from* Work: Rethinking Labour Rights' (2021) 160(2) International Labour Review 311

Bueno N, 'From Productive Work to Capability-Enhancing Work: Implications for Labour Law and Policy' (2022) 23(3) Journal of Human Development and Capabilities 354
Cholbi M, 'The Duty to Work' (2018) 21(5) Ethical Theory and Moral Practice 1119
Condé-Ruiz JI and Gonzalez CI, 'From Bismarck to Beveridge: The Other Pension Reform in Spain' (2016) 7 SERIEs 461.
Cylus J and others, 'Consumption and Tax Gains Attributable to Covid-19 Vaccinations in 12 EU Countries with Low Vaccination Rates' (2023) 33(2) European Journal of Public Health 228
Dermine E, 'Activation Policies for the Unemployed and the International Human Rights Case Law on the Right to a Freely Chosen Work' in Elise Dermine and Daniel Dumont (eds), *Activation Policies for the Unemployed, the Right to Work and the Duty to Work* (Peter Lang 2014)
Dermine E and Dumont D, 'A Renewed Critical Perspective on Social Law: Disentangling Its Ambivalent Relationship With Productivism' (2022) 38(3) International Journal of Comparative Labour Law and Industrial Relations 237
Dumont D, 'Universal Basic Income as a Source of Inspiration for the Future of Social Protection Systems? A Counter-Agenda' (2022) 24(4) European Journal for Social Security Law 299
Geldon MA, 'John P. Humphrey and the Drafting of the Universal Declaration of Human Rights' (2000) 2 Journal of the History of International Law 250
Gestrich A, Grüner E, and Hahn S (eds), *Poverty in Modern Europe* (OUP 1986)
Guinanne TW, Job TA, and Strep J, 'Bismarcks Sozialversicherung und ihr Einfluss auf Deutschlands demografischen Wandel' (2021) 101(4) Zeitschrift für Wirtschaftspolitik 246
Harvey P, 'Human Rights and Economic Policy Discourse: Taking Economic and Social Rights Seriously' (2002) 33(2) Columbia Human Rights Law Review 363
Heredero AG, *Social Security as a Human Right* (Council of Europe Publishing 2007)
Hiessl C, 'Working, Yet Poor: A Comparative Appraisal' in Luca Ratti (ed), *In Work Poverty in Europe: Vulnerable and Under-Represented Persons in a Comparative Perspective* (Kluwer 2022)
Kotlikoff LJ, 'Fixing Social Security: What Would Bismarck Do?' (2011) 64(2.1) National Tax Journal 415
Mantouvalou V, 'Legal Construction of Structures of Exploitation' in H Collins, G Lester, and V Mantouvalou (eds), *Philosophical Foundations of Labour Law* (OUP 2012)
Meyer T and Bridgen P, 'Towards German Liberalism and British Social Democracy: The Evolution of Two Public Occupational Pension Regimes from 1945 to 2009' in J Clasen (ed), *Converging Worlds of Welfare? British and German Social Policy in the 21st Century* (OUP 2011)
More T, *De optimo statu reipublicae deque nova insula Utopia* (Dirk Martens 1516)
Morsink J, *The Universal Declaration of Human Rights: Origins, Drafting, and Intent* (Pennsylvania Press 1999)
Paz-Fuchs A, 'The Right to Work and the Duty to Work' in V Mantouvalou (ed), *The Right to Work. Legal and Philosophical Perspectives* (Hart Publishing 2015)
Piketty T, *Le Capital au XXI siècle* (Editions du Seuil 2013)
Raworth K, *Doughnut Economics: Seven Ways to Think Like a 21st-Century Economist* (Chelsea Green Publishing 2017)
Rohwer A, 'Bismarck versus Beveridge: ein Vergleich von Sozialversicherungssystemen in Europa' (2008) 61(21) ifo Schnelldienst 26

Schoukens P, Barrio A, and De Becker E, 'Platform Economy and the Risk of in-Work Poverty: A Research Agenda for Social Security Lawyers' in V Di Stefano and others (eds), *A Research Agenda for the Gig Economy and Society* (Edward Elgar 2022)
Van Langendonck J and others, *Handboek Socialezekerheidsrecht* (10th edn, Intersentia 2020)
Vives JL, *De subventione pauperum* (De Crook 1526)

12

Utopia, Power, and Free Labour

Sergio Gamonal C.

Power tends to corrupt and absolute power corrupts absolutely[1]

Lord Acton

In an industrial undertaking, there is, to begin with, a distinction analogous to that between citizens and slaves in antiquity. The citizens are those who have invested capital in the undertaking, while the slaves are the employees. I do not wish to press that analogy. The employee differs from a slave in the fact that he is free to change his job is he can, and in his right to spend his non-working hour as a pleases. The analogy that I wish to bring out is in relation to government[2]

Bertrand Russell

I. Introduction

Human beings can be defined as entities with utopian perspectives, always trying to improve their situation, changing their environment, and attaining new and better goals. As Ortega y Gasset affirmed, human beings are idealistic, constantly driven towards a purpose that mobilizes them, even if they never reach their objectives.[3]

No matter how far from our current reality, the utopian perspective always urges us to go forward towards action and the possibility of change. Notwithstanding its impossible or unachievable nature, utopia always has a certain impact on reality,[4] with a critical intention.[5]

[1] John Emerich Edward Dalberg Acton, *Essays on Freedom and Power* (The Free Press 1949) 364.
[2] Bertrand Russell, *Power. A New Social Analysis* (first published 1938, Routledge 2004) 159.
[3] José Ortega y Gasset 'Prólogo a Historia de la Filosofía, de Émile Bréhier (Ideas para una historia de la filosofía)' in José Ortega y Gasset, *Obras Completas T. VI* (first published 1942, Taurus 2017) 171.
[4] Antonio Poch, 'Estudio preliminar' in Tomás Moro, *Utopía* (5th edn, Tecnos 2017) lxxxiii–lxxxix.
[5] ibid lxviii.

Sergio Gamonal C., *Utopia, Power, and Free Labour* In: *Labour Law Utopias.* Edited by: Nicolas Bueno, Beryl ter Haar, and Nuna Zekić, Oxford University Press. © Oxford University Press 2024. DOI: 10.1093/oso/9780198889755.003.0012

Utopia is not the same as dystopia, which refers to a general situation where everything is undesirable, usually in works of fiction.[6] Although utopia and dystopia may seem like antonyms, both notions can overlap in fictional narrative and historical reality. In other words, many revolutionary processes begin with the pursuit of a utopian ideal which ends up being a dystopia.

A few years ago, Rutger Bregman, in his provocative book *Utopia for Realists*, posed the need, once again, to enchant ourselves with the future,[7] thinking of weak utopias that mobilize us as they aspire for new proposals of change in society.[8] Bregman cites a phrase by Oscar Wilde on how humanity occasionally lands on the country of Utopia, and when it does, it looks to the horizon and discovers a better country and sails again. In this way, progress arises from the constant pursuit of utopia, for pursuing our dreams. If we were to over-interpret Wilde, it is possible to imagine that whenever humanity lands on Utopia, the latter rapidly becomes Dystopia, which is why we need to dream again. And this transition from utopia to dystopia probably has to do with power and the propensity of those who exercise it to abuse it.

This chapter is structured in two sections and aims to provide an overview of power in relation to utopia and labour law, as well as to propose a concrete utopian path for labour law. Section II deals with power and utopia and is structured as follows. Section A starts with a brief outline of the notion of power before elaborating on two important relations between power and utopia: the struggle for power for utopia and the entropy of power in utopia. Finally, it analyses how labour law sets a limit to power. Section III will outline a labour utopia for the twenty-first century, inspired by the *Free Labour* perspective of the radical republican movement of the mid-nineteenth century in the US, identified by its opposition to the domination and abuses of power inherent to subordinate labour.

[6] María Moliner, *Diccionario de uso español* (Gredos 2016).

[7] Rutger Bregman, *Utopía para Realistas* (Salamandra 2017).

[8] ibid 20–21. A weak, open and unrigid utopia, ie, rather than a completed and rigid project that is often totalitarian and dystopic, such as *Ciudad del Sol* of Campanella, which is consistent with a closed utopian model.

II. Power and Utopia

A. Notions of Power

Power is a complex notion[9] with often incompatible meanings, which, according to Han, leads to theoretical chaos.[10] The concept of power, from an intuitive perspective, is related to the notion of force or coercion, that is, being imprisoned or killed. That is what Russell calls direct physical power over an individual's body (naked power).[11] From this approach, power can be defined as the production of the desired effects. It is a quantitative notion of power.[12]

One of the most influential analyses of power is that of Max Weber, who defines it as 'the probability that one actor within a social relationship will be in a position to carry out his own will despite resistance, regardless of the basis on which this probability rests'.[13] Nonetheless, Weber believes this notion of power is too broad and amorphous from a sociological point of view. Hence, to get a more precise notion, he works with the concept of domination,[14] understood as 'the probability that a command with a given specific content will be obeyed by a given group of persons'.[15]

Domination always implies the presence of someone efficiently commanding another person.[16] In Weber's sociology, domination is a special form of power because it requires a certain degree of consent from the compliant one.[17]

Some authors often make the distinction between coerciveness and power. Luhmann, for instance, explains that power influences the actions or omissions of those affected by power, and power is stronger if it is capable of prevailing over other attractive alternatives available for those subject to power.[18] Power operates over the behaviour of those subject to power, unlike coerciveness or physical strength, where there is no action from those subject to coercion but from those who exercise it.[19] In this way, coerciveness is exerted in the absence of power.[20]

[9] Byung-Chul Han, *Sobre el poder* (Herder 2018) 11.
[10] ibid 9.
[11] Russell, *Power* (n 2) 24.
[12] ibid 23.
[13] Max Weber, in Guenther Roth and Claus Wittich (eds), *Economy and Society* (University of California Press 1978) 53.
[14] ibid.
[15] ibid.
[16] ibid.
[17] Xavier Coller, *Canon sociológico* (Tecnos 2003) 173.
[18] Niklas Luhmann, *Poder* (Anthropos Editorial 2005) 14–15.
[19] ibid 14.
[20] ibid.

Lukes lays down a bidimensional perspective of power, showing that certain groups control the agenda through which the public becomes aware of certain decisions. In other words, power is exerted with the full exclusion of certain issues discussed in politics,[21] which is a nuance concerning the unidimensional approach of power based on the interests and influence of an individual over another individual, as it turns 'no decisions' into a form of decision-making, by preventing decisions on controversial issues from being taken.[22] Furthermore, Lukes suggests a tridimensional or radical approach to power focused on the manipulation and modelling of the needs and desires of people as well, thus leading to a power model that goes beyond the decisions of individuals and the need for conflict.[23]

Foucault sustains an even more radical approach by studying the mechanisms through which obedience is exerted[24] and relating power and knowledge in an original manner, including the power mechanisms regarding the different areas of social sciences.[25]

As Bourdieu points out, power can become invisible and symbolic, exerted with the complicity of those who do not want to know that they are subject to it or even exert it.[26] In other words, a superior power is the one that shapes the future of somebody else, not the one that blocks it.[27]

B. The Path of Utopia: The Struggle for Power

Whoever desires a utopian social change must find a way to influence others and gain power. Violence, coerciveness, and force can be ways of gaining power, but due to their nature are unstable and rudimentary. One must evolve to subtler forms of power, such as symbolic power, to achieve a permanent change. That is easy to say in theory but very difficult in practice, albeit not impossible. For instance, notwithstanding the difficulties, there have been

[21] Anthony Giddens and Philip W Sutton, *Conceptos Esenciales de Sociología* (Alianza Editorial 2015) 319.

[22] Steven Lukes, *El Poder. Un enfoque radical* (Siglo XXI 2007) 15–16.

[23] ibid 16–22.

[24] ibid 103.

[25] ibid 103–04.

[26] Pierre Bourdieu, *Intelectuales, política y poder* (Eudeba 2014) 66.

[27] Han, *Sobre el poder* (n 9) 14. Additionally, the most complex forms of power, the stealthiest ones, imply a certain degree of reciprocity of power, ie a certain dependence of the individual who is being dominated, which leads to the 'dialectic of power': the more power the ruler has, the more he depends on his own subjects. ibid 16–17.

significant changes in the world with the end of slavery, which seemed impossible to modify in the eighteenth century.

Paradoxically, operating at a symbolic level should be easier in this globalized and hyperconnected world. But excessive information can also lead to ignorance. Bregman explains how many political decisions ignore evidence, for example, in matters of basic income[28] or migration.[29] Moreover, a key aspect in the spread of ideas is money, which acts as a magnet, directing research and ideas.[30] Neutrality is lost to the pursuit of research funds.[31] In other words, if academic research often depends on private funds, academics' independence is limited by the decisions of those who manage that money.

An interesting approach is that of Erik Olin Wright, who proposes paths of utopias within the interstices of the system through *real utopias*, that is, utopian ideals based on the actual potentials of humanity, utopian destinations with accessible intermediate stops, utopian plans for institutions that are capable of informing our practical tasks of navigating in a world of imperfect conditions for social change.[32] Wright proposes that this path be taken through Wikipedia,[33] basic income,[34] cooperatives,[35] etc.

The question, within the scope of this edited book, is what could be the *real utopia* of labour law scholars? In order to build a real utopia for labour law scholars, first, there is a need to adopt a critical perspective and focus more on non-specialized readers.

I believe that as academics, we are required to cultivate a critical perspective; that is to say, we must constantly examine or reconsider ideas, narratives, and paradigms, trying to compare or prove the affirmations or certainties thereof by analysing their causes, elements, and consequences. In other words, we must constantly defy symbolic power and beliefs. The critical perspective is characterized by constantly questioning the dominant paradigms, which are often reductionist, and methodologies imported from 'hard or exact sciences' through an explanatory model that ignores the complexities of the legal phenomenon.[36] The critical perspective must question the over-rationalization of

[28] Bregman, *Utopía* (n 7) 46–47.
[29] ibid 205–11.
[30] David Colander, 'Money and the Spread of Ideas' in David Colander and Alfred W Coats (eds), *The Spread of Economic Ideas* (CUP 1993) 229.
[31] ibid 233.
[32] Erik Olin Wright, *Construyendo utopías reales* (Akal 2015) 22.
[33] ibid 204.
[34] ibid 225.
[35] ibid 243.
[36] Carlos María Cárcova, 'Notas acerca de la Teoría Crítica del Derecho' in Christian Courtis (ed), *Desde otra mirada* (Eudeba 2009) 22.

certain approaches,[37] asking awkward questions: for instance, criticizing the criterion of the *homo economicus* in legal analysis[38] or questioning whether legal training is neutral or serves the interests of domination?[39] In the economic sphere, post-growth approaches are doing this critical exercise, for example by deconstructing the idea of over-rationalization and the concept of *homo economicus* and proposing new concepts to replace them.[40]

In my opinion, as scholars, we must also focus more on the general non-specialist public if we are to contest the space of symbolic power. The faith in Bregman's ideas is inspiring,[41] and our potential actions or omissions regarding symbolic power pose a significant responsibility on us.

Currently, scholars and researchers might find it overwhelming to publish in indexed and specialized journals, which tend to have little relevance in the public debate. On the contrary, books criticized by scholars at one time for being aimed at the general public rather than the specialized one have significantly influenced social changes. For example, in 1944, the book *The Road to Serfdom* by Frederich Hayek was highly criticized by his colleagues at the London School of Economics, such as Professor Durbin,[42] and, as Hayek himself stated in the prologue to the 1976 edition: 'most of my social science colleagues made me feel as if I had wasted my knowledge'.[43]

Nevertheless, I am not suggesting that we should abandon academia, but rather that we must stop being encapsulated in our expertise and start discussing ideas in forums, in the press, in books for non-specialists, etc, such as the initiative of Professors Ferreras, Battilana, and Méda of The Working Manifesto: *Democratize, Decommodify, Remediate*.[44]

[37] ibid 23.

[38] Elizabeth Anderson, 'Beyond Homo Economicus: New Developments in Theories of Social Norms' (2000) 29 Philosophy & Public Affairs 170, 170–200.

[39] Duncan Kennedy, 'Legal Education and the Reproduction of Hierarch' (1982) 32 Journal of Legal Education 591, 591–615.

[40] Tim Jackson, *Prosperity Without Growth. Economics for a Finite Planet* (Earthscan 2009) chs 3, 4; Kate Raworth, *Economía de la Rosquilla* (Paidós 2018) chs 1, 3, 7.

[41] Bregman, *Utopía* (n 7) 220–21.

[42] Evan Frank Mottram Durbin, 'Professor Hayek on Economic Planning and Political Liberty' (1945) 55 The Economic Journal 357, 358–70.

[43] Frederich A Hayek, *Camino de servidumbre* (first published 1944, Alianza Editorial 2000) 25.

[44] Isabelle Ferreras, Julie Battilana, and Dominique Méda, *Democratize Work, The Case for Reorganizing the Economy* (Miranda Richmond Mouillot tr, The University of Chicago Press 2022)

C. Utopia and Entropy: The Evanescent of Power

Power acts as a poison. As Lord Acton said well: 'Power tends to corrupt and absolute power corrupts absolutely.'[45] Every utopia that intends to survive must address the problem of power. Gaining the power to install a utopia is not sufficient. Once installed, the distribution of power must be balanced. Part of the current political breakdown and crisis is due to power imbalances.

Perhaps labour law can show us how to deal with power, which can be useful once utopian ideas have been consolidated.

Labour law has always grappled with power at different levels. From the naked power mentioned by Russell, comparing workers to slaves,[46] to the symbolic power of management theories and the economic analysis of law. Making visible the way these dimensions of power operate in the employment contract is certainly a contribution.

Firstly, we have naked power, which, according to Luhmann, is not power but just coerciveness. The master key of power clearly lies in the disciplinary powers of the employer and, ultimately, in dismissal.

There is a lot of literature about corporate authoritarianism. The followers of the *Critical Legal Studies* movement have criticized the lack of democracy in modern society, emphasizing the many uncontrolled private spaces, such as companies, hospitals, and schools.[47] Most recently, Andersen condemned the current authoritarianism within companies,[48] and not surprisingly, in this context, Wright often defines them as relations of domination.[49]

As the German economist Brentano said in the late nineteenth century, in a rather grim fashion, human work is a commodity, but a very special one that requires specific regulations.[50] For this reason, he concluded that the solution to the labour problem was to conjugate two types of regulations within companies: that of lawmakers and the law of unions.[51]

Secondly, this naked power of employers or companies grew more sophisticated during the twentieth century as a kind of domination, as described by Weber. One of the expressions of this metamorphosis is the staff policies adopted by employers within companies, which build a 'corporate culture'

[45] Acton, *Essays* (n 1) 364.
[46] Russell, *Power* (n 2) 159.
[47] Roberto Mangabeira Unger, 'The Critical Legal Studies Movement' (1983) 96 Harvard Law Review 561, 589.
[48] Elizabeth Anderson, *Private Government* (Princeton UP 2017) 37.
[49] Wright, *Construyendo* (n 32) 66.
[50] Lujo Brentano, *The Relation of Labor to the Law of Today* (G.P. Putnam's Sons 1891) 169–78.
[51] ibid 300.

meant to increase the workers' loyalty and improve their productivity through their mental or spiritual welfare.

Criticism has also been made of the fact that, while labour conditions and salaries drop, these policies aimed at increasing loyalty (leading workers to surrender their bodies and souls) aim to camouflage the deterioration of objective working conditions. In this way, we can see large companies treating their workers as 'associates or partners' or as 'managers', even if they earn the minimum wage. Warde says that although salaries drop, *psychic salaries* increase and the exaggeration of positions compensates for the reduction of buying power.[52]

Another criticism comes from the social science scholars who created the school of thought called *Critical Management Studies* (CMS) or critical studies of corporate management, which questions the management practices of current organizations and the notion of management itself.[53] It has been stated that 'corporate cultures' can turn into excessive or totalitarian control as they tend to steal the hearts and minds of workers, guiding their thoughts and feelings and not only their behaviour.[54] In the words of Willcott, governing the soul of workers becomes a key element for corporate strategies aimed at obtaining a comparative advantage.[55] This corporate domination clashes head-on with workers' human rights.

Thirdly, since the 1990s, the symbolic power of neoliberal economists, identified with the Chicago School, has pervaded the political and academic arenas. Not only are we faced with bidimensional power (with issues that are permanently out of the agenda, such as unionism), but with tridimensional power (Lukes), which manipulates and models the needs and desires of people, thus explaining the strength of the economic analysis of law and its attacks against labour law. The most shocking thing is that economics is not an exact science; worse, it tends to operate dogmatically.[56] Labour law was built without attending to business claims against protective regulations, as many protective laws would supposedly lead to the ruin of companies. Indeed, the more radical

[52] Ibrahim Warde, 'Estados Unidos y la "religión" del trabajo' in *El Trabajo* (Editorial Aún Creemos en Sueños 2007) 42.

[53] Carlos Jesús Fernández Rodríguez, 'Postmodernidad y Teoría Crítica de la Empresa: Una presentación de los *Critical Management Studies*' in Carlos Fernández (ed), *Vigilar y Organizar, Una introducción a los Critical Management Studies* (Siglo XXI 2007) 1.

[54] Hugh Willmott, 'La fuerza es la ignorancia, la esclavitud es la libertad: la gestión de la cultura en las organizaciones modernas' in Carlos Fernández (ed), *Vigilar y Organizar, Una introducción a los Critical Management Studies* (Siglo XXI 2007) 106.

[55] ibid 108.

[56] Sergio Gamonal, 'Labor Law, Economic Narrative and Law & Economics: The Method is the Problem' (2018) 35 Hofstra Labour & Employment Law Journal 317, 317–36.

economists' view did not prevail for much of the twentieth century, and labour law was consolidated with the support of Keynesian economists and became a pillar of the welfare state. After the 1980s, labour law began to be strongly attacked by neoliberal ideas, and, to some extent, it became a victim of its success[57] (many workers voted for Reagan and Thatcher[58]), and we are currently not only faced with the threat of the effects of the Covid-19 pandemic but also an alarming increase of inequality worldwide with its subsequent instability.

That is how power dynamics have operated in labour law. This example helps us with any future utopia or path to utopia.

D. Labour Law as a Limit to Power

The optics of power can also be useful in analysing labour law techniques. If the parties are allowed to operate their autonomy 'freely', as they did during the first Industrial Revolution (1770, Great Britain, steam engine), naked power (Russell) and coerciveness start to govern the workers. Private law of the nineteenth century was blind to social differences and workers' lack of power. Sinzheimer illustrated this reality very well in the 1930s: 'The man introduced to us by Civil Law is not a real man, but as gender.'[59] On the contrary, Sinzheimer believes that 'Labour Law orders the notion of man according to its reality'.[60]

Labour law's traditional technique to mitigate the impact of naked power is public order laws, a minimum floor that cannot be waived by contractual agreement unless it benefits workers. This non-waivability mechanism assumes that the workers lack bargaining power.[61] Many flexibility techniques introduced in the 1980s promote the return to free will in employment contracts and the individualization of the employment relationship as if the workers did not then lack power and were able to negotiate at arm's length. The result is well known

[57] ibid 335. The welfare state, the result of a protective labour law among others, generated the illusion that legal protections were unnecessary, and that deregulation would create greater prosperity for all.

[58] In 1992, the economist John Kenneth Galbraith published his book *The Culture of Contentment*, where he analysed how, once middle classes attain welfare, they tend to vote against regulations and tax increases, as they adhere to a short-term culture of immediate gratification, which leads to contentment and hinders long-term progress. See John Kenneth Galbraith, *The Culture of Contentment* (Princeton UP 2017).

[59] Hugo Sinzheimer, *Crisis Económica y Derecho del trabajo. Cinco estudios sobre la problemática humana y conceptual del Derecho del Trabajo* (Instituto de Estudios del Trabajo y de la Seguridad Social 1984) 106.

[60] ibid 111.

[61] Sergio Gamonal and César Rosado Marzán, *Principled Labor Law. U.S. Labor Law through a Latin American Method* (OUP 2019) 93–106.

to us all since deregulation and flexibility have been relevant factors in the increase of precariousness and inequality in developed countries.[62]

Public order laws are imperfect protection for workers because they do not impact domination (Weber), tridimensional power (Lukes), or symbolic power (Bourdieu), and additionally, for them to work, they require an inspection system and labour courts with efficient and brief procedures. And all of this does not happen often. For this reason, public order laws are supplemented and improved by the power of trade unions and workers' right to strike. In academic writing, there seems to exist consensus that collective bargaining was the better protection mechanism of labour law in the mid-twentieth century.[63]

The right to strike is the key to the trade unions' power, and it is the most controversial and counter-intuitive right from the state approach. It is a limited counter-power of workers at the level of naked power (Russell).

During the twentieth century, unions seemed to hold more power because of their participation in the 'industrial democracy' in developed countries. Unions can be the voice of workers within the company through discussion, voting, union elections, and collective bargaining[64] in matters as relevant as safety, promotion processes, benefits, salary levels, etc.[65] From its inception, collective bargaining has served as a way for workers to participate in decision-making processes within the company, that is, it has facilitated workers' right to participate in establishing employment conditions that will govern them.

This function of industrial democracy of the collective bargaining processes is generally absent in weak unions, in underdeveloped countries, and even in developed countries with union decline, such as the US. And symbolic power threatens industrial democracy, especially considering unions can legitimize managerial decisions, thus improperly representing its members.[66] In current times of union decline around the world, industrial democracy seems to be far from becoming a reality.

[62] There is much literature in this regard: for example, Thomas Piketty, *El capital en el siglo XXI* (Fondo de Cultura Económica 2014); Guy Standing, *Precariado. Una carta de derechos* (Capitán Swing 2014).

[63] Otto Kahn-Freund, *Labour and the Law* (3rd edn, by Paul Davies, Mark Freedland, Stevens & Sons 1983); Ruth Dukes, *The Labour Constitution. The Enduring Idea of Labour Law* (OUP 2014).

[64] Christopher Schenk, *Unions and Democracy* (Canadian Centre of Political Alternatives 2014) 6.

[65] ibid 7.

[66] Karl Klare, 'The Horizons of Transformative *Labour* and Employment Law' in Joanne Conaghan, Richard Fisch, and Karl Klare (eds), *Labour Law in an Era of Globalization* (OUP 2004) 12.

III. Building the Utopia of Free Labour

Power, in all its forms, is linked to the domination and exploitation of people. That is why we are interested in the approaches of twentieth-century neo-republicanism and the radical republicanism of the nineteenth century to propose a utopia based on a reinterpretation of the *Free Labour* vision of the mid-nineteenth century.

The notions of domination and exploitation can serve not only as a philosophical foundation for labour law,[67] but also to build real utopias if we link them with the *Free Labour* paradigm of the radical republicanism of the nineteenth century.[68]

Pettit, the strongest proponent of the neo-republicanism paradigm, argues for a concept of freedom as non-domination different from the classic dichotomy between negative and positive freedom (Berlin). Freedom as non-domination implies the lack of domination by others (absence of mastery by others)[69] or the lack of servitude according to the republican tradition.[70] Domination is clearly present in the relationship between master and slave or servant, where the master may interfere arbitrarily in the choices of the dominated person with complete impunity.[71] We need not exert domination for it to exist. In other words, even if the master is benevolent or docile with the submissive, domination and the possibility of arbitrary interference are always eventually present.[72] That may be referred to as the 'panoptic character of domination',[73] which is very relevant.

[67] On domination as the basis of labour law, see Alan Bogg, *The Democratic Aspects of Trade Recognition* (Hart Publishing 2009) 144–49; Alan Bogg and Cynthia Estlund, 'Freedom of Association and the Right to Contest' in Alan Bogg and Tonia Novitz (eds), *Voices at Work. Continuity and Change in the Common Law World* (OUP 2014) 151–53; David Cabrelli and Rebecca Zahn, 'Civic Republican Political Theory and *Labour* Law' in Hugh Collins, Gillian Lester, and Virginia Mantouvalou (eds), *Philosophical Foundations of Labour Law* (OUP 2018) 104–21.

On the notion of exploitation see Virginia Mantouvalou, 'The Right to Non-Exploitative Work' in Virginia Mantouvalou (ed), *The Right to Work. Legal and Philosophical Perspectives* (Hart Publishing 2015) 48–53, exposing how legal regulations favour the exploitation of legal and illegal migrants. See also Virginia Mantouvalou, 'Legal Construction of Structures of Exploitation' in Hugh Collins, Gillian Lester, and Virginia Mantouvalou (eds), *Philosophical Foundations of Labour Law* (OUP 2018) 188–204, exposing the need to broaden the notion of exploitation beyond slavery and servitude.

On the different conceptions of this notion see Jonathan Wolff, 'Structures of Exploitation' in Hugh Collins, Gillian Lester, and Virginia Mantouvalou (eds), *Philosophical Foundations of Labour Law* (OUP 2018) 175–87.

[68] The labour movement in the US that would postulate the *Free Labour* vision originated around 1820. See Rebecca Zietlow, *The Forgotten Emancipator. James Mitchell Ashley and the Ideological Origins of Reconstructions* (CUP 2018) 44– 67.

[69] Philip Pettit, *Republicanism. A Theory of Freedom and Government* (OUP 1997) 22.

[70] ibid.

[71] ibid.

[72] ibid 22–23.

[73] Bentham's architectural idea (borrowed from his brother) of the Panopticon is based on the fact that each individual feels watched even though he is really not. This *apparent omnipresence* of the

Pettit poses the capricious dismissal of workers as an example of arbitrary power[74] because even if an employer is nice—very considerate with his employees—they all know they can be fired if there is a conflict. That means that the 'panoptic nature of domination' affects workers directly. Although Pettit's notion of non-domination[75] seems to be very relevant for labour law, its labour implications are rather modest, if not disappointing, focusing mainly on universal basic income and leaving aside the state guardianship once the employment contract is terminated, and also workers' right to speak and the right to strike.[76] Other neo-republican proposals have also been criticized, such as Frank Lovett's suggestion centred around universal basic income[77] or Robert Taylor's proposal centred around the exit right.[78] This neo-republican approach has also been criticized as insufficient to guarantee freedom from work (the freedom of individuals to perform work that has an intrinsic value); in other words, as Bueno points out, not being dominated by an employer is not equivalent to being able to choose a meaningful work.[79]

Gourevitch's approach is more consistent with the nineteenth-century republicanism but also limited regarding labour law,[80] even though his perspective on the right to strike is more favourable to union power, and radical.[81] Also,

watchman or inspector is the genius of his proposal. See Jeremy Bentham, *El panóptico* (first published 1791, Editorial Quadrata 2004) 50, 59.

[74] Pettit, *Republicanism* (n 69) 57.

[75] For a critical view of Pettit on non-domination and political theory see Ian Shapiro, 'On Non-Domination' (2012) 62 University of Toronto Law Journal 293, 293–335.

[76] Alan Bogg, 'Republican Non Domination and *Labour* Law: New Normativity or Trojan Horse?' (2017) 33 International Journal of Comparative Labour Law and Industrial Relations 391, 403–09. For a critique in the same vein, see David Cabrelli and Rebecca Zahn, 'Theories of Domination and *Labour* Law: An Alternative Conception for Intervention?' (2017) 33 International Journal of Comparative Labour Law and Industrial Relations 339, 341, 343, 358.

[77] Frank Lovett, 'Domination and Distributive Justice' (2009) 71 The Journal of Politics 817, 817–30; Frank Lovett, 'Civic Republicanism and Social Justice' (2016) 44 Political Theory 687, 687–96; Keith Breen, 'Non-Domination, Workplace Republicanism, and the Justification of Worker Voice and Control' (2017) 33 International Journal of Comparative Labour Law and Industrial Relations 419, 419–39.

[78] Bogg, 'Republican Non Domination' (n 76) 409–13.

[79] Nicolas Bueno, 'Freedom at, *through* and *from* Work: Rethinking Labour Rights' (2021) 160 International Labour Review 311, 313, 319.

[80] Goutrevitch also looks askance at the protective techniques of labour law, insisting on the cooperative route. See Bogg, 'Republican Non Domination' (n 76) 413–15. In any case, Gourevitch's criticism of paternalism of labour law, from the approach of non-domination, is genuine. It treats workers as a dependent class in need of state protection. Rather than being against labour law and its techniques, Gourevitch wishes to overcome the structural cause of domination. From this perspective, although labour law intends to rebalance employment relationships, it does not seek a radical change in the system. See Alex Gourevitch, *From Slavery to the Cooperative Commonwealth. Labor and Republican Liberty in the Nineteenth Century* (CUP 2015) 174–85.

[81] Alex Gourevitch, 'Quitting Work but not the Job: Liberty and the Right to Strike' (2016) 14 Perspectives on Politics 307, 307–23; Alex Gourevitch, 'A Right to Strike: A Radical View' (2018) 112 American Political Science Review 905, 905–17.

unlike Pettit, Lovett, and Taylor, Gourevitch is highly critical of universal basic income.[82] In short, he argues that the republican theory of non-domination is broader than the one defended by current neo-republican authors.[83] His approach is based on 'labour republicanism' in the US in the second half of the nineteenth century, which attacked 'structural domination' at work, claiming changes towards a cooperative production system. In other words, the working class in the nineteenth century took on republican ideals.[84] Gourevitch focuses mainly on the activism of the Knight of Labour of the late nineteenth century.[85]

During the nineteenth century, several republicans fought not only slavery in the US but also the abuses of the industrial system, as they believed it was contrary to republican ideals.[86] The free worker who was hired by an employer was the victim of a system of economic domination that they called 'wage slavery', characterized not only by harassment and abuses but also by the submission of the worker to an industrial organization controlled by the employer.[87] Domination in the wage slavery system was structural since workers who had no land or tools were forced to sell their work to employers in order to survive, earning low wages for excessive working hours.[88] Northern labour activists used the image of slaves to describe their working conditions.[89] What solution did these labour activists propose? Moving towards a cooperative system[90] using state power to regulate the employment contract, limiting working hours, nationalizing transportation and communications, and redistributing land, credit and property to encourage the creation of cooperatives owning stores and industries.[91] This approach is clearly more complete than that of the neo-republicanism of Pettit, Lovett, and Taylor because it shows more accurately the domination of subordinate labour, which was denounced by *Free Labour* activists as 'wage slavery' since the first half of the nineteenth century.[92]

[82] Alex Gourevitch, 'The Limits of a Basic Income: Means and Ends of Workplace Democracy' (2016) 11 Basic Income Studies 17, 17–28.

[83] Alex Gourevitch, 'Labor Republicanism and the Transformation of Work' (2013) 41 Political Theory 591, 592, 598.

[84] ibid 593.

[85] ibid 594–98.

[86] ibid 594–95.

[87] ibid 595.

[88] ibid 596.

[89] Zietlow, *The Forgotten Emancipator* (n 68) 44, 57, 62; Gourevitch, *From Slavery* (n 80) 85.

[90] On current proposals for cooperatism, see Wright, *Construyendo* (n 32) 243.

[91] Gourevitch, 'Labor Republicanism' (n 83) 597.

[92] Labour transformations in the US were vertiginous, given the nascent industrial system, accompanied by the decline of the 'indentured service' system and the massification of the figure of the free worker who had to be employed to survive ('wage slavery'). This worker earned little, worked a lot, and did not have the possibility of purchasing land or becoming independent. The law applied contractual discipline to them, and the courts quickly applied some principles of the Master and Servant law to the

However, my approach will go back in time a little further, focusing on the republican perspective of *Free Labour* before the American Civil War[93] and then developed during the discussion of Amendment XIII of the US Constitution in 1865, as it provides a broader insight than that of the late nineteenth century. We must consider that by the end of the nineteenth century, the industrial production system was consolidated, unlike the time when the *Free Labour* vision was born in 1820,[94] where on the one hand, we had slavery, and on the other, subordinated labour, with several intermediate and fluid categories in between them, such as rented slaves, self-hiring slaves, indentured servants, redemptioners, apprentices, prisoners, children, etc.[95] For this reason, the original *Free Labour* paradigm is more complete than an approach of domination limited to the employment contract, and it allows for proposals that are more appropriate today in the face of the precariousness and segmentation of the labour market.

There are several meanings for *Free Labour* that range from a formalist vision linked to freedom of contract to a more substantive one linked to the actual freedom of workers. In fact, the idea of *Free Labour*[96] was interpreted differently from its inception to the Reconstruction period after the Civil War, in the Lochner era from 1905 to 1937 and in the New Deal era.[97] In this chapter, I will focus on the more substantive notion of *Free Labour*, which can be found in the discussion about the scope of Amendment XIII prohibiting slavery and involuntary servitude.[98]

As Vander Velde pointed out, the legislative discussion of Amendment XIII shows that some legislators understood *Free Labour* as being an extensive notion, comprising not only the right to resign from work but also the state guarantee of labour autonomy, freeing the worker from the dominion and control

detriment of the autonomy of these workers, who were subject to the discipline and control of their employers. See Christopher Tomlins, *Law, Labor, and Ideology in the Early American Republic* (CUP 1993) 259–92.

[93] Alex Gourevitch, 'Labor and Republican Liberty' (2011) 18 Constellations 431, 437.

[94] Zietlow, *The Forgotten Emancipator* (n 68) 44–67.

[95] Adelle Blackett, 'Emancipation in the Idea of *Labour* Law' in Guy Davidov and Brian Langille (eds), *The Idea of Labour Law* (OUP 2011) 424–25. Blackett bases her work on historians like Seth Rockman and Christopher L Tomlins.

[96] Tomlins, *Law, Labor, and Ideology* (n 92) 289; William Forbath, 'The Ambiguities of Free Labor: Labor and the Law in the Gilded Age' [1985] Wisconsin Law Review 767, 767–817.

[97] Risa Goluboff, 'The Thirteenth Amendment in Historical Perspective' (2009) 11 University of Pennsylvania Journal of Consttitutional Law 1451, 1459–60.

[98] For many citizens, hierarchical practices in employment relations violated the basic equality promised in the American Revolution. See Robert Steinfeld, *The Invention of Free Labor—The Employment Relations in English & American Law and Culture, 1350–1870* (The University of North Carolina Press 1991).

of the employer.[99] These legislators were part of a radical republicanism[100] that held that the degradation of one worker entailed the degradation of all workers,[101] and, therefore, their proposal included people of colour, Chinese workers, natives, immigrants, serfs, apprentices, or other disadvantaged groups so that all workers could enjoy the result of their jobs, upgrading their status by recognizing the dignity of labour and setting a minimum floor of rights and the autonomy of workers from the employer's control.[102]

How should the utopia of *Free Labour* be in the twenty-first century? I believe that the idea of Free Labour posed by the radical republicanism of the nineteenth century can be given a new interpretation nowadays with a more global approach,[103] that is, not only relevant to the US[104] but for all five continents, based on the notion of freedom as non-domination: absence of domination or servitude by others, excluding all arbitrary interferences.[105]

If we interpret *Free Labour* as radical republicanism, labour autonomy must be guaranteed, freeing the worker from the domination and control of the employer,[106] favouring their emancipation.[107] This liberation must include anyone who works beyond the nation-state and beyond subordinate labour[108] since the degradation of one worker leads to the degradation of them all.[109] In other words, a twenty-first-century utopia based on *Free Labour* must encompass all those who work for another person or entity, for example subordinate workers, migrants (formal and informal), domestic workers, prisoners, and care workers on zero-hour contracts.[110] And it should also include reproductive labour[111] and workers in the sharing economy.

[99] Lea VanderVelde, 'The Labor Vision of the Thirteenth Amendment' (1989) 138 University of Pennsylvania Law Review 437, 437–504.

[100] ibid 445. These ideals were also expressed through 'popular constitutionalism' in the nineteenth century, see Rebecca Zietlow, 'The Ideological Origins of the Thirteenth Amendment' (2012) 49 Houson Law Review 393, 393–458.

[101] VanderVelde, 'The Labor Vision' (n 99) 445. Before the Civil War, it was argued that slavery degraded the rights of white workers who had to compete with southern slaves (Free labor), see ibid 466.

[102] ibid 445–48, 460; Steinfeld, *The Invention of Free Labor* (n 98) 159.

[103] Adelle Blackett, 'Theorizing Emancipatory Transnational Futures of International Labor Law' (2019) 113 American Journal of International Law Unbound 390, 394–95.

[104] It has been emphasized, with respect to the Thirteenth Amendment, that it is the only guarantee of the American Constitution that attacks relations of subjugation, exploitation, and domination. See James Gray Pope, 'What's Different about the Thirteenth Amendment, and Why does it Matter?' (2011) 71 Maryland Law Review 189, 196–97; William Forbath, 'The New Deal Constitution in Exile' (2001) 51 Duke Law Jorunal 165, 165–222.

[105] Pettit, *Republicanismo* (n 69) 22.

[106] VanderVelde, 'The Labor Vision' (n 99) 437–504.

[107] Blackett, 'Emancipation' (n 95) 420–36; Bueno, 'Freedom at' (n 79) 311–29.

[108] See Chapter 4 by Zekić in this book.

[109] VanderVelde, 'The Labor Vision' (n 99) 445.

[110] Mantouvalou, 'Legal Construction' (n 67) 198–203.

[111] Judy Fudge, '*Labour* as a 'Fictive Commodity': Radically Reconceptualizing *Labour* Law' in Guy Davidov and Brian Langille (eds), *The Idea of Labour Law* (OUP 2011) 131.

Precursors to this broad sense of *Free Labour*[112] are Lea VanderVelde on *Free Labour* and the need for a broad interpretation of Amendment XIII,[113] Maria L Ontiveros on immigrants,[114] James Gray Pope on immigrants, and victims of human trafficking and sex trafficking,[115] and Rebecca E Zietlow on the new forms of exploitation of workers in the gig economy.[116]

Free Labour utopia must also address structural domination, especially the one fostered by labour legislation, for example in the case of migrant workers.[117]

Free Labour utopia should be global. If issues such as free trade, intellectual property, or the recent agreement to raise corporate taxes (2021)[118] can have a global facet, *Free Labour* utopia should also be global.

The utopia of *Free Labour* should aim to abolish domination, especially in subordinate labour.[119] There is no one defined path for this, and the cooperative proposal of radical republicanism or other routes of utopia that may be in line with *Free Labour* should be seriously taken into account.[120]

How are *Free Labour* and radical republicanism linked to power? Certainly in multiple ways. The *Free Labour* utopia will have to deal with naked or coercive power (Russell), as it had to deal with slavery in the nineteenth century and as it must today with exploited workers and forced labour. It must also fight domination (Weber) fostered above all by the precariousness of people, that is in the face of unemployment many are happy with a stable subordinate job (under the employer's hierarchy) without questioning the domination

[112] Papers by authors such as Pope, VanderVelde, Goluboff, and Zietlow are part of a group of writings that show the renewed interest in Amendment XIII. This interest has been displayed in various academic meetings and seminars that originated in the 2006 symposium 'A New Birth of Freedom: The Thirteenth Amendment-Past, Present and Future', organized by Rebecca E Zietlow at the University of Toledo College of Law. The papers presented are published in (2007) the University of Toledo Law Review 38(3).

[113] VanderVelde, 'The Labor Vision' (n 99) 437–504.

[114] Maria Ontiveros, 'Immigrant Workers' Rights in a Post-*Hoffman* Word-Organizing Around the Thirteenth Amendment' (2005) 18 Gerogetown Inmigration Law Journal 651, 651–80.

[115] James Gray Pope, 'A Free Labor Approach to Human Trafficking' (2010) 158 University of Pennsylvania Law Review 1849, 1849–76.

[116] Rebecca Zietlow, 'The New Peonage: Liberty and Precarity for Workers in the Gig Economy' (2020) 55 Wake Forest Law Review 1087, 1087–142.

[117] Mantouvalou, 'The Right to' (n 67) 49–51.

[118] <https://www.nytimes.com/2021/10/30/world/europe/g20-biden-corporate-tax-agreement.html> accessed 4 December 2022.

[119] On the contradiction between liberal values and the employment contract and hierarchy within the firm, see Hugh Collins, 'Is the Contract of Employment Illiberal?' in Hugh Collins, Gillian Lester, and Virginia Mantouvalou (eds), *Philosophical Foundations of Labour Law* (OUP 2018) 48–67.

[120] See Chapter 8 by Tomassetti, on *labour* law and the utopia of the commons; Chapter 11 by De Becker and Claus on the connection between the right to laziness, right to work, and right to self-determination; Chapter 3 by ter Haar on Doughnut economics utopia; and Chapter 4 by Zekić regarding the meaning of work and the post-growth future, all in this book. See also Bueno, 'Freedom at' (n 79) 321–25; Onni Hirvonen Keith Breen, 'Recognitive Arguments for Workplace Democracy' (2020) 27 Constellation 716, 716–31; Nien-he Hsieh, 'Justice at Work: Arguing for Property-Owning Democracy' (2009) 40 Journal of Social Philosophy 397, 397–411.

involved. It must also confront subtle and symbolic power (Luhmann, Lukes, Han, Bourdieu) that may propose rival utopias or cloister *Free Labour* in the category of unattainable utopia or manipulate the utopian narrative.[121] Finally, it must deal with bidimensional power (Lukes), where the hardships of workers and the possibilities of transformation are excluded from public agendas. In short, the narrative does matter.[122]

What strategy should one adopt in the face of power? I propose a gradual one. A transformative agenda should focus on the most serious cases, such as exploitation and forced labour. In parallel, democracy should be promoted within the company without neglecting traditional labour rights (state protection, the right of association, and the right to strike).

What can we, as academics, do? As we suggested above, we can encourage critical thinking, go out of our schools to debate in the real world, with books, presence in the press, forums, conferences, etc, and never lose faith in the possibility of real transformations.

IV. Conclusions

In this chapter, I have studied the relationship between power, utopia, and labour law, proposing a utopia for the twenty-first century based on *Free Labour* in radical republicanism.

The deployment of power, from its most rudimentary forms, such as coercion (Russell), to the more sophisticated ones, such as subtle and symbolic power (Luhmann, Lukes, Han, Bourdieu), is of relevance for any utopian path. The link between power and utopia provides perspectives that must be considered if one wishes to walk a utopian path in labour law. Labour law has tried to deal with power, but not as successfully as we would have wished. Industrial democracy has not spread in many countries, and the right to strike, a bulwark for workers, operates at the most rustic level of power.

The utopia of *Free Labour* that is proposed in this chapter is ambitious and must be gradually achieved through many battles with a global approach. For this very reason, academics have no room for boredom since much is yet to be done—as each chapter of this book has tried to show with possible paths of change and realization.

[121] See Chapter 8 by Tomassetti in this book.
[122] Blackett, 'Emancipation' (n 95) 421; Fudge, '*Labour* as a "Fictive Commodity"' (n 111) 120–36.

Bibliography

Acton J, *Essays on Freedom and Power* (The Free Press 1949)
Anderson E, 'Beyond Homo Economicus: New Developments in Theories of Social Norms' (2000) 29 Philosophy & Public Affairs 170
Anderson E, *Private Government* (Princeton UP 2017)
Bentham J, *El panóptico* (first published 1791, Editorial Quadrata 2004)
Blackett A, 'Emancipation in the Idea of *Labour* Law' in G Davidov and B Langille (eds), *The Idea of Labour Law* (OUP 2011)
Blackett A, 'Theorizing Emancipatory Transnational Futures of International Labor Law' (2019) 113 AJIL Unbound 390
Bogg A, *The Democratic Aspects of Trade Recognition* (Hart Publishing 2009)
Bogg A, 'Republican Non Domination and *Labour* Law: New Normativity or Trojan Horse?' (2017) 33 International Journal of Comparative Labour Law and Industrial Relations 39
Bogg A and Estlund C, 'Freedom of Association and the Right to Contest' in A Bogg and T Novitz (eds), *Voices at Work. Continuity and Change in the Common Law World* (OUP 2014)
Bourdieu P, *Intelectuales, política y poder* (Eudeba 2014)
Breen K, 'Non-Domination, Workplace Republicanism, and the Justification of Worker Voice and Control' (2017) 33 International Journal of Comparative Labour Law and Industrial Relations 419
Bregman R, *Utopía para Realistas* (Salamandra 2017)
Brentano L, *The Relation of Labor to the Law of Today* (G.P. Putnam's Sons 1891)
Bueno N, 'Freedom at, *through* and *from* Work: Rethinking Labour Rights' (2021) 160 International Labour Review 311
Cabrelli D, 'Civic Republican Political Theory and *Labour* Law' in H Collins, G Lester, and V Mantouvalou (eds), *Philosophical Foundations of Labour Law* (OUP 2018)
Cabrelli D and Zahn R, 'Theories of Domination and *Labour* Law: An Alternative Conception for Intervention?' (2017) 33 International Journal of Comparative Labour Law and Industrial Relations 339
Cárcova C, 'Notas acerca de la Teoría Crítica del Derecho' in C Courtis (ed), *Desde otra mirada* (Eudeba 2009)
Colander D, 'Money and the Spread of Ideas' in D Colander and A Coats (eds), *The Spread of Economic Ideas* (CUP 1993)
Coller X, *Canon sociológico* (Tecnos 2003)
Collins H, 'Is the Contract of Employment Illiberal?' in H Collins, G Lester, and V Mantouvalou (eds), *Philosophical Foundations of Labour Law* (OUP 2018)
Dukes R, *The Labour Constitution. The Enduring Idea of Labour Law* (OUP 2014)
Durbin E, 'Professor Hayek on Economic Planning and Political Liberty' (1945) 55 The Economic Journal 357
Fernández C, 'Postmodernidad y Teoría Crítica de la Empresa: Una presentación de los *Critical Management Studies*' in C Fernández (ed), *Vigilar y Organizar, Una introducción a los Critical Management Studies* (Siglo XXI 2007)
Ferreras I, Battilana J, and Méda D, *Democratize Work, The Case for Reorganizing the Economy* (Richmond-Mouillot M tr, The University of Chicago Press 2022)
Forbath W, 'The Ambiguities of Free Labor: Labor and the Law in the Gilded Age' [1985] Wisconsin Law Review 767
Forbath W, 'The New Deal Constitution in Exile' (2001) 51 Duke Law Journal 165

Fudge J, '*Labour* as a "Fictive Commodity": Radically Reconceptualizing *Labour* Law' in G Davidov and B Langille (eds), *The Idea of Labour Law* (OUP 2011)
Galbraith J, *The Culture of Contentment* (Princeton UP 2017)
Gamonal S, 'Labor Law, Economic Narrative and Law & Economics: The Method is the Problem' (2018) 35 Hofstra Labour & Employment Law Journal 317
Gamonal S and Marzán C, *Principled Labor Law. U.S. Labor Law through a Latin American Method* (OUP 2019)
Giddens A and Sutton P, *Conceptos Esenciales de Sociología* (Alianza Editorial 2015)
Goluboff R, 'The Thirteenth Amendment in Historical Perspective' (2009) 11 University of Pennsylvania Journal of Constitutional Law 1451
Gourevitch A, 'Labor and Republican Liberty' (2011) 18 Constellations 431
Gourevitch A, 'Labor Republicanism and the Transformation of Work' (2013) 41 Political Theory 591
Gourevitch A, *From Slavery to the Cooperative Commonwealth. Labor and Republican Liberty in the Nineteenth Century* (CUP 2015)
Gourevitch A, 'Quitting Work but not the Job: Liberty and the Right to Strike' (2016) 14 Perspectives on Politics 307
Gourevitch A, 'The Limits of a Basic Income: Means and Ends of Workplace Democracy' (2016) 11 Basic Income Studies 17
Gourevitch A, 'A Right to Strike: A Radical View' (2018) 112 American Political Science Review 905
Han B, *Sobre el poder* (Herder 2018)
Hayek F, *Camino de servidumbre* (first published 1944, Alianza Editorial 2000)
Hirvonen O and Breen K, 'Recognitive Arguments for Workplace Democracy' (2020) 27 Constellation 716
Hsieh N, 'Justice at Work: Arguing for Property-Owning Democracy' (2009) 40 Journal of Social Philosophy 397
Jackson T, *Prosperity Without Growth. Economics for a Finite Planet* (Earthscan 2009)
Kahn-Freund O, *Labour and the Law* (3rd edn, by Davies P, Freedland M, Stevens & Sons 1983)
Kennedy D, 'Legal Education and the Reproduction of Hierarch' (1982) 32 Journal of Legal Education 591
Klare K, 'The Horizons of Transformative *Labour* and Employment Law' in J Conaghan, R Fisch, and K Klare (eds), *Labour Law in an Era of Globalization* (OUP 2004)
Lovett F, 'Domination and Distributive Justice' (2009) 71 The Journal of Politics 817
Lovett F, 'Civic Republicanism and Social Justice' (2016) 44 Political Theory 687
Luhmann N, *Poder* (Anthropos Editorial 2005)
Lukes S, *El Poder. Un enfoque radical* (Siglo XXI 2007)
Mantouvalou V, 'The Right to Non-Exploitative Work' in V Mantouvalou (ed), *The Right to Work. Legal and Philosophical Perspectives* (Hart Publishing 2015)
Mantouvalou V, 'Legal Construction of Structures of Exploitation' in H Collins, G Lester, and V Mantouvalou (eds), *Philosophical Foundations of Labour Law* (OUP 2018)
Moliner M, *Diccionario de uso español* (Gredos 2016)
Ontiveros M, 'Immigrant Workers' Rights in a Post-*Hoffman* Word-Organizing Around the Thirteenth Amendment' (2005) 18 Georgetown Immigration Law Journal 651
Ortega y Gasset J, 'Prólogo a Historia de la Filosofía, de Émile Bréhier (Ideas para una historia de la filosofía)' in J Gasset, *Obras Completas T. VI* (first published 1942, Taurus 2017)
Pettit P, *Republicanism. A Theory of Freedom and Government* (OUP 1997)
Piketty T, *El capital en el siglo XXI* (Fondo de Cultura Económica 2014)

Poch A, Estudio preliminar' in T Moro, *Utopía* (5th edn, Tecnos 2017)
Pope J, 'A Free Labor Approach to Human Trafficking' (2010) 158 University pf Pennsylvania Law Review 1849
Pope J, 'What's Different about the Thirteenth Amendment, and Why does it Matter?' (2011) 71 Maryland Law Review 189
Raworth K, *Economía de la Rosquilla* (Paidós 2018)
Russell B, *Power. A New Social Analysis* (first published 1938, Routledge 2004)
Schenk C, *Unions and Democracy* (Canadian Centre of Political Alternatives 2014)
Shapiro I, 'On Non-Domination' (2012) 62 University of Toronto Law Journal 293
Sinzheimer H, *Crisis Económica y Derecho del trabajo. Cinco estudios sobre la problemática humana y conceptual del Derecho del Trabajo* (Instituto de Estudios del Trabajo y de la Seguridad Social 1984)
Standing G, *Precariado. Una carta de derechos* (Capitán Swing 2014)
Steinfeld R, *The Invention of Free Labor—The Employment Relations in English & American Law and Culture, 1350–1870* (The University of North Carolina Press 1991)
Tomlins C, Law, Labo*r, and Ideology in the Early American Republic* (CUP 1993)
Unger R, 'The Critical Legal Studies Movement' (1983) 96 Harvard Law Review 561
VanderVelde L, 'The Labor Vision of the Thirteenth Amendment' (1989) 138 University of Pennsylvania Law Review 437
Warde I, 'Estados Unidos y la "religión" del trabajo' in *El Trabajo* (Editorial Aún Creemos en Sueños 2007)
Weber M, in G Roth and C Wittich (eds), *Economy and Society* (University of California Press 1978)
Willmott H, 'La fuerza es la ignorancia, la esclavitud es la libertad: la gestión de la cultura en las organizaciones modernas' in C Fernández (ed), *Vigilar y Organizar, Una introducción a los Critical Management Studies* (Siglo XXI 2007)
Wolff J, 'Structures of Exploitation' in H Collins, G Lester, and V Mantouvalou (eds), *Philosophical Foundations of Labour Law* (OUP 2018)
Wright E, *Construyendo utopías reales* (Akal 2015)
Zietlow R, 'The Ideological Origins of the Thirteenth Amendment' (2012) 49 Houson Law Review 393
Zietlow R, *The Forgotten Emancipator. James Mitchell Ashley and the Ideological Origins of Reconstructions* (CUP 2018)
Zietlow R, 'The New Peonage: Liberty and Precarity for Workers in the Gig Economy' (2020) 55 Wake Forest Law Review 1087

13
Conclusion
Utopias for an Ecological Social Law and How to Get There

Élise Dermine and Daniel Dumont

I. Introduction

The aim of this thought-provoking and refreshing book was to sketch out renewed labour law utopias; more specifically, it examined alternative approaches to the growth-driven market economy, namely post-growth and post-(productive) work approaches. For the first time, this effort was carried out by legal scholars. In doing so, they have made a valuable contribution to the ongoing debates in the socioeconomic literature on post-growth and post-(productive) work.

In this concluding chapter, we will first provide a synthesized overview of the labour law utopias that have been presented in the book. We will underscore that the different chapters reflect a broadening of the context in which the debates on the meaning and the centrality of work unfold. Whereas these discussions in the 1980s were based on the observation that post-industrial societies could not overcome the dilemma between the persistence of structural unemployment and the development of in-work poverty, they now include the need to shift away from the growth paradigm to achieve the ecological transition (Section II).

As explained in the book's Introduction, conceptualizing utopias for labour law aimed to put 'dots' on the horizon to open the realm of the imaginary and thereby contribute to social change. In this concluding chapter, we propose to travel back downstream and suggest some modest guidelines on how we could start to build transition paths from where we are to the dots on the horizon, through the progressive transformation of social law. The authors in this book understand labour law broadly, often including social security law and employment policy law.[1] To indicate this all-encompassing approach, we will use

[1] The expression 'employment policy law' constitutes an attempt to translate the French notion of *droit de l'emploi*, an emerging branch of social law that covers all measures—whether in the field of tax

Élise Dermine and Daniel Dumont, *Conclusion* In: *Labour Law Utopias*. Edited by: Nicolas Bueno, Beryl ter Haar, and Nuna Zekić, Oxford University Press. © Oxford University Press 2024. DOI: 10.1093/oso/9780198889755.003.0013

the term 'social law' since, in most continental European countries, the term labour law is understood in a more restricted sense that is limited to employment contracts and industrial relations. Since the various contributions to the book share a post-growth background, in that they recognize the limits of growth, we propose more specifically to sketch out some initial thoughts on how to pave the way towards 'sustainable (or ecological) social law'. By this, we mean a system of social law that continues to meet the challenges of social justice but without transgressing planetary boundaries and endangering ecosystems.[2] We will do this at the levels of ideas (Section III.A) and then policies (Section III.B).

II. Post-(Productive) Work Utopias: From the Fordist Crisis to the Imperative of Ecological Transition

Fuelled by the fading horizon of full employment in most Western countries, a series of reflections were conducted in the 1980s and 1990s on the relationship between work and non-work, that is, between the labour market activities on the one hand and the wide range of activities performed outside of it on the other. These were based on a critique of the centrality and contours of work in the context of de-industrialization.[3] However, with the economic recovery and the decrease in unemployment at the end of the 1990s in most Western countries, this line of research found little echo in the policies carried out in these countries during the 2000s. Despite the severe economic crisis caused by the instability of the banking and financial system in 2008, the dominant political agenda, notably due to the influence of the European Union (EU), has remained more than ever focused on the cardinal objective of raising employment rates through activation measures, that is, by coercively increasing

law, economic law, labour law, or social security law—aimed at creating, adapting, sharing, or safeguarding jobs. See eg Franck Petit and Dirk Baugard, *Droit de l'emploi. Etudes juridiques des politiques d'emploi* (Gualino 2010).

[2] For further elaboration, see Élise Dermine, 'Towards a Sustainable Social Law: What Role for Legal Scholars?' (2023) 39(3–4) International Journal of Comparative Labour Law and Industrial Relations 315–36. See also, from the perspective of social policy scholars, Fiona Dukelow and Mary Murphy, 'Building the Future from the Present: Imagining Post-Growth, Post-Productivist Ecosocial Policy' (2022) 51(3) Journal of Social Policy 504–18. See yet Frédéric Géa, 'Droit du travail et écologie' (2024) 1 Revue de droit du travail 17–29.

[3] Fred Block, *Postindustrial Possibilities. A Critique of Economic Discourse* (University of California Press 1990); Claus Offe and Rolf G Heinze, *Beyond Employment: Time, Work, and the Informal Economy* (Polity Press 1992).

transitions from social security to the labour market,[4] and growth-oriented macroeconomic policies. Lately, however, an important shift is observable in ideas on our social model's future and our economies' environmental impact. The post-productivist agenda is indeed strongly re-incentivized by the growing scientific consensus on the empirical need to break away from the growth obsession, as the present book shows.

After Langille (Chapter 2) reminds us of the importance of designing new utopias for labour law, Ter Haar (Chapter 3) outlines a shift in socioeconomic thinking. As she shows, some economic thinkers are moving away from the growth-driven free market economic paradigms towards a 'social and environmental wellbeing paradigm'. This new paradigm will fundamentally alter the meaning, value, and position work has in society. Zekić (Chapter 4) and Carelli (Chapter 5) address this economic shift away from economic growth with more concrete ideas about work and labour law. Zekić discusses the centrality and meaning of work within the necessity of a degrowth agenda to respect the boundaries and needs of the planet. The traditional concept of decent work in labour law needs to be broadened to respect planetary boundaries, and its objective should be to contribute to individual flourishing. In addition, labour law must fundamentally reassess its purpose of redistributing labour, income, and wealth more fairly. Carelli drafts lines for an ecological labour law, which is to be universal and, in his view, encompasses all human activities (productive and non-productive, formal and informal, generating material and immaterial wealth, etc). Moreover, he argues ecological labour law is essential for degrowth because there will be no degrowth without resolving social problems, including anti-colonial struggles and attention to the Global South. Deva and Anand (Chapter 6) share this concern for workers in the Global South. As they demonstrate, the globalized economy has linked the Global North to the Global South, particularly through global supply chains. Hence, any strategy developed in the North, such as degrowth, must consider the needs and aspirations of workers in the Global South. Therefore, Deva and Anand plea for a differentiated degrowth model that combines a changed purpose of corporations in societies and more accountable transnational corporations. Lastly, like Carelli, they make a point that international labour standards for decent work need to be adapted and made more universal to include, among others, informal work.

[4] Élise Dermine and Daniel Dumont (eds), *Activation Policies for the Unemployed, the Right to Work and the Duty to Work* (P.I.E.-Peter Lang 2014).

Moving from the purpose of the economy as a whole to a post-productive work approach that reconsiders the quality of work for people and the planet beyond its mere economic value, Bueno (Chapter 7) dives deeper into the meaning of work for society and the individual. As Bueno illustrates, the market cares little for the social value of work and its impact on people's wellbeing and the environment. To change this, he proposes a labour law system that revalorizes non-market work that is essential for society, individuals, and the environment and, simultaneously, deters high-paid market work that negatively impacts societal basic needs and the environment, such as speculation on housing prices and food.

Focusing on the essential needs of society, individuals, and the environment is currently difficult since our economic system is strongly grounded in the idea that property rights and preferences are mainly given by markets, which creates a wedge between private and public interests. Therefore, Tomassetti (Chapter 8) explores the idea of a real utopia of the commons based on a collectivistic and participative reconfiguration between the public and the private, which should create the space for a socioeconomic paradigm that will focus on the essential needs of society and the environment. Moreover, Tomassetti explains that labour in the commons is relational and solidarity-based, which would be supportive and consistent with new forms of non-market work in which social relations and ecological values are a priority. Encinas de Muñagorri (Chapter 9) continues on essential needs by addressing the heavily undervalued non-market care work in productivity-driven markets, despite the fact that its value for society as a whole is largely undisputed. Embracing ideas for a wellbeing economy, Encinas de Muñagorri explores how social law systems can be adjusted to protect paid and unpaid care work for its intrinsic societal value. Albin (Chapter 10) shows how this logic of property rights and productivism impacts the role of technology at work. To change this, she proposes a labour law system in which technology fulfils an accommodating role to workers (similar to an employer's obligation to provide reasonable accommodation for disabled workers). Thus, instead of technology serving the employer's interests of productivity and profits, it should be developed and used to accommodate the needs and wellbeing of workers and improve labour relations.

While the previous ideas are mostly based on a post-productive work approach, albeit in different ways, De Becker and Claus (Chapter 11) adopt a more radical post-work approach, as also envisioned by Carelli, by looking at the quantity of work that is needed in society. They explore paths to shift from a right to work to a freedom not to work, coupled with a right to laziness.

The right to laziness distinguishes itself from the right to leisure since it is not about a time to recover from work; instead, it is a right not to engage in work. According to De Becker and Claus, getting there entails breaking the connection between work and social security by introducing a universal basic income. A basic income would liberate everyone from the need to work and, therefore, the risk of exploitation. On the issue of exploitation, Gamonal (Chapter 12) elaborates on non-domination approaches to labour law and suggests extending this approach to all those who work for another person or entity, from subordinated workers to migrants, domestic, prison, formal, informal, and paid as well as unpaid care workers. He suggests that this requires a better understanding of relations of power in these contexts, and a starting point for partly achieving it would be democratizing work environments through labour rights, such as the freedom of association and the right to strike.

III. From Utopias to Reality: Achieving Ecological Social Law

The utopias presented in this book give a general direction towards a future social model emancipated from the growth paradigm that takes planetary boundaries into account.[5] In other words, they underline the need, as we would like to put it, for an ecological social law. In the remainder of this conclusion, we propose to explore the potential for an ecological transition of the current work and welfare legal system. Working with utopias opens the realm of the imaginary (see Langille in Chapter 2) and, therefore, of possibilities for achieving the desired social changes. However, identifying the transition paths is an important part of achieving it. How to achieve sustainable social law? We aim to illustrate with our conclusions how the ideas presented in this book could be used to set paths for such a transition.

To identify these transition paths, we suggest basing our approach on Bloch's formula of 'objectively real possibilities'.[6] This approach suggests that while having 'dots' on the horizon of the future is stimulating, in the end, the transition cannot come from a top-down remodelling of existing structures. Instead, a prospective approach gains from taking root more directly in our present

[5] See also Dominique Méda, 'Work and Employment in a Post-Growth Era' in Isabelle Cassiers, Kevin Maréchal, and Dominique Méda (eds), *Post-Growth Economics and Society: Exploring the Paths of a Social and Ecological Transition* (Routledge 2018) 13.

[6] Ernst Bloch, *The Principle of Hope* (MIT Press 1986). The original version was edited between 1954 and 1959 (three volumes) and was entitled *Das Prinzip Hoffnung*.

situation in order to develop proposals with a higher threshold of social acceptability, which are thus more likely to be reappropriated by social actors while turning these into reality. Especially since the law is plural, at its margins, there are already mechanisms and devices at work that break with the dominant growth paradigm and which could be progressively extended and systematized. Herein lies a 'latent utopia', with a possible future.[7] This 'interstitial' strategy is also followed by some of the authors in this book (eg Tomassetti) and the one defended by the sociologist Erik Olin Wright in his pivotal book *Envisioning Real Utopias*.[8] It is an approach that will lead us to formulate post-productive work proposals rather than envisioning a post-work society. We will conclude that social law should be emancipated from the economic growth paradigm without getting rid of work altogether; we will explain why.

Let us now turn first to the field of ideas (Section A) and then to that of policies (Section B).

A. The Right to Ecosocially Useful Work as Guiding Principle

The human right to work, which lies at the basis of all our social law, has been mainly limited to productive work, meaning work that contributes to economic growth. But at the same time, the right to work includes a right to free choice of employment. Although choices depend on the labour market, this freedom served as a safeguard against the exacerbation of the duty to work. The right to work has thus emerged both as an instrument of the growth paradigm and a means of recognizing aspirations for self-fulfilment.[9]

As explored by several authors in this book, in the world of tomorrow, the right to work could become the legal forum for a democratic reflection on finding a way out of the growth paradigm. Such debate may confirm that our post-industrial economies are effectively trapped in an insoluble dilemma between the persistence of structural unemployment and the rise of in-work

[7] See Loren Goldman, *The Principle of Political Hope* (OUP 2023), more specifically ch 2, 'Bloch and Latent Utopia' (62–85).

[8] Erik Olin Wright, *Envisioning Real Utopias* (Verso 2010).

[9] Élise Dermine and Daniel Dumont, 'A Renewed Critical Perspective on Social Law: Disentangling its Ambivalent Relationship with Productivism' (2022) 38(3) International Journal of Comparative Labour Law and Industrial Relations 237, 256–59. See also Élise Dermine, 'The Right to Work: A Justification for Welfare-to-Work?' in Anja Eleveld and others (eds), *Welfare to Work in Contemporary European Welfare States: Legal, Sociological and Philosophical Perspectives on Justice and Domination* (Bristol UP 2020) 49. On the dependence of the social and economic fundamental rights on economic growth in the international system, more generally, see Matthias Petel and Norman Vander Putten, 'Economic, Social, and Cultural Rights and Their Dependence on the Economic Growth Paradigm: Evidence from the ICESCR System' (2021) 39(1) Netherlands Quarterly of Human Rights 53–72.

poverty, which would lead to a debate redefining the contours of the right to work. A possible outcome of those debates may be that it is impossible to offer the entire working population employment that is both productive and freely chosen, which may lead to a path in which our societies could legitimately decide to untie the right to work from the growth paradigm. Beyond the social dimension, the question of reformulating the right to work should also fit more broadly into the ecological transition imperative. In the framework of a new social contract, the right to work would no longer be concerned only with economically productive work but with any socially valued activity, regardless of whether or not this activity contributes to economic growth while paying, by contrast, due attention to its social usefulness and environmental impact (cf Ter Haar, Zekić, and Carelli).

Emancipating the right to work from the economic growth imperative would not, in our view, imply abandoning the promotion of work, provided that it should be conceived in a much broader perspective than is currently the case (as evoked in many chapters). Some advocate the pure and simple discarding of the right to work, as it is considered both alienating for its 'beneficiaries' and fictitious for those excluded, in favour of a right to a guaranteed income. That would mean replacing the right to work with a right to be freed from work (or even with a right to laziness, as proposed by De Becker and Claus).[10] This argument is often based on libertarian premises and the consideration that work has no value in itself: each individual should be free to determine the importance they attach to work.[11]

Like most authors in this book, we do not think that getting rid of work should be the goal per se. Indeed, in our (Western) societies, individual fulfilment and self-esteem remain profoundly linked to the feeling of usefulness and social recognition provided by activities, among which work plays an important role.[12] For this reason, one should be careful not to celebrate too quickly 'the disintegration of our Great Integrator, work'.[13] In any case, the formula seems to be wrong on a factual level, in the sense that the scientific research available

[10] David Frayne, *The Refusal of Work. The Theory and Practice of Resistance to Work* (Zed Books 2015). In a much-praised article, Bueno floated the notion of 'freedom from work': Nicolas Bueno, 'From the Right to Work to Freedom from Work: Introduction to the Human Economy' (2017) 33(4) International Journal of Comparative Labour Law and Industrial Relations 463–87.

[11] See eg Philippe Van Parijs, 'Why Surfers Should Be Fed: The Liberal Case for an Unconditional Basic Income' (1991) 20(2) Philosophy and Public Affairs 101–31.

[12] cf among many others, Amartya Sen, 'Inequality, Unemployment, and Contemporary Europe' (1997) 136(2) International Labour Review 155–71 and Dominique Méda and Patricia Vendramin, *Reinventing Work in Europe. Values, Generations and Labour* (Palgrave Macmillan/Springer 2017) 49–91, and the many surveys mobilized.

[13] Yvan Barel, 'Le Grand Intégrateur' (1990) 56(1) Connexions 94.

invalidates for the moment the repeated apocalyptic prophecies about 'the end of work', even if the digitalization of the economy clearly represents a major challenge given its more marked impact on low-skilled workers.[14] In the same vein, empirical data do not show that we would be witnessing an explosion in the number of 'bullshit jobs', to use the expression popularized by David Graeber; quite the contrary, even if the existence of meaningless jobs is obviously a social ill that needs to be tackled.[15]

What would make sense is seeking to enshrine a form of right for everyone to freely engage in various socially useful activities throughout their life, with an intensity and in ways that vary across time and with each of them 'backed up by protection for living'.[16] That is also the general direction in which most of the contributors to this book are heading. When reconstructed in this way, work would no longer be a purely economic issue; it would also become a political question,[17] since it would become necessary to define the activities deemed valuable for the community through democratic deliberation rather than by referring to the market.[18] It is along this view that Bueno (Chapter 7) suggests a new role for labour law to identify and promote undervalued essential jobs in the market and, conversely, deter high-paid market jobs that increase the costs of essential needs and, therefore, the costs of living and ultimately the need to work more to fuel the growth.

For us, the shift towards a right to a guaranteed income that is not linked to integration runs the risk of 'disembedding the economic from the social', to use Karl Polanyi's terminology,[19] and of a democratic disinvestment of the market sphere. Therefore, the right to an ecosocially valued activity appears, compared to the libertarian version of the right to a basic income, more aligned with a philosophy of rights that conceives rights as a forum for exchange and debate on the construction of the common, rather than a source of fragmentation of

[14] See eg the convergence, on this point, between the otherwise very different analyses of Melanie Arntz, Terry Gregory, and Ulrich Zierahn, 'The Risk of Automation for Jobs in OECD Countries. A Comparative Analysis', OECD Social, Employment, and Migration Working Papers no 189 (OECD 2016) 34 p; and Christophe Degryse, 'Digitalisation of the Economy and its Impact on Labour Markets', ETUI Working Papers no 2016/2 (European Trade Union Institute 2016) 80p.

[15] Magdalena Soffia, Alex Wood, and Brendan Burchell, 'Alienation is Not "Bullshit": An Empirical Critique of Graeber's Theory of BS Jobs' (2021) 36(5) Work, Employment & Society 816–40.

[16] Chantal Nicole-Drancourt, 'Activation de la protection sociale: un droit à revenu universel de type nouveau?' (2013) 73(1) Mouvements 122, 124 (our translation).

[17] For an argument in the same vein, but from a different perspective to the one defended here since it focuses on the company level, see Isabelle Ferreras, *Firms as Political Entities* (CUP 2017).

[18] On the importance of politicizing the definition of the contours of work, Francesco Laruffa, 'Rethinking Work and Welfare for the Social-Ecological Transformation' (2022) 16(1) Sociologica 123, 133–36.

[19] Karl Polanyi, *The Great Transformation* (Rinehart 1944).

society into strictly individual aspirations.[20] Perhaps this formula—that of a right to ecosocially useful work as a guiding principle—is likely to bring together and crystallize what is present in embryonic form in most of the chapters.

B. How Social Law Can Valorize Ecosocially Useful Activities

How can the right to engage freely in ecosocially valued activities be realized in practice? How can social law better value care and activities that do not produce value in an economic sense but other values for people and the planet? Which path should we follow?

In this quest, there is one proposal that has become inescapable today, and it is the subject of a particularly lively international debate, notably in the degrowth movement: that is, instituting a universal basic income, a minimum floor income that would be totally unconditional.[21] While some proponents of the universal basic income see it as the materialization of a right to income that is disconnected from work—and we have just laid down our argument about this, others who are committed to maintaining the right to work argue that guaranteeing such an unconditional income would be the best way to effectively secure the possibility of engaging in socially useful activities.[22]

Avenues other than the basic income, which are less present in the discussion, seem more 'latent' in our social model and, therefore, more likely to break through. They deal with the promotion and protection of activities beyond paid employment. On the rewriting of our legal grammar of socio-occupational integration, the 'Supiot Report'[23] seems very useful for starting to rethink the

[20] See Claude Lefort, 'Droits de l'homme et politique' in *L'invention démocratique* (Fayard 1981) 45–84); Élise Dermine, 'Social Rights Adjudication and the Future of the Welfare State' in Christina Binder and others (eds), *Research Handbook on International Law and Social Rights* (Edward Elgar 2020) 375–92.

[21] Among many others, Philippe Van Parijs and Yannick Vanderborght, *Basic Income. A Radical Proposal for a Free Society and a Sane Economy* (Harvard UP 2017).

[22] For a discussion of this widely debated idea, to which we will not return here, see Daniel Dumont, 'Universal Basic Income as a Source of Inspiration for the Future of Social Protection Systems? A Counter-Agenda' (2022) 24(4) European Journal of Social Security 299–318.

[23] Alain Supiot and others, *Beyond Employment. Changes in Work and the Future of Labour Law in Europe* [1999] (OUP 2001) 50–57. For discussion, see David Marsden and Hugh Stephenson (eds), 'Labour Law and Social Insurance in the New Economy: A Debate on the Supiot Report', CEP Discussion Paper no 500 (London School of Economics and Political Science, Centre for Economic Performance 2001), esp 45–60 (interventions by Jane Lewis and Simon Deakin). See also Michael Wynn and Amir Paz-Fuchs, 'Flexicurity Outside the Employment Relationship? Re-Engineering Social Security for the New Economy' in Mies Westerveld and Marius Oliver (eds), *Social Security Outside the Realm of the Employment Contract. Informal Work and Employee-like Workers* (Edward Elgar 2019) 47–48.

practicalities of a post-growth social law—although it primarily intended to respond to the social challenges that the Fordist compromise was no longer able to meet in post-industrial societies. As its title, *Beyond Employment*, suggests, the key idea is that work should no longer be reduced to employment, which is, after all, but one facet of it, namely that of work rented out on the market. Work, in fact, as presented above and by many authors in this book, encompasses many other types of human activities referred to as non-market values and are carried out outside the market: vocational training, political commitment, community involvement, family care, etc. On the basis of this observation, the report proposes to allocate to individuals diversified 'social drawing rights',[24] which would allow each person to finance different forms of work outside the market while benefitting from a certain continuity of protection. The aim would be to accommodate the multiplicity of human aspirations in order to increase opportunities to engage in activities other than those geared towards production and consumption, thus increasing their freedom in work and throughout their working lives.

Although this would be only a beginning, as more structural questions regarding the purpose of our economies, their relation to the environment, and the meaning and value of work must continue to be addressed, as done in this book, we believe that this line of thinking is based on objectively real possibilities. Indeed, certain legal provisions already present in the toolkit of social law systems encourage the development of socially useful activities, even if in a very hesitant way and without any real overarching logic: leaves of absence allowing for a better reconciliation between private and family life and professional life, salarization of useful but not very economically productive activities, exemptions from the obligation to look for work for non-employment benefit recipients, etc. In one sense, 'the cart has gone before the horse, with elements of a new welfare architecture being ... developed in the absence of an ecosocial blueprint'.[25] Already present for a long time in the interstices of our social law but little conceptualized, and even less coordinated, these mechanisms are all potentialities waiting to be amplified in the perspective of a relaxation of the productivist paradigm under the banner of an enlarged right to work.

In this perspective, Nicole-Drancourt proposes 'to inscribe socially useful activities in a legal bond that would elevate them to the rank of "work", without a hierarchy of recognition'.[26] That would imply formally recognizing

[24] This expression translates the original French formula *droits de tirage sociaux*.
[25] Dukelow and Murphy, 'Building the Future' (n 2) 514.
[26] Nicole-Drancourt, 'Activation de la protection sociale' (n 16) 124 (our translation).

the contribution to the construction of a sustainable society of a whole range of human activities that do not fit the matrix of productive work in the economic sense, precisely by attaching social rights to them (as in Zekić's chapter). Whereas, at present, social protection is still largely tied to productive work, tomorrow, it could be a socially useful activity—whether productive or not—that would be the trigger.[27] In other words, the vector of eligibility to entitlements would become the contribution to social and ecological utility rather than to GDP growth.

Let it be clear, however, that in our view, not all ecosocially useful activities should necessarily give rise to the same rights in an undifferentiated way (as advocated, eg, by Carelli). Rather, it is a matter of ensuring a continuum of protection, with a view to better accommodating the idea that every human being is, at least potentially, a producer, a citizen, and an individual engaged in private and family life. Accordingly, while an ambitious reform of social law must undoubtedly 'take greater account of non-market work, in particular child-raising and care work for elderly parents, which is as vital to society as it is ignored by economic indicators'[28] (as also outlined by Encinas de Muñagorri), the aim of full participation in economic and social life must not be pursued to the detriment of equal access to the labour market. Rather, it should encompass the latter in a broader yet coherent package. Diversifying social rights should thus constitute a means of simultaneously meeting the aspiration of many women to achieve greater fulfilment in the professional sphere and that of many men to reduce its grip on their lives. In the same way, it should also be a way of meeting the often-thwarted desires at the top and bottom of the social ladder for greater equality in the various spheres of activity, typically (classic) employment for those who are excluded from it or live on its margins.

Setting the path into new directions and understandings is obviously a huge undertaking, the plan and execution of which still have to be elaborated. All the more so since, politically, productivism is one of the few 'invariants' of social democracy:[29] 'the general idea remains firmly anchored that our social systems

[27] Compare this with the more radically universal agenda as sketched, but in the context of informal economies, by Laura Alfers, Francie Lund, and Rachel Moussié, 'Approaches to Social Protection for Informal Workers: Aligning Productivist and Human Rights-Based Approaches' (2017) 70(4) International Social Security Review 67–85.

[28] Alain Supiot, 'Et si l'on refondait le droit du travail' (2017) 10 Le Monde Diplomatique 23 (our translation).

[29] See the political scientist Fabien Escalona's comparative analyses, *La reconversion partisane de la social-démocratie européenne. Du régime social-démocrate keynésien au régime social-démocrate de marché* (Dalloz 2018), that highlight the abandonment of Keynesianism in almost all European social-democratic formations during the 1990s, coupled with a reinforcement of the productivist horizon, seen as the condition of possibility for redistribution. The author goes on to underline the increasingly untenable nature, including electorally, of this social-liberal stance— with not taking into account the

depend on growth to survive'.[30] We will not enter this discussion here except to underscore that this path could constitute an 'offensive' response to the surge of the tough variant of activation policies. Faced with the reinforcement of counterpart demands indexed on the sole perspective of a short-term reintegration into the labour market, social democrats sometimes tend to retreat into a very defensive posture, denying any merit, even potential, to the logic of activation in order to take refuge in incantatory calls to restore the 'post-World War II moment'. Instead of falling into what Habermas described as the 'fundamentalism of the great refusal',[31] it would be a matter of proposing, on the basis of orientations that are, in fact, already budding in our positive law, another type of activation, an activation that is ecosocial and innovation-friendly,[32] that is, one that encourages and supports the diversity of contributions, lifestyles, experiences, and choices—in short, autonomy.

IV. Conclusion

To make a future less dependent on growth happen, 'the challenge is to join the dots making the connection between prefigurative experimentation, somewhat siloed reform proposals and the welfare imaginary, ... making more concrete the ambition of a decommodified, post-growth and post-productivist ecosocial welfare world'.[33] Thanks to the editors' efforts, the contributions gathered in this pioneering book have set very valuable reference points on the horizon that can help move our legal grammar away from the productivist paradigm towards one that fits an ecological social law. In this way, they help to reduce the feeling of paralysis that we may be experiencing at the moment: we

ecological challenge—since the economic crisis of 2008 and the entry into a period of persistently flat growth.

[30] Dominique Méda, 'Stratégies de croissance et environnement: quelle conciliation?' (2016) 70(1) Revue française des affaires sociales 279, 282 (our translation).

[31] Jurgen Habermas, 'The New Obscurity: The Crisis of the Welfare State and the Exhaustion of Utopian Energies' (1986) 11(2) Philosophy & Social Criticism 1, 14.

[32] Olivier De Schutter, 'Activation Policies for the Unemployed: Redefining a Human Rights Response' in Élise Dermine and Daniel Dumont (eds), *Activation Policies for the Unemployed, the Right to Work and the Duty to Work* (P.I.E.-Peter Lang 2014) 275; reiterated in Olivier De Schutter, 'Welfare State Reform and Social Rights' (2015) 33(2) Netherlands Quarterly of Human Rights 123, 159; Fiona Dukelow, 'What Role for Activation in Eco-Social Policy?' (2022) 21(3) Social Policy and Society 496–507. See also Anja Eleveld, 'Re-interpreting Basic Values Underlying Social Security Law in Times of Ecological Crisis' (2024) European Journal of Social Security, forthcoming.

[33] Dukelow and Murphy, 'Building the Future' (n 2) 514.

are now at a less embryonic stage in the sketching out of proposals and the effective construction of renewed labour and social security law utopias.

Bibliography

Alfers L, Lund F, and Moussié R, 'Approaches to Social Protection for Informal Workers: Aligning Productivist and Human Rights-Based Approaches' (2017) 70(4) International Social Security Review 67

Arntz M, Gregory T, and Zierahn U, 'The Risk of Automation for Jobs in OECD Countries. A Comparative Analysis', OECD Social, Employment, and Migration Working Papers no 189 (OECD 2016)

Barel Y, 'Le Grand Intégrateur' (1990) 56(1) Connexions 94

Bloch E, *The Principle of Hope* (MIT Press 1986)

Block F, *Postindustrial Possibilities. A Critique of Economic Discourse* (University of California Press 1990)

Bueno N, 'From the Right to Work to Freedom from Work: Introduction to the Human Economy' (2017) 33(4) International Journal of Comparative Labour Law and Industrial Relations 463

Degryse C, 'Digitalisation of the Economy and its Impact on Labour Markets', ETUI Working Papers no 2016/2 (European Trade Union Institute, 2016)

Dermine E, 'Social Rights Adjudication and the Future of the Welfare State' in C Binder and others (eds), *Research Handbook on International Law and Social Rights* (Edward Elgar 2020)

Dermine E, 'The Right to Work: A Justification for Welfare-to-Work?' in A Eleveld and others (eds), *Welfare to Work in Contemporary European Welfare States: Legal, Sociological and Philosophical Perspectives on Justice and Domination* (Bristol UP 2020)

Dermine E, 'Towards a Sustainable Social Law: What Role for Legal Scholars?' (2023) 39(3–4) International Journal of Comparative Labour Law and Industrial Relations 315

Dermine E and Dumont D (eds), *Activation Policies for the Unemployed, the Right to Work and the Duty to Work* (P.I.E.-Peter Lang 2014)

Dermine E and Dumont D, 'A Renewed Critical Perspective on Social Law: Disentangling its Ambivalent Relationship with Productivism' (2022) 38(3) International Journal of Comparative Labour Law and Industrial Relations 237

De Schutter O, 'Activation Policies for the Unemployed: Redefining a Human Rights Response' in E Dermine and D Dumont (eds), *Activation Policies for the Unemployed, the Right to Work and the Duty to Work* (P.I.E.-Peter Lang 2014)

De Schutter O, 'Welfare State Reform and Social Rights' (2015) 33(2) Netherlands Quarterly of Human Rights 123

Dukelow F, 'What Role for Activation in Eco-Social Policy?' (2022) 21(3) Social Policy and Society 496.

Dukelow F and Murphy M, 'Building the Future from the Present: Imagining Post-Growth, Post-Productivist Ecosocial Policy' (2022) 51(3) Journal of Social Policy 504

Dumont D, 'Universal Basic Income as a Source of Inspiration for the Future of Social Protection Systems? A Counter-Agenda' (2022) 24(4) European Journal of Social Security 299

Eleveld A, 'Re-interpreting Basic Values Underlying Social Security Law in Times of Ecological Crisis' (2024) European Journal of Social Security, forthcoming

Escalona F, *La reconversion partisane de la social-démocratie européenne: Du régime social-démocrate keynésien au régime social-démocrate de marché* (Dalloz 2018)
Ferreras I, *Firms as Political Entities* (CUP 2017)
Frayne D, *The Refusal of Work. The Theory and Practice of Resistance to Work* (Zed Books 2015)
Géa F, 'Droit du travail et écologie' (2024) 1 Revue de droit du travail 17
Goldman L, *The Principle of Political Hope* (OUP 2023)
Habermas J, 'The New Obscurity: The Crisis of the Welfare State and the Exhaustion of Utopian Energies' (1986) 11(2) Philosophy & Social Criticism 1
Laruffa F, 'Re-thinking Work and Welfare for the Social-Ecological Transformation' (2022) 16(1) Sociologica 123
Lefort C, 'Droits de l'homme et politique' in *L'invention démocratique* (Fayard 1981)
Marsden D and Stephenson H (eds), 'Labour Law and Social Insurance in the New Economy: A Debate on the Supiot Report', CEP Discussion Paper no 500 (London School of Economics and Political Science, Centre for Economic Performance 2001)
Méda D, 'Stratégies de croissance et environnement: quelle conciliation?' (2016) 70(1) Revue française des affaires sociales 279
Méda D, 'Work and Employment in a Post-Growth Era' in I Cassiers, K Maréchal, and D Méda (eds), *Post-Growth Economics and Society: Exploring the Paths of a Social and Ecological Transition* (Routledge 2018)
Méda D and Vendramin P, *Reinventing Work in Europe. Values, Generations and Labour* (Palgrave Macmillan/Springer 2017)
Nicole-Drancourt C, 'Activation de la protection sociale: un droit à revenu universel de type nouveau?' (2013) 73(1) Mouvements 122
Offe C and Heinze RG, *Beyond Employment: Time, Work, and the Informal Economy* (Polity Press 1992)
Petel M and Vander Putten N, 'Economic, Social, and Cultural Rights and their Dependence on the Economic Growth Paradigm: Evidence from the ICESCR System' (2021) 39(1) Netherlands Quarterly of Human Rights 53
Petit F and Baugard D, *Droit de l'emploi. Etudes juridiques des politiques d'emploi* (Gualino 2010)
Polanyi K, *The Great Transformation* (Rinehart 1944)
Sen A, 'Inequality, Unemployment, and Contemporary Europe' (1997) 136(2) International Labour Review 155
Soffia M, Wood A, and Burchell B, 'Alienation Is Not "Bullshit": An Empirical Critique of Graeber's Theory of BS Jobs' (2021) 36(5) Work, Employment & Society 816
Supiot A, 'Et si l'on refondait le droit du travail' (2017) 10 Le Monde Diplomatique 23
Supiot A and others, *Beyond Employment. Changes in Work and the Future of Labour Law in Europe* (OUP 2001)
Van Parijs P, 'Why Surfers Should be Fed: The Liberal Case for an Unconditional Basic Income' (1991) 20(2) Philosophy and Public Affairs 101
Van Parijs P and Vanderborght Y, *Basic Income. A Radical Proposal for a Free Society and a Sane Economy* (Harvard UP 2017)
Wright EO, *Envisioning Real Utopias* (Verso 2010)
Wynn M and Paz-Fuchs A, 'Flexicurity Outside the Employment Relationship? Re-Engineering Social Security for the New Economy' in M Westerveld and M Oliver (eds), *Social Security Outside the Realm of the Employment Contract. Informal Work and Employee-like Workers* (Edward Elgar 2019)

Index

For the benefit of digital users, indexed terms that span two pages (e.g., 52–53) may, on occasion, appear on only one of those pages.